FOR THE KID I SAW IN MY Dreams ⑦

KEI SANBE

TRANSLATION: SHELDON DRZKA ✦ LETTERING: ABIGAIL BLACKMAN

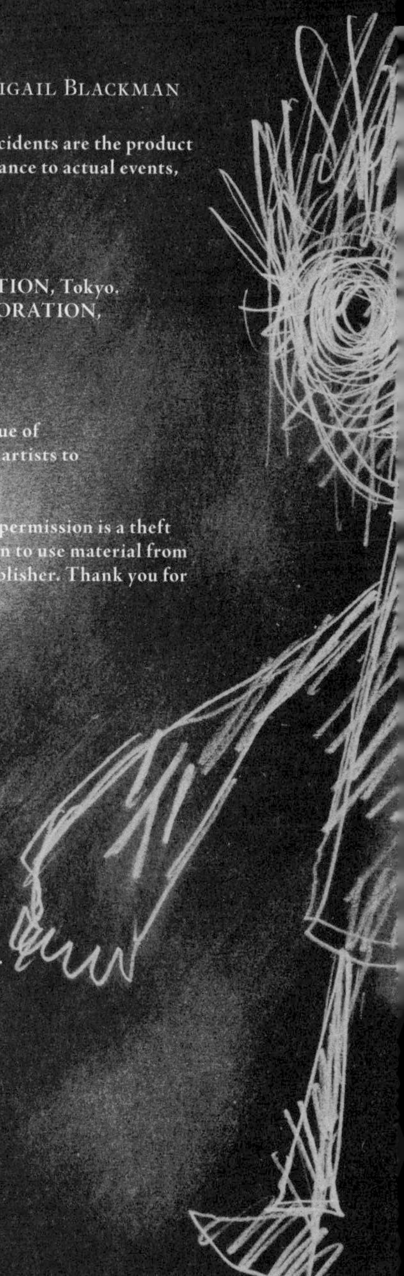

YUME DE MITA ANO KO NO TAME NI Volume 7
© Kei Sanbe 2020.
First published in Japan in 2020 by KADOKAWA CORPORATION, Tokyo.
English translation rights arranged with KADOKAWA CORPORATION,
Tokyo through TUTTLE-MORI AGENCY INC., Tokyo.

English translation © 2021 by Yen Press, LLC

Yen Press
150 West 30th Street, 19th Floor
New York, NY 10001

Visit us at yenpress.com
facebook.com/yenpress
twitter.com/yenpress
yenpress.tumblr.com
instagram.com/yenpress

First Yen Press Edition: November 2021

Yen Press is an imprint of Yen Press, LLC.
The Yen Press name and logo are trademarks of Yen Press, LLC.

Library of Congress Control Number: 2018958636

ISBNs: 978-1-9753-3679-0 (hardcover)
        978-1-9753-3680-6 (ebook)

10 9 8 7 6 5 4 3 2 1

WOR

Printed in the United States of America

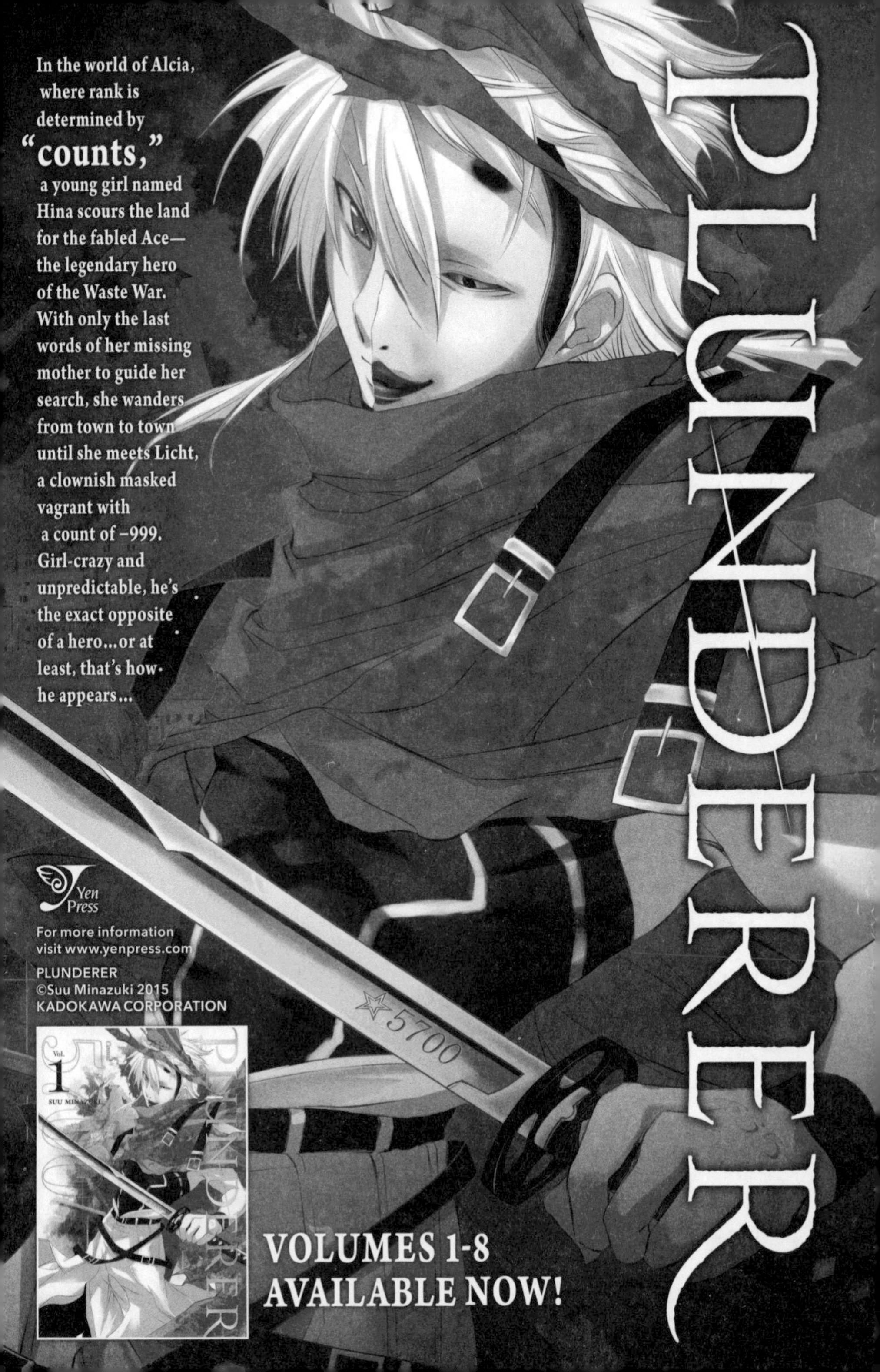

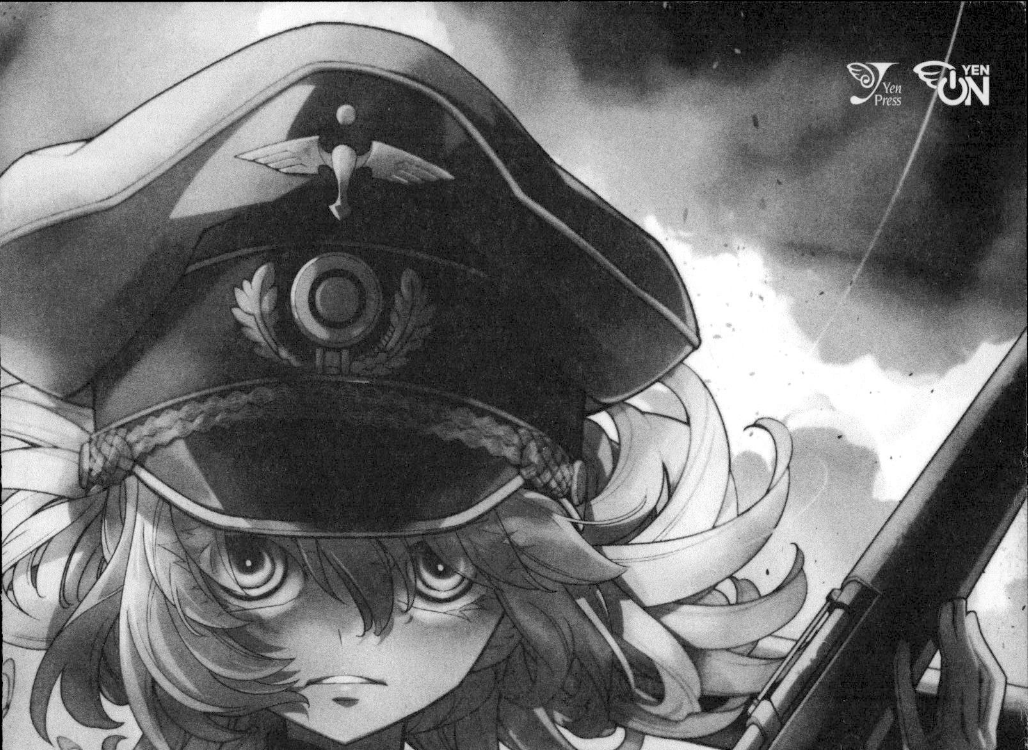

THE SAGA OF TANYA THE EVIL

Her name is Tanya Degurechaff and she is the Devil of the Rhine, one of the greatest soldiers the Empire has ever seen! But inside her mind lives a ruthless, calculating ex-salaryman who enjoyed a peaceful life in Japan until he woke up in a war-torn world. Reborn as a destitute orphaned girl with nothing to her name but memories of a previous life, Tanya will do whatever it takes to survive, even if she can find it only behind the barrel of a gun!

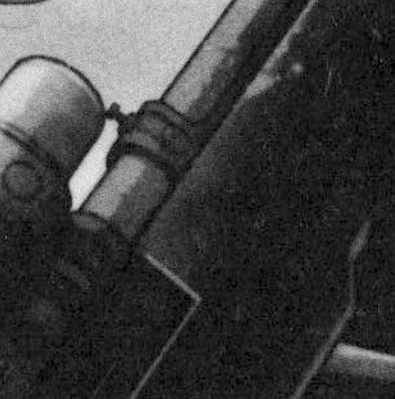

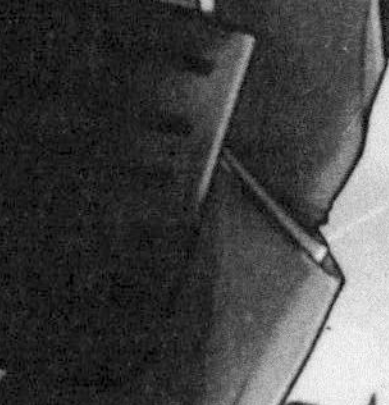

LIGHT NOVEL VOL. 1-8 AND MANGA VOL. 1-15 AVAILABLE NOW!

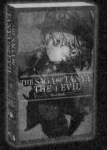

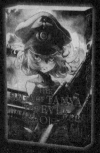

The Detective Is Already Dead

When the story begins without its hero

Kimihiko Kimizuka has always been a magnet for trouble and intrigue. For as long as he can remember, he's been stumbling across murder scenes or receiving mysterious attaché cases to transport. When he met Siesta, a brilliant detective fighting a secret war against an organization of pseudohumans, he couldn't resist the call to become her assistant and join her on an epic journey across the world.

...Until a year ago, that is. Now he's returned to a relatively normal and tepid life, knowing the adventure must be over. After all, the detective is already dead.

Volume 1 available wherever books are sold!

YenPress.com

TANTEI HA MO, SHINDEIRU. Vol. 1
©nigozyu 2019
Illustration: Umibouzu
KADOKAWA CORPORATION

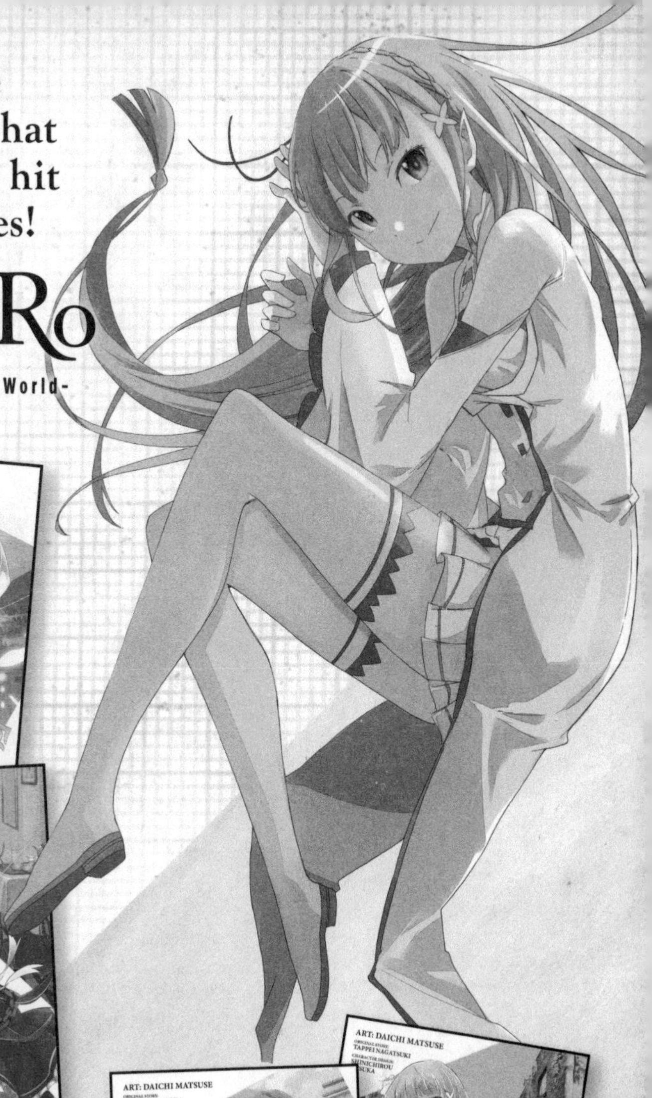
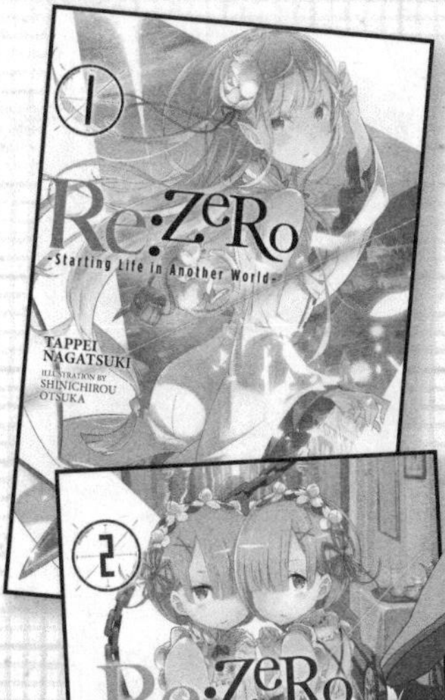

1
Re:ZeRo
-Starting Life in Another World-
TAPPEI NAGATSUKI
ILLUSTRATION BY SHINICHIROU OTSUKA
2
Re:ZeRo
-Starting Life in Another World-
TAPPEI NAGATSUKI
ILLUSTRATION BY SHINICHIROU OTSUKA

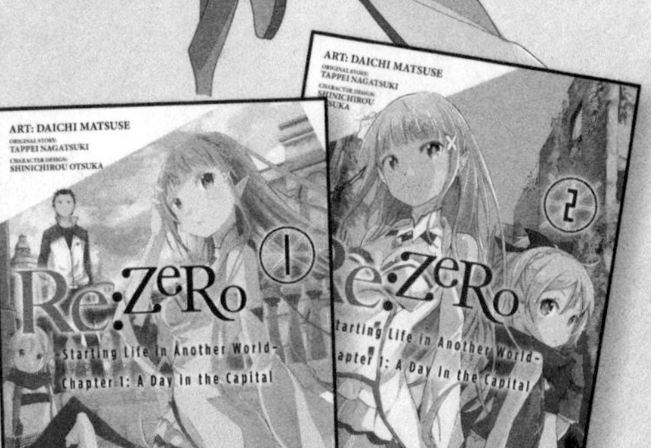

ART: DAICHI MATSUSE
ORIGINAL STORY: TAPPEI NAGATSUKI
CHARACTER DESIGN: SHINICHIROU OTSUKA
1
Re:ZeRo
-Starting Life in Another World-
Chapter 1: A Day in the Capital
ART: DAICHI MATSUSE
2
Re:ZeRo

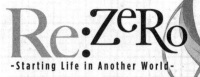

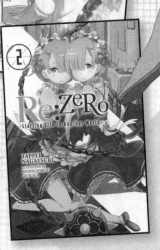

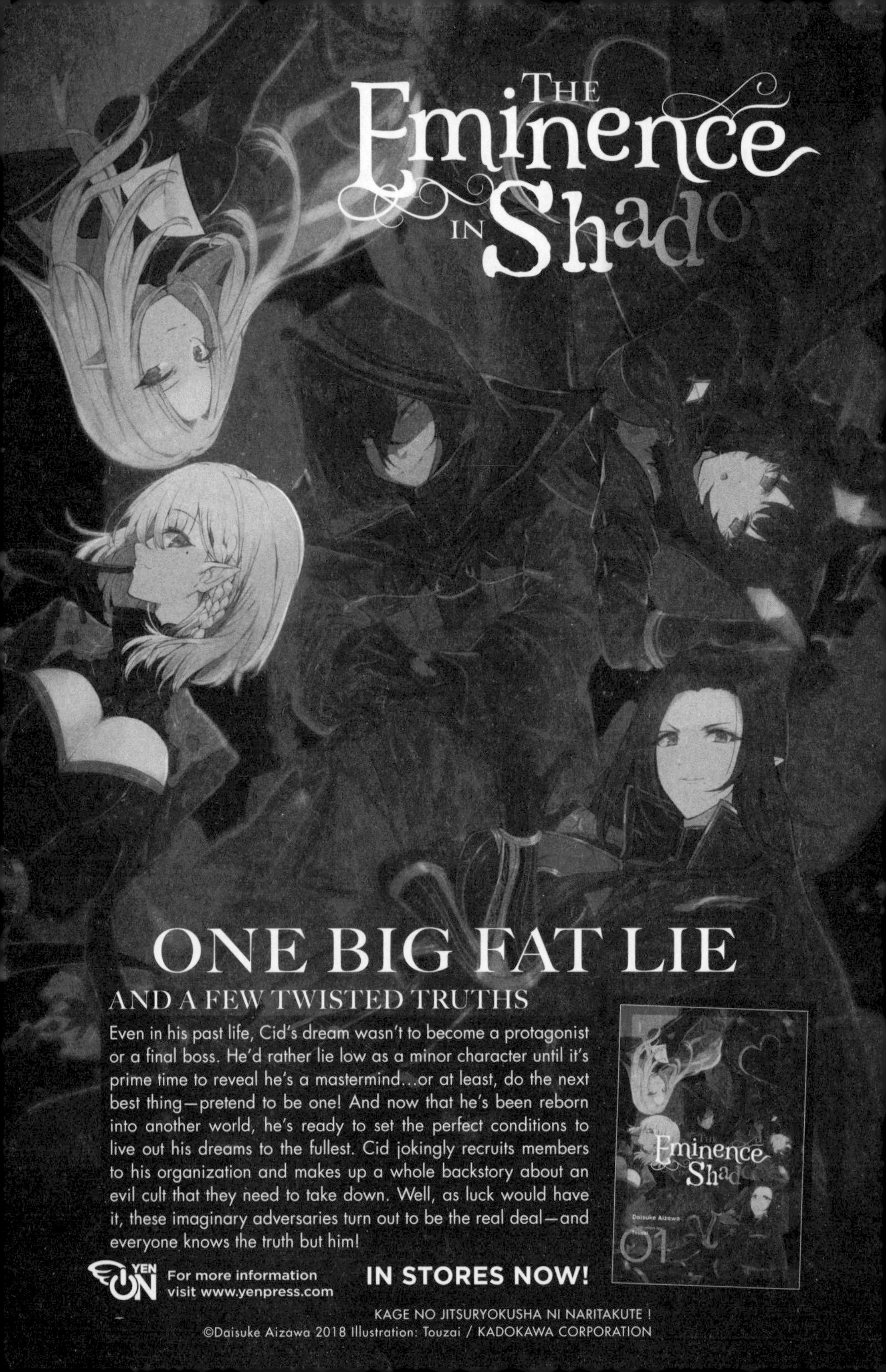
THE Eminence IN Shadow
ONE BIG FAT LIE
AND A FEW TWISTED TRUTHS
Even in his past life, Cid's dream wasn't to become a protagonist or a final boss. He'd rather lie low as a minor character until it's prime time to reveal he's a mastermind…or at least, do the next best thing—pretend to be one! And now that he's been reborn into another world, he's ready to set the perfect conditions to live out his dreams to the fullest. Cid jokingly recruits members to his organization and makes up a whole backstory about an evil cult that they need to take down. Well, as luck would have it, these imaginary adversaries turn out to be the real deal—and everyone knows the truth but him!
The Eminence in Shadow
Daisuke Aizawa
01
YEN ON
For more information visit www.yenpress.com
IN STORES NOW!
KAGE NO JITSURYOKUSHA NI NARITAKUTE !
©Daisuke Aizawa 2018 Illustration: Touzai / KADOKAWA CORPORATION

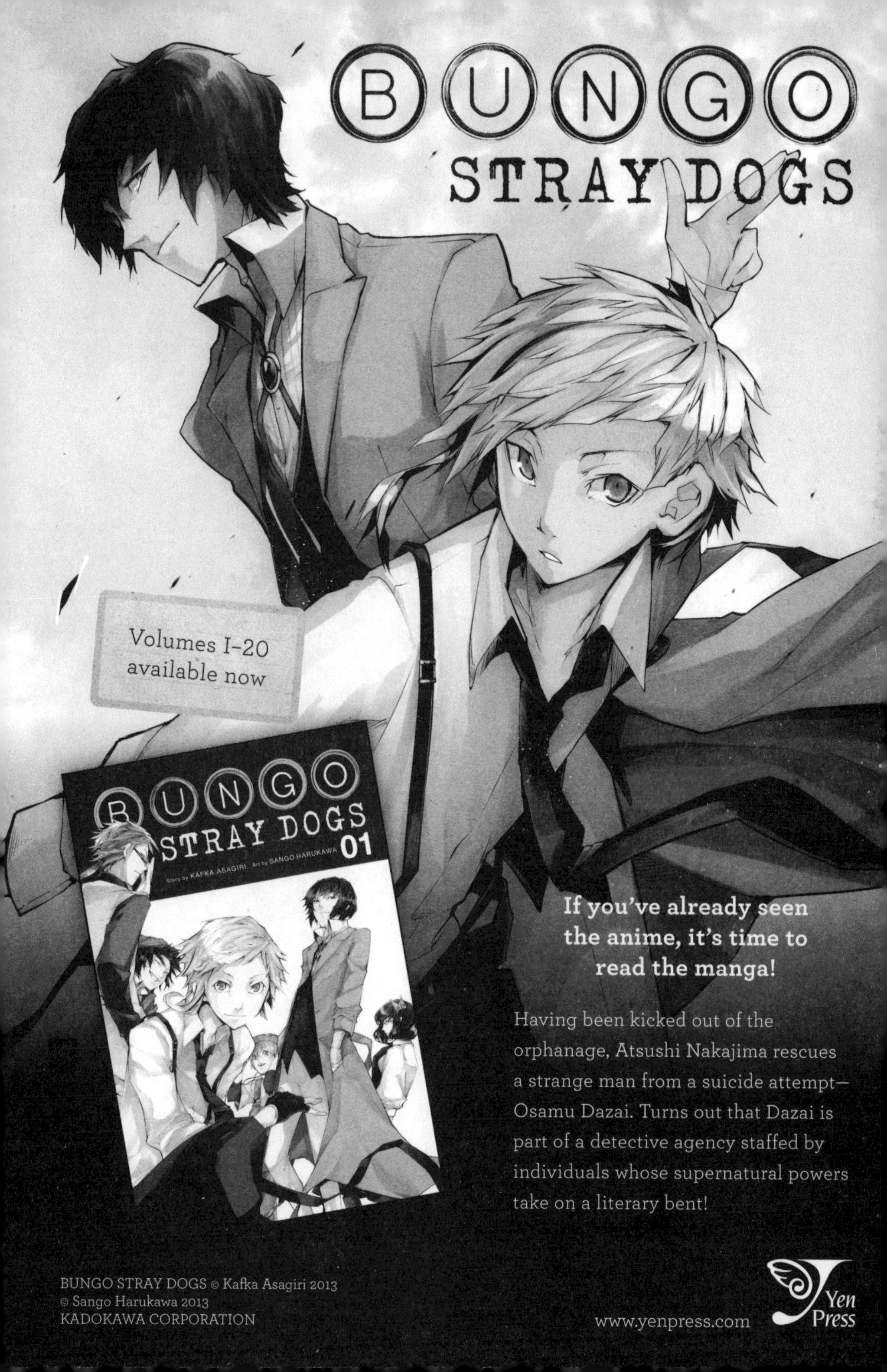
BUNGO
STRAY DOGS
Volumes 1–20
available now
BUNGO
STRAY DOGS
01
Story by KAFKA ASAGIRI Art by SANGO HARUKAWA
If you've already seen
the anime, it's time to
read the manga!
Having been kicked out of the
orphanage, Atsushi Nakajima rescues
a strange man from a suicide attempt—
Osamu Dazai. Turns out that Dazai is
part of a detective agency staffed by
individuals whose supernatural powers
take on a literary bent!
BUNGO STRAY DOGS © Kafka Asagiri 2013
© Sango Harukawa 2013
KADOKAWA CORPORATION
www.yenpress.com
Yen
Press

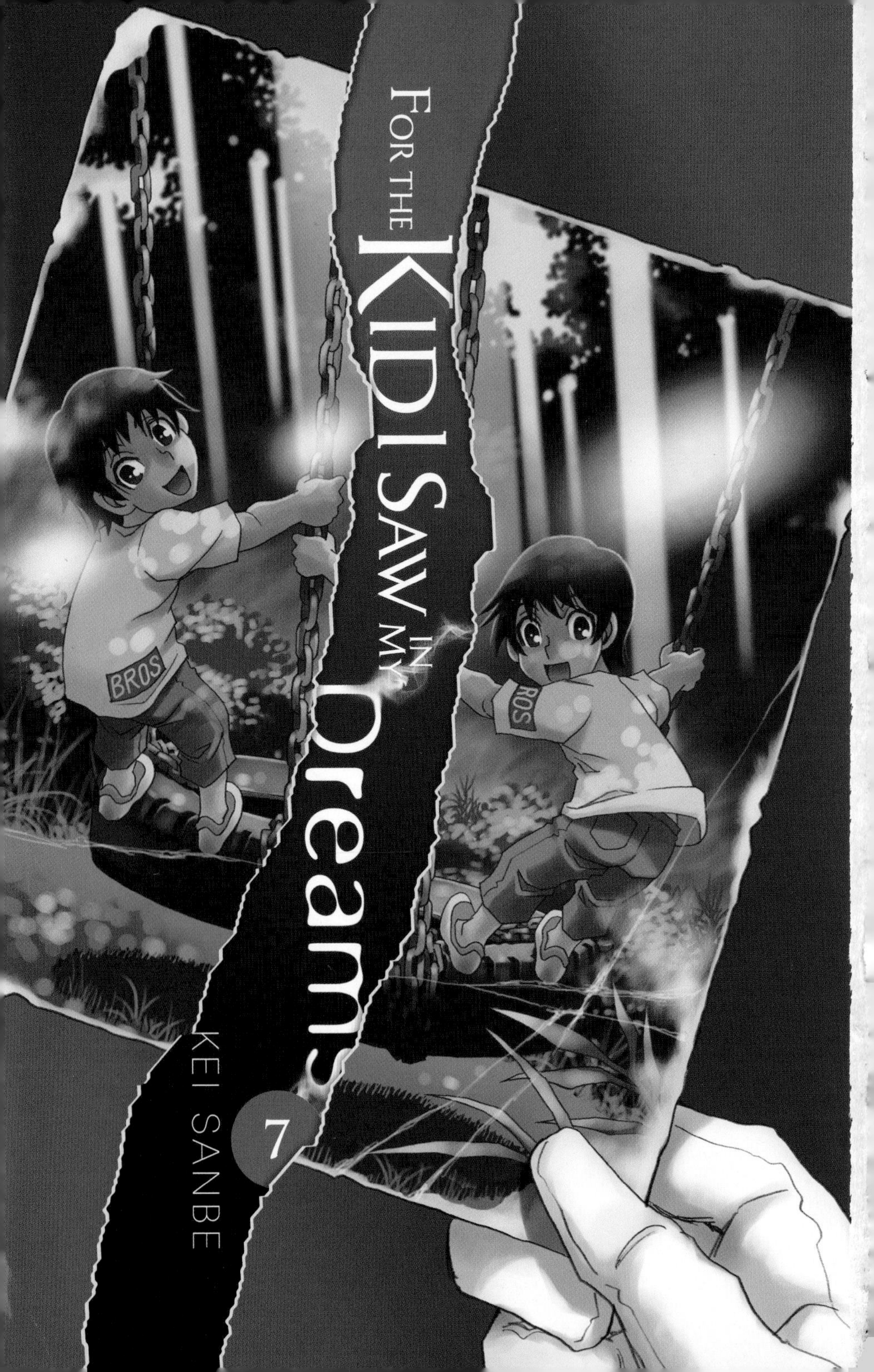
FOR THE KID I SAW IN MY Dreams
7
KEI SANBE
BROS
ROS

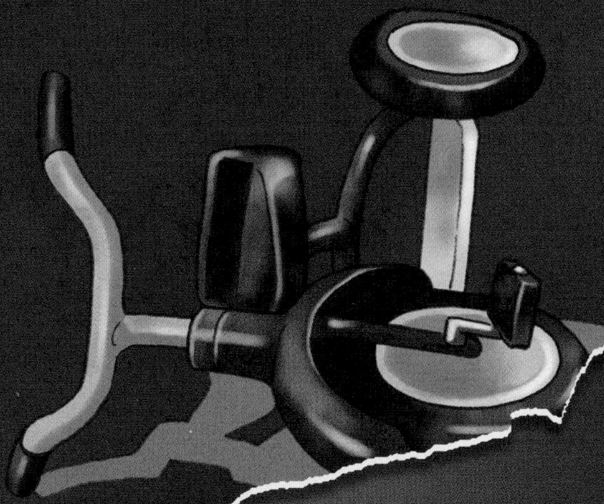

CONTENTS

#33 A Letter from Kazuto————————3

#34 Crime of a Five-Year-Old————41

#35 Photo of a Memory————————77

#36 Something to Cling To————115

#37 Gift————153

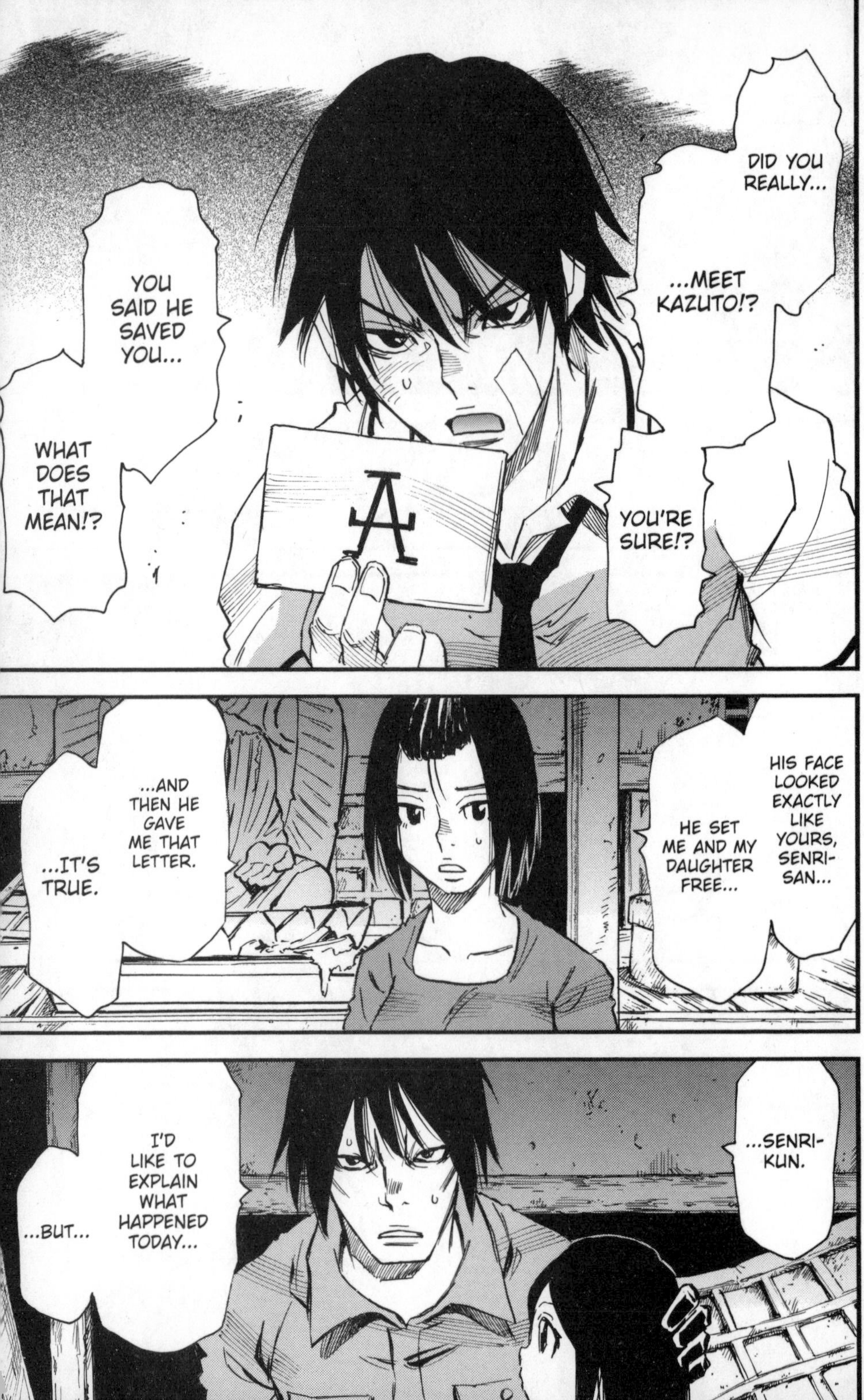
DID YOU REALLY...
...MEET KAZUTO!?
YOU'RE SURE!?
YOU SAID HE SAVED YOU...
WHAT DOES THAT MEAN!?
HIS FACE LOOKED EXACTLY LIKE YOURS, SENRI-SAN...
HE SET ME AND MY DAUGHTER FREE...
...AND THEN HE GAVE ME THAT LETTER.
...IT'S TRUE.
...SENRI-KUN.
I'D LIKE TO EXPLAIN WHAT HAPPENED TODAY...
...BUT...

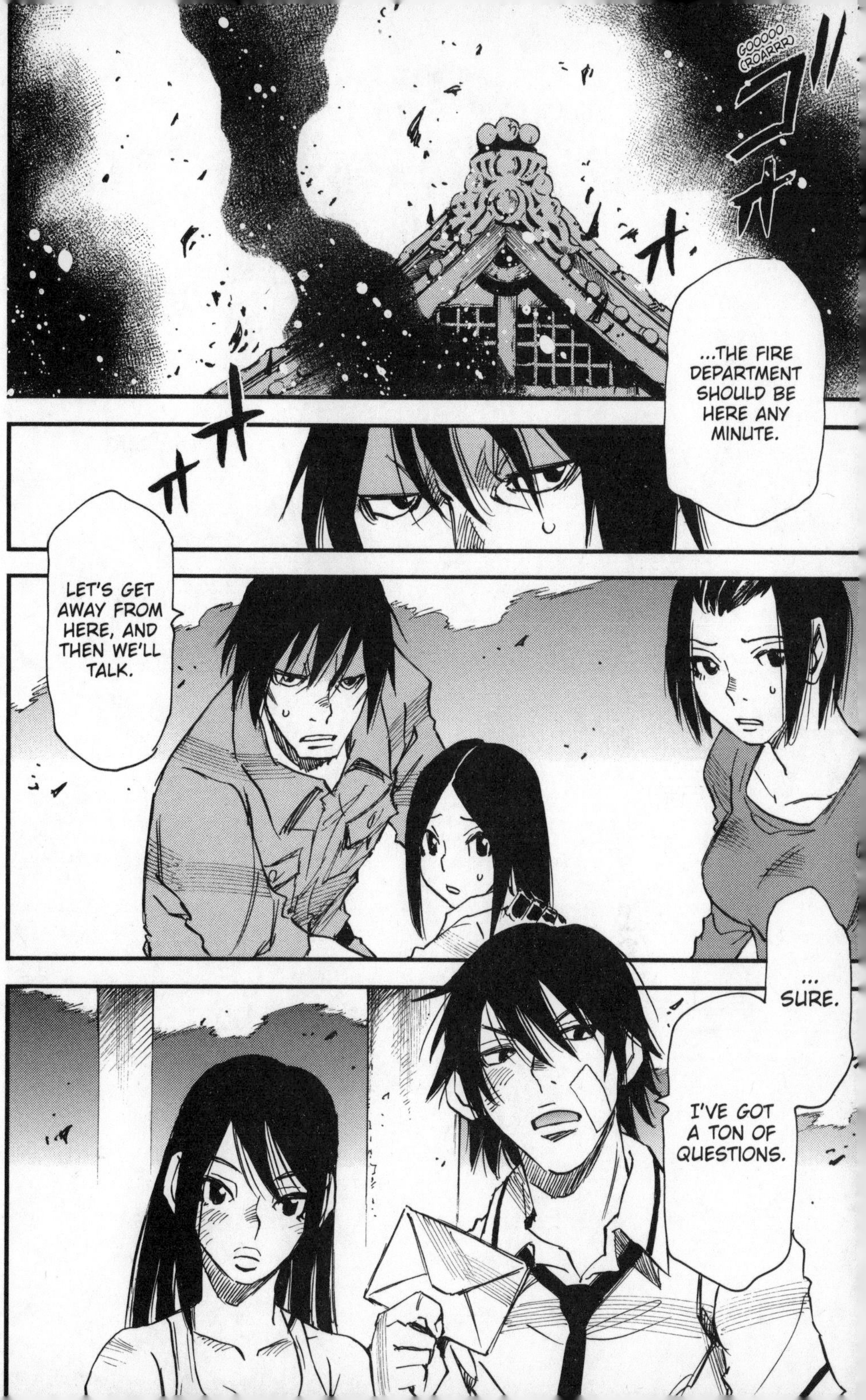
GOOOOO (ROARRR)
...THE FIRE DEPARTMENT SHOULD BE HERE ANY MINUTE.
LET'S GET AWAY FROM HERE, AND THEN WE'LL TALK.
... SURE.
I'VE GOT A TON OF QUESTIONS.

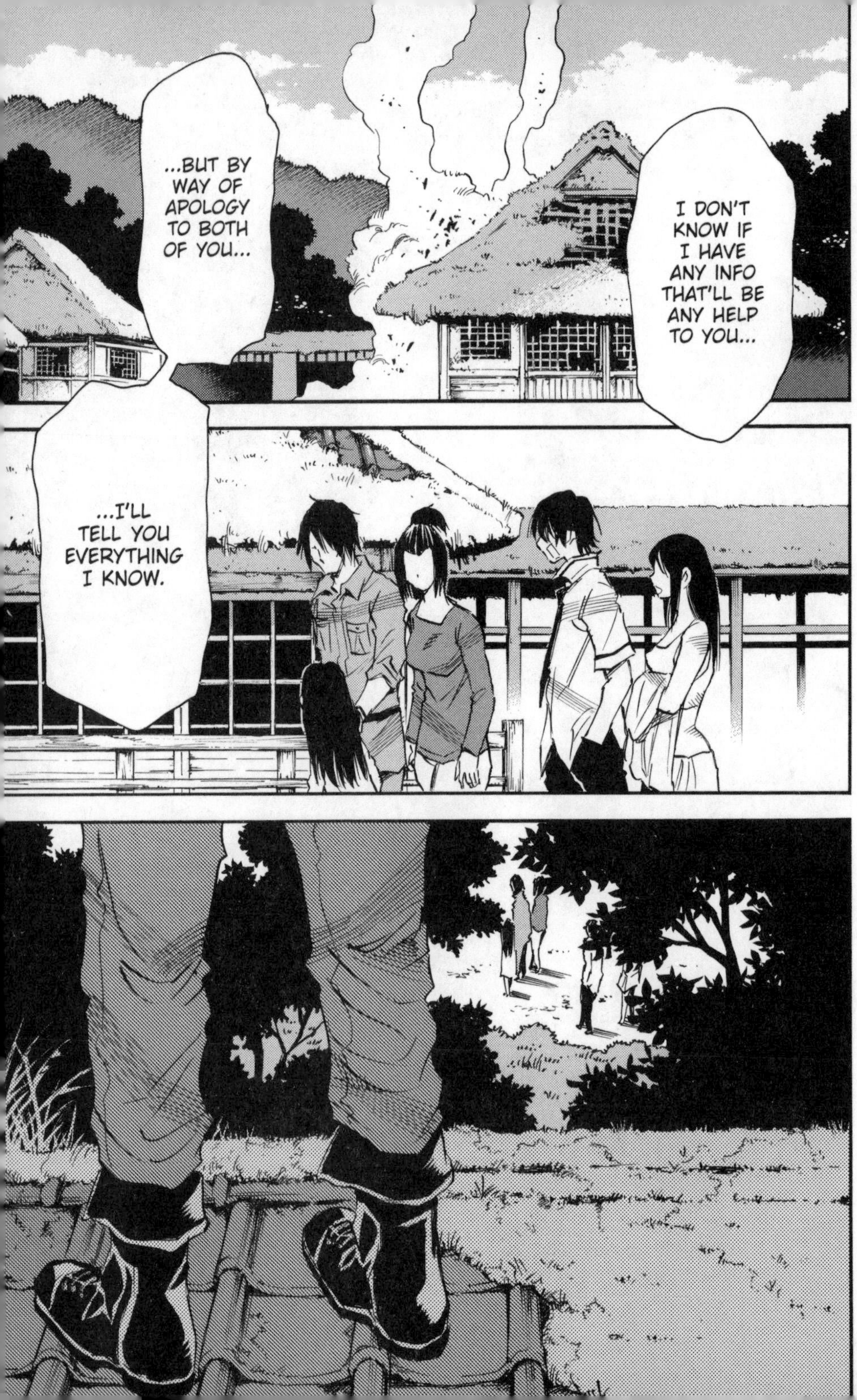
I DON'T KNOW IF I HAVE ANY INFO THAT'LL BE ANY HELP TO YOU...
...BUT BY WAY OF APOLOGY TO BOTH OF YOU...
...I'LL TELL YOU EVERYTHING I KNOW.

#33 A Letter from Kazuto

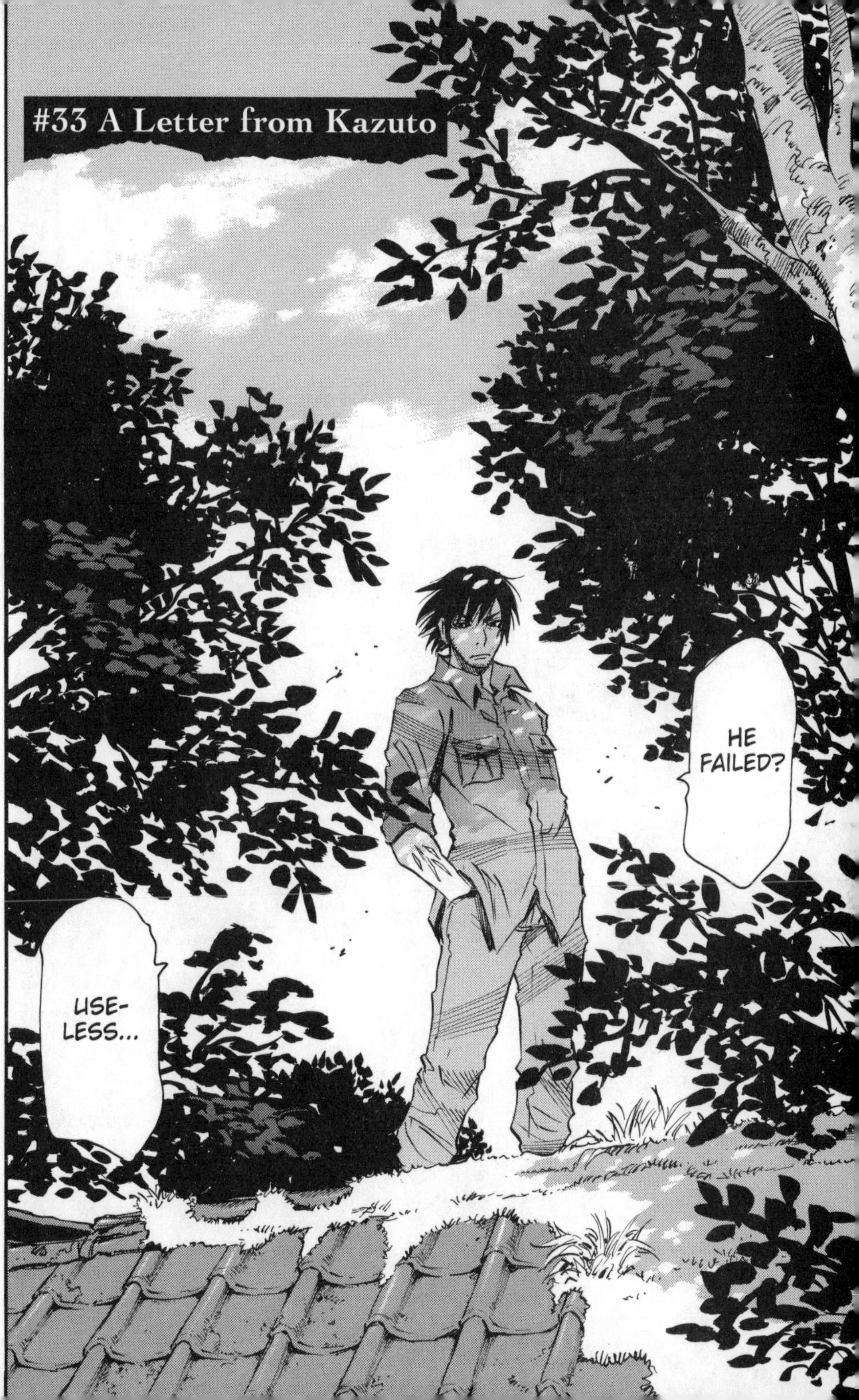
HE FAILED?
USE-LESS...

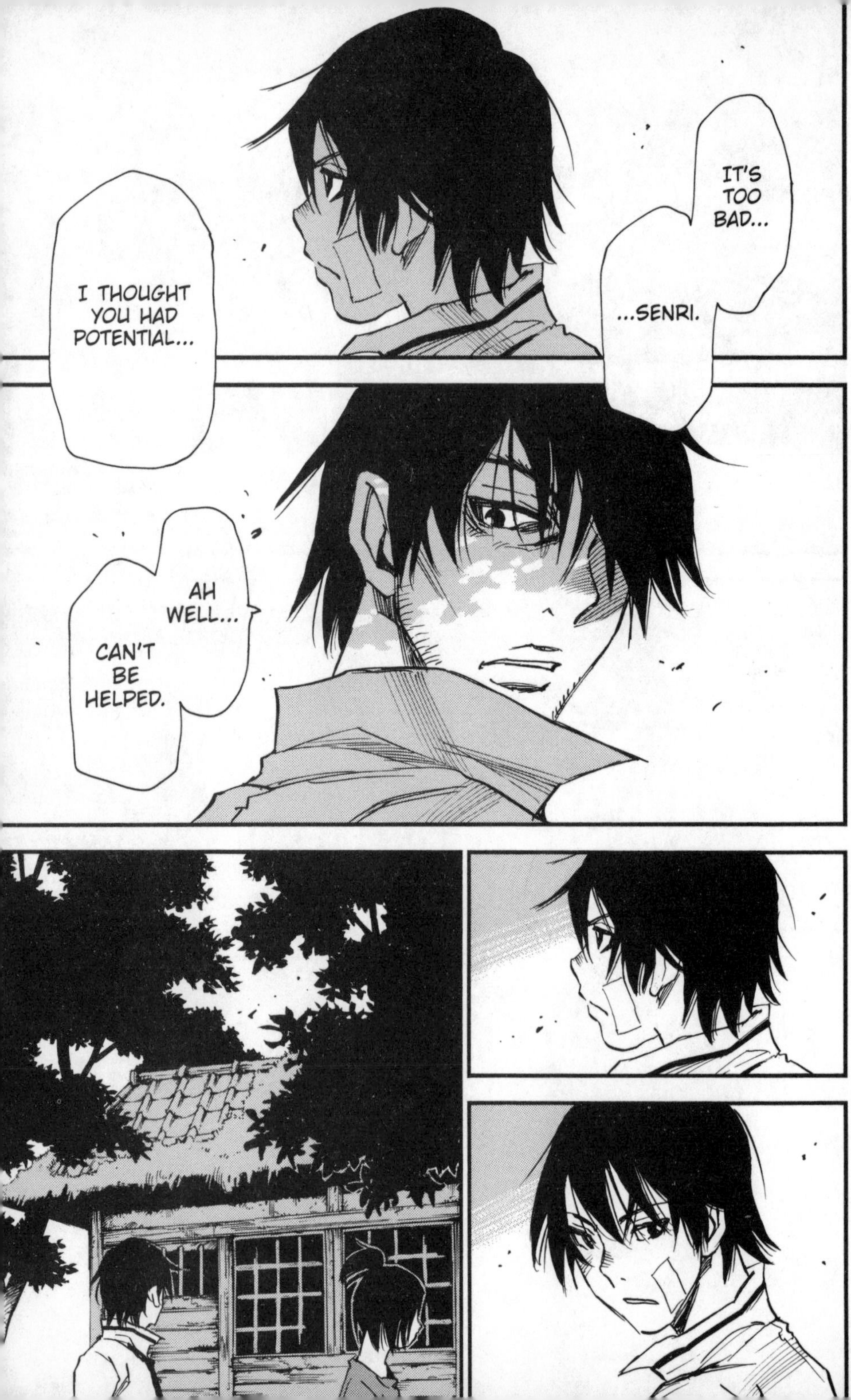
IT'S TOO BAD... ...SENRI.
I THOUGHT YOU HAD POTENTIAL...
AH WELL... CAN'T BE HELPED.

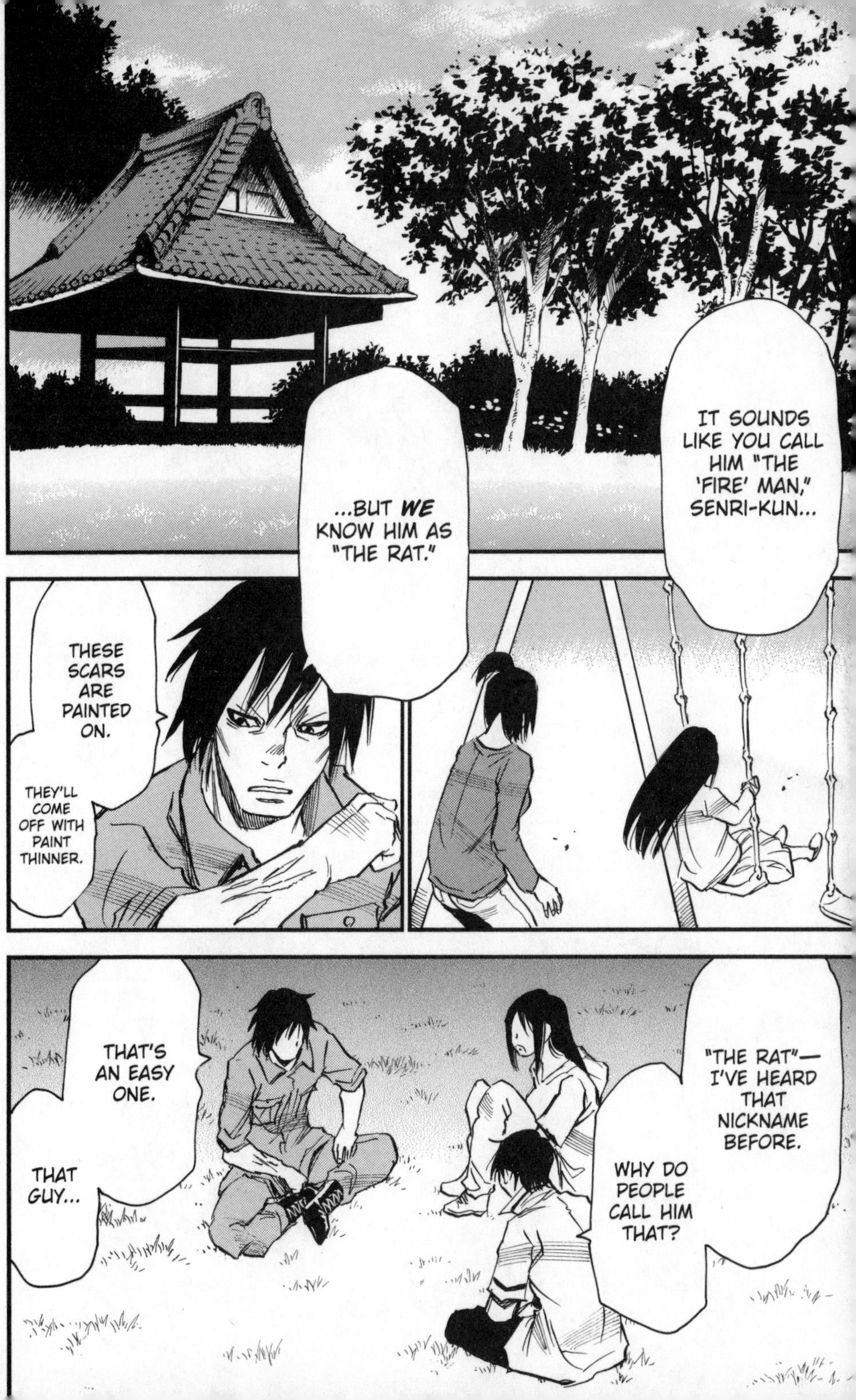
IT SOUNDS LIKE YOU CALL HIM "THE 'FIRE' MAN," SENRI-KUN...
...BUT ***WE*** KNOW HIM AS "THE RAT."
THESE SCARS ARE PAINTED ON.
THEY'LL COME OFF WITH PAINT THINNER.
"THE RAT"—I'VE HEARD THAT NICKNAME BEFORE.
WHY DO PEOPLE CALL HIM THAT?
THAT'S AN EASY ONE.
THAT GUY...

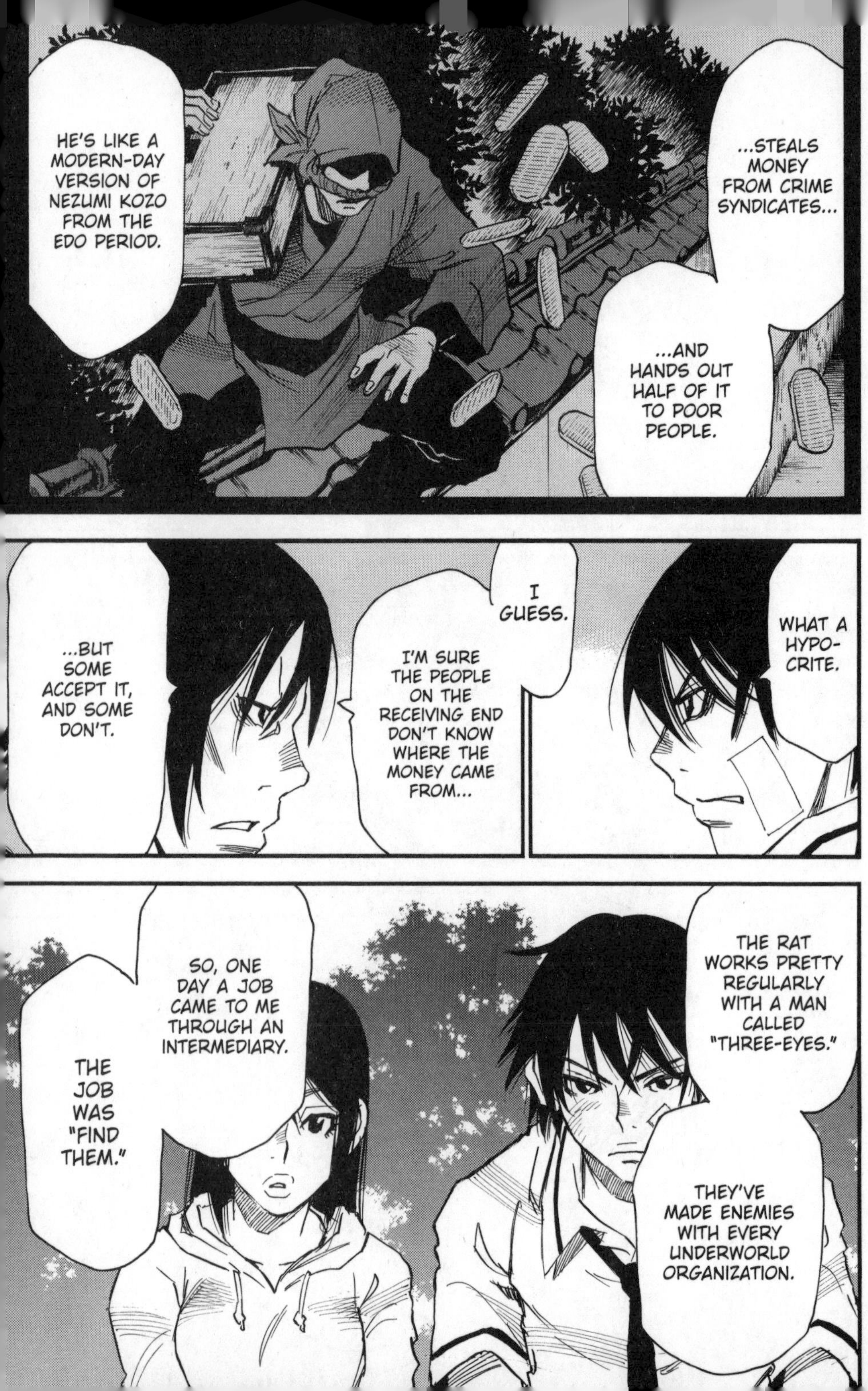
...STEALS MONEY FROM CRIME SYNDICATES...
...AND HANDS OUT HALF OF IT TO POOR PEOPLE.
HE'S LIKE A MODERN-DAY VERSION OF NEZUMI KOZO FROM THE EDO PERIOD.
WHAT A HYPO-CRITE.
I GUESS.
I'M SURE THE PEOPLE ON THE RECEIVING END DON'T KNOW WHERE THE MONEY CAME FROM...
...BUT SOME ACCEPT IT, AND SOME DON'T.
THE RAT WORKS PRETTY REGULARLY WITH A MAN CALLED "THREE-EYES."
THEY'VE MADE ENEMIES WITH EVERY UNDERWORLD ORGANIZATION.
SO, ONE DAY A JOB CAME TO ME THROUGH AN INTERMEDIARY.
THE JOB WAS "FIND THEM."

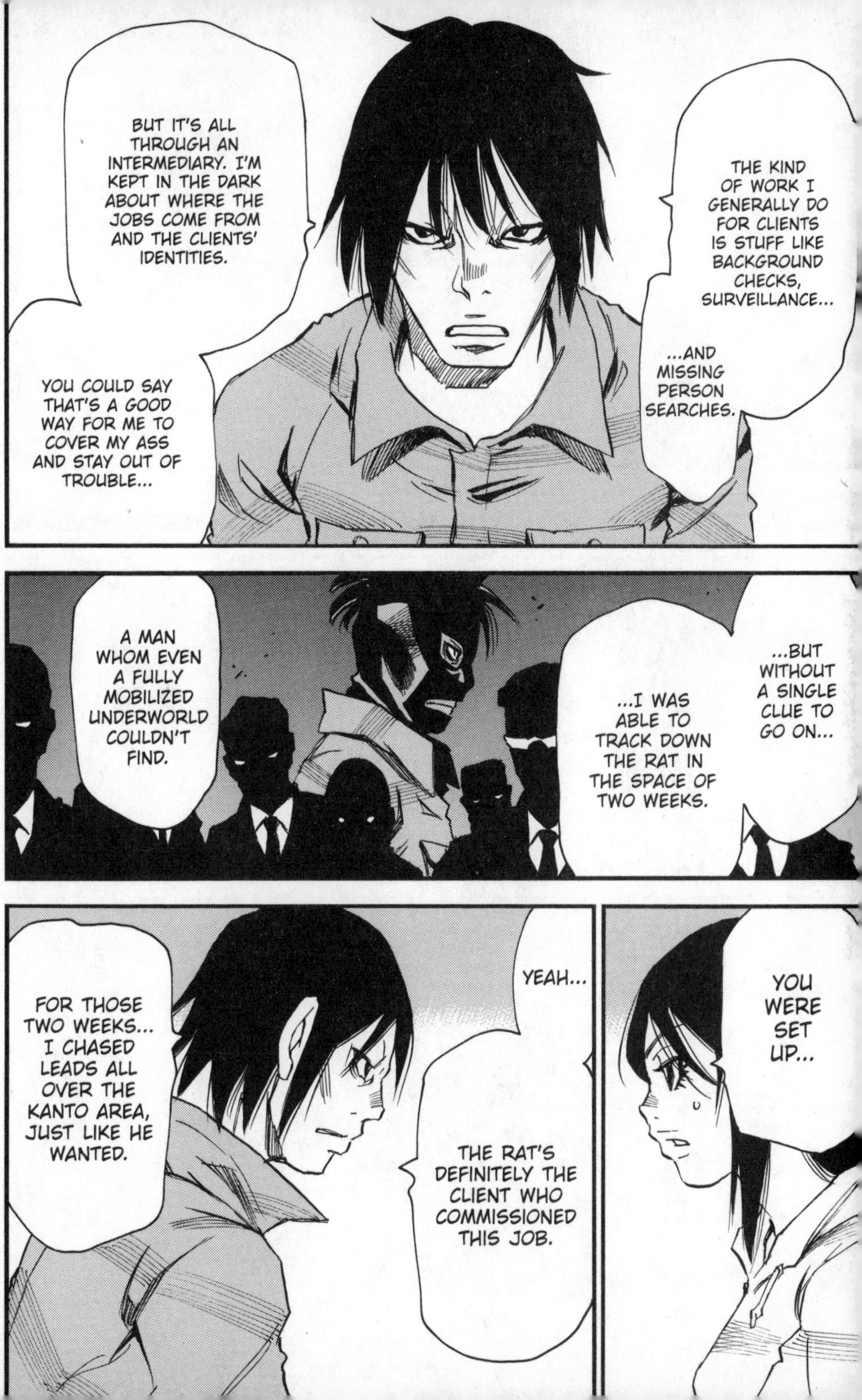
THE KIND OF WORK I GENERALLY DO FOR CLIENTS IS STUFF LIKE BACKGROUND CHECKS, SURVEILLANCE...
...AND MISSING PERSON SEARCHES.
BUT IT'S ALL THROUGH AN INTERMEDIARY. I'M KEPT IN THE DARK ABOUT WHERE THE JOBS COME FROM AND THE CLIENTS' IDENTITIES.
YOU COULD SAY THAT'S A GOOD WAY FOR ME TO COVER MY ASS AND STAY OUT OF TROUBLE...
...BUT WITHOUT A SINGLE CLUE TO GO ON...
...I WAS ABLE TO TRACK DOWN THE RAT IN THE SPACE OF TWO WEEKS.
A MAN WHOM EVEN A FULLY MOBILIZED UNDERWORLD COULDN'T FIND.
YOU WERE SET UP...
YEAH...
THE RAT'S DEFINITELY THE CLIENT WHO COMMISSIONED THIS JOB.
FOR THOSE TWO WEEKS... I CHASED LEADS ALL OVER THE KANTO AREA, JUST LIKE HE WANTED.

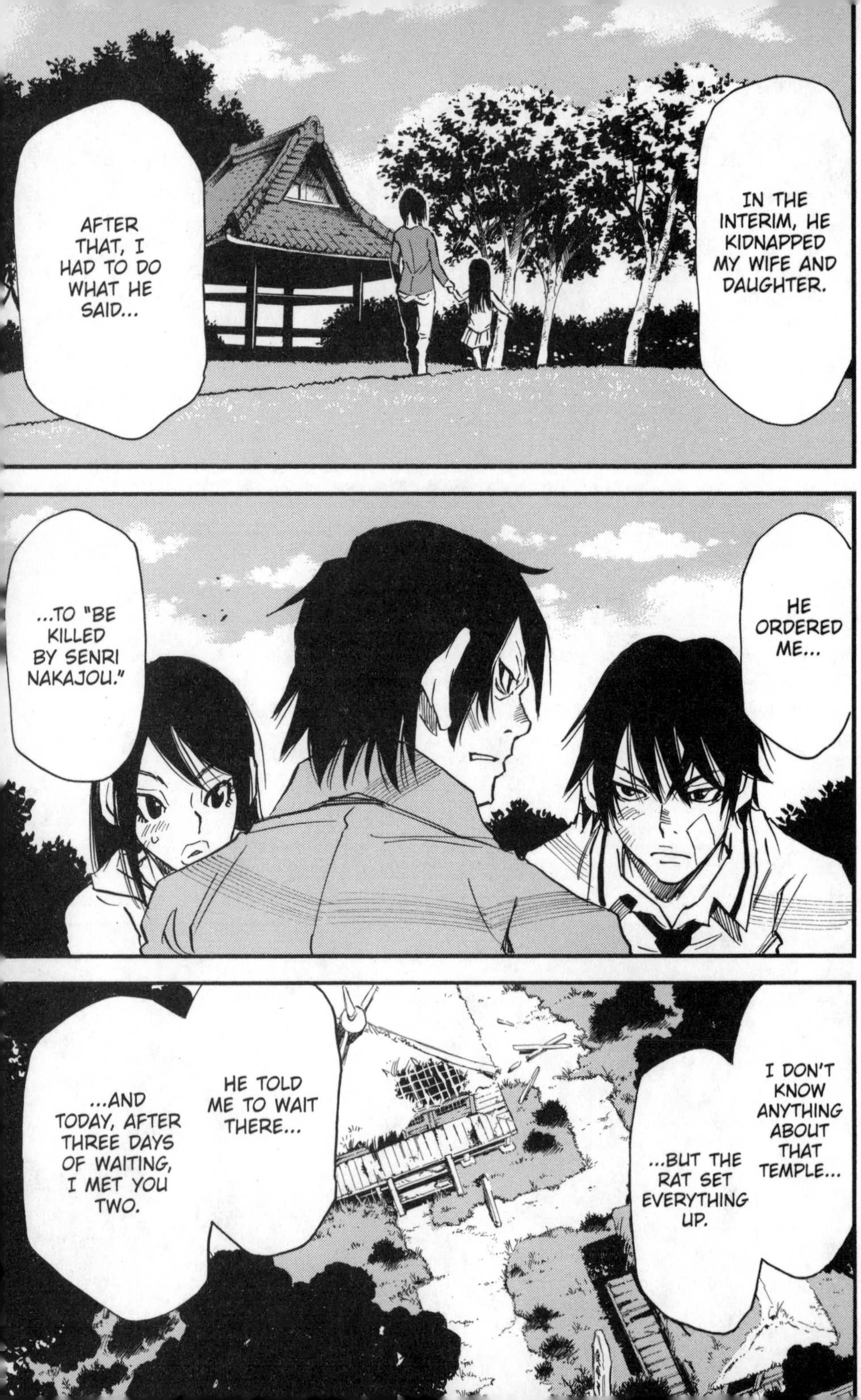
IN THE INTERIM, HE KIDNAPPED MY WIFE AND DAUGHTER.
AFTER THAT, I HAD TO DO WHAT HE SAID...
HE ORDERED ME...
...TO "BE KILLED BY SENRI NAKAJOU."
I DON'T KNOW ANYTHING ABOUT THAT TEMPLE...
...BUT THE RAT SET EVERYTHING UP.
HE TOLD ME TO WAIT THERE...
...AND TODAY, AFTER THREE DAYS OF WAITING, I MET YOU TWO.

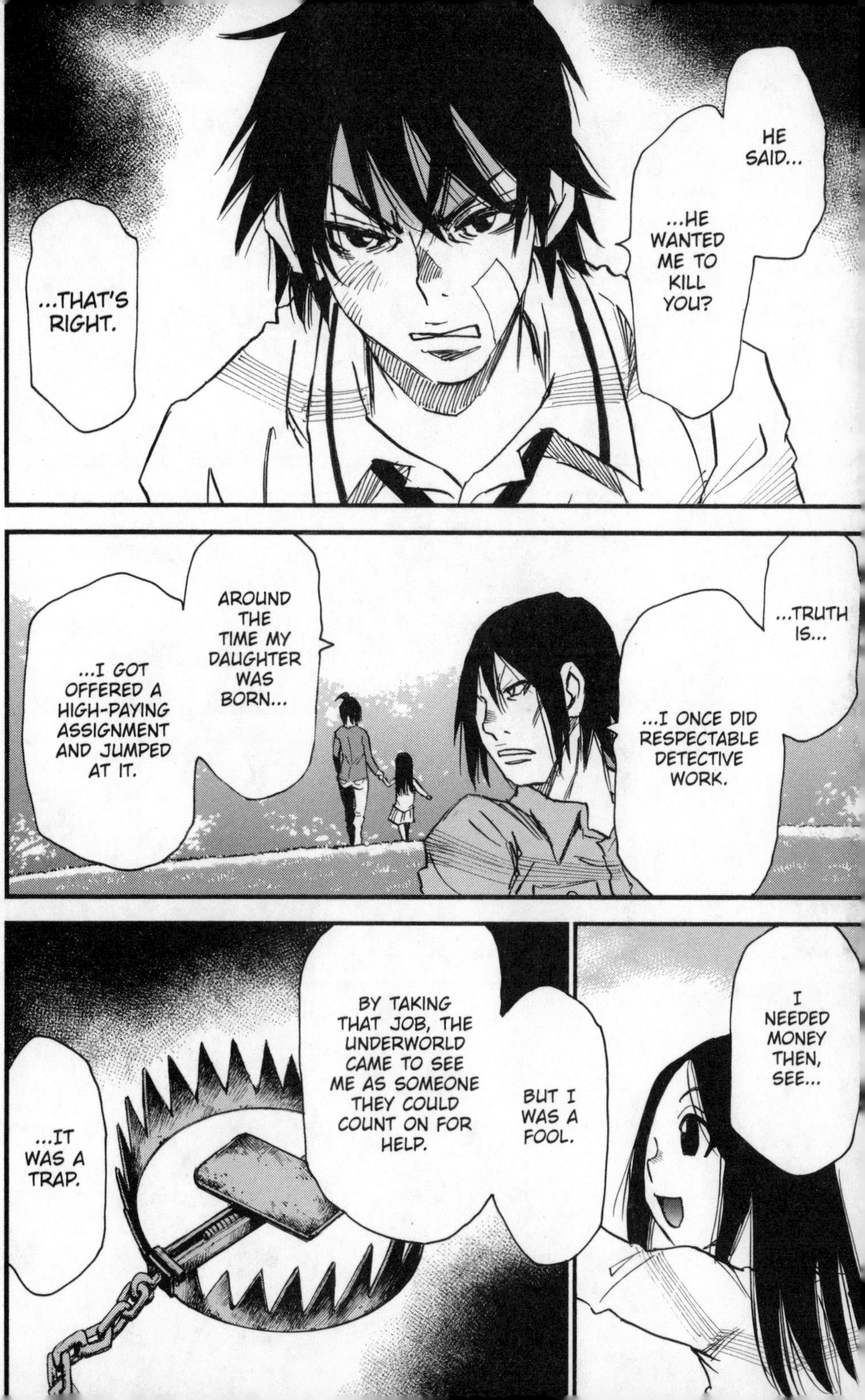
HE SAID...
...HE WANTED ME TO KILL YOU?
...THAT'S RIGHT.
...TRUTH IS...
...I ONCE DID RESPECTABLE DETECTIVE WORK.
AROUND THE TIME MY DAUGHTER WAS BORN...
...I GOT OFFERED A HIGH-PAYING ASSIGNMENT AND JUMPED AT IT.
I NEEDED MONEY THEN, SEE...
BUT I WAS A FOOL.
BY TAKING THAT JOB, THE UNDERWORLD CAME TO SEE ME AS SOMEONE THEY COULD COUNT ON FOR HELP.
...IT WAS A TRAP.

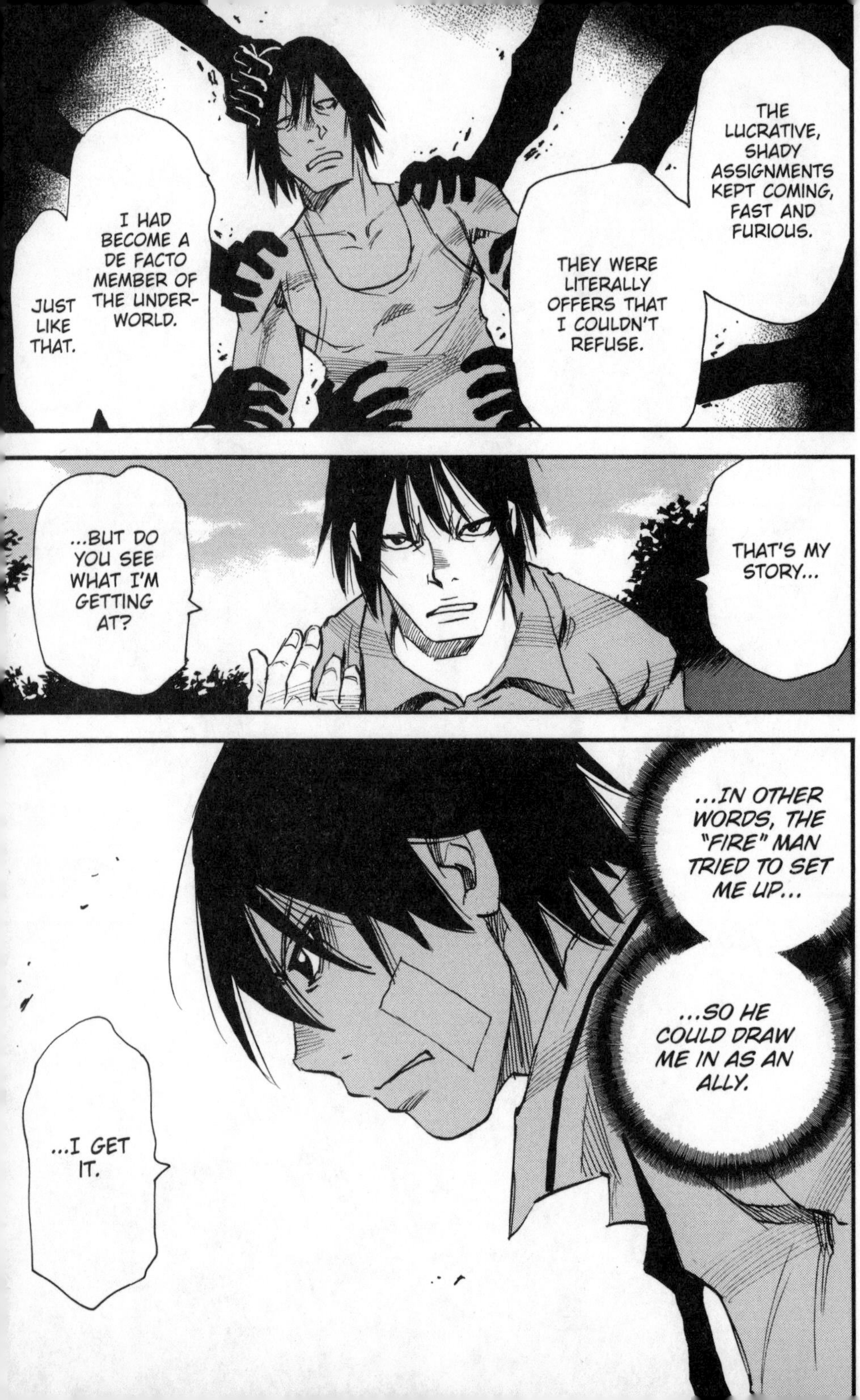
THE LUCRATIVE, SHADY ASSIGNMENTS KEPT COMING, FAST AND FURIOUS.
THEY WERE LITERALLY OFFERS THAT I COULDN'T REFUSE.
I HAD BECOME A DE FACTO MEMBER OF THE UNDER-WORLD.
JUST LIKE THAT.
THAT'S MY STORY...
...BUT DO YOU SEE WHAT I'M GETTING AT?
...IN OTHER WORDS, THE "FIRE" MAN TRIED TO SET ME UP...
...SO HE COULD DRAW ME IN AS AN ALLY.
...I GET IT.

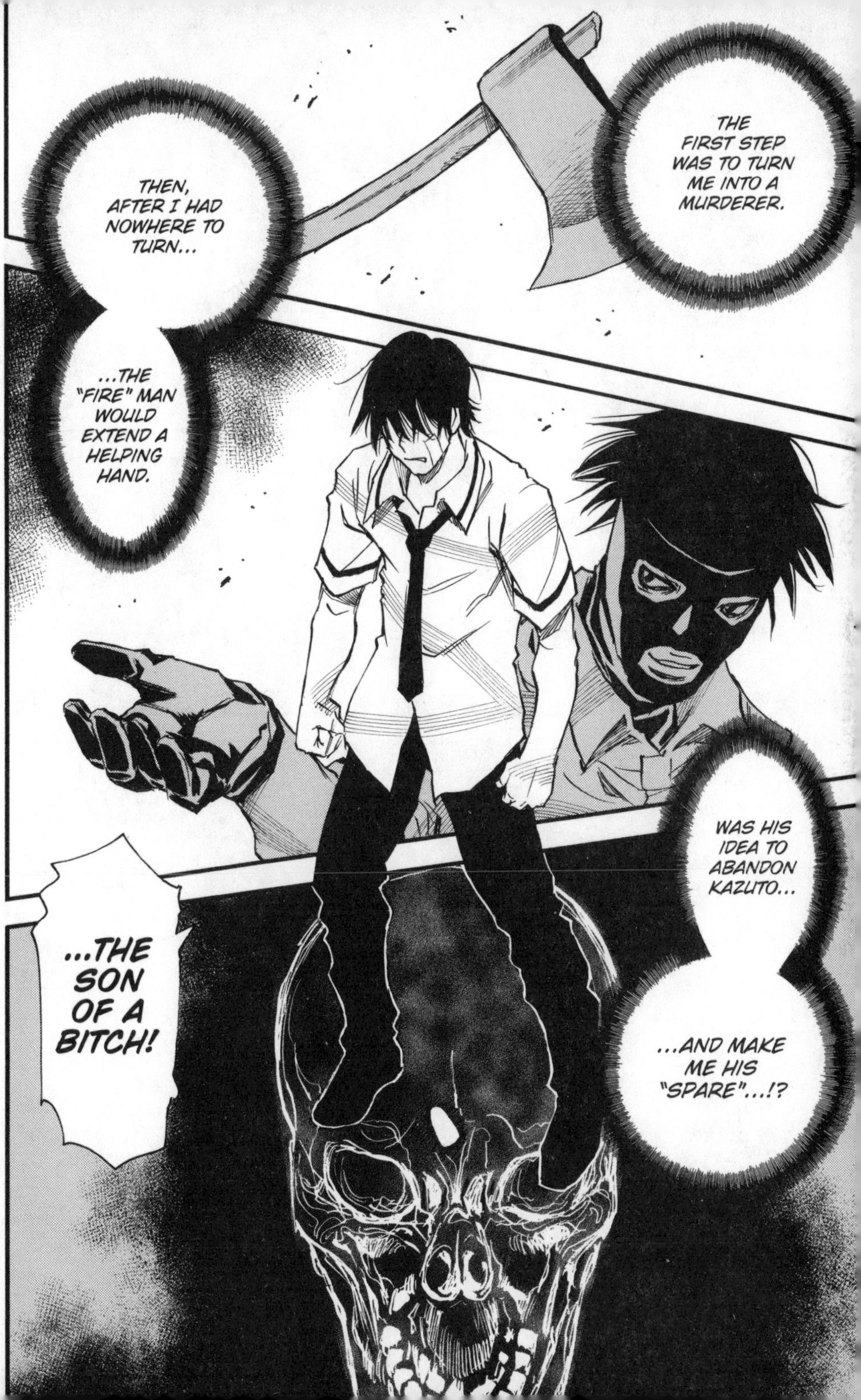
THE FIRST STEP WAS TO TURN ME INTO A MURDERER.
THEN, AFTER I HAD NOWHERE TO TURN...
...THE "FIRE" MAN WOULD EXTEND A HELPING HAND.
WAS HIS IDEA TO ABANDON KAZUTO...
...AND MAKE ME HIS "SPARE"...!?
...THE SON OF A BITCH!

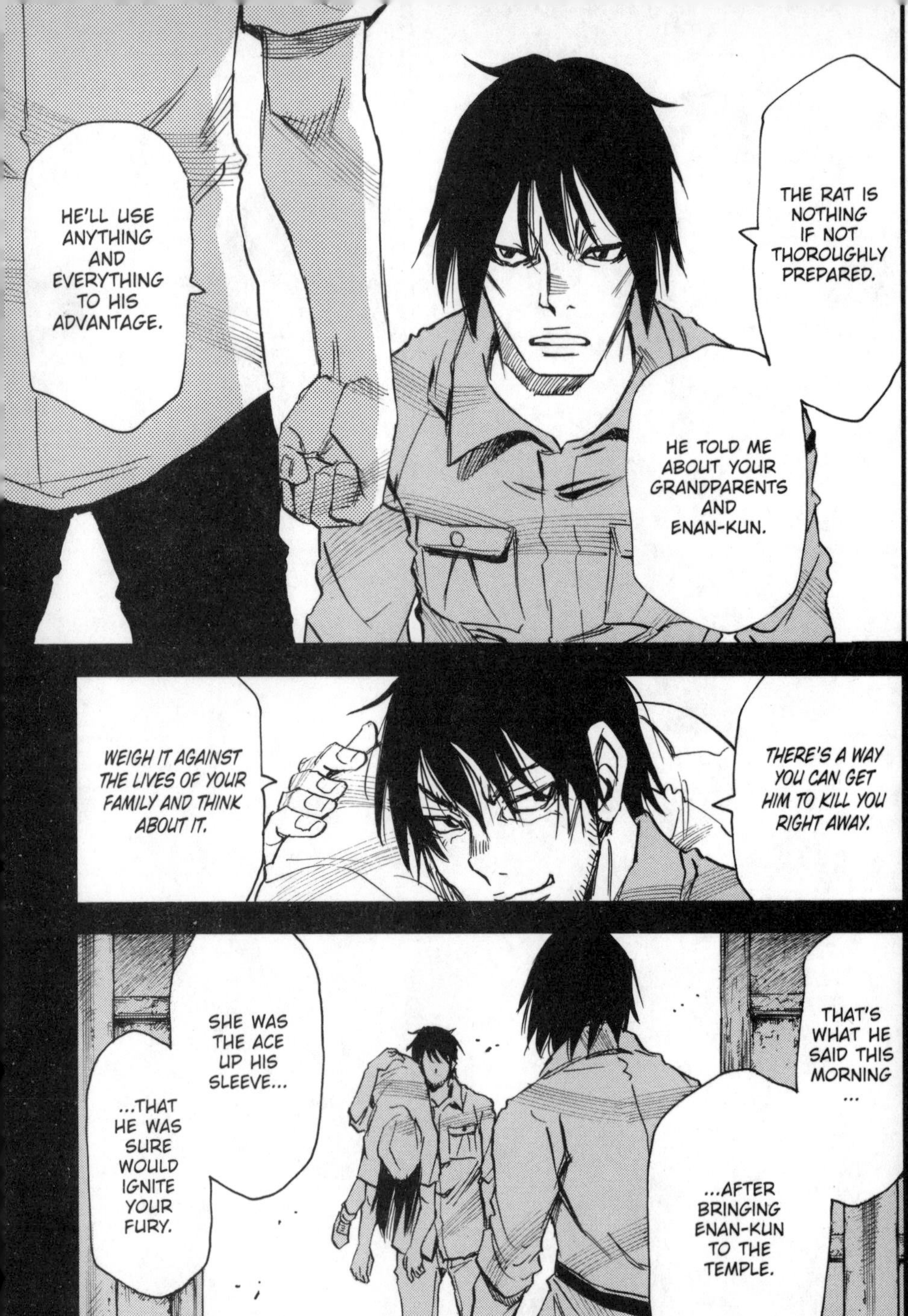
THE RAT IS NOTHING IF NOT THOROUGHLY PREPARED.
HE TOLD ME ABOUT YOUR GRANDPARENTS AND ENAN-KUN.
HE'LL USE ANYTHING AND EVERYTHING TO HIS ADVANTAGE.
THERE'S A WAY YOU CAN GET HIM TO KILL YOU RIGHT AWAY.
WEIGH IT AGAINST THE LIVES OF YOUR FAMILY AND THINK ABOUT IT.
THAT'S WHAT HE SAID THIS MORNING ...
...AFTER BRINGING ENAN-KUN TO THE TEMPLE.
SHE WAS THE ACE UP HIS SLEEVE...
...THAT HE WAS SURE WOULD IGNITE YOUR FURY.

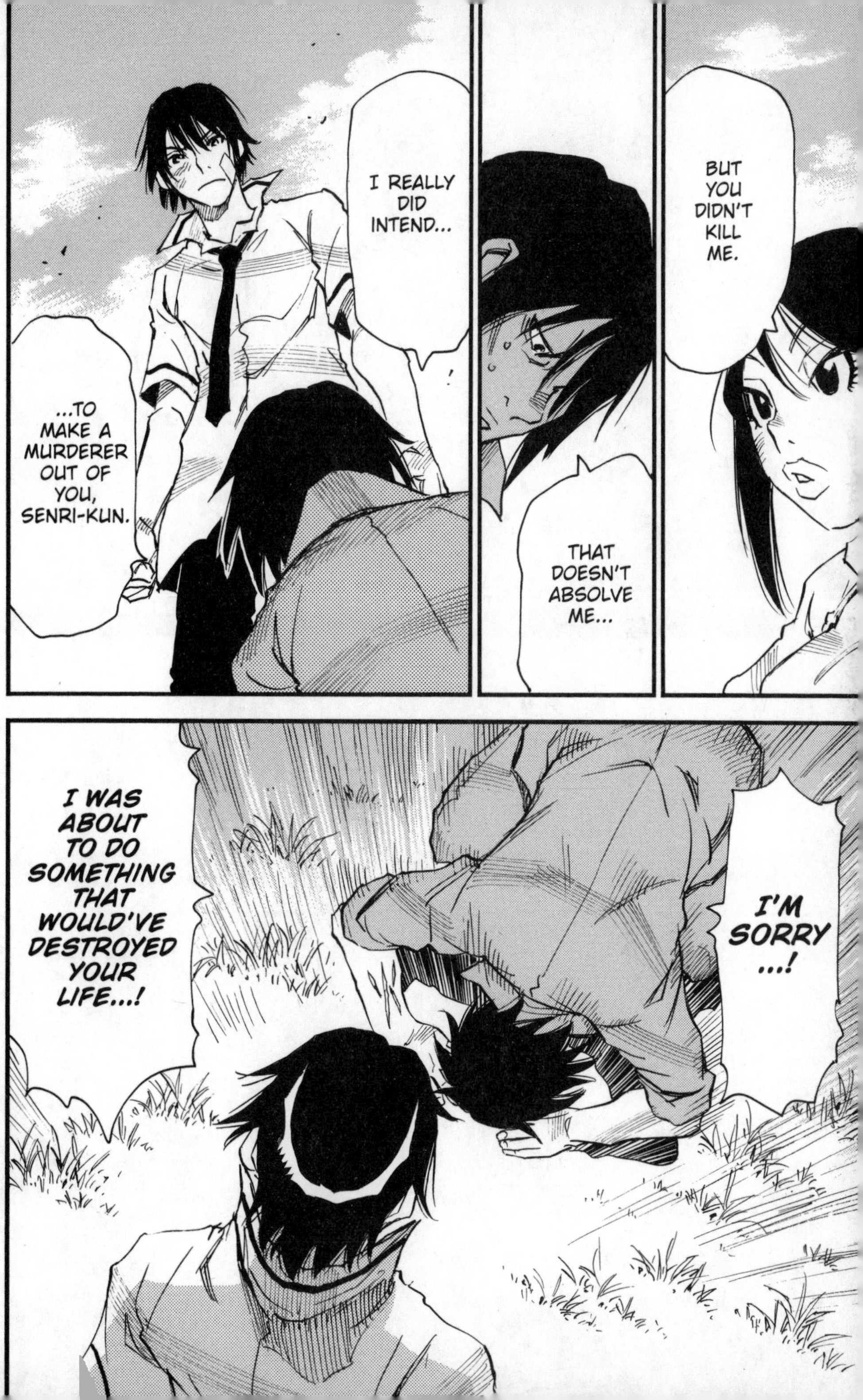
BUT YOU DIDN'T KILL ME.
THAT DOESN'T ABSOLVE ME...
I REALLY DID INTEND...
...TO MAKE A MURDERER OUT OF YOU, SENRI-KUN.
I'M SORRY...!
I WAS ABOUT TO DO SOMETHING THAT WOULD'VE DESTROYED YOUR LIFE...!

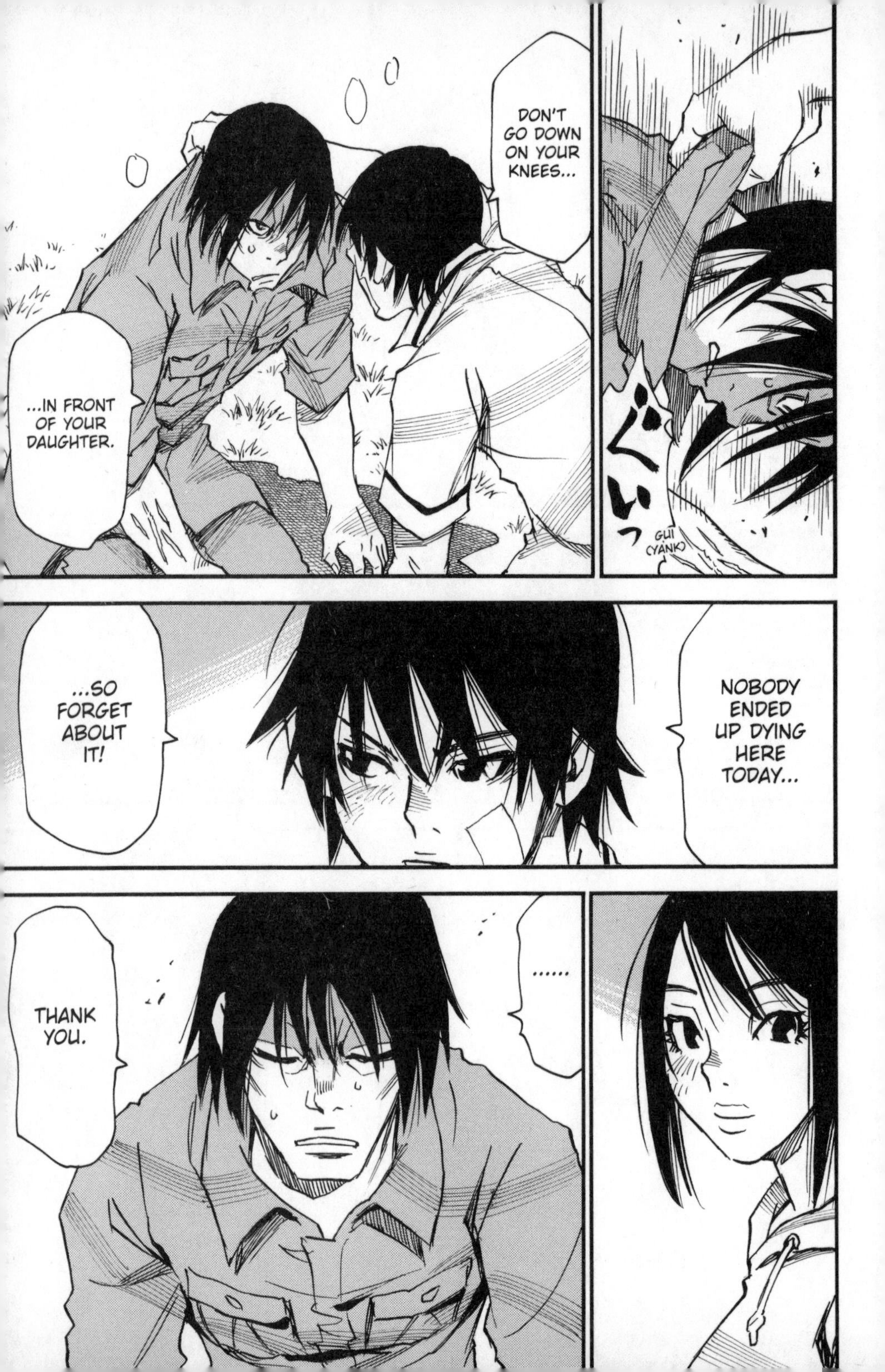
ぐいっ
GUI (YANK)
DON'T GO DOWN ON YOUR KNEES...
...IN FRONT OF YOUR DAUGHTER.
NOBODY ENDED UP DYING HERE TODAY...
...SO FORGET ABOUT IT!
......
THANK YOU.

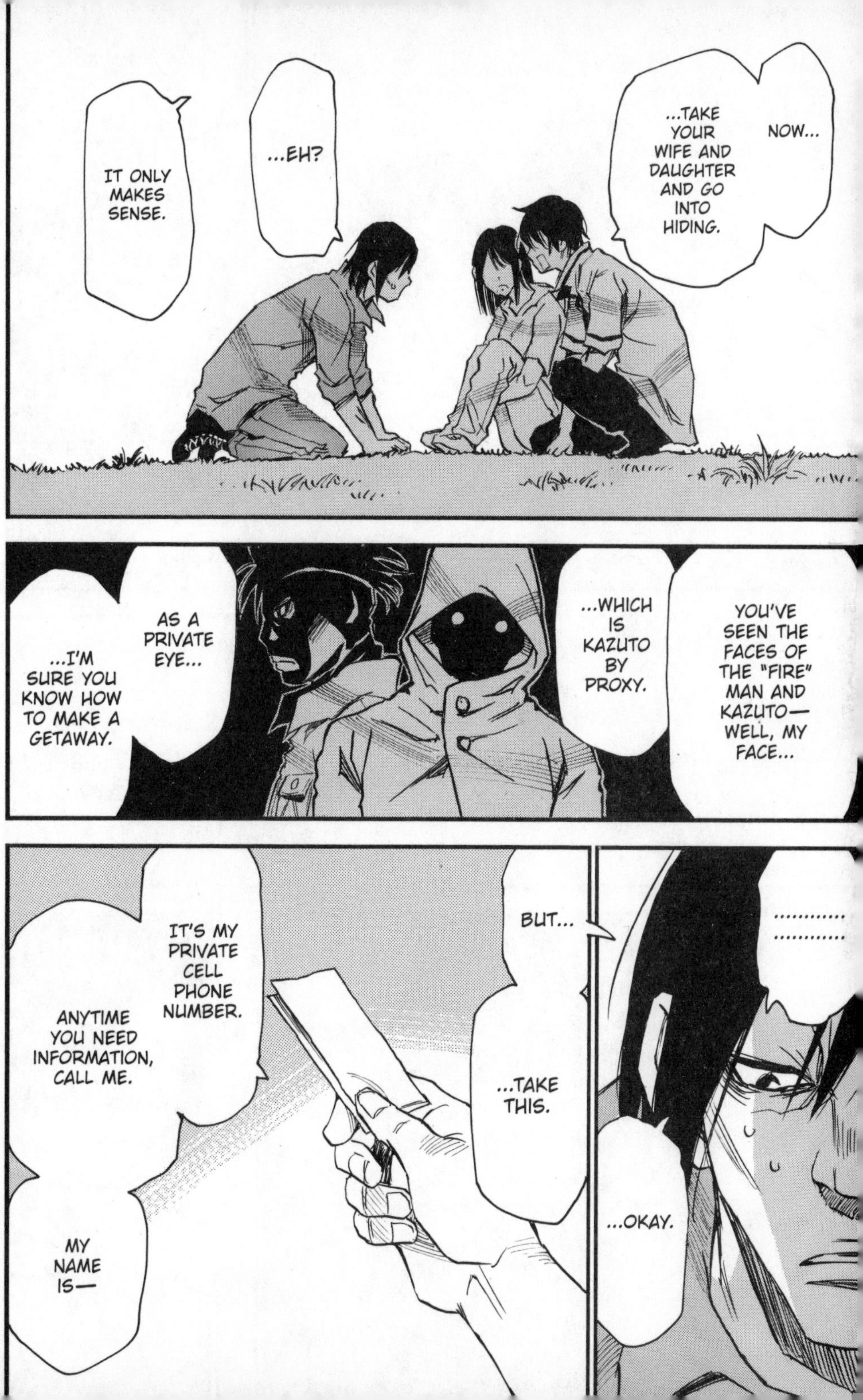
NOW...
...TAKE YOUR WIFE AND DAUGHTER AND GO INTO HIDING.
...EH?
IT ONLY MAKES SENSE.
YOU'VE SEEN THE FACES OF THE "FIRE" MAN AND KAZUTO—WELL, MY FACE...
...WHICH IS KAZUTO BY PROXY.
AS A PRIVATE EYE...
...I'M SURE YOU KNOW HOW TO MAKE A GETAWAY.
....
...OKAY.
BUT...
...TAKE THIS.
IT'S MY PRIVATE CELL PHONE NUMBER.
ANYTIME YOU NEED INFORMATION, CALL ME.
MY NAME IS—

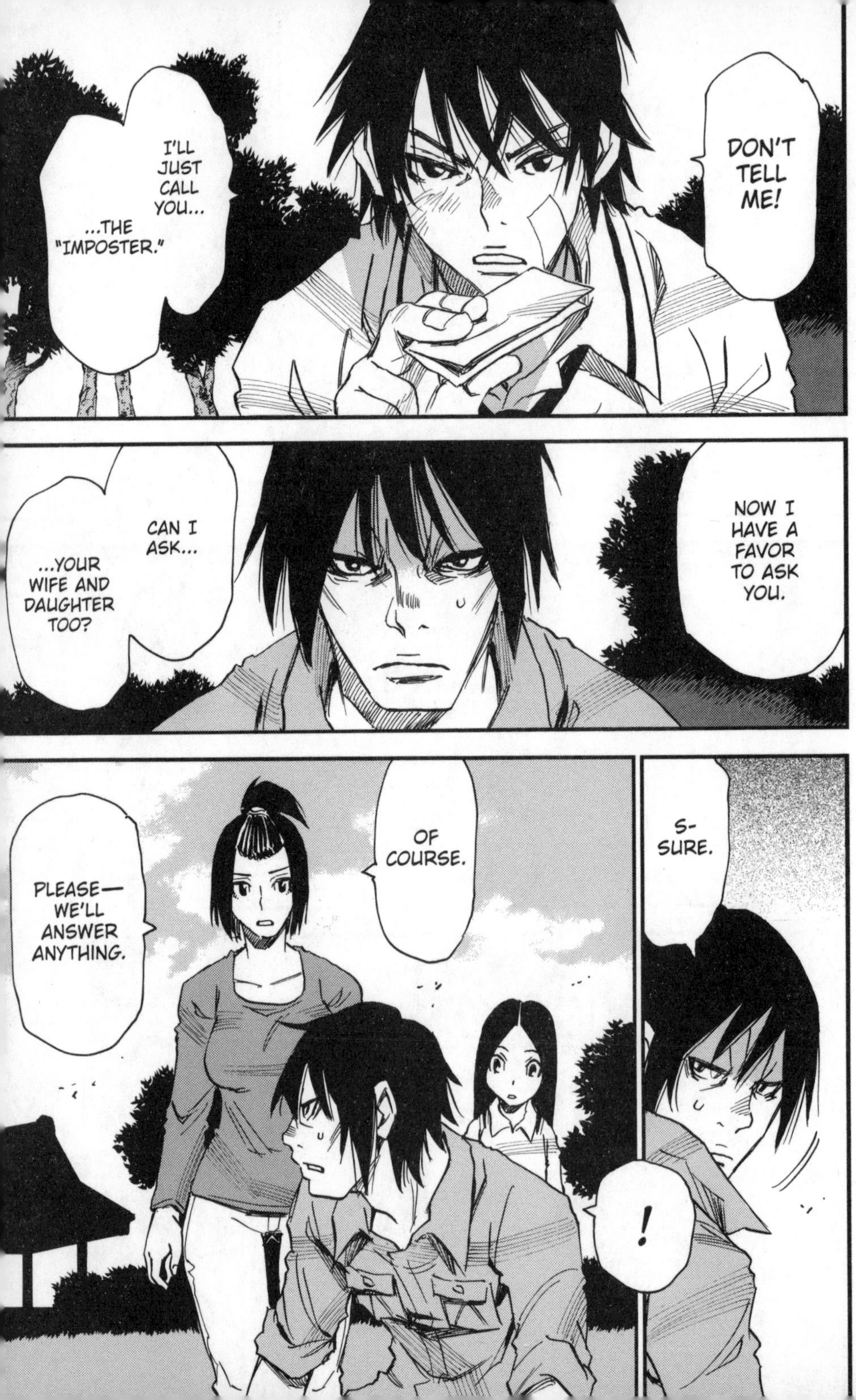
DON'T TELL ME!
I'LL JUST CALL YOU...
...THE "IMPOSTER."
NOW I HAVE A FAVOR TO ASK YOU.
CAN I ASK...
...YOUR WIFE AND DAUGHTER TOO?
S-SURE.
!
OF COURSE.
PLEASE—WE'LL ANSWER ANYTHING.

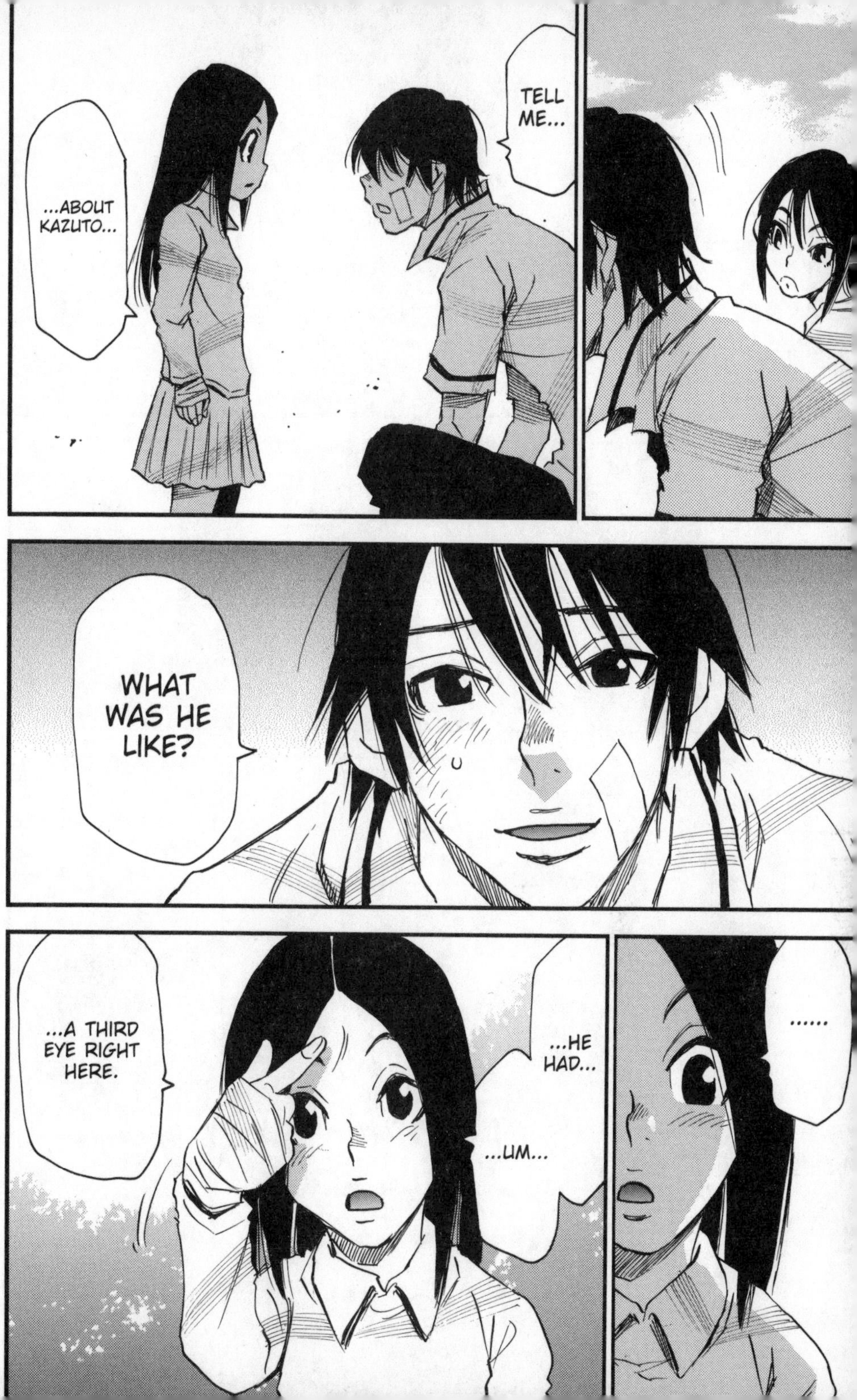
TELL ME...
...ABOUT KAZUTO...
WHAT WAS HE LIKE?
......
...HE HAD...
...UM...
...A THIRD EYE RIGHT HERE.

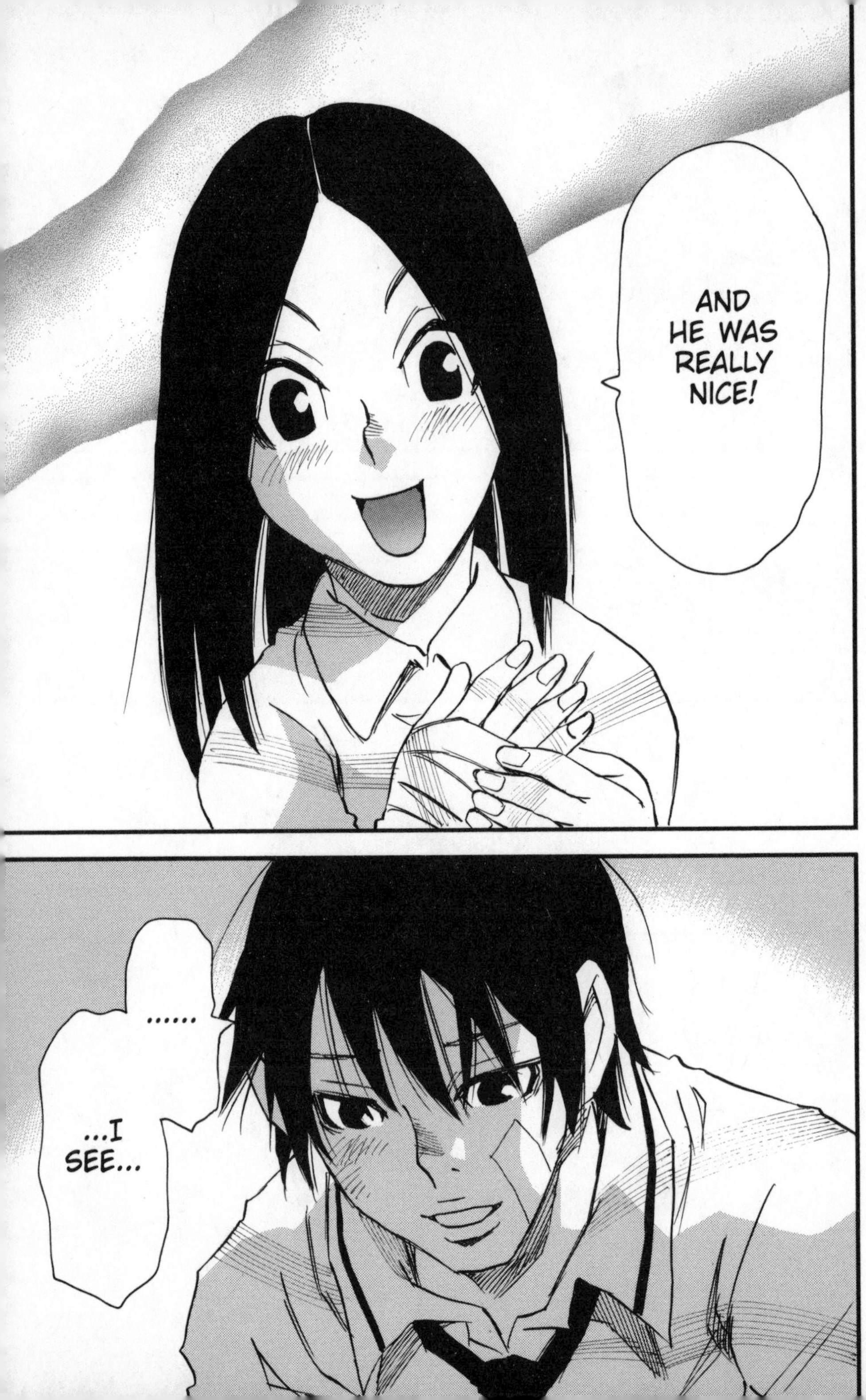
AND HE WAS REALLY NICE!
......
...I SEE...

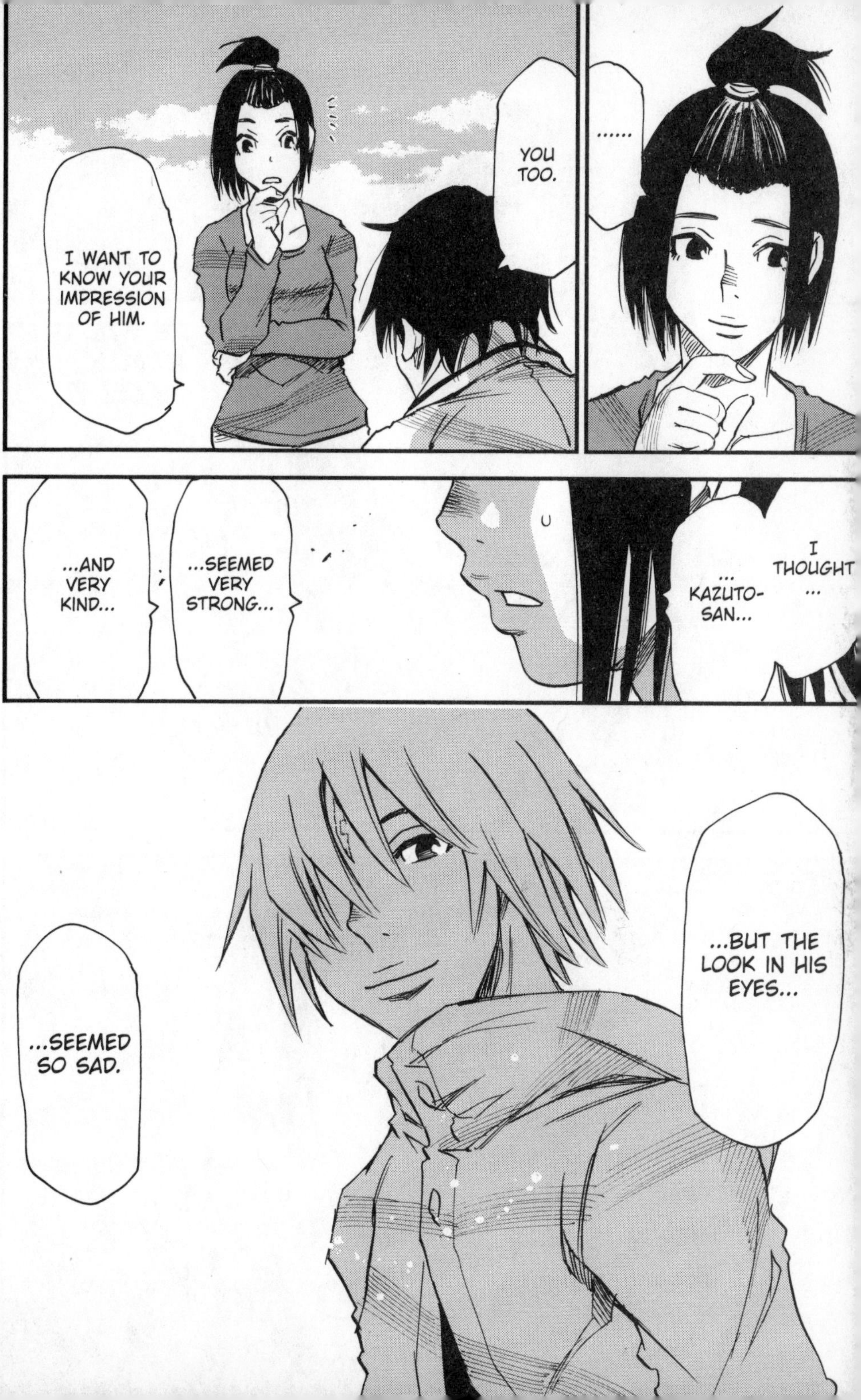
......
YOU TOO.
I WANT TO KNOW YOUR IMPRESSION OF HIM.
I THOUGHT ...
... KAZUTO-SAN...
...SEEMED VERY STRONG...
...AND VERY KIND...
...BUT THE LOOK IN HIS EYES...
...SEEMED SO SAD.

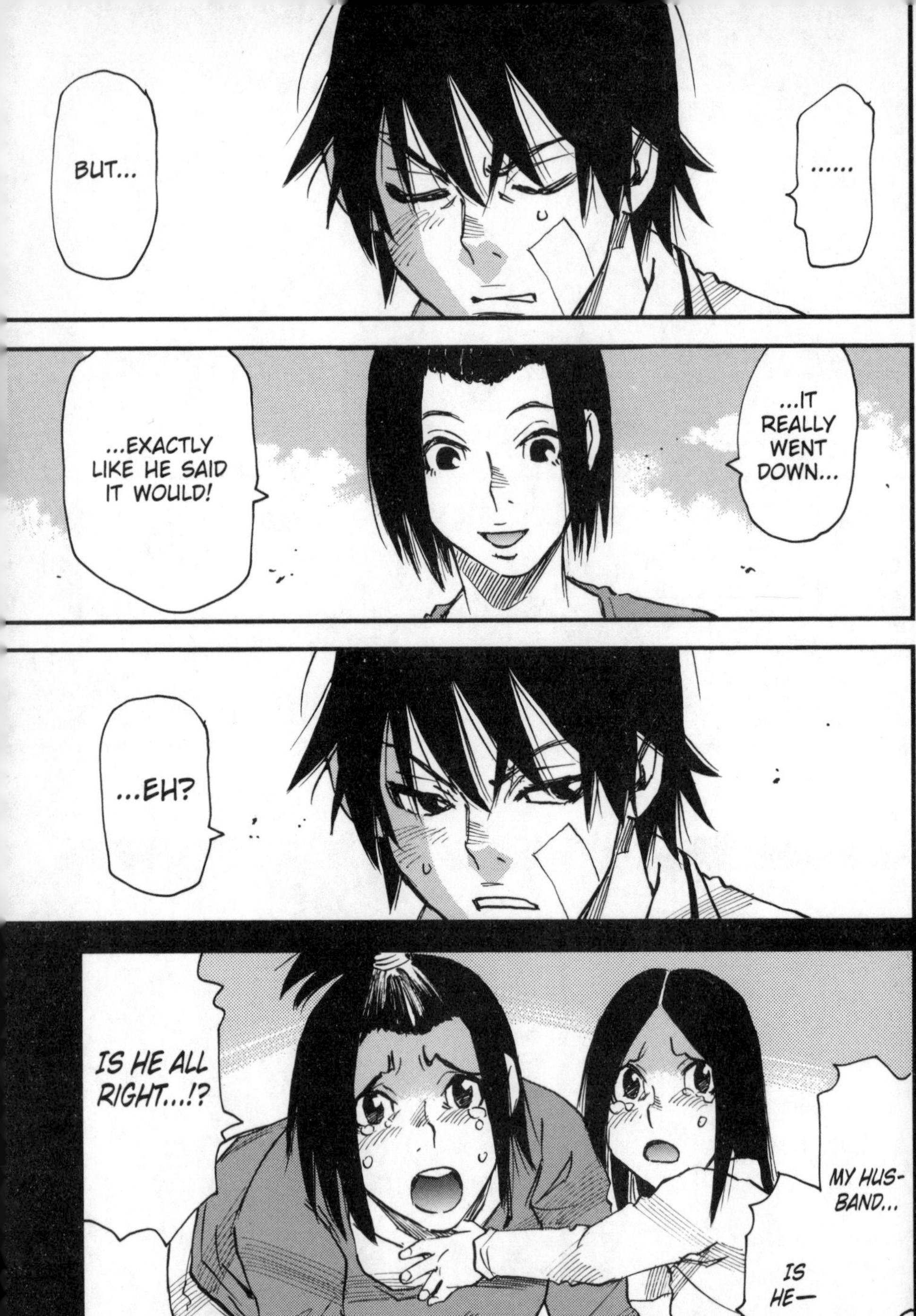
......
BUT...
...IT REALLY WENT DOWN...
...EXACTLY LIKE HE SAID IT WOULD!
...EH?
IS HE ALL RIGHT...!?
MY HUS-BAND...
IS HE—

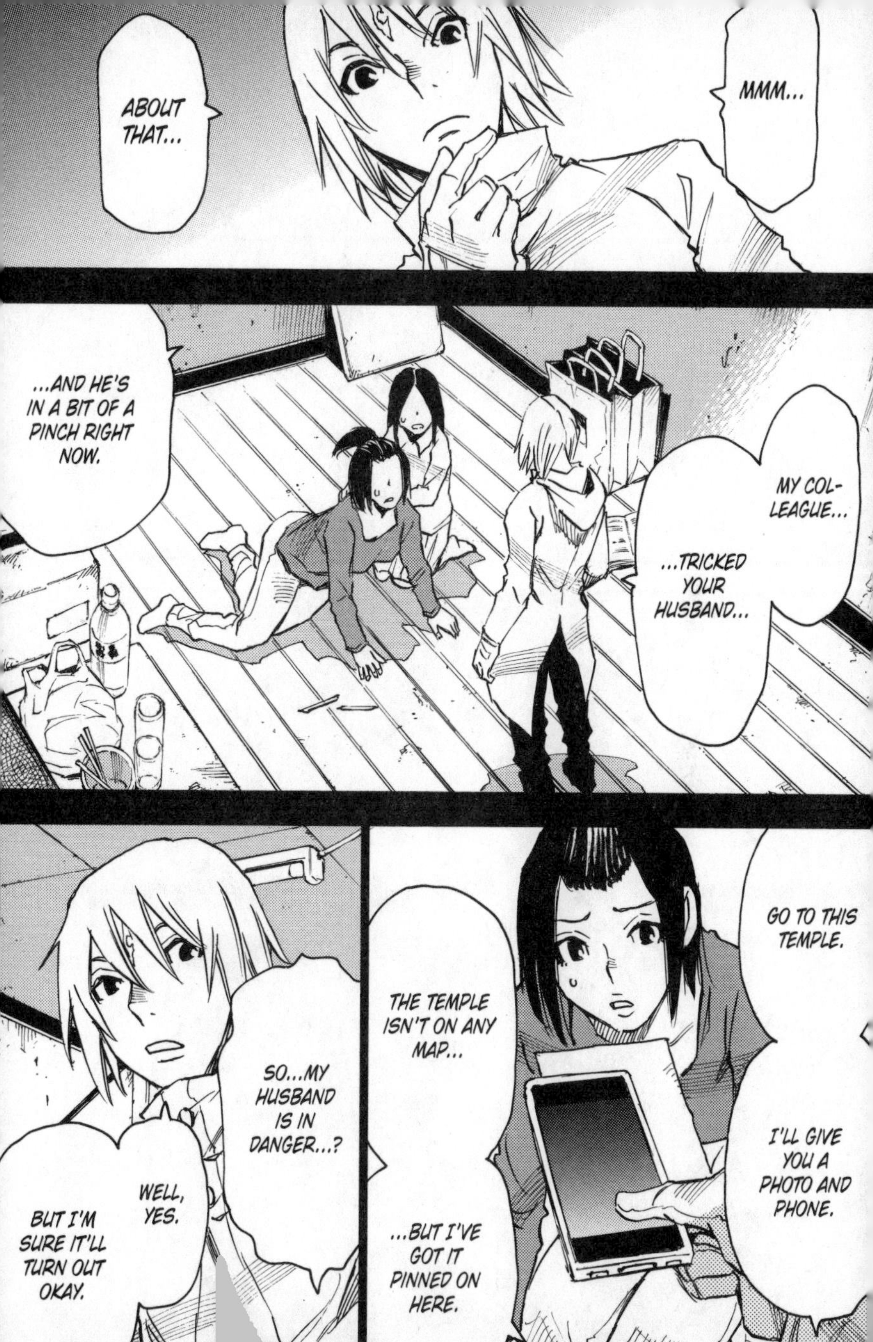
MMM...
ABOUT THAT...
MY COLLEAGUE...
...TRICKED YOUR HUSBAND...
...AND HE'S IN A BIT OF A PINCH RIGHT NOW.
GO TO THIS TEMPLE.
I'LL GIVE YOU A PHOTO AND PHONE.
THE TEMPLE ISN'T ON ANY MAP...
...BUT I'VE GOT IT PINNED ON HERE.
SO...MY HUSBAND IS IN DANGER...?
WELL, YES.
BUT I'M SURE IT'LL TURN OUT OKAY.

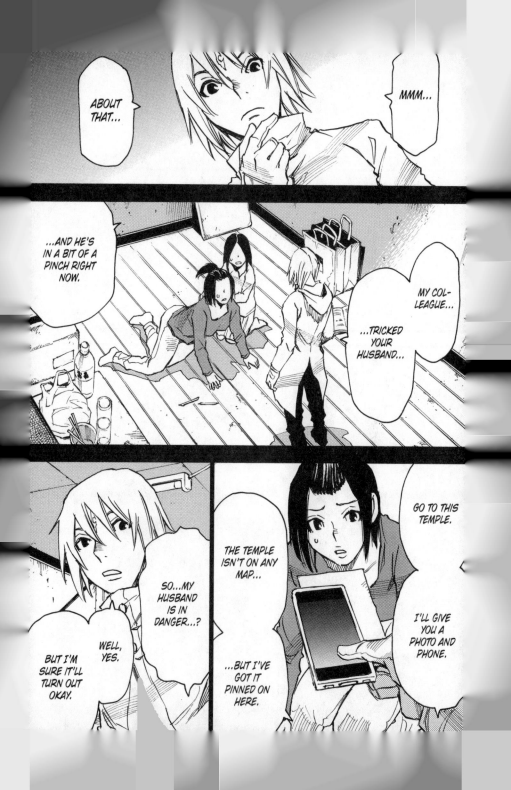

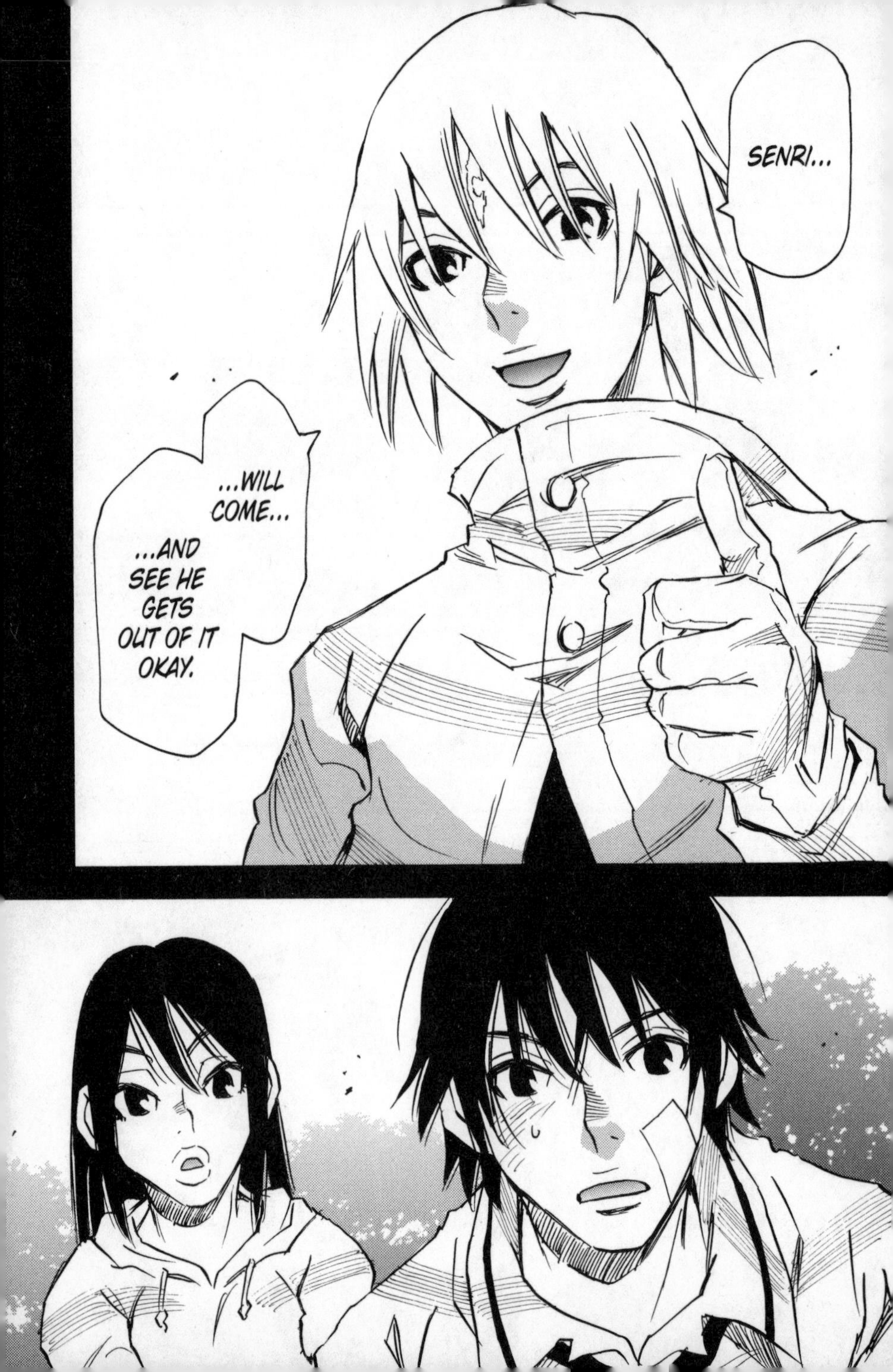
SENRI...
...WILL COME...
...AND SEE HE GETS OUT OF IT OKAY.

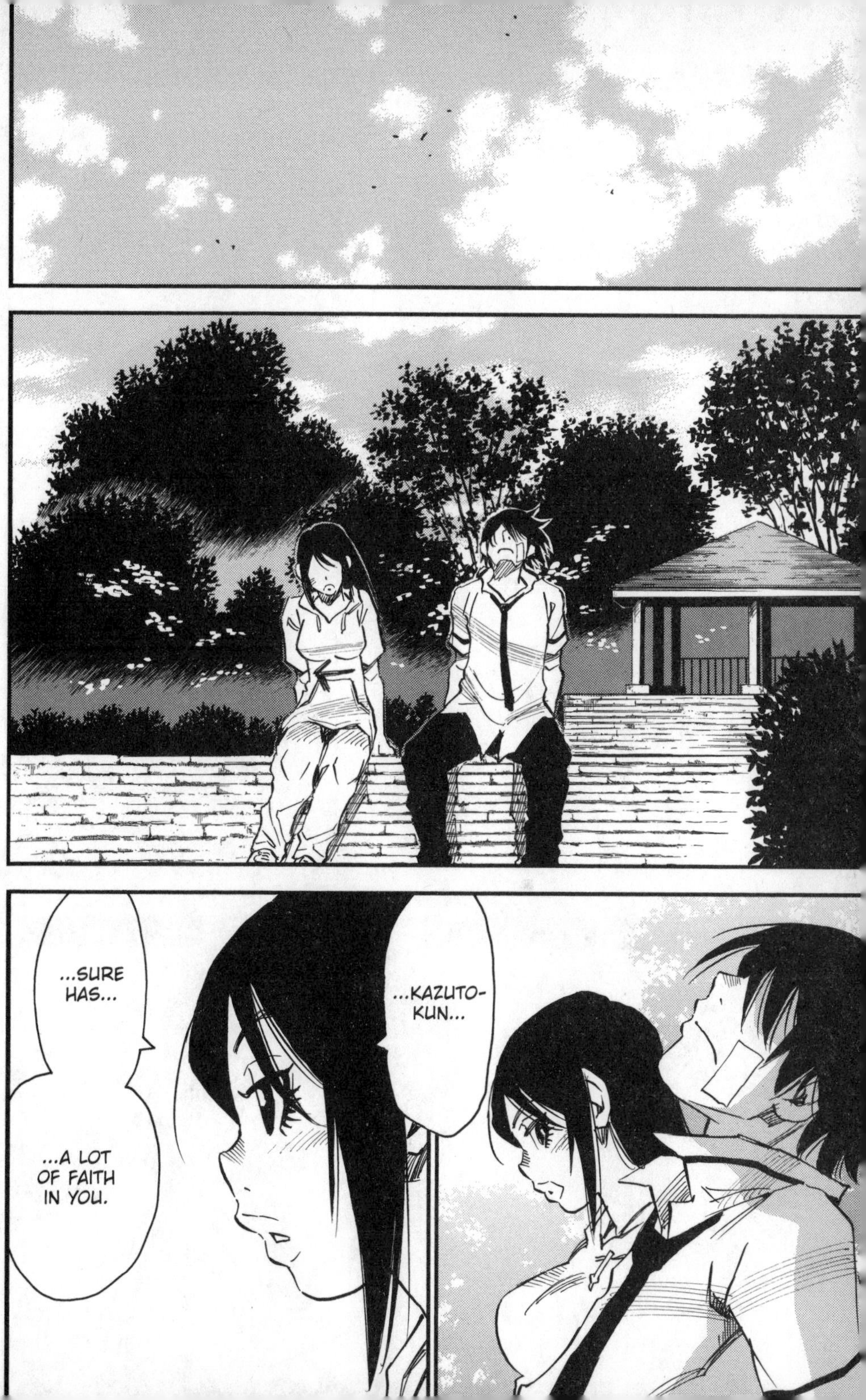
...KAZUTO-KUN...
...SURE HAS...
...A LOT OF FAITH IN YOU.

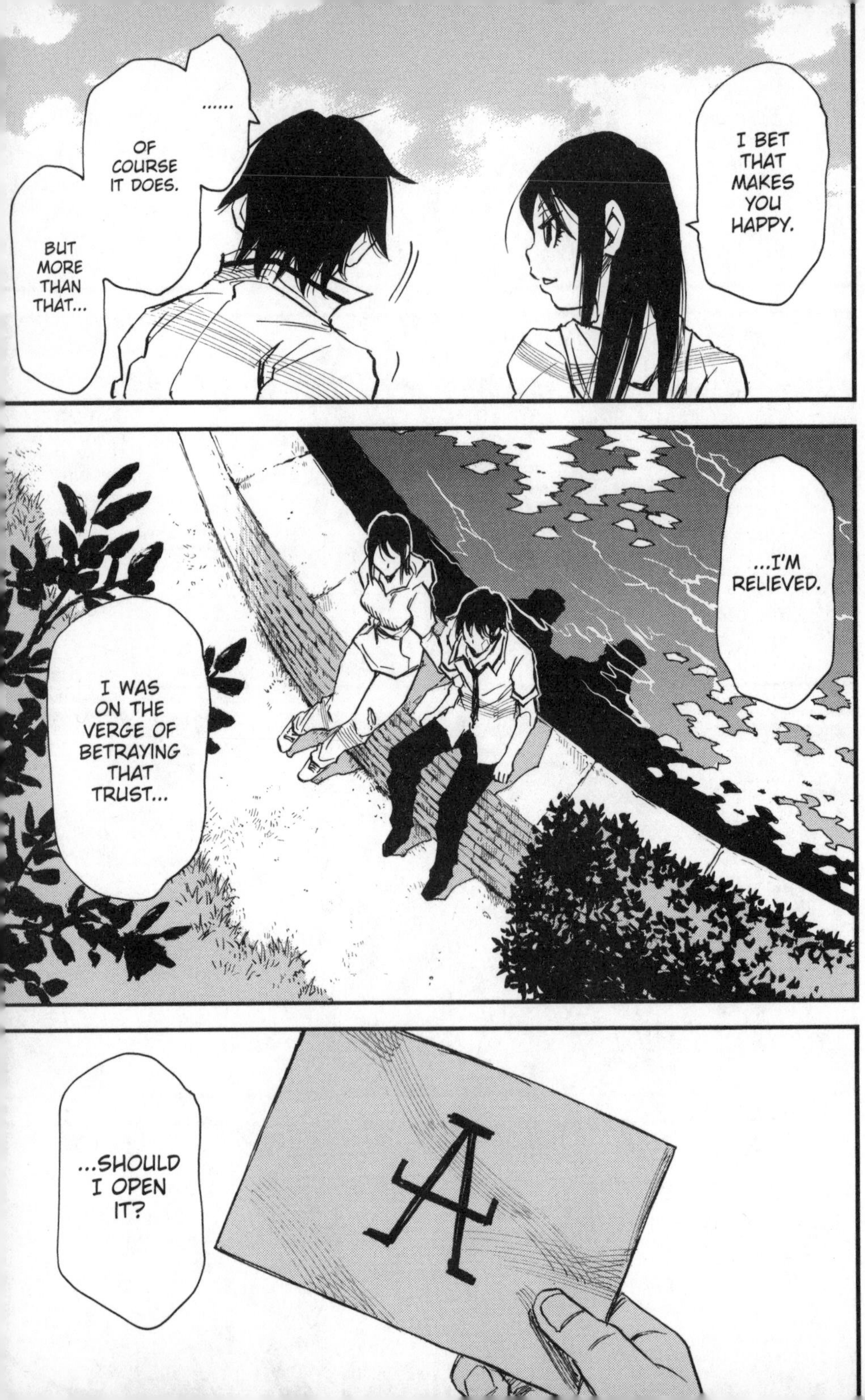
I BET THAT MAKES YOU HAPPY.
......
OF COURSE IT DOES.
BUT MORE THAN THAT...
...I'M RELIEVED.
I WAS ON THE VERGE OF BETRAYING THAT TRUST...
...SHOULD I OPEN IT?

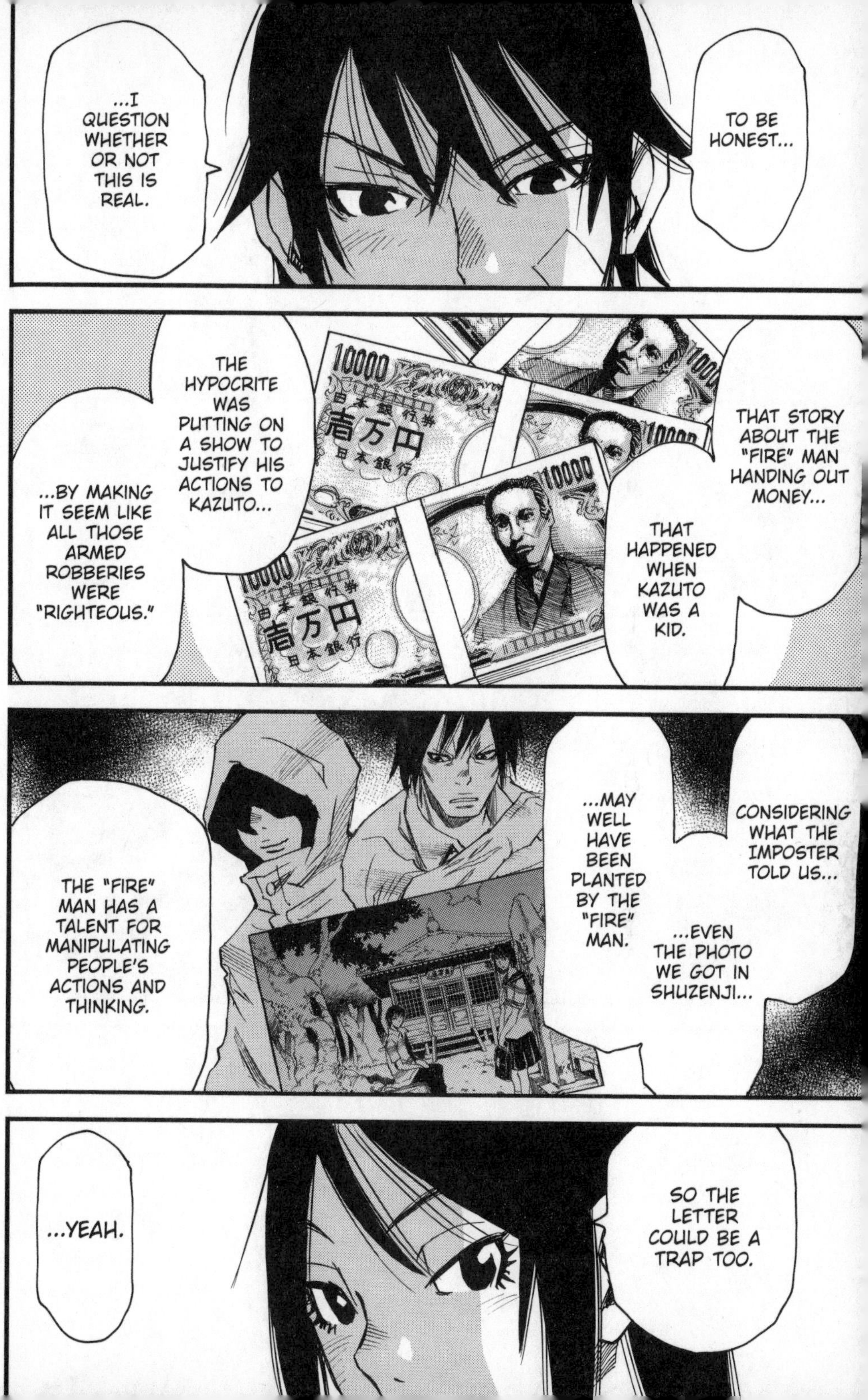
TO BE HONEST...
...I QUESTION WHETHER OR NOT THIS IS REAL.
THAT STORY ABOUT THE "FIRE" MAN HANDING OUT MONEY...
THAT HAPPENED WHEN KAZUTO WAS A KID.
THE HYPOCRITE WAS PUTTING ON A SHOW TO JUSTIFY HIS ACTIONS TO KAZUTO...
...BY MAKING IT SEEM LIKE ALL THOSE ARMED ROBBERIES WERE "RIGHTEOUS."
CONSIDERING WHAT THE IMPOSTER TOLD US...
...EVEN THE PHOTO WE GOT IN SHUZENJI...
...MAY WELL HAVE BEEN PLANTED BY THE "FIRE" MAN.
THE "FIRE" MAN HAS A TALENT FOR MANIPULATING PEOPLE'S ACTIONS AND THINKING.
SO THE LETTER COULD BE A TRAP TOO.
...YEAH.

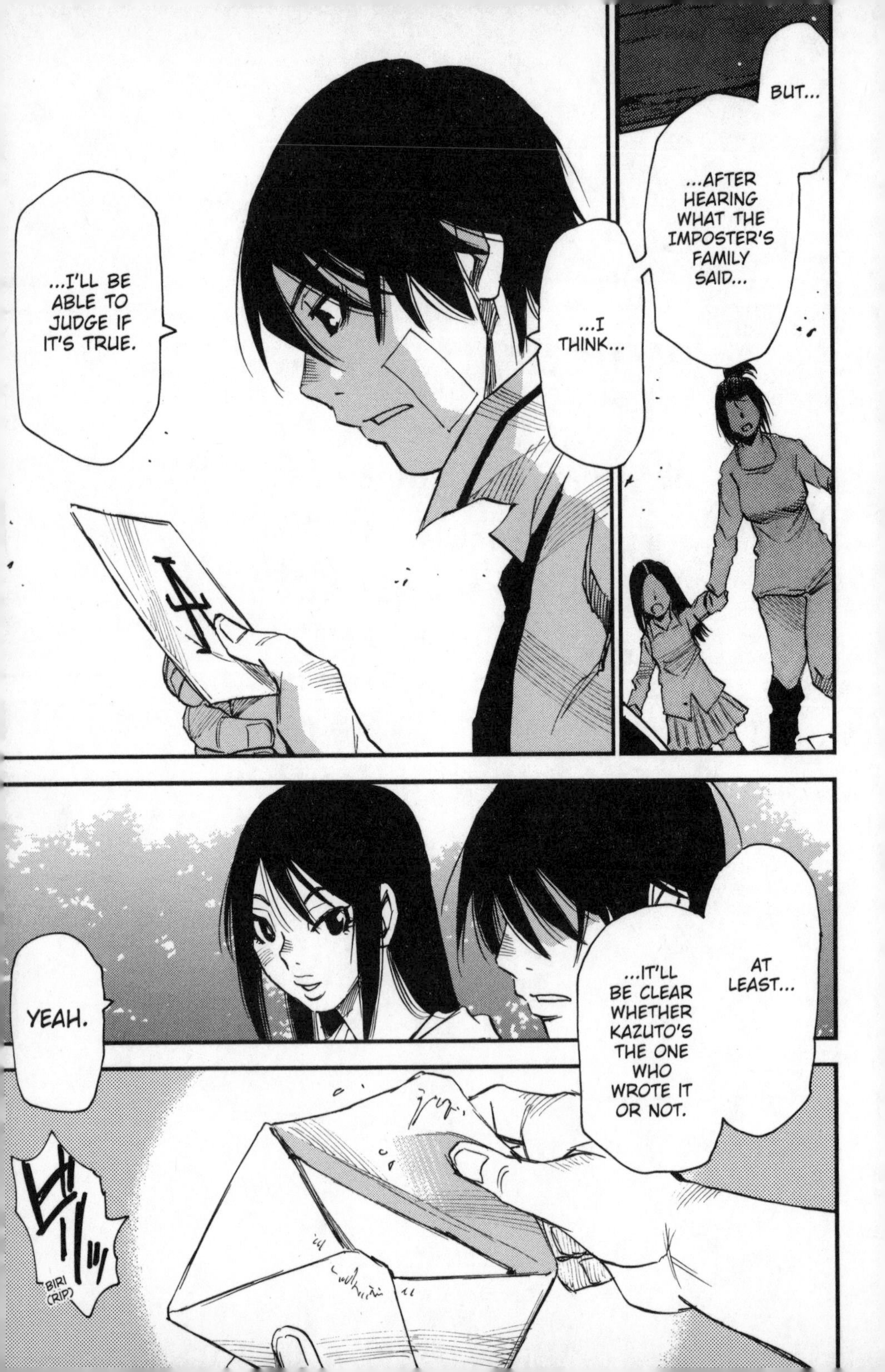
BUT...
...AFTER HEARING WHAT THE IMPOSTER'S FAMILY SAID...
...I THINK...
...I'LL BE ABLE TO JUDGE IF IT'S TRUE.
AT LEAST...
...IT'LL BE CLEAR WHETHER KAZUTO'S THE ONE WHO WROTE IT OR NOT.
YEAH.
BIRI (RIP)

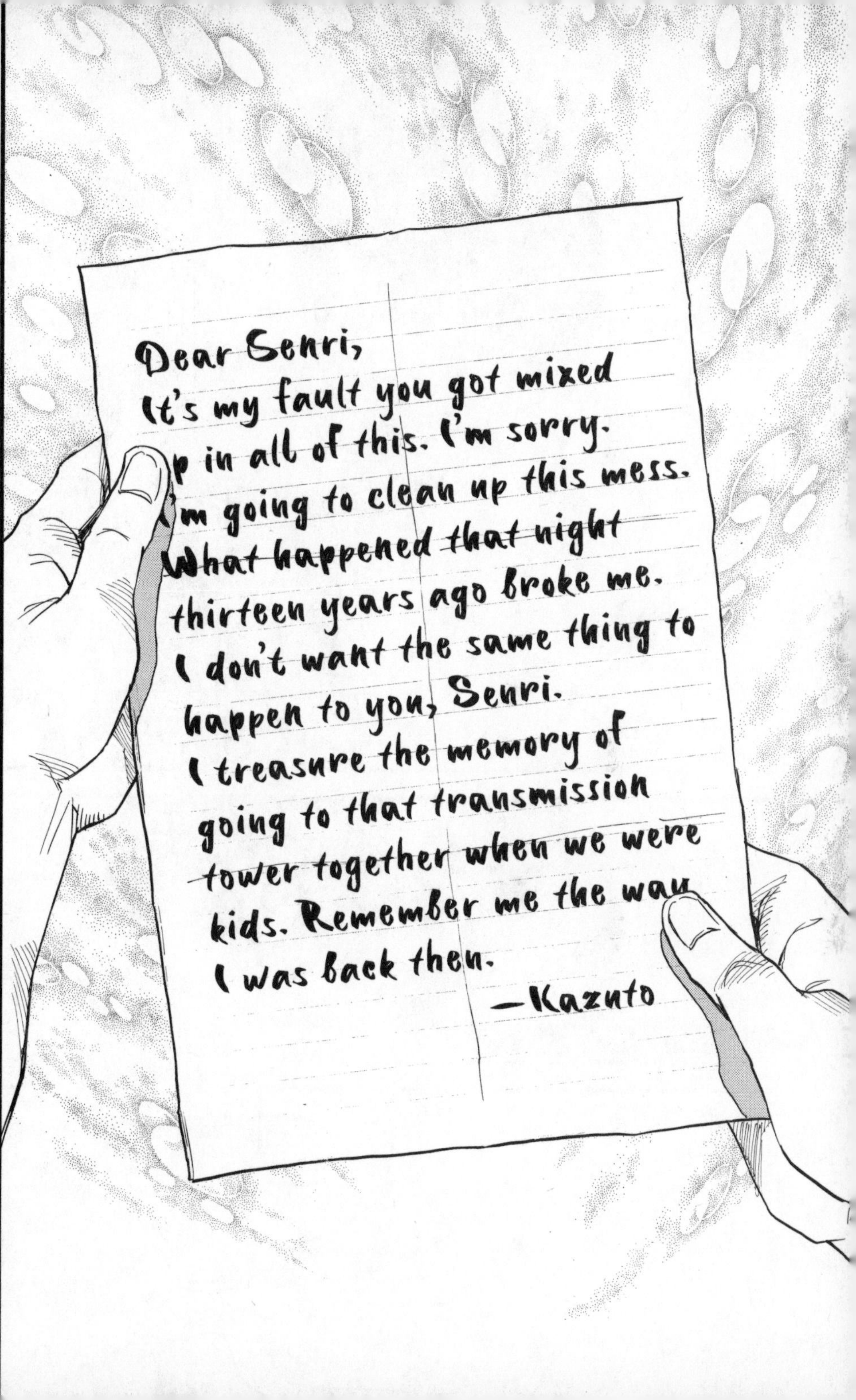
Dear Senri,
It's my fault you got mixed
p in all of this. I'm sorry.
m going to clean up this mess.
What happened that night
thirteen years ago broke me.
I don't want the same thing to
happen to you, Senri.
I treasure the memory of
going to that transmission
tower together when we were
kids. Remember me the way
I was back then.
—Kazuto

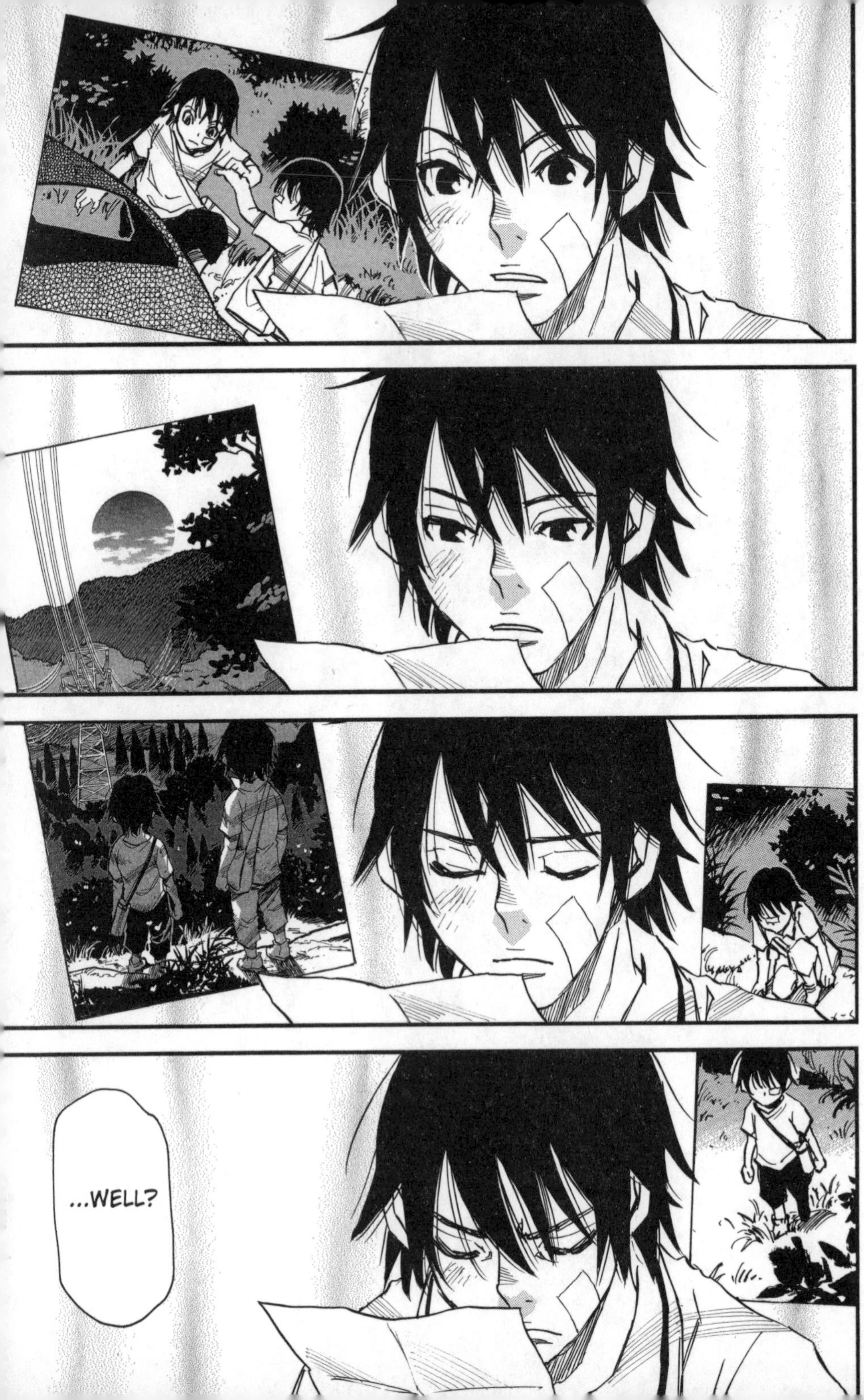
...WELL?

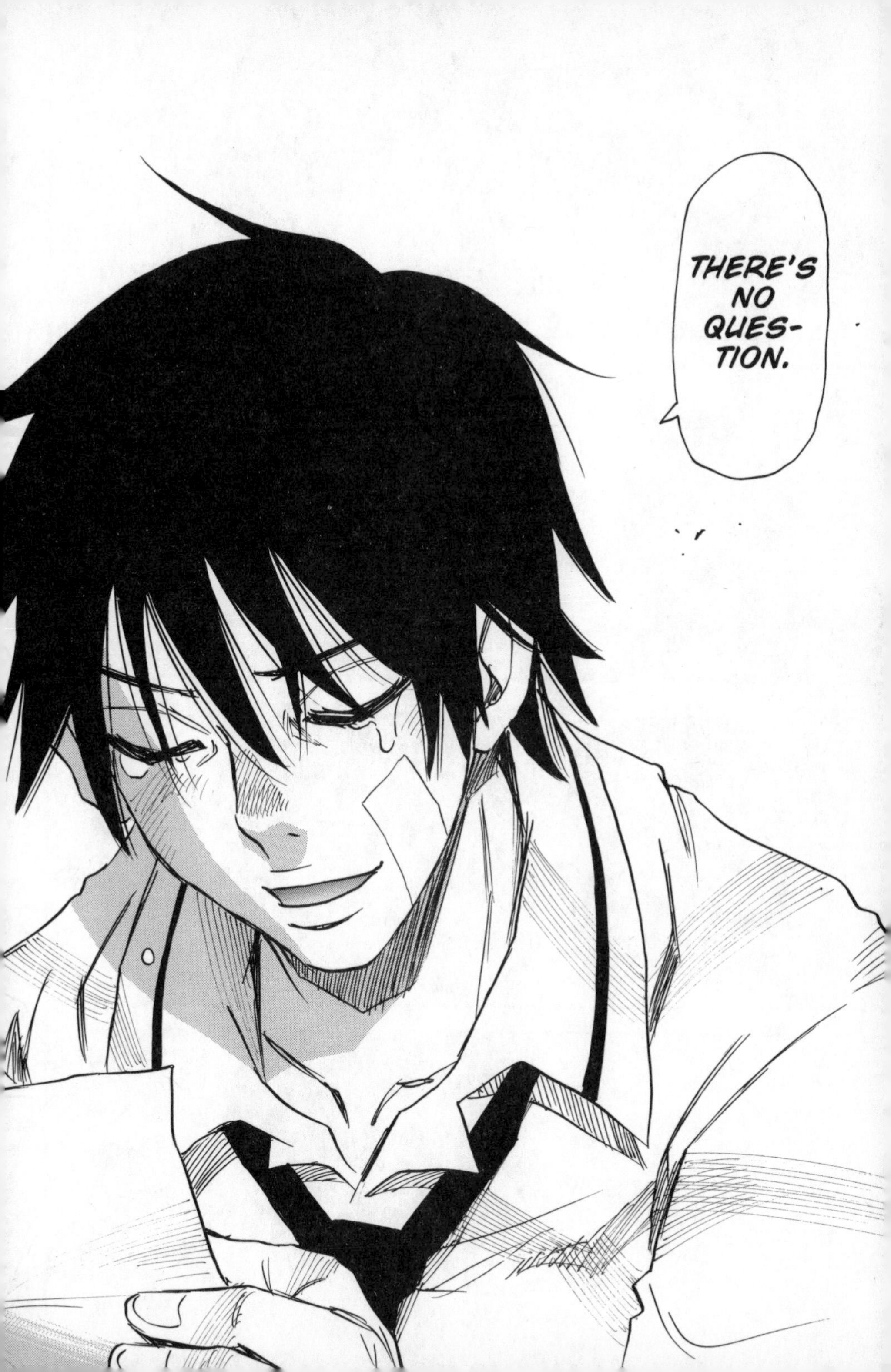
THERE'S NO QUES-TION.

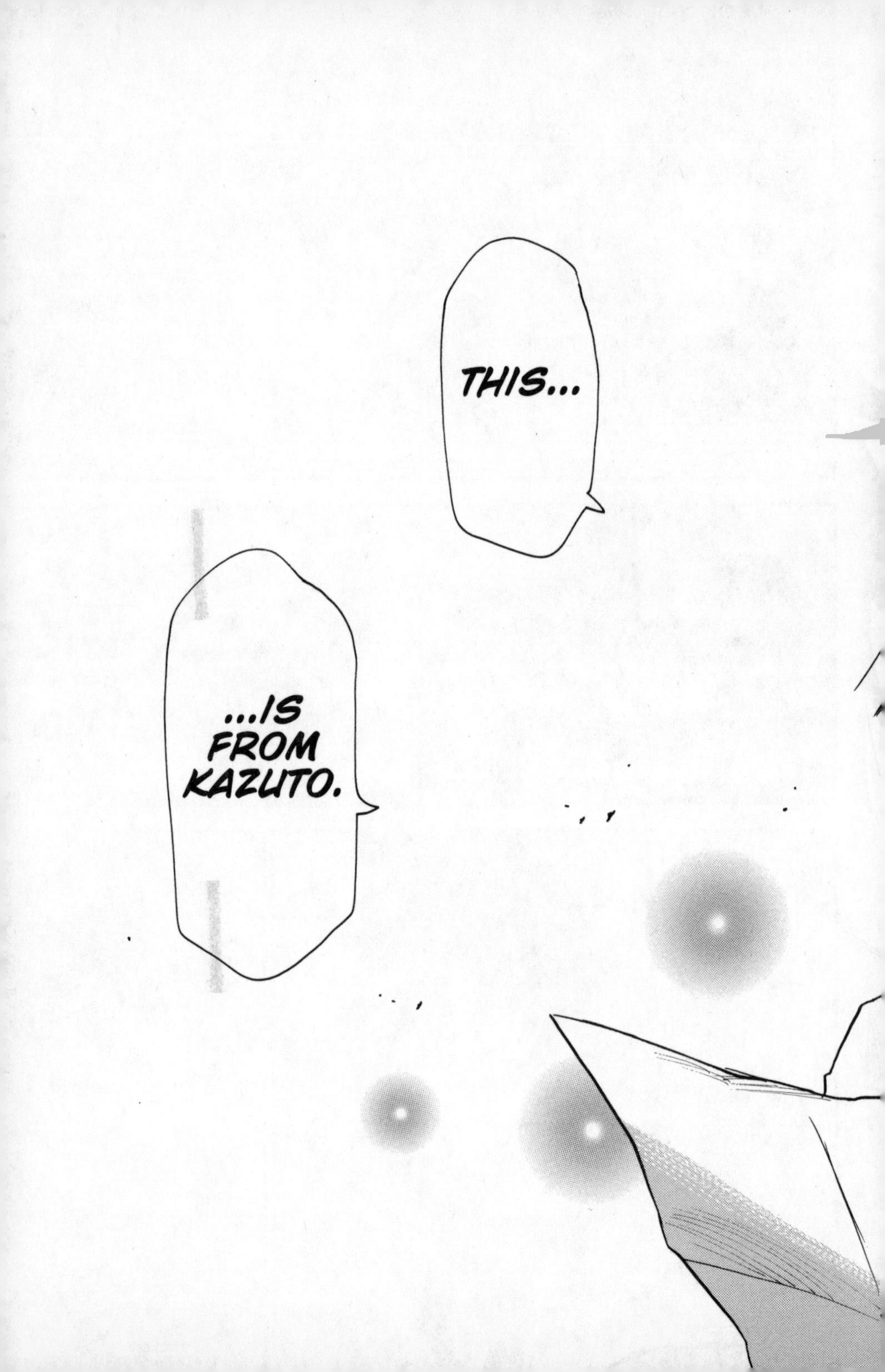
THIS...
...IS FROM KAZUTO.

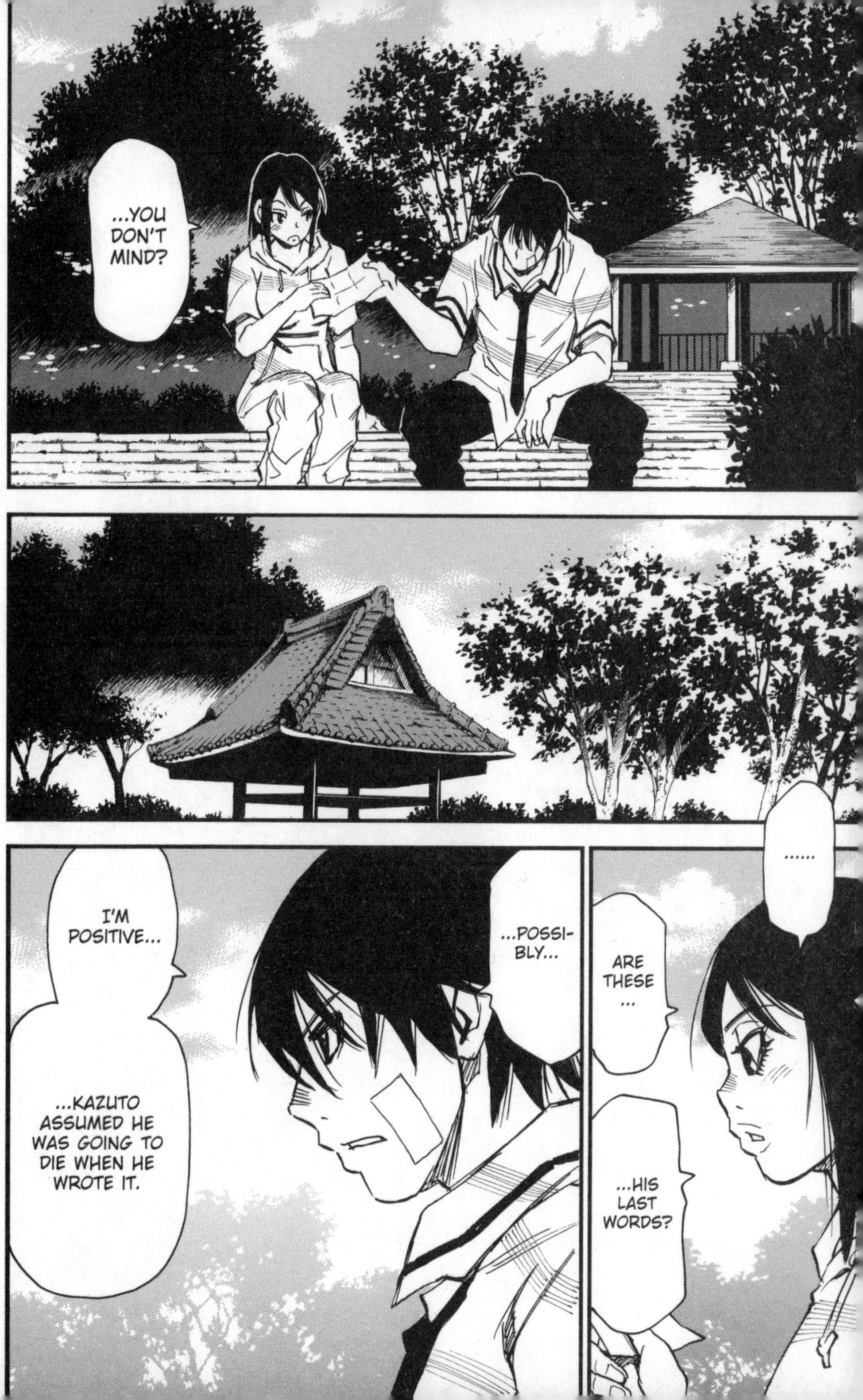
...YOU DON'T MIND?
......
ARE THESE ...
...HIS LAST WORDS?
...POSSIBLY...
I'M POSITIVE...
...KAZUTO ASSUMED HE WAS GOING TO DIE WHEN HE WROTE IT.

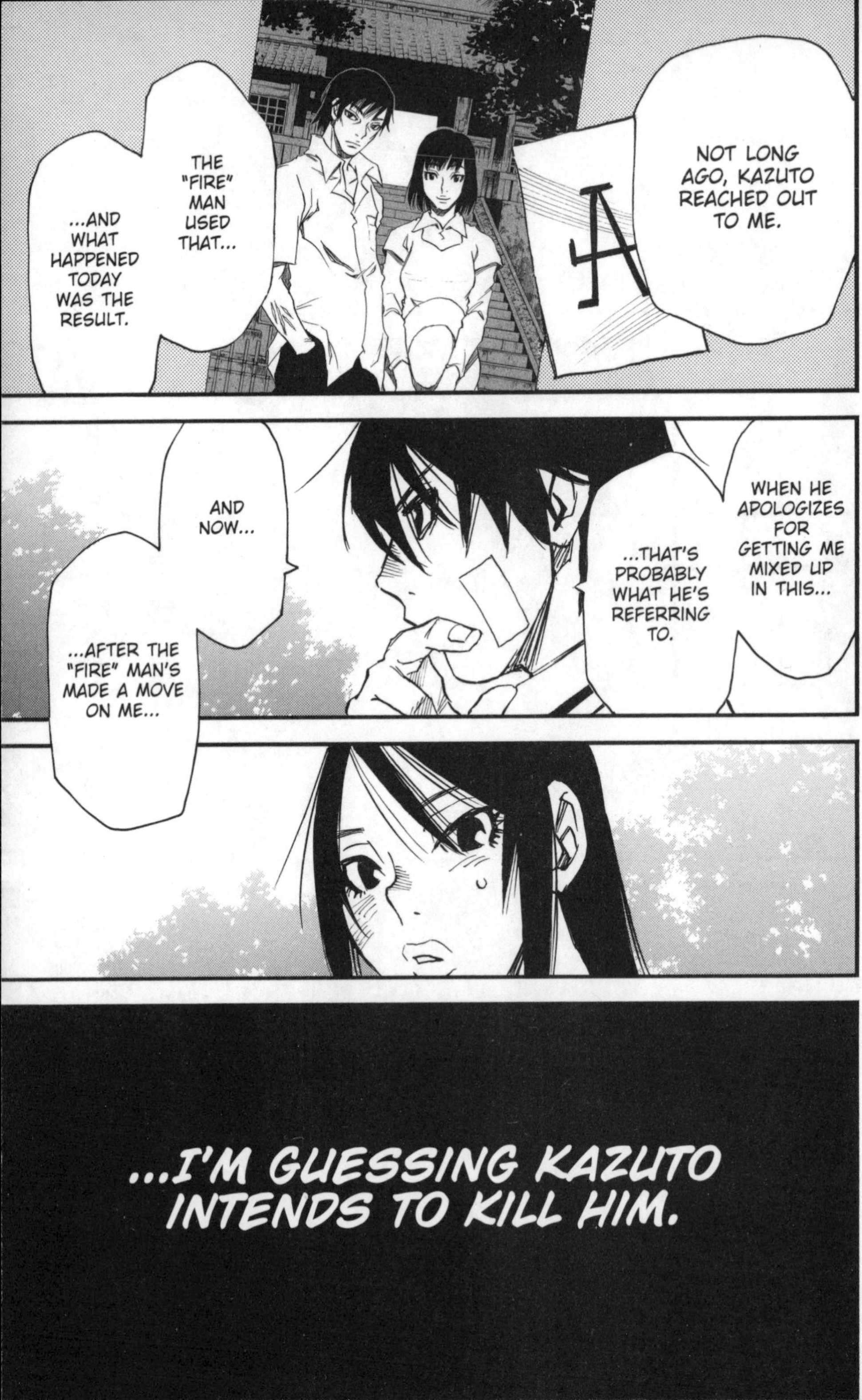
NOT LONG AGO, KAZUTO REACHED OUT TO ME.
THE "FIRE" MAN USED THAT...
...AND WHAT HAPPENED TODAY WAS THE RESULT.
WHEN HE APOLOGIZES FOR GETTING ME MIXED UP IN THIS...
...THAT'S PROBABLY WHAT HE'S REFERRING TO.
AND NOW...
...AFTER THE "FIRE" MAN'S MADE A MOVE ON ME...
...I'M GUESSING KAZUTO INTENDS TO KILL HIM.

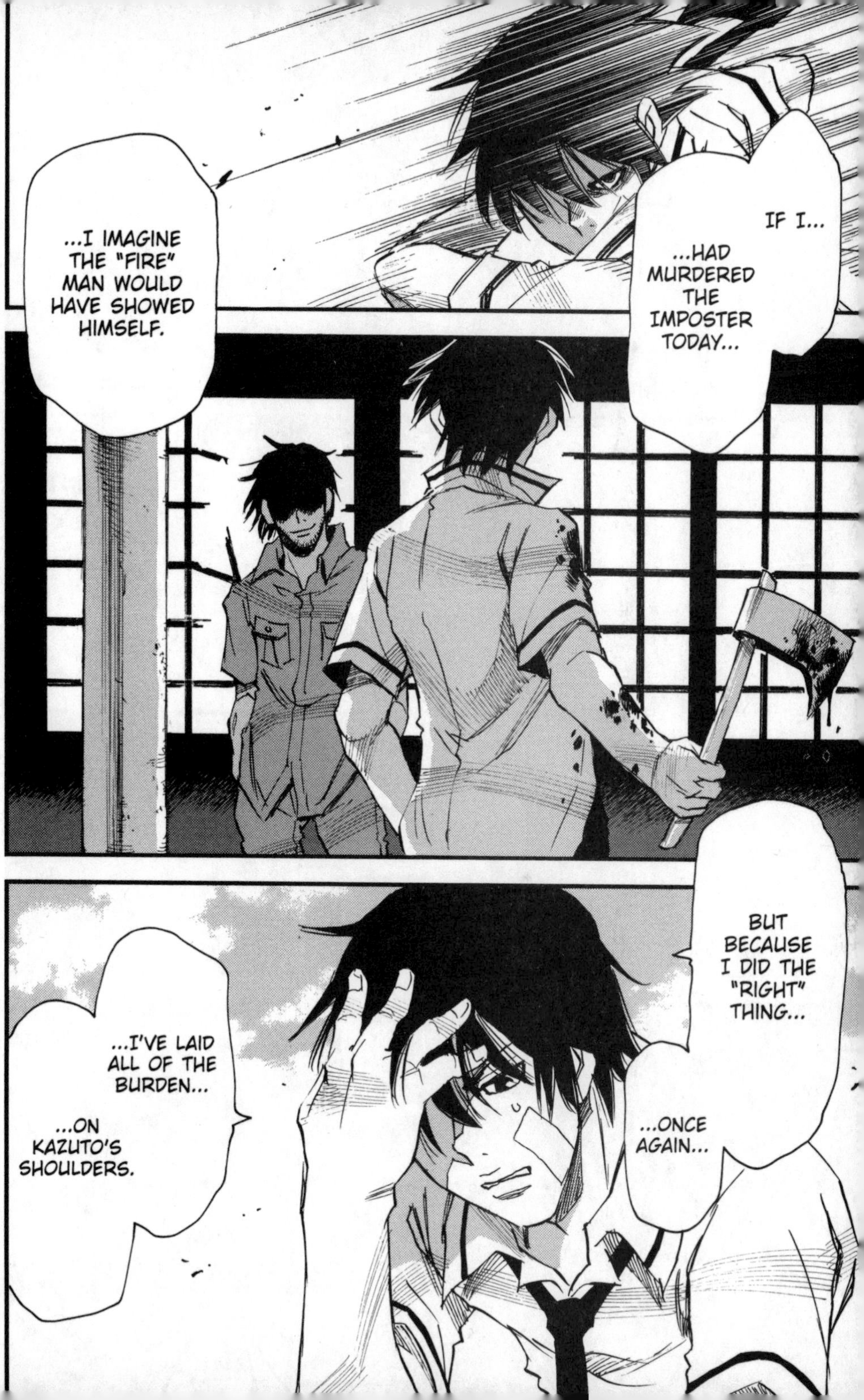
IF I...
...HAD MURDERED THE IMPOSTER TODAY...
...I IMAGINE THE "FIRE" MAN WOULD HAVE SHOWED HIMSELF.
BUT BECAUSE I DID THE "RIGHT" THING...
...ONCE AGAIN...
...I'VE LAID ALL OF THE BURDEN...
...ON KAZUTO'S SHOULDERS.

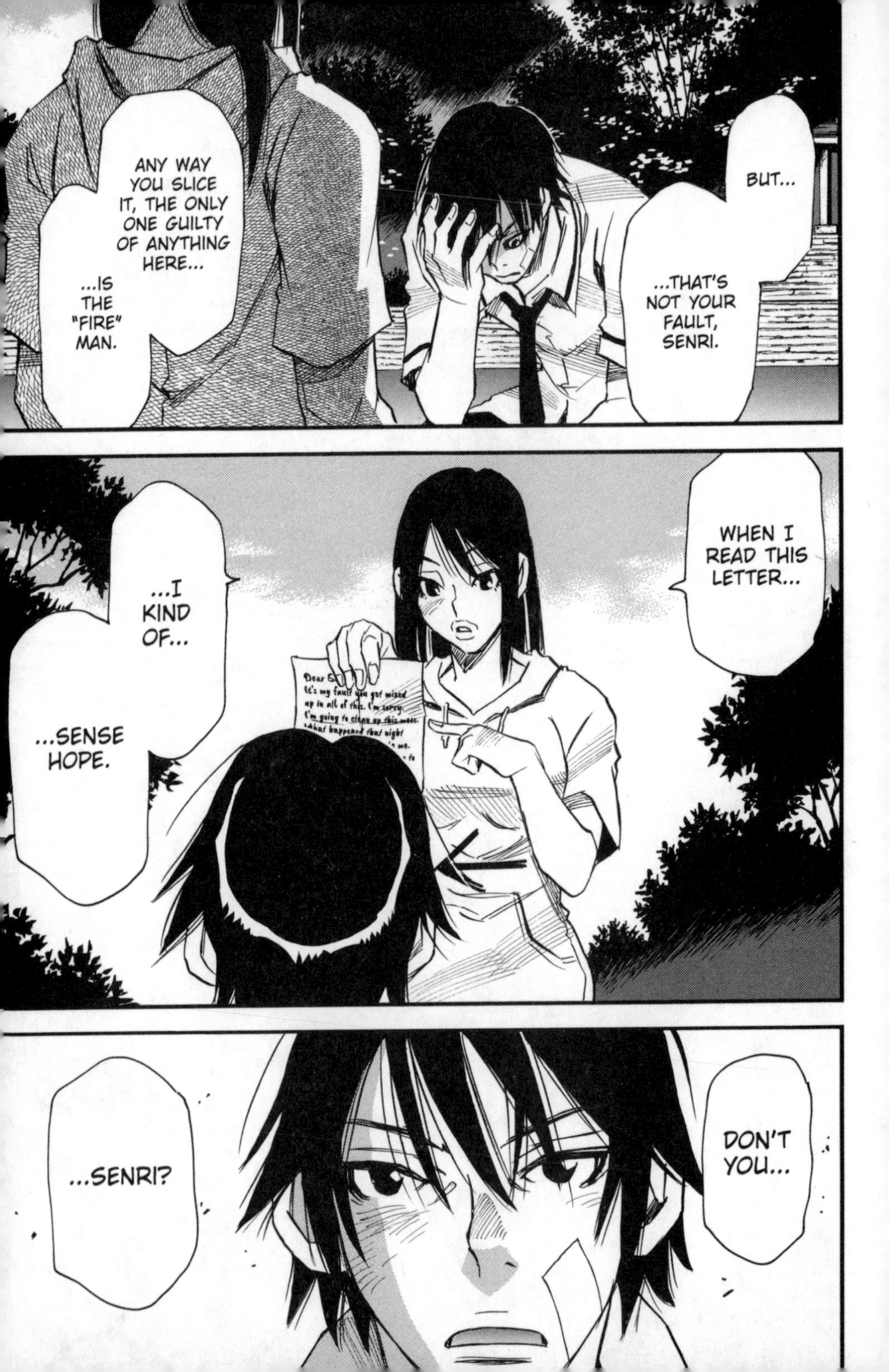
BUT...
...THAT'S NOT YOUR FAULT, SENRI.
ANY WAY YOU SLICE IT, THE ONLY ONE GUILTY OF ANYTHING HERE...
...IS THE "FIRE" MAN.
WHEN I READ THIS LETTER...
It's my fault you got mixed
up in all of this. I'm sorry.
I'm going to clean up this mess.
...I KIND OF...
...SENSE HOPE.
DON'T YOU...
...SENRI?

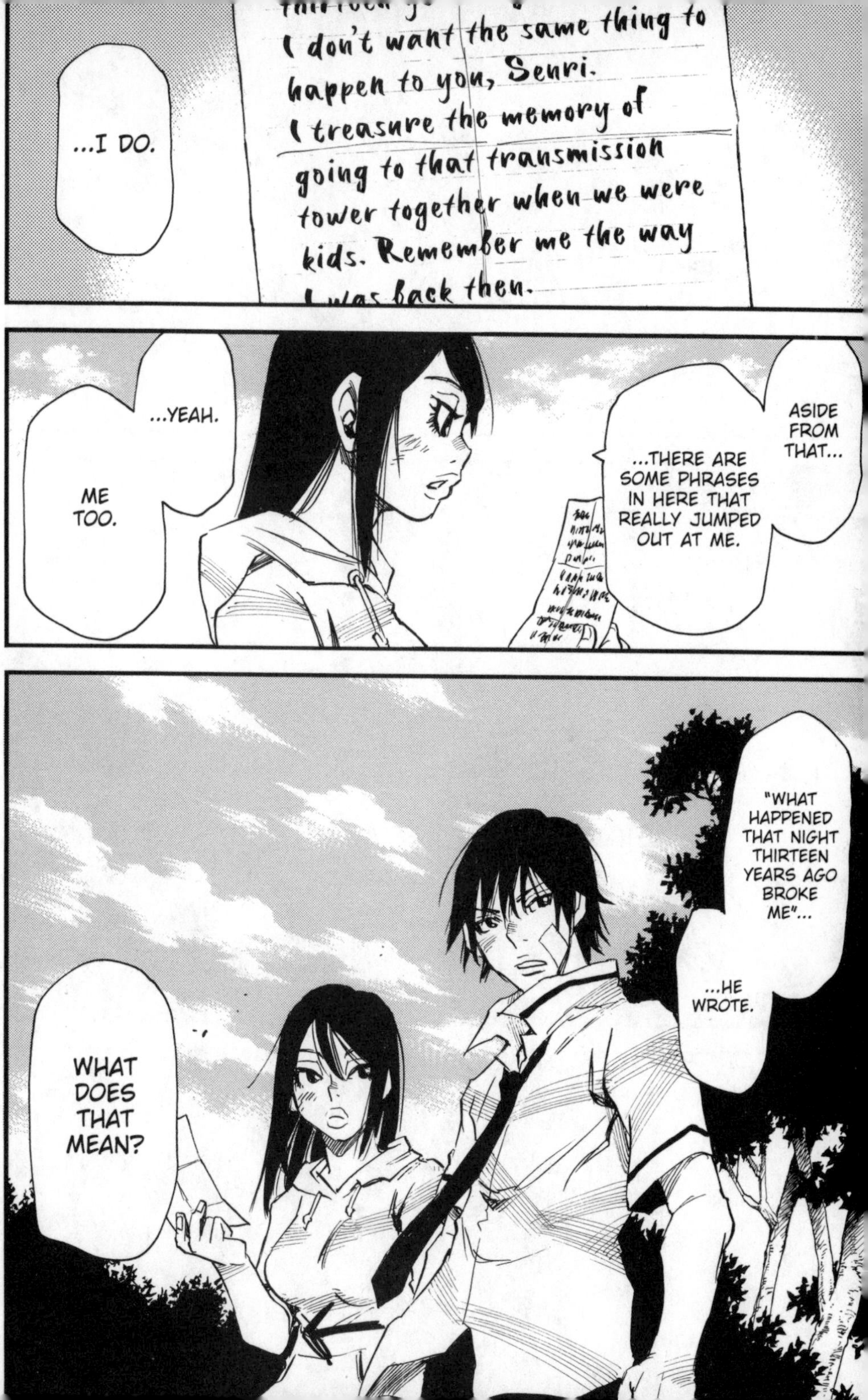
I don't want the same thing to happen to you, Senri.
I treasure the memory of going to that transmission tower together when we were kids. Remember me the way I was back then.
...I DO.
ASIDE FROM THAT...
...THERE ARE SOME PHRASES IN HERE THAT REALLY JUMPED OUT AT ME.
...YEAH.
ME TOO.
"WHAT HAPPENED THAT NIGHT THIRTEEN YEARS AGO BROKE ME"...
...HE WROTE.
WHAT DOES THAT MEAN?

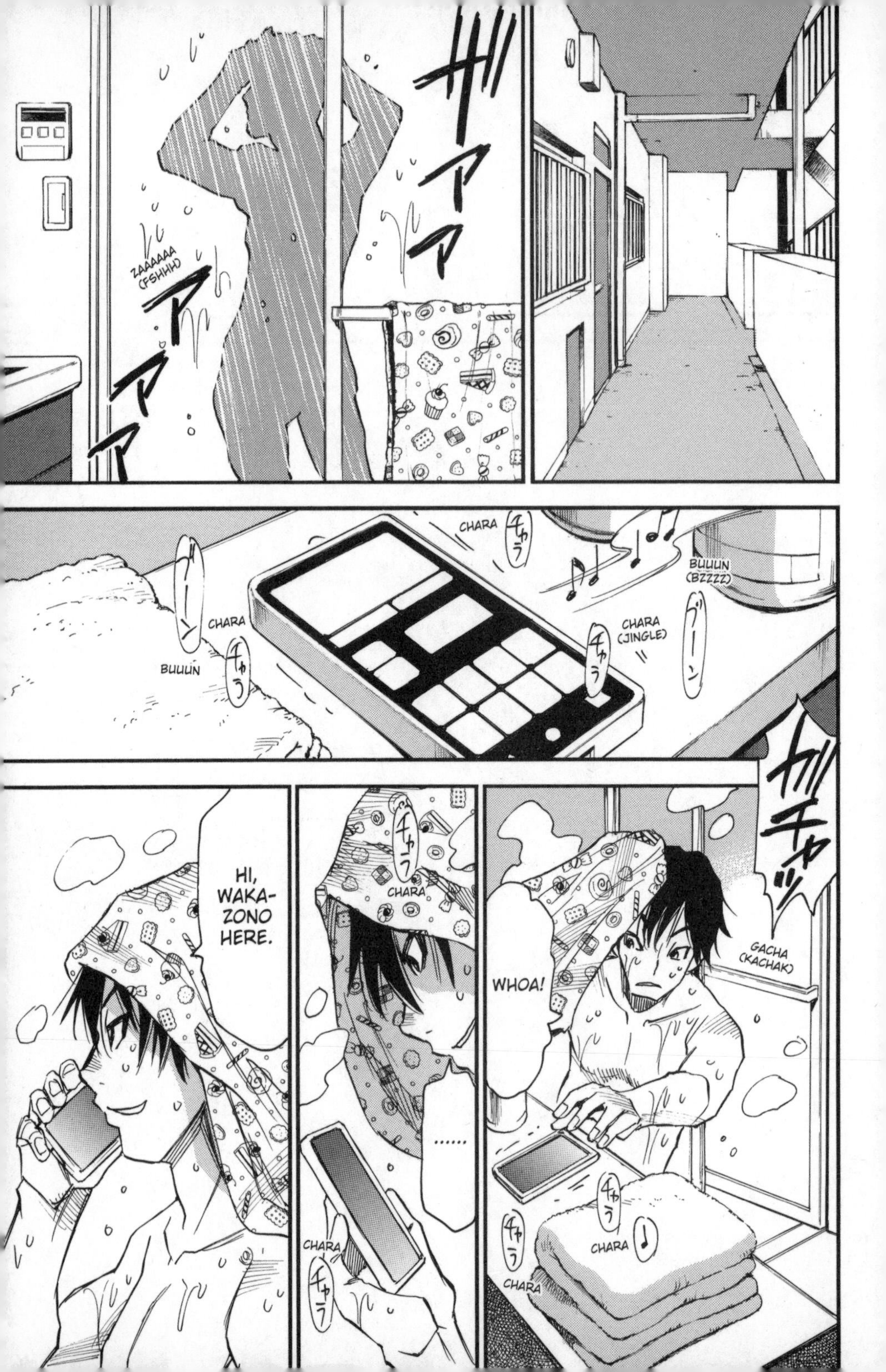
ザァァァ
ZAAAAAA (FSHHH)
ザァァァ
チャラ
CHARA
ブーン
BUUUN (BZZZZ)
チャラ
CHARA (JINGLE)
チャラ
CHARA
ブーン
BUUUN
ガチャッ
GACHA (KACHAK)
WHOA!
チャラ
CHARA
チャラ
CHARA
チャラ
CHARA
......
チャラ
CHARA
HI, WAKA-ZONO HERE.

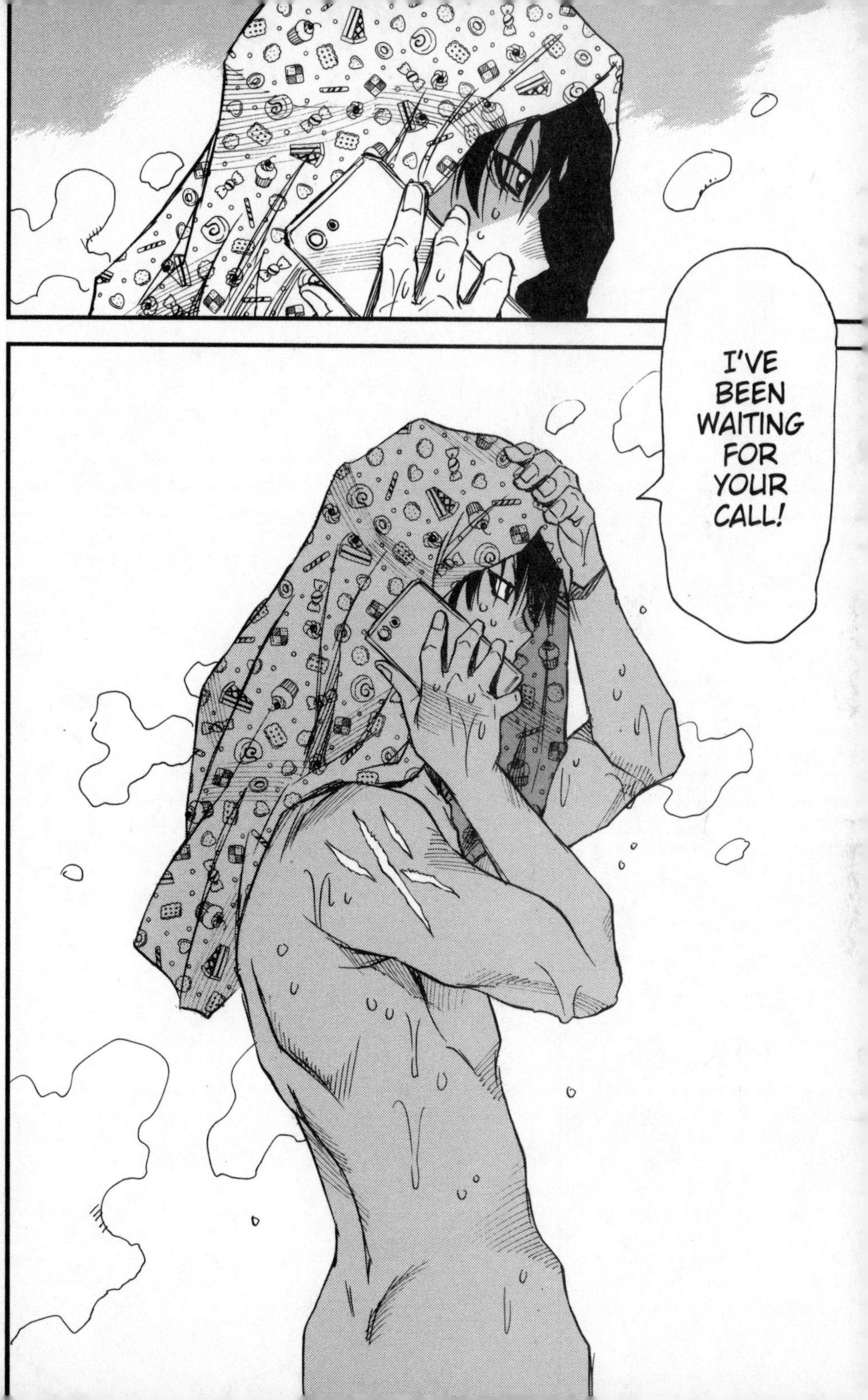
I'VE BEEN WAITING FOR YOUR CALL!

#33 END

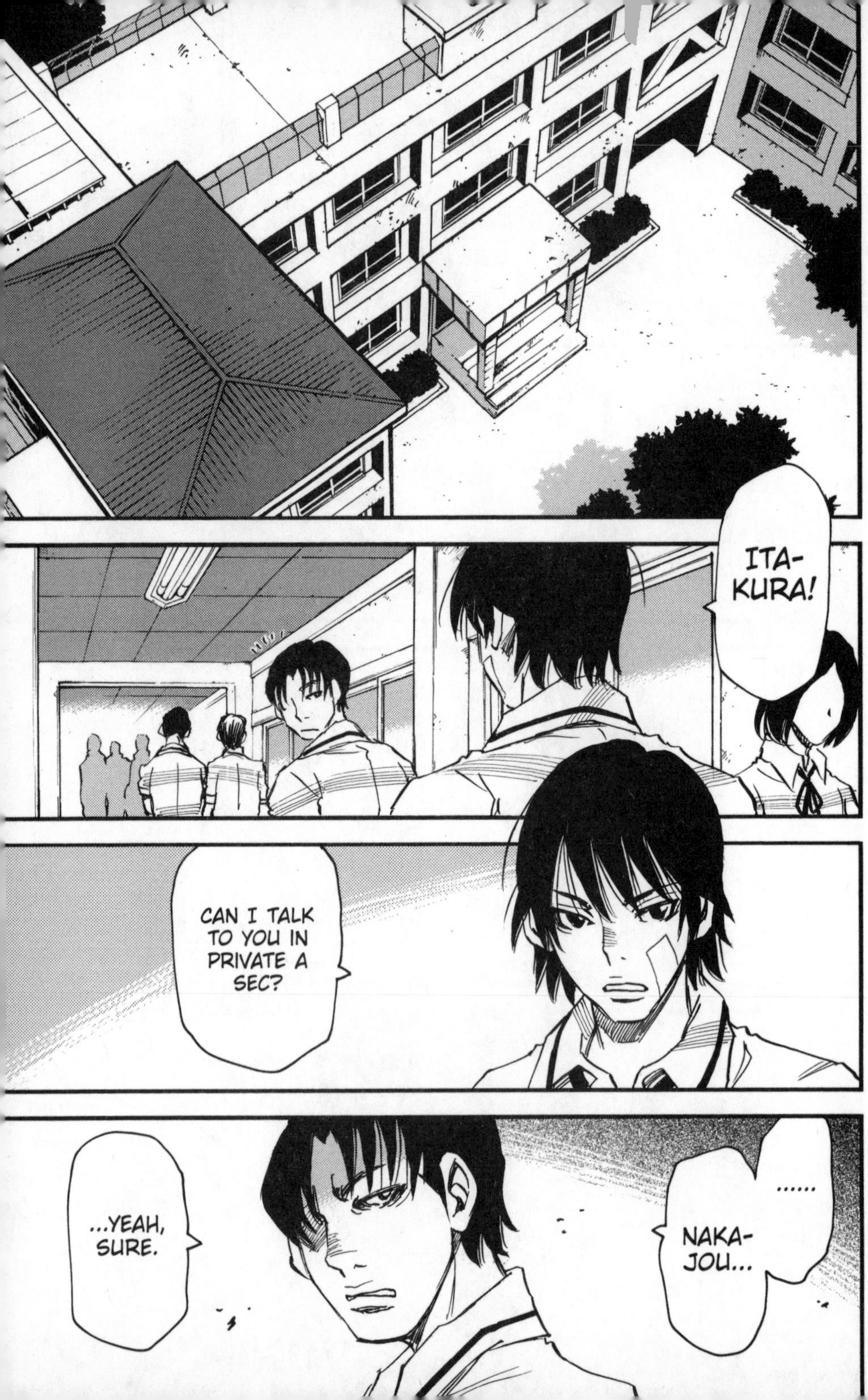
ITA-KURA!
CAN I TALK TO YOU IN PRIVATE A SEC?
......
NAKA-JOU...
...YEAH, SURE.

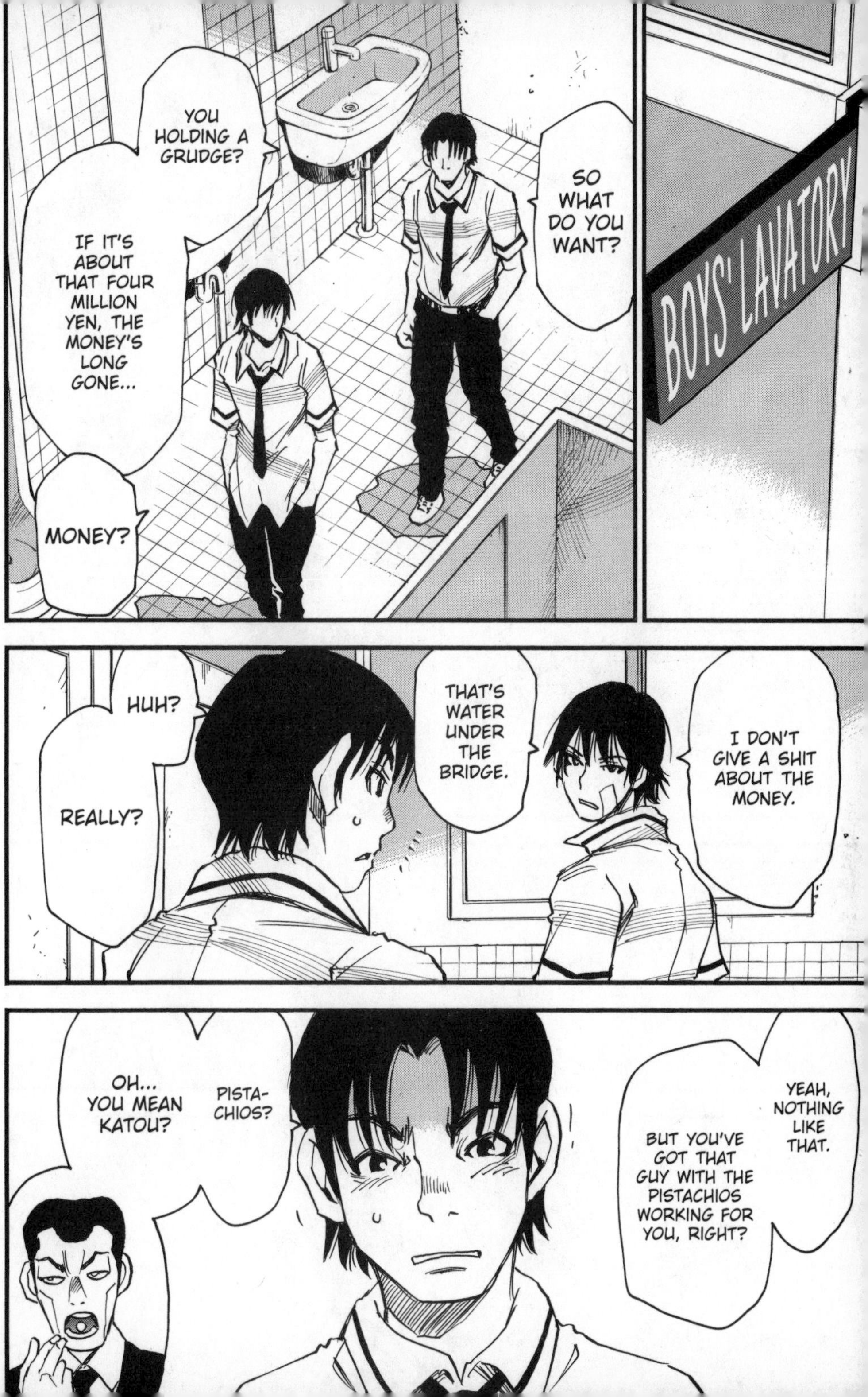
BOYS' LAVATORY
SO WHAT DO YOU WANT?
YOU HOLDING A GRUDGE?
IF IT'S ABOUT THAT FOUR MILLION YEN, THE MONEY'S LONG GONE...
MONEY?
I DON'T GIVE A SHIT ABOUT THE MONEY.
THAT'S WATER UNDER THE BRIDGE.
HUH?
REALLY?
YEAH, NOTHING LIKE THAT.
BUT YOU'VE GOT THAT GUY WITH THE PISTACHIOS WORKING FOR YOU, RIGHT?
PISTA-CHIOS?
OH... YOU MEAN KATOU?

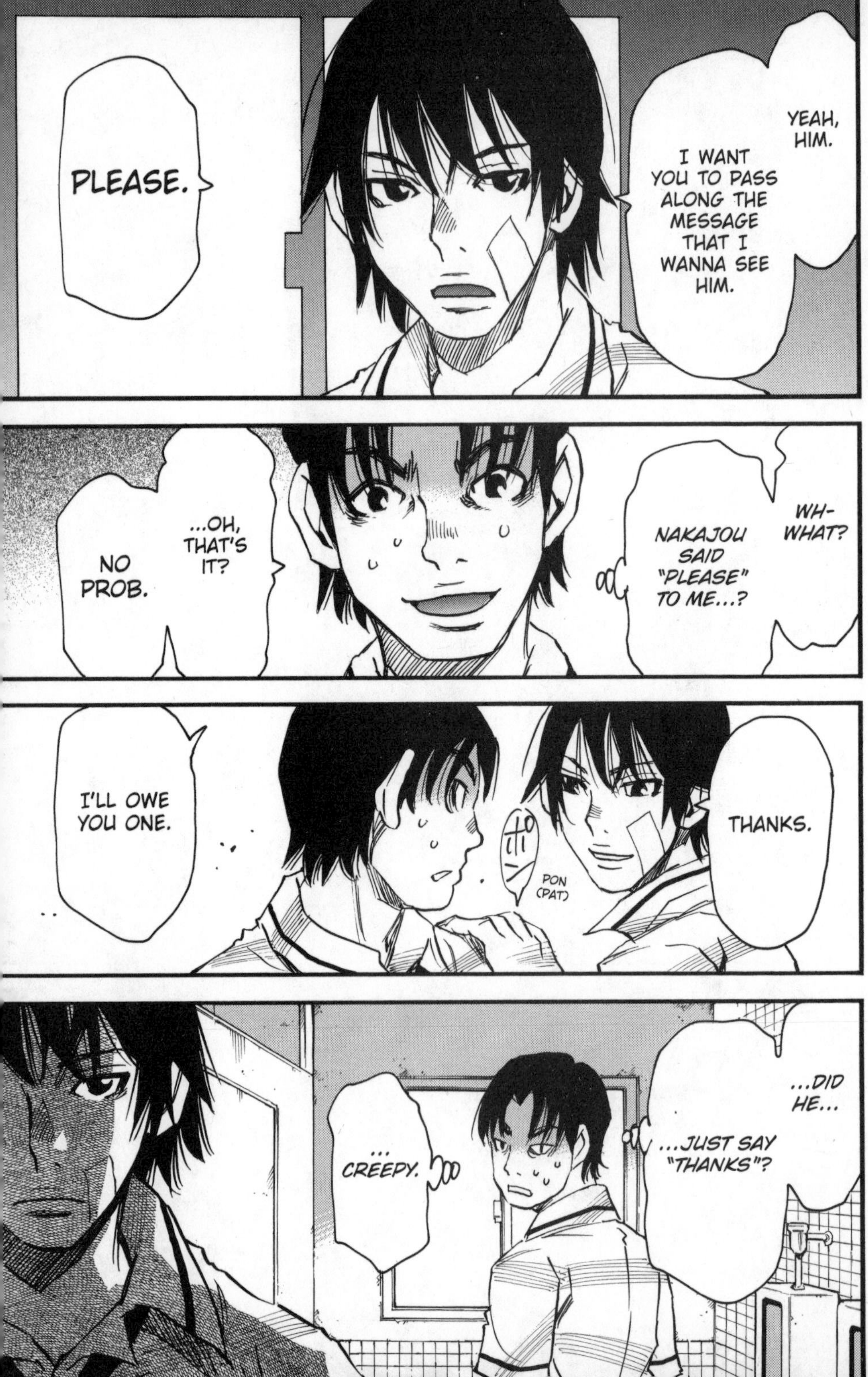
YEAH, HIM.
I WANT YOU TO PASS ALONG THE MESSAGE THAT I WANNA SEE HIM.
PLEASE.
WH- WHAT?
NAKAJOU SAID "PLEASE" TO ME...?
...OH, THAT'S IT?
NO PROB.
THANKS.
PON (PAT)
I'LL OWE YOU ONE.
...DID HE...
...JUST SAY "THANKS"?
...CREEPY.

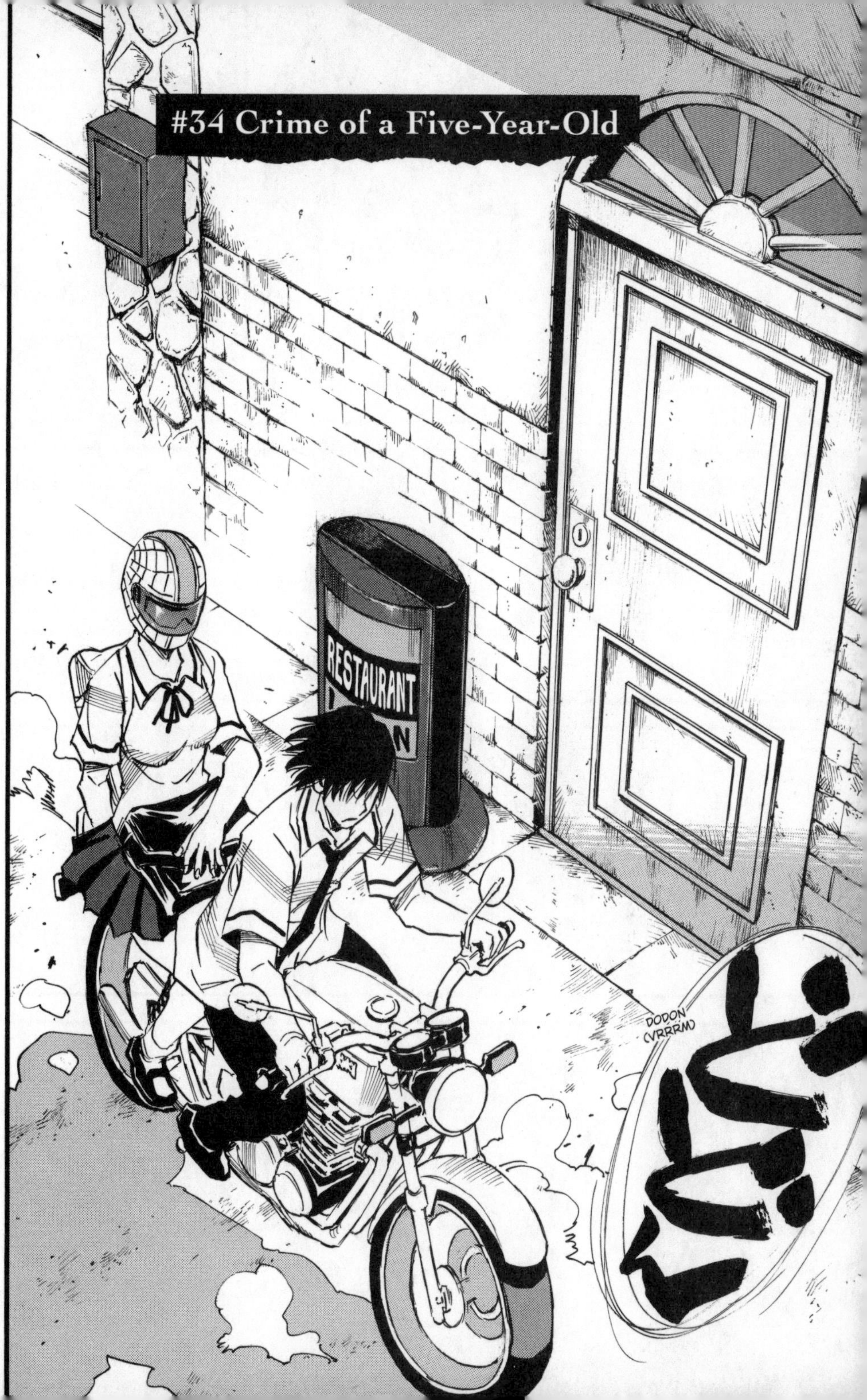
#34 Crime of a Five-Year-Old
RESTAURANT
DODON
(VRRRM)

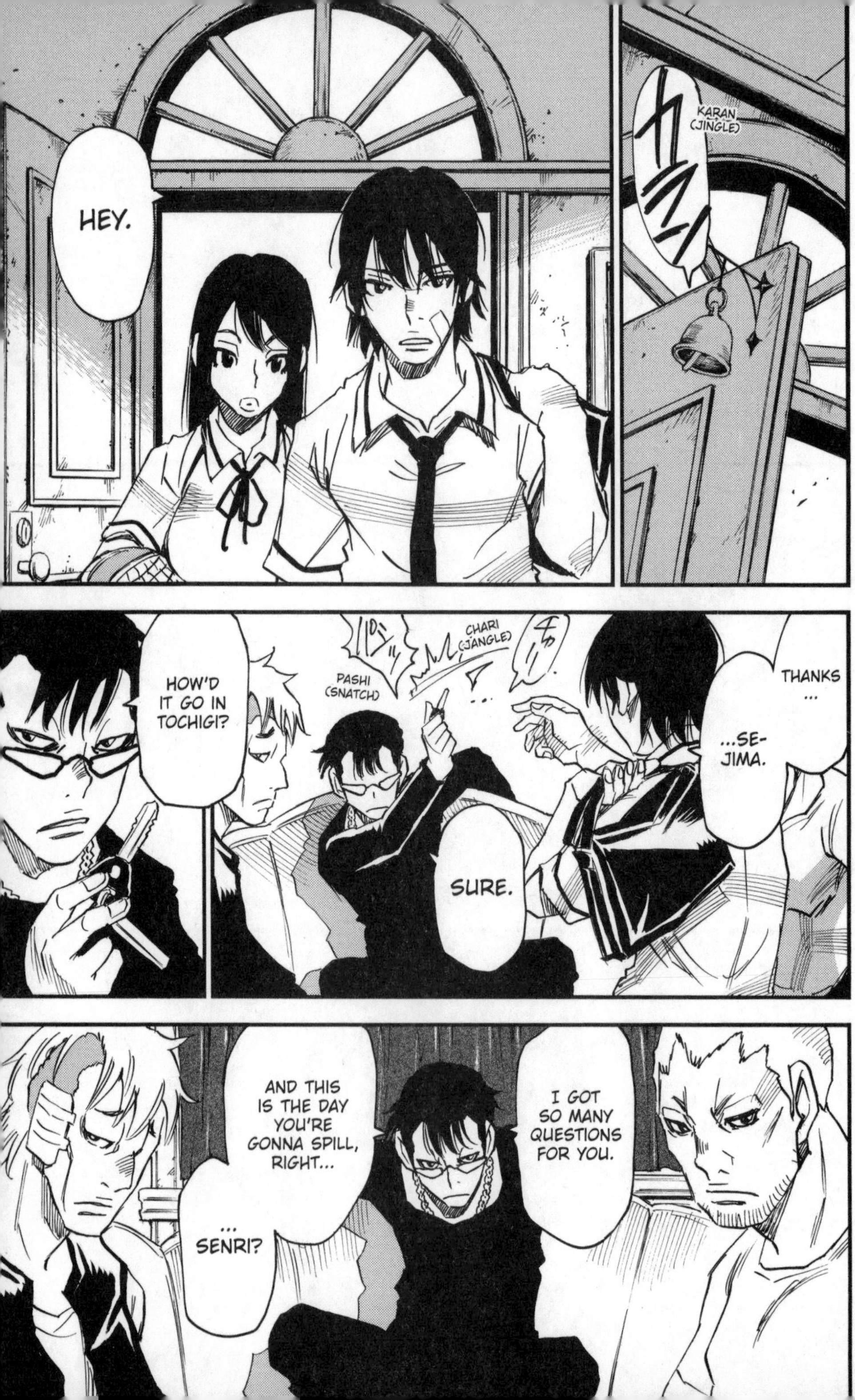
KARAN (JINGLE)
HEY.
THANKS ...
...SE-JIMA.
CHARI (JANGLE)
PASHI (SNATCH)
SURE.
HOW'D IT GO IN TOCHIGI?
I GOT SO MANY QUESTIONS FOR YOU.
AND THIS IS THE DAY YOU'RE GONNA SPILL, RIGHT...
... SENRI?

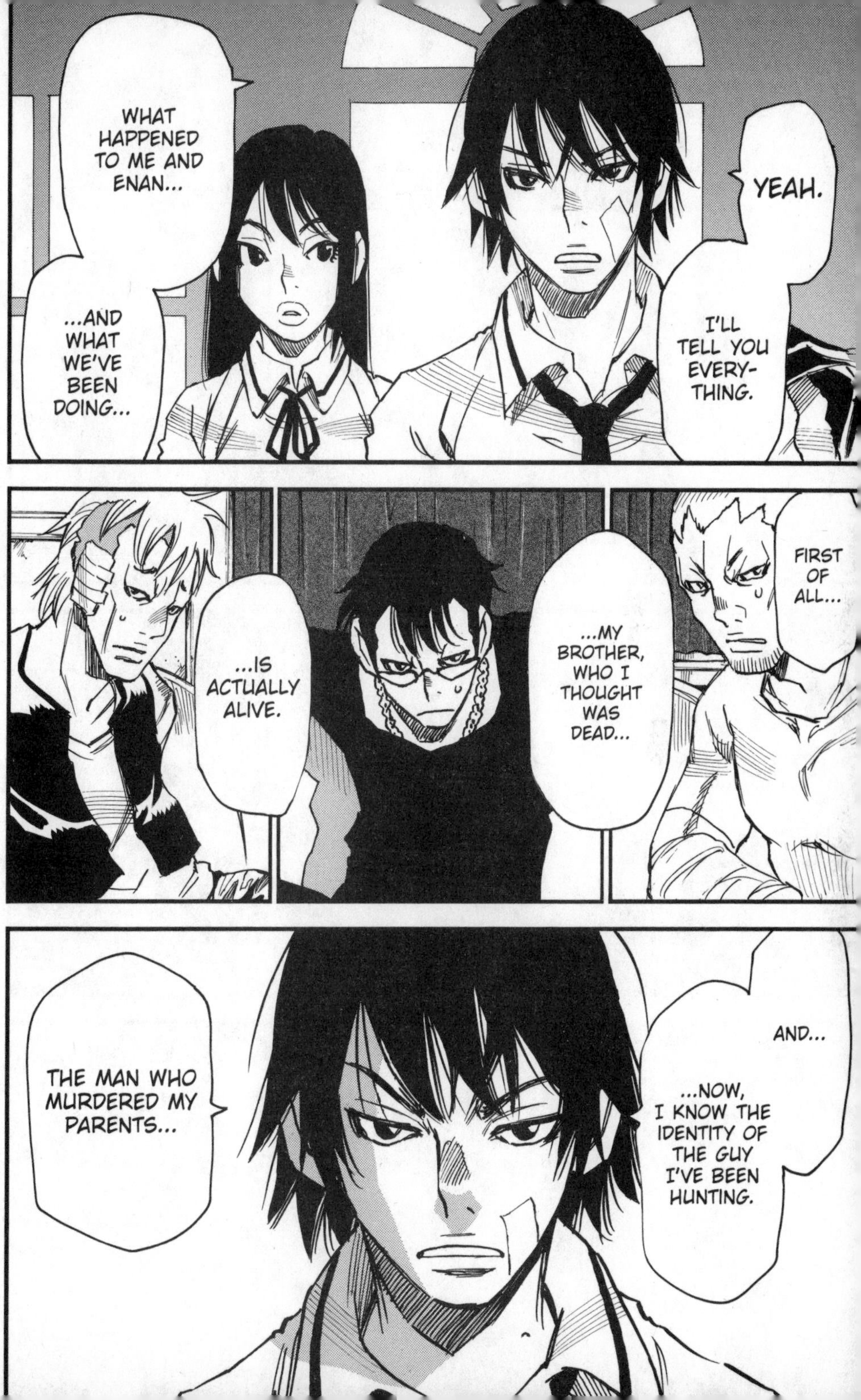
YEAH.
I'LL TELL YOU EVERY-THING.
WHAT HAPPENED TO ME AND ENAN...
...AND WHAT WE'VE BEEN DOING...
FIRST OF ALL...
...MY BROTHER, WHO I THOUGHT WAS DEAD...
...IS ACTUALLY ALIVE.
AND...
...NOW, I KNOW THE IDENTITY OF THE GUY I'VE BEEN HUNTING.
THE MAN WHO MURDERED MY PARENTS...

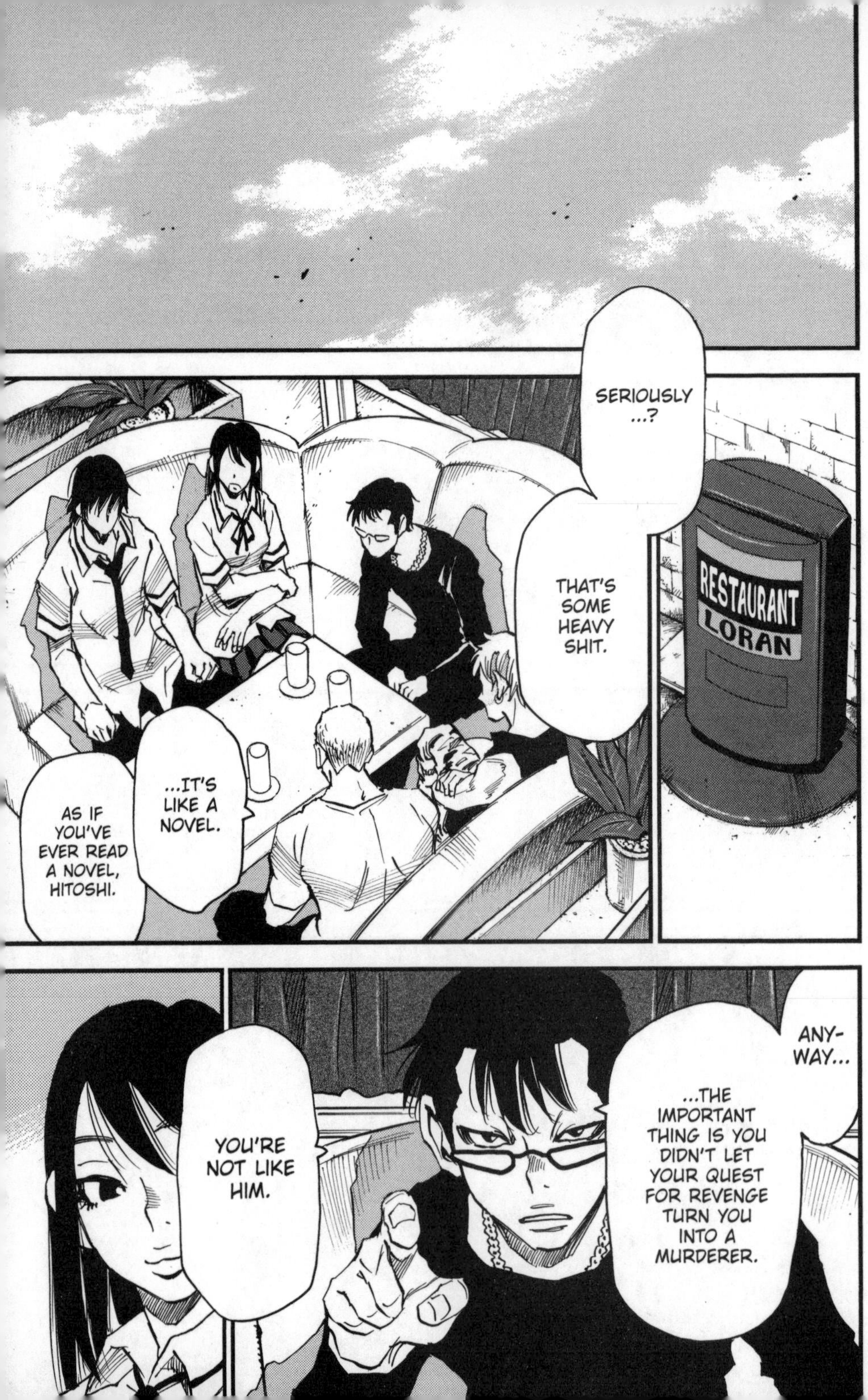
SERIOUSLY ...?
THAT'S SOME HEAVY SHIT.
RESTAURANT LORAN
...IT'S LIKE A NOVEL.
AS IF YOU'VE EVER READ A NOVEL, HITOSHI.
ANY-WAY...
...THE IMPORTANT THING IS YOU DIDN'T LET YOUR QUEST FOR REVENGE TURN YOU INTO A MURDERER.
YOU'RE NOT LIKE HIM.

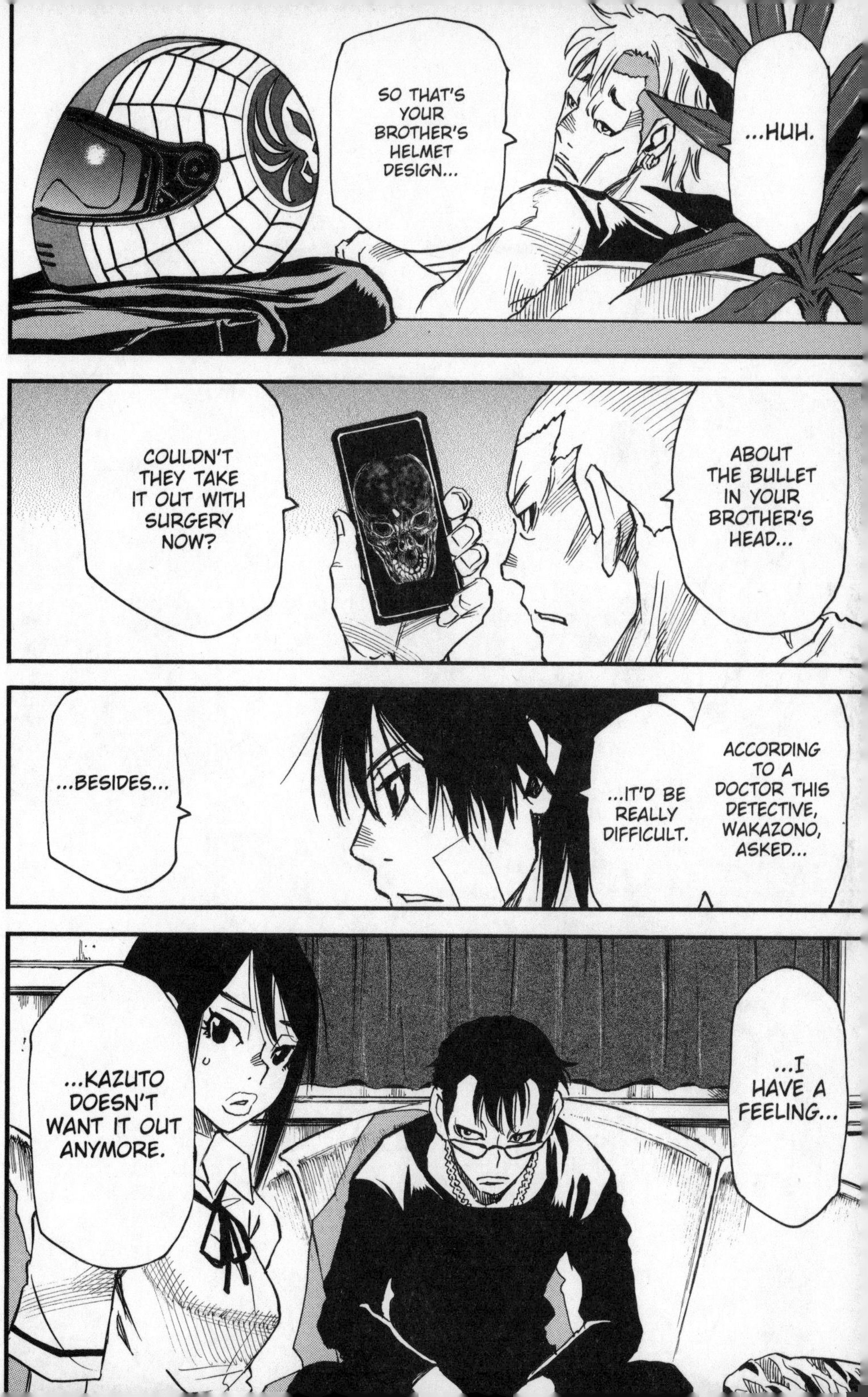
...HUH.
SO THAT'S YOUR BROTHER'S HELMET DESIGN...
ABOUT THE BULLET IN YOUR BROTHER'S HEAD...
COULDN'T THEY TAKE IT OUT WITH SURGERY NOW?
ACCORDING TO A DOCTOR THIS DETECTIVE, WAKAZONO, ASKED...
...IT'D BE REALLY DIFFICULT.
...BESIDES...
...I HAVE A FEELING...
...KAZUTO DOESN'T WANT IT OUT ANYMORE.

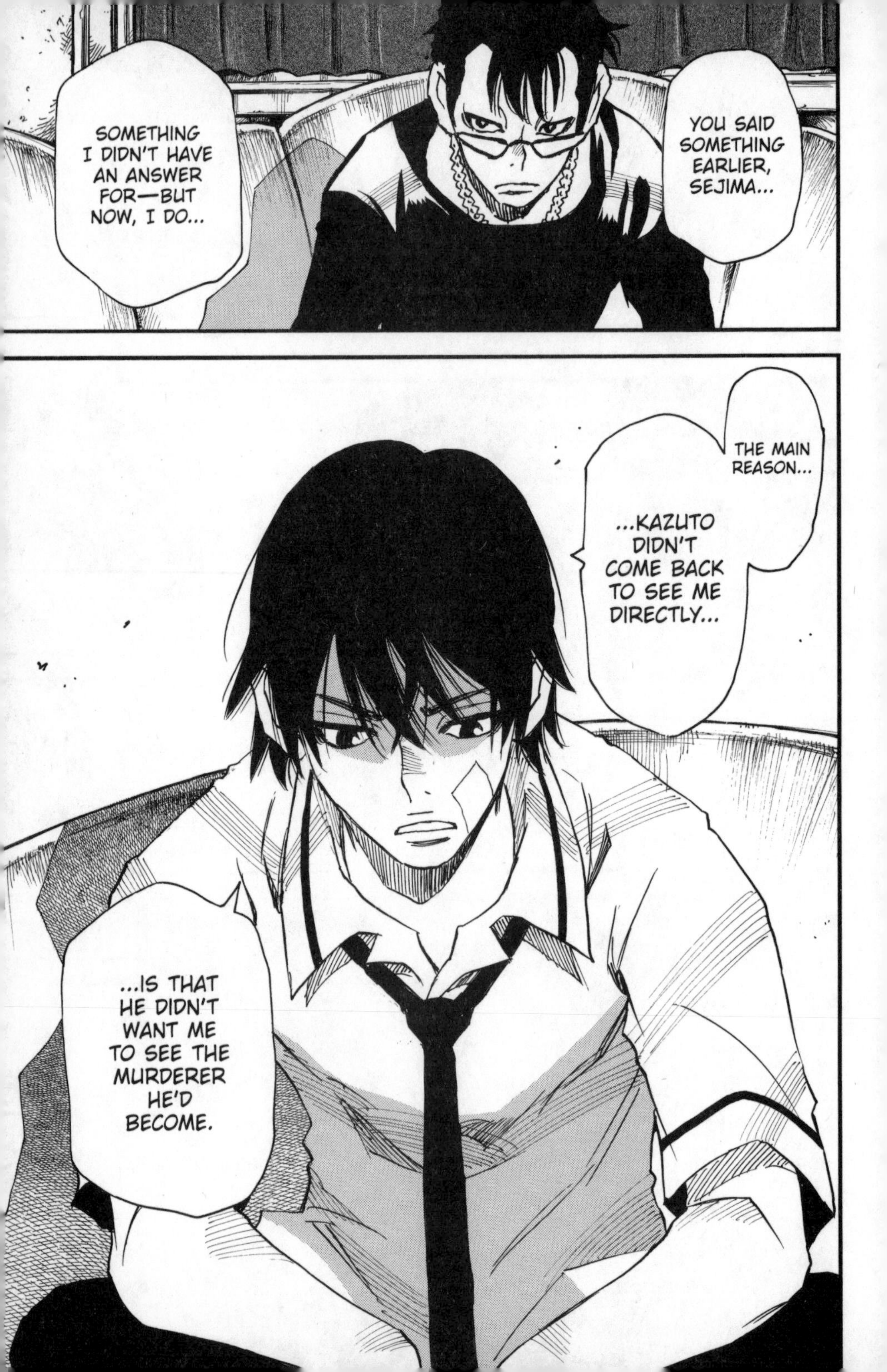
YOU SAID SOMETHING EARLIER, SEJIMA...
SOMETHING I DIDN'T HAVE AN ANSWER FOR—BUT NOW, I DO...
THE MAIN REASON...
...KAZUTO DIDN'T COME BACK TO SEE ME DIRECTLY...
...IS THAT HE DIDN'T WANT ME TO SEE THE MURDERER HE'D BECOME.

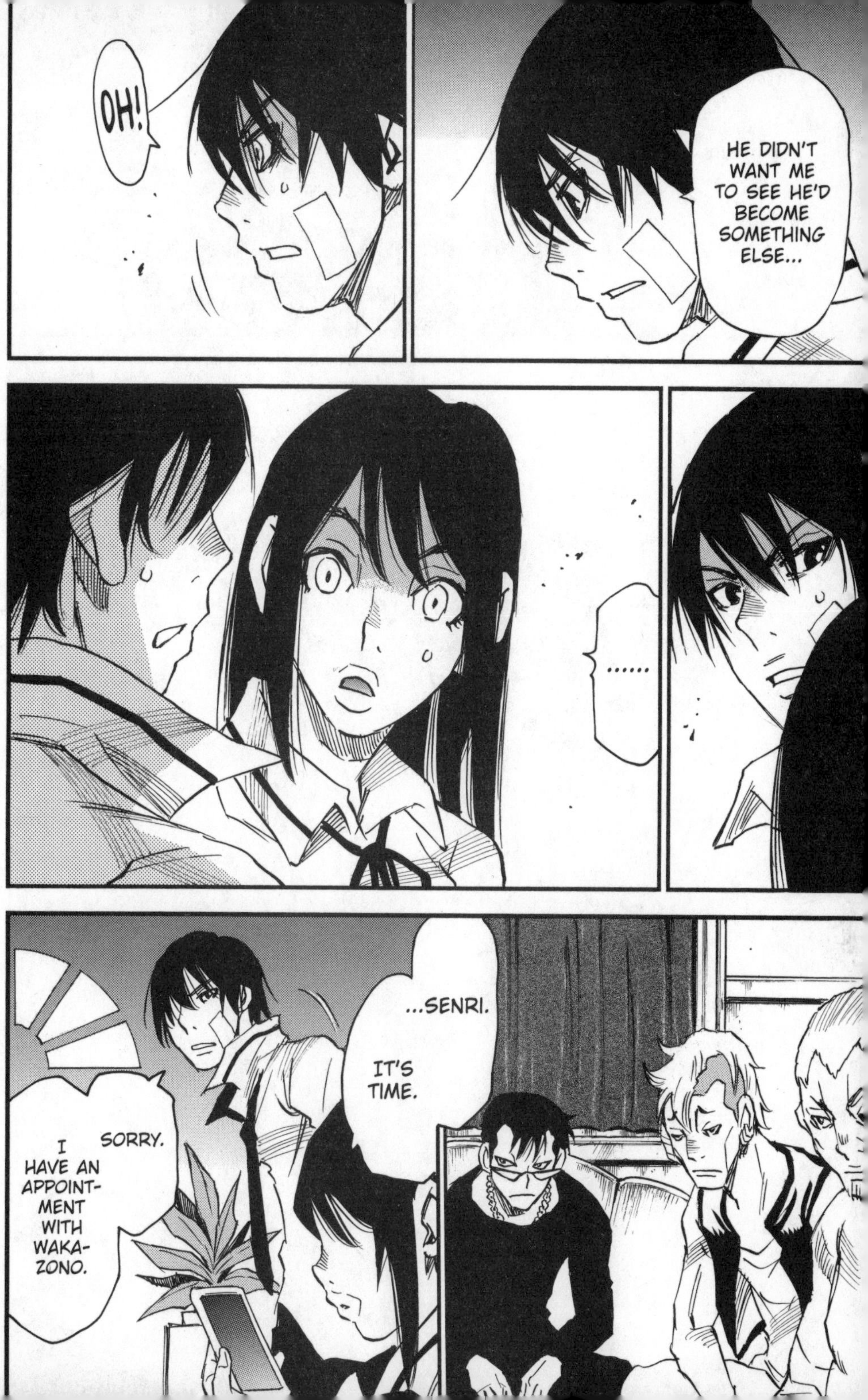
HE DIDN'T WANT ME TO SEE HE'D BECOME SOMETHING ELSE...
OH!
......
...SENRI.
IT'S TIME.
SORRY. I HAVE AN APPOINTMENT WITH WAKAZONO.

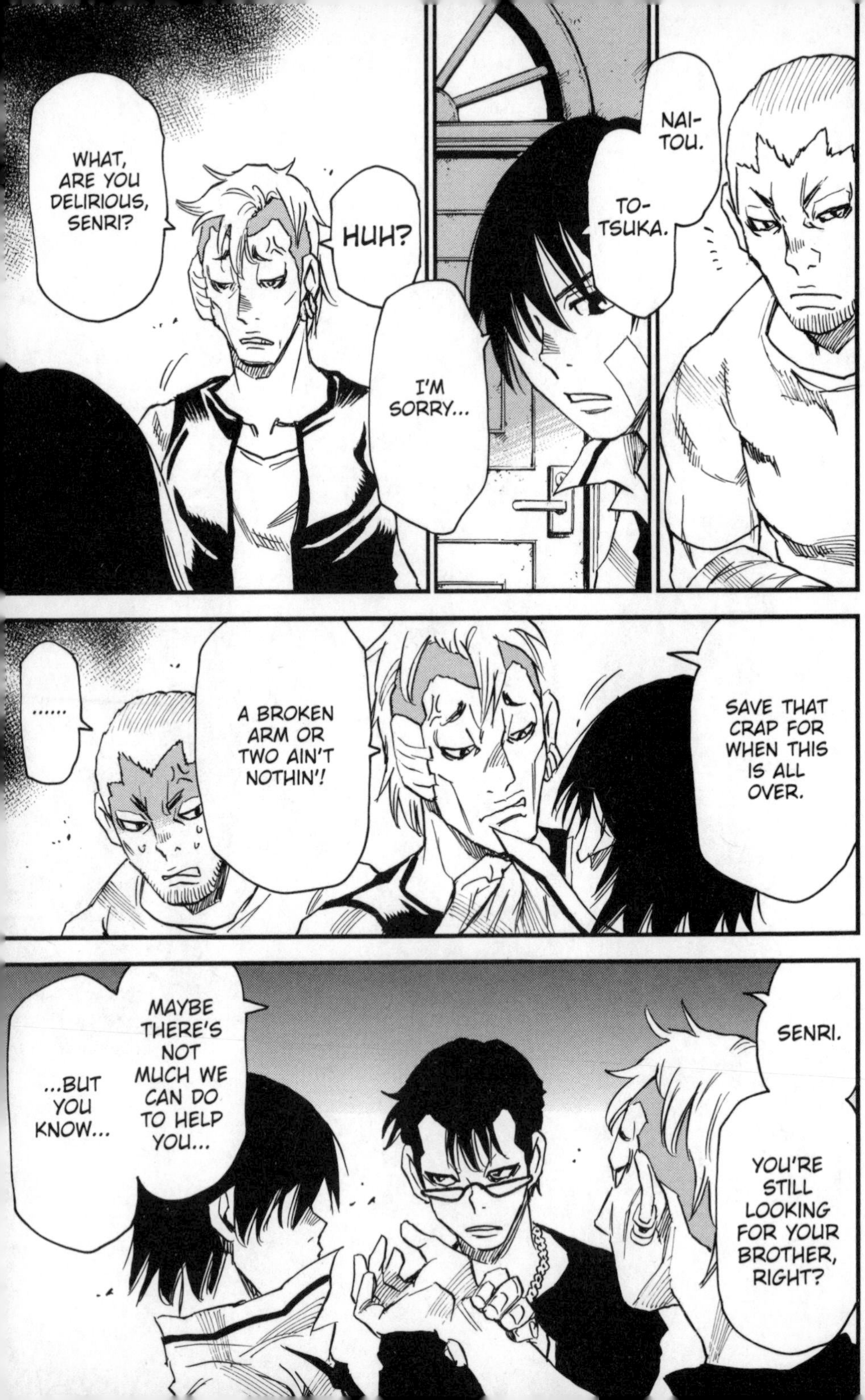
NAI-TOU.
TO-TSUKA.
I'M SORRY...
HUH?
WHAT, ARE YOU DELIRIOUS, SENRI?
SAVE THAT CRAP FOR WHEN THIS IS ALL OVER.
A BROKEN ARM OR TWO AIN'T NOTHIN'!
......
SENRI.
YOU'RE STILL LOOKING FOR YOUR BROTHER, RIGHT?
MAYBE THERE'S NOT MUCH WE CAN DO TO HELP YOU...
...BUT YOU KNOW...

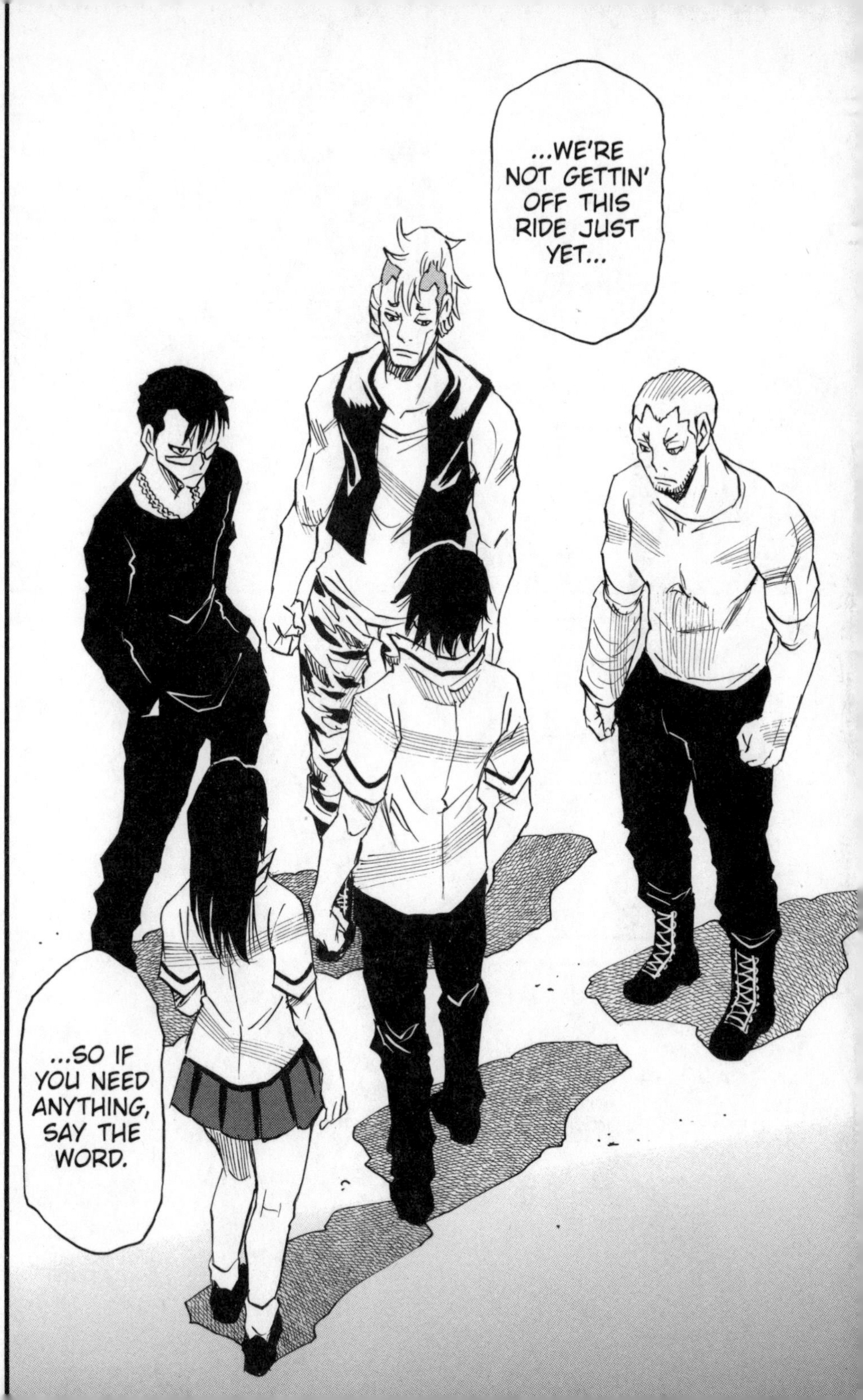
...WE'RE NOT GETTIN' OFF THIS RIDE JUST YET...
...SO IF YOU NEED ANYTHING, SAY THE WORD.

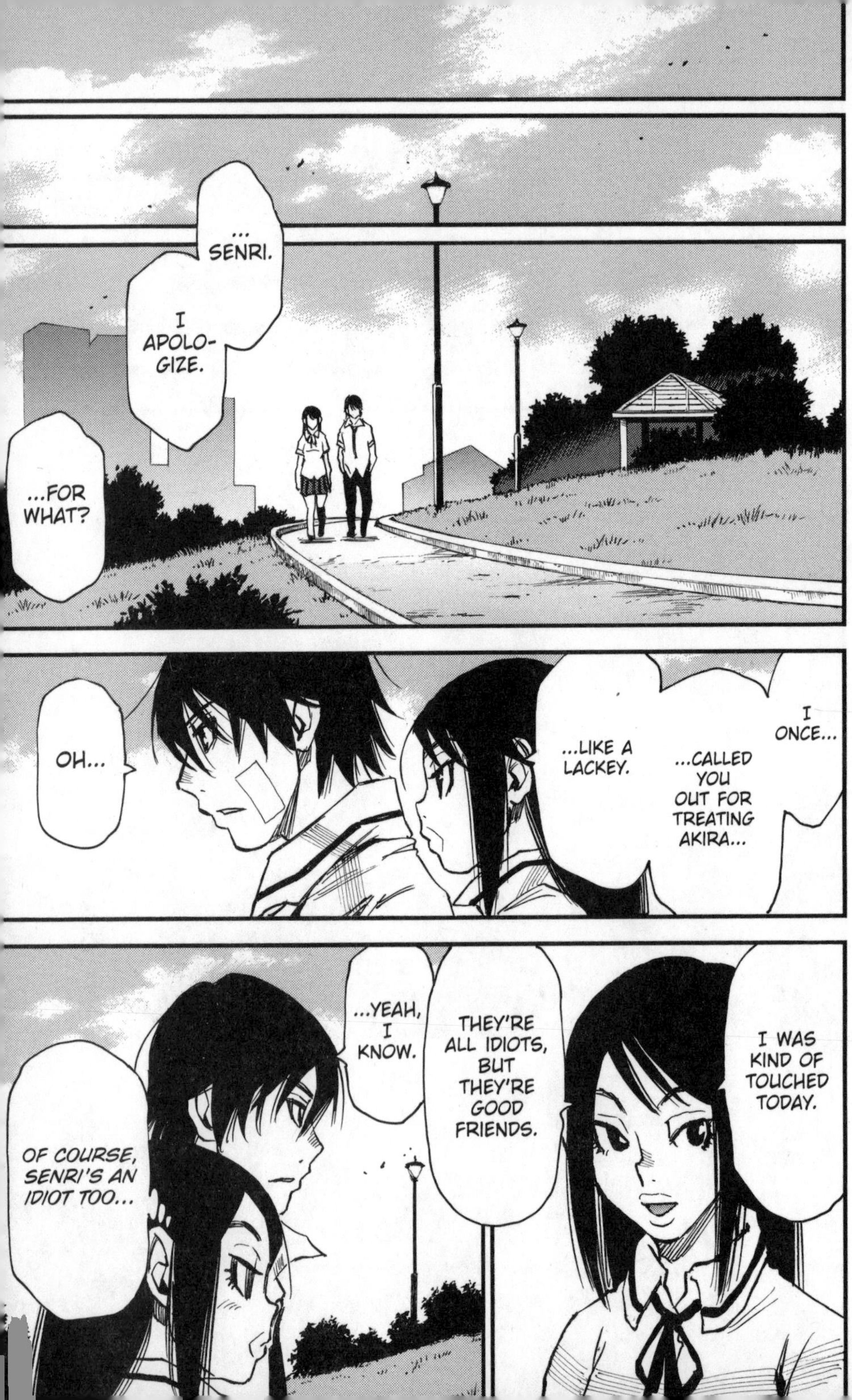
... SENRI.
I APOLOGIZE.
...FOR WHAT?
I ONCE...
...CALLED YOU OUT FOR TREATING AKIRA...
...LIKE A LACKEY.
OH...
I WAS KIND OF TOUCHED TODAY.
THEY'RE ALL IDIOTS, BUT THEY'RE GOOD FRIENDS.
...YEAH, I KNOW.
OF COURSE, SENRI'S AN IDIOT TOO...

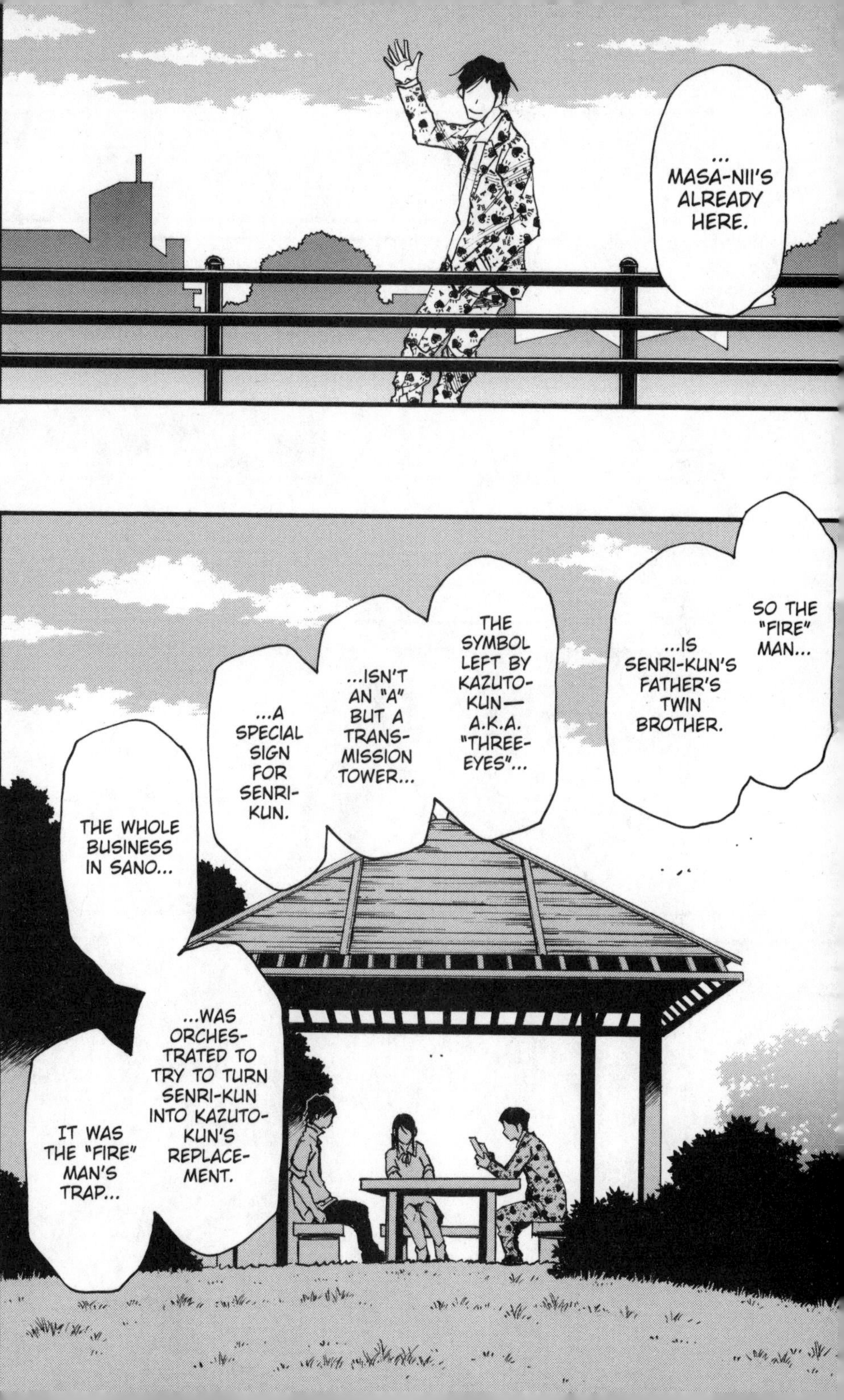
...MASA-NII'S ALREADY HERE.
SO THE "FIRE" MAN...
...IS SENRI-KUN'S FATHER'S TWIN BROTHER.
THE SYMBOL LEFT BY KAZUTO-KUN—A.K.A. "THREE-EYES"...
...ISN'T AN "A" BUT A TRANSMISSION TOWER...
...A SPECIAL SIGN FOR SENRI-KUN.
THE WHOLE BUSINESS IN SANO...
...WAS ORCHESTRATED TO TRY TO TURN SENRI-KUN INTO KAZUTO-KUN'S REPLACEMENT.
IT WAS THE "FIRE" MAN'S TRAP...
...

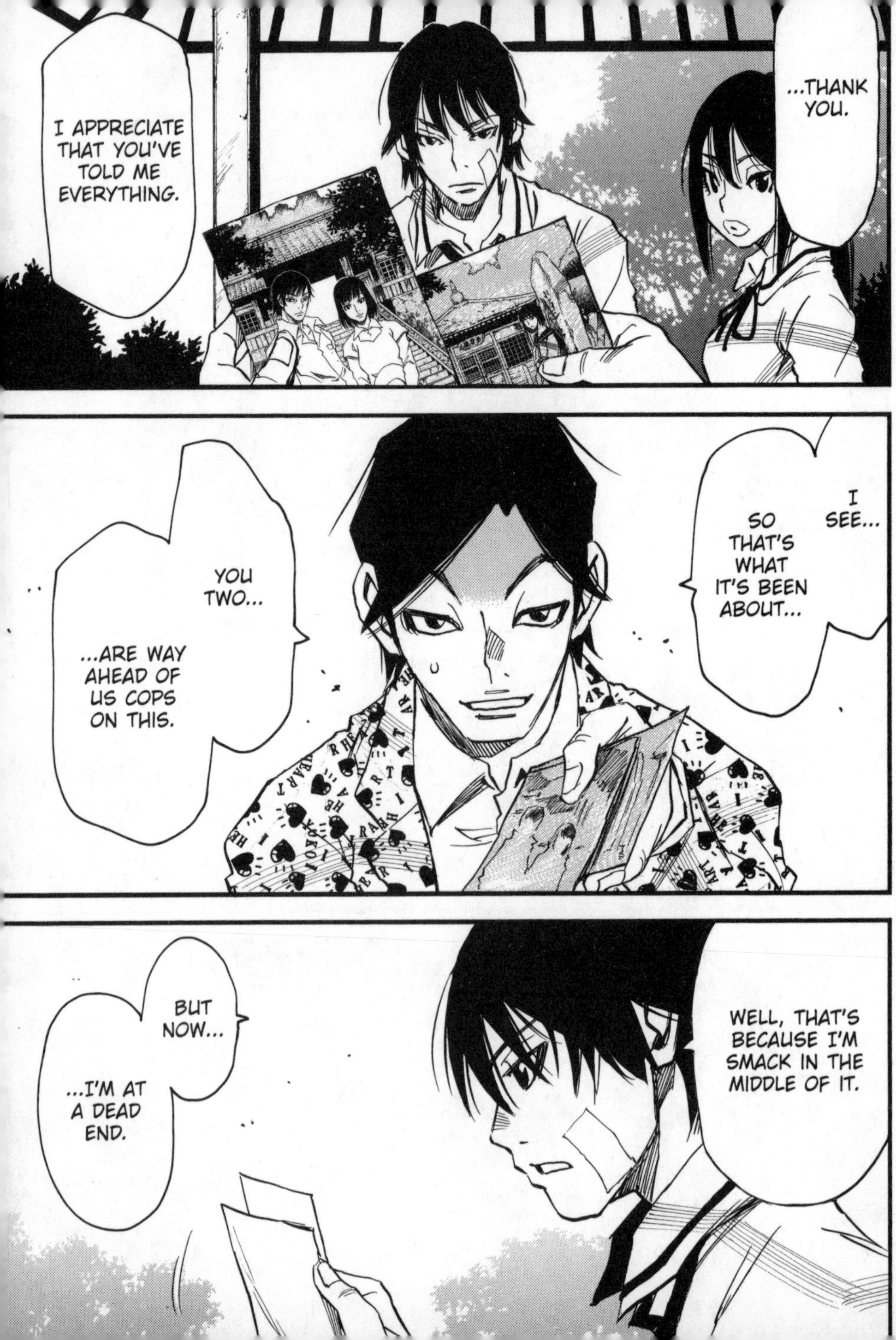
...THANK YOU.
I APPRECIATE THAT YOU'VE TOLD ME EVERYTHING.
I SEE...
SO THAT'S WHAT IT'S BEEN ABOUT...
YOU TWO...
...ARE WAY AHEAD OF US COPS ON THIS.
WELL, THAT'S BECAUSE I'M SMACK IN THE MIDDLE OF IT.
BUT NOW...
...I'M AT A DEAD END.

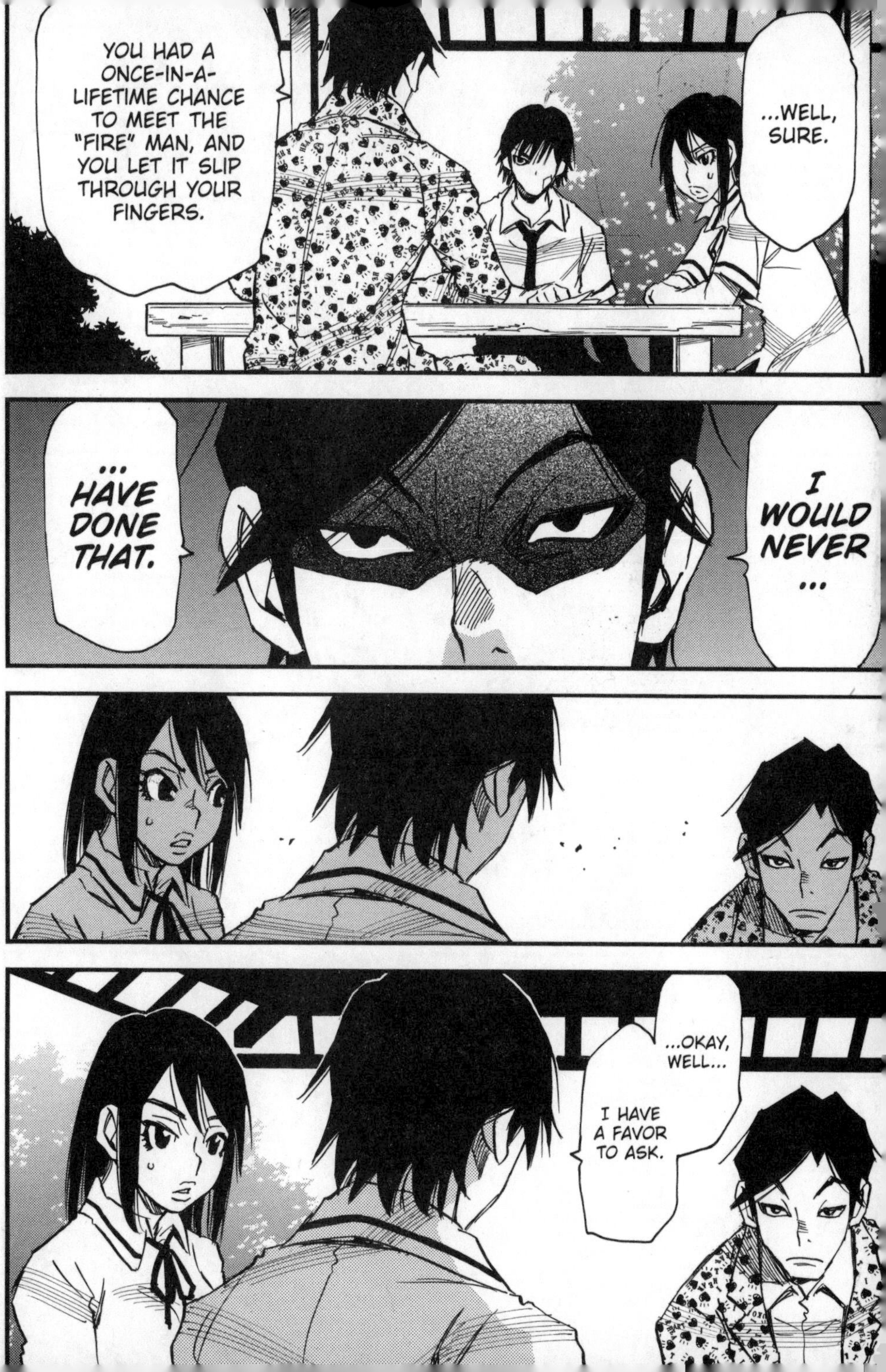
...WELL, SURE.
YOU HAD A ONCE-IN-A-LIFETIME CHANCE TO MEET THE "FIRE" MAN, AND YOU LET IT SLIP THROUGH YOUR FINGERS.
I WOULD NEVER ...
... HAVE DONE THAT.
...OKAY, WELL...
I HAVE A FAVOR TO ASK.

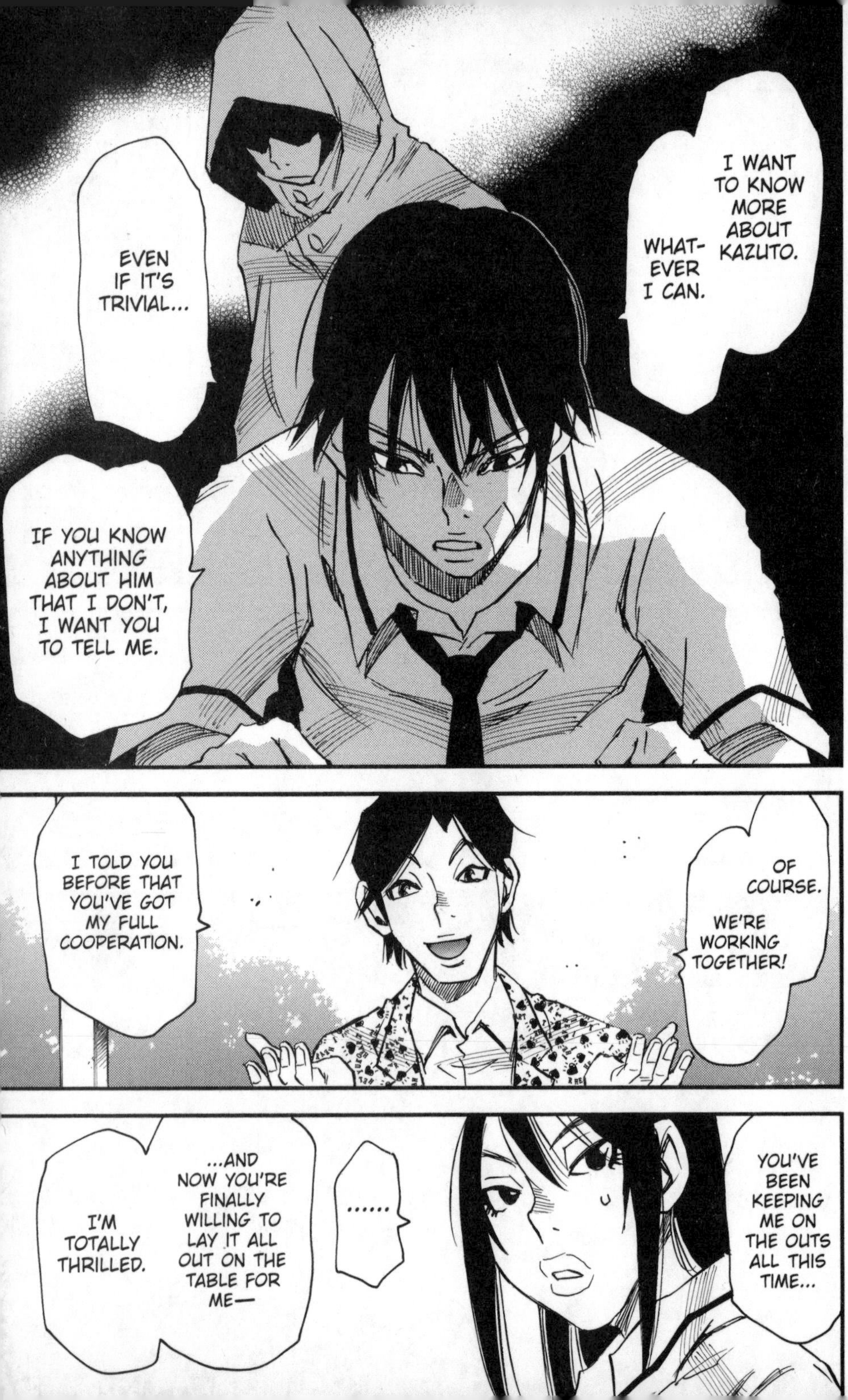
I WANT TO KNOW MORE ABOUT KAZUTO.
WHAT-EVER I CAN.
EVEN IF IT'S TRIVIAL...
IF YOU KNOW ANYTHING ABOUT HIM THAT I DON'T, I WANT YOU TO TELL ME.
OF COURSE.
WE'RE WORKING TOGETHER!
I TOLD YOU BEFORE THAT YOU'VE GOT MY FULL COOPERATION.
YOU'VE BEEN KEEPING ME ON THE OUTS ALL THIS TIME...
......
...AND NOW YOU'RE FINALLY WILLING TO LAY IT ALL OUT ON THE TABLE FOR ME—
I'M TOTALLY THRILLED.

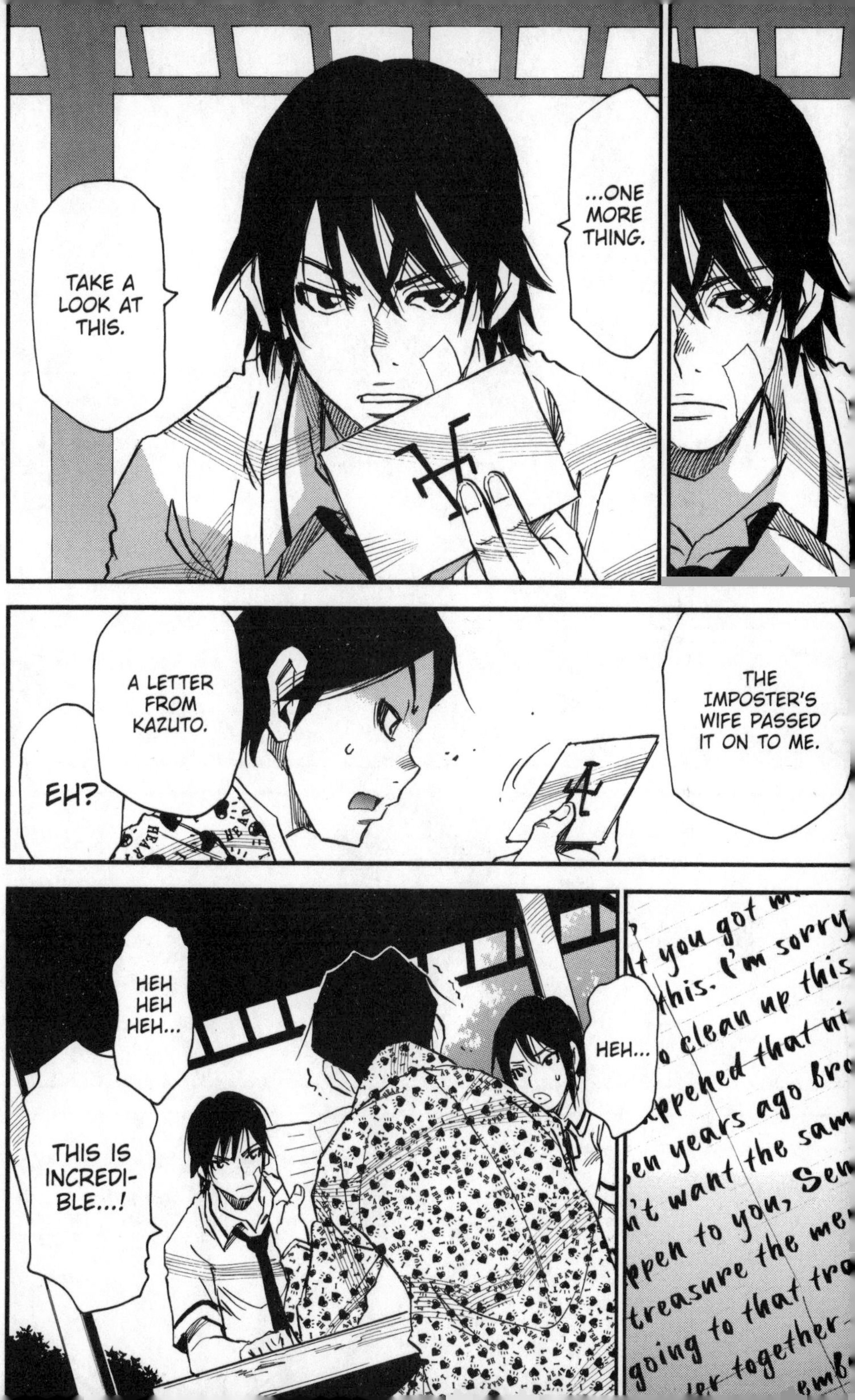
...ONE MORE THING.
TAKE A LOOK AT THIS.
THE IMPOSTER'S WIFE PASSED IT ON TO ME.
A LETTER FROM KAZUTO.
EH?
you got
this. I'm sorry
clean up this
ppened that
en years ago
t want the sam
pen to you, Sen
treasure the me
going to that tr
together
HEH...
HEH HEH HEH...
THIS IS INCREDIBLE...!

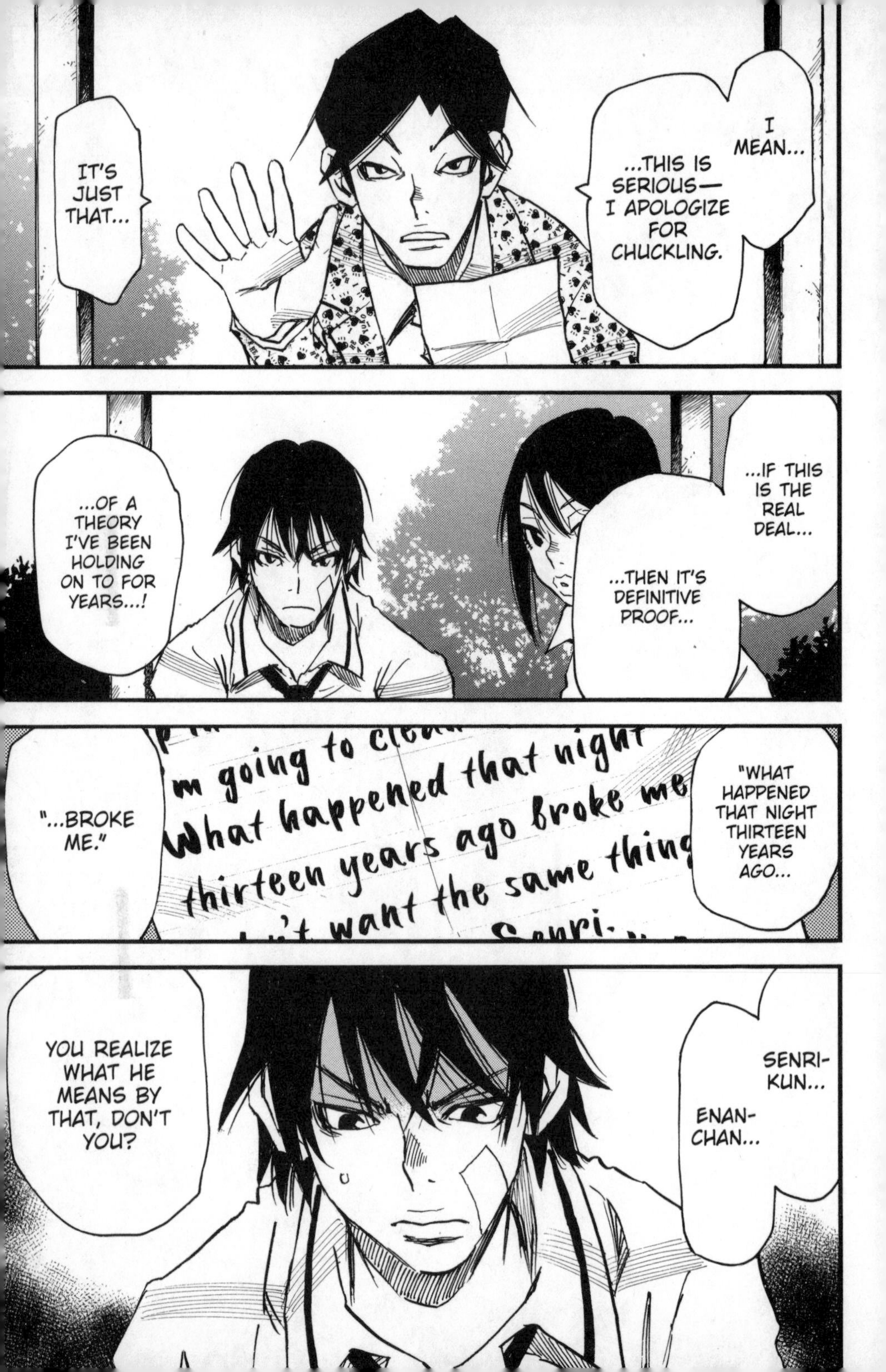
I MEAN...
...THIS IS SERIOUS—I APOLOGIZE FOR CHUCKLING.
IT'S JUST THAT...
...IF THIS IS THE REAL DEAL...
...THEN IT'S DEFINITIVE PROOF...
...OF A THEORY I'VE BEEN HOLDING ON TO FOR YEARS...!
"WHAT HAPPENED THAT NIGHT THIRTEEN YEARS AGO...
m going to
What happened that night
thirteen years ago broke me
want the same thing
"...BROKE ME."
SENRI-KUN...
ENAN-CHAN...
YOU REALIZE WHAT HE MEANS BY THAT, DON'T YOU?

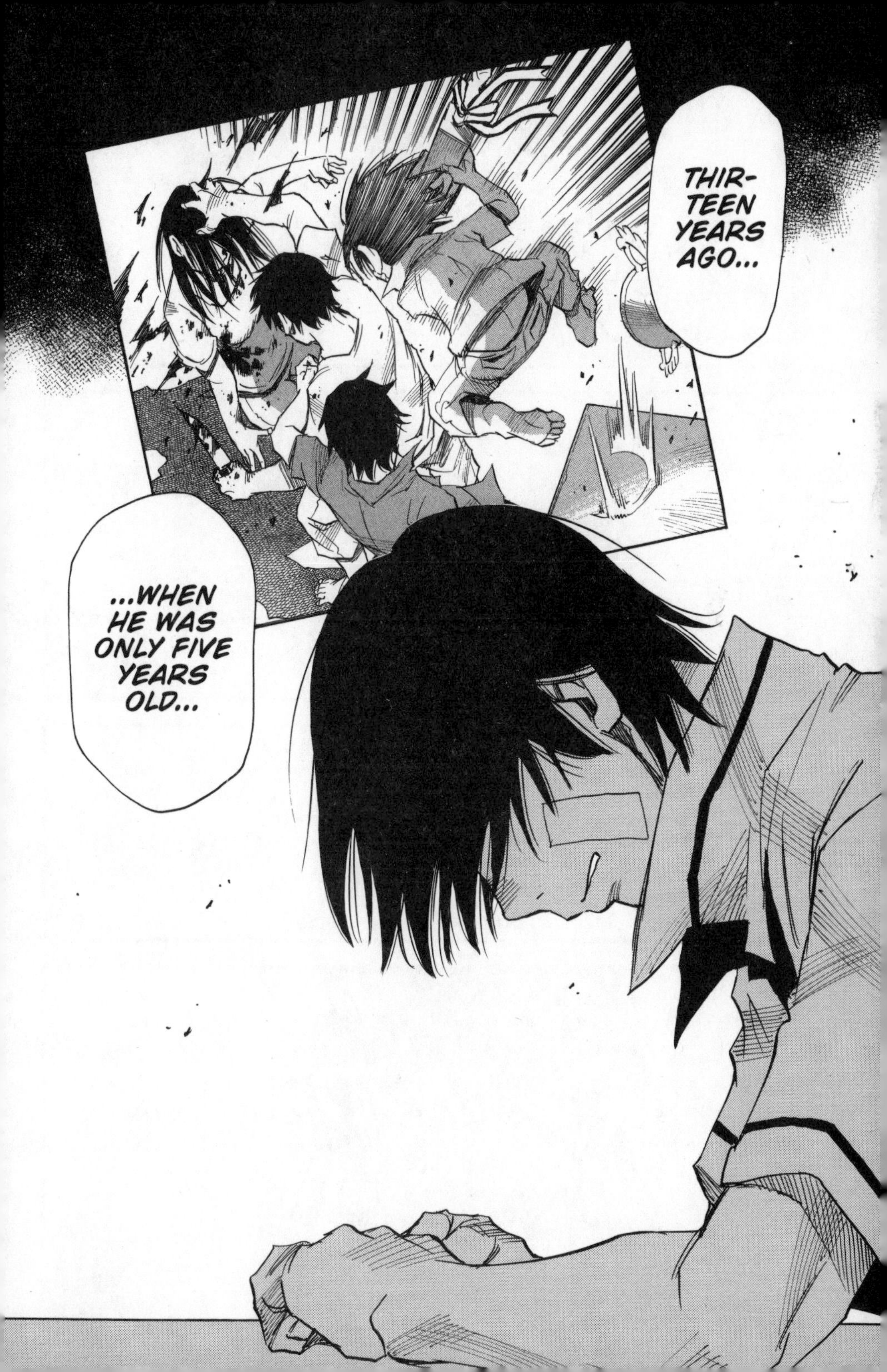
THIR-
TEEN
YEARS
AGO...
...WHEN
HE WAS
ONLY FIVE
YEARS
OLD...

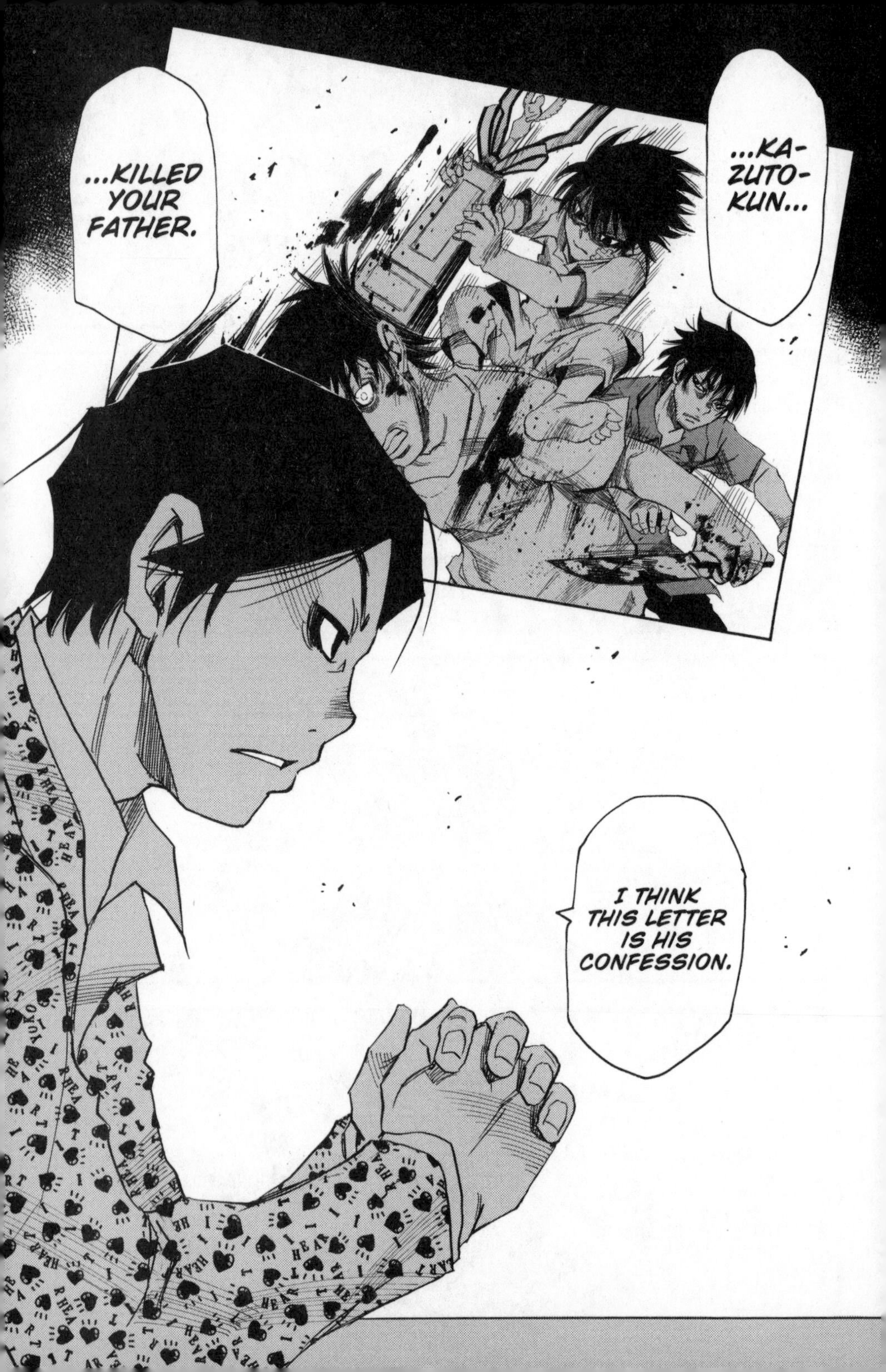
...KA-ZUTO-KUN...
...KILLED YOUR FATHER.
I THINK THIS LETTER IS HIS CONFESSION.

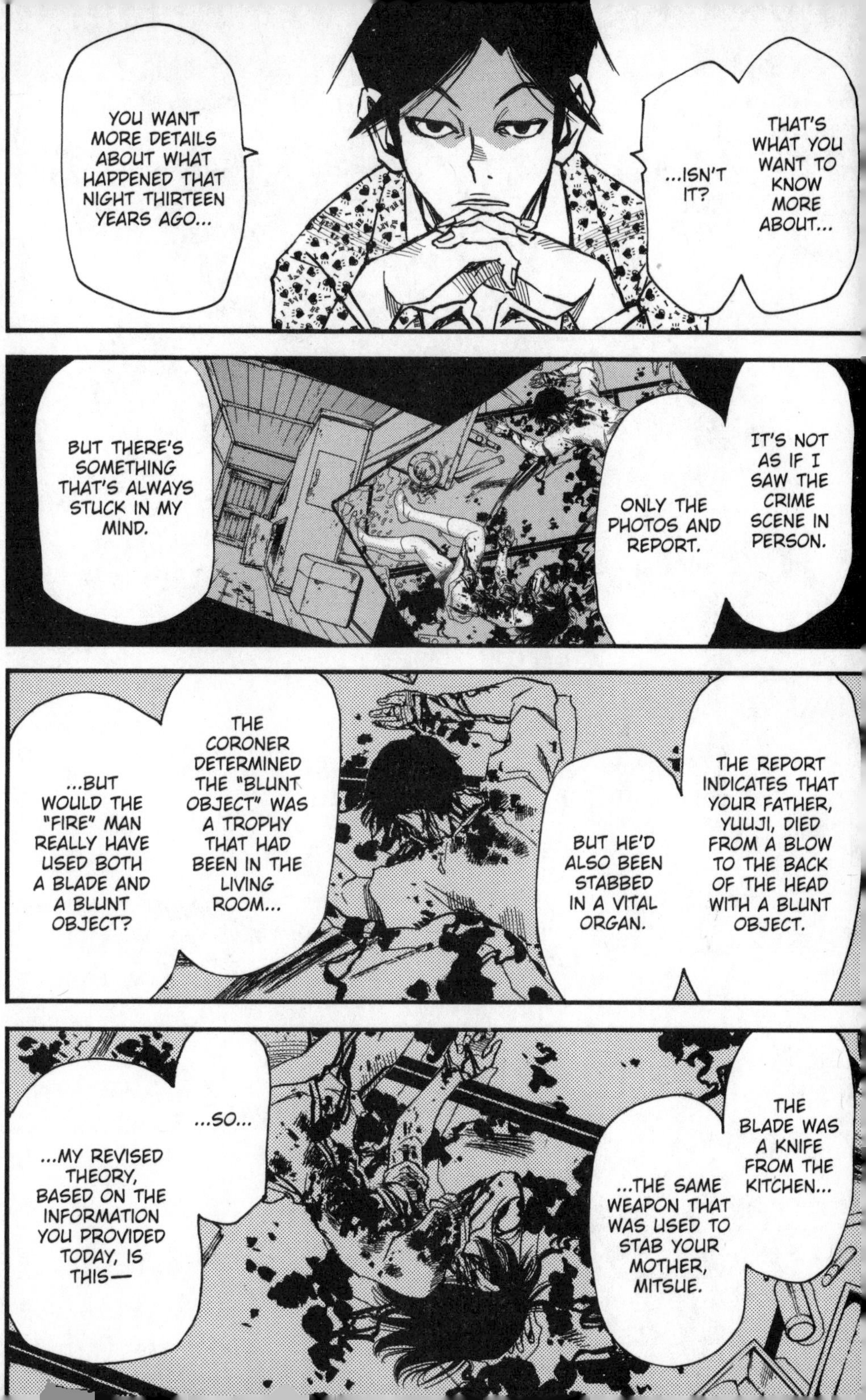
THAT'S WHAT YOU WANT TO KNOW MORE ABOUT...
...ISN'T IT?
YOU WANT MORE DETAILS ABOUT WHAT HAPPENED THAT NIGHT THIRTEEN YEARS AGO...
IT'S NOT AS IF I SAW THE CRIME SCENE IN PERSON.
ONLY THE PHOTOS AND REPORT.
BUT THERE'S SOMETHING THAT'S ALWAYS STUCK IN MY MIND.
THE REPORT INDICATES THAT YOUR FATHER, YUUJI, DIED FROM A BLOW TO THE BACK OF THE HEAD WITH A BLUNT OBJECT.
BUT HE'D ALSO BEEN STABBED IN A VITAL ORGAN.
THE CORONER DETERMINED THE "BLUNT OBJECT" WAS A TROPHY THAT HAD BEEN IN THE LIVING ROOM...
...BUT WOULD THE "FIRE" MAN REALLY HAVE USED BOTH A BLADE AND A BLUNT OBJECT?
THE BLADE WAS A KNIFE FROM THE KITCHEN...
...THE SAME WEAPON THAT WAS USED TO STAB YOUR MOTHER, MITSUE.
...SO...
...MY REVISED THEORY, BASED ON THE INFORMATION YOU PROVIDED TODAY, IS THIS—

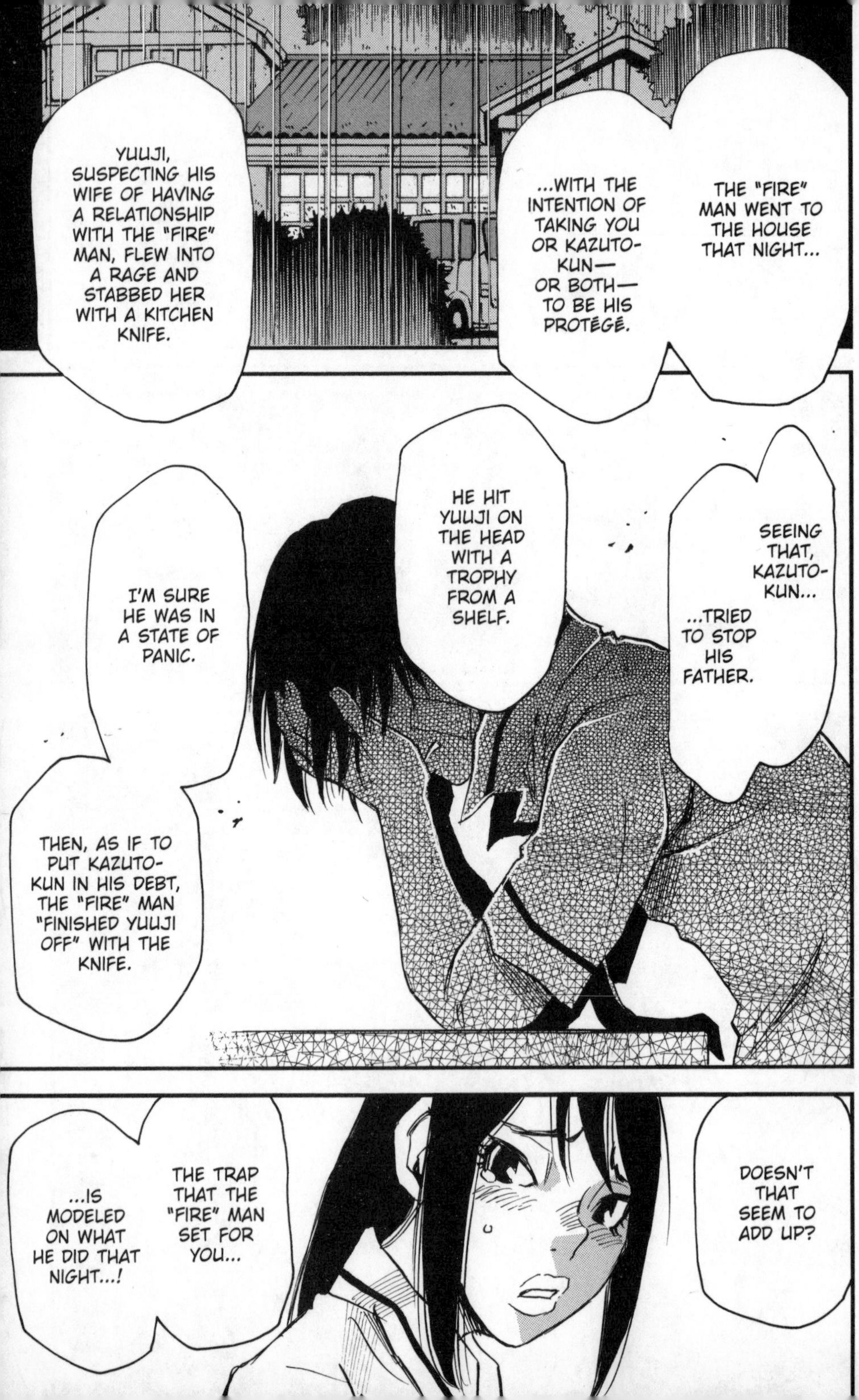
THE "FIRE" MAN WENT TO THE HOUSE THAT NIGHT...
...WITH THE INTENTION OF TAKING YOU OR KAZUTO-KUN— OR BOTH— TO BE HIS PROTÉGÉ.
YUUJI, SUSPECTING HIS WIFE OF HAVING A RELATIONSHIP WITH THE "FIRE" MAN, FLEW INTO A RAGE AND STABBED HER WITH A KITCHEN KNIFE.
SEEING THAT, KAZUTO-KUN...
...TRIED TO STOP HIS FATHER.
HE HIT YUUJI ON THE HEAD WITH A TROPHY FROM A SHELF.
I'M SURE HE WAS IN A STATE OF PANIC.
THEN, AS IF TO PUT KAZUTO-KUN IN HIS DEBT, THE "FIRE" MAN "FINISHED YUUJI OFF" WITH THE KNIFE.
DOESN'T THAT SEEM TO ADD UP?
THE TRAP THAT THE "FIRE" MAN SET FOR YOU...
...IS MODELED ON WHAT HE DID THAT NIGHT...!

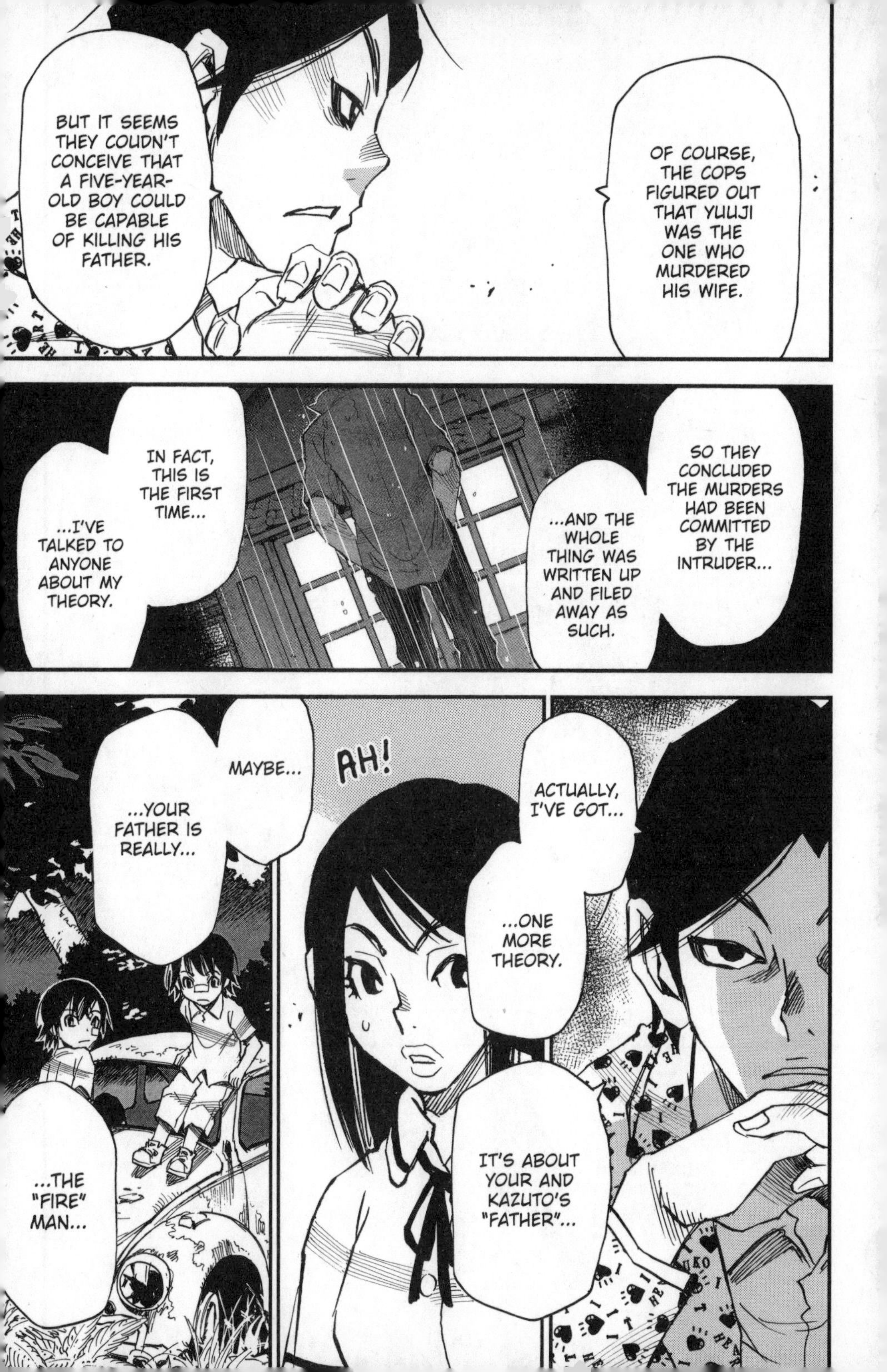
OF COURSE, THE COPS FIGURED OUT THAT YUUJI WAS THE ONE WHO MURDERED HIS WIFE.
BUT IT SEEMS THEY COUDN'T CONCEIVE THAT A FIVE-YEAR-OLD BOY COULD BE CAPABLE OF KILLING HIS FATHER.
SO THEY CONCLUDED THE MURDERS HAD BEEN COMMITTED BY THE INTRUDER...
...AND THE WHOLE THING WAS WRITTEN UP AND FILED AWAY AS SUCH.
IN FACT, THIS IS THE FIRST TIME...
...I'VE TALKED TO ANYONE ABOUT MY THEORY.
ACTUALLY, I'VE GOT...
...ONE MORE THEORY.
IT'S ABOUT YOUR AND KAZUTO'S "FATHER"...
AH!
MAYBE...
...YOUR FATHER IS REALLY...
...THE "FIRE" MAN...

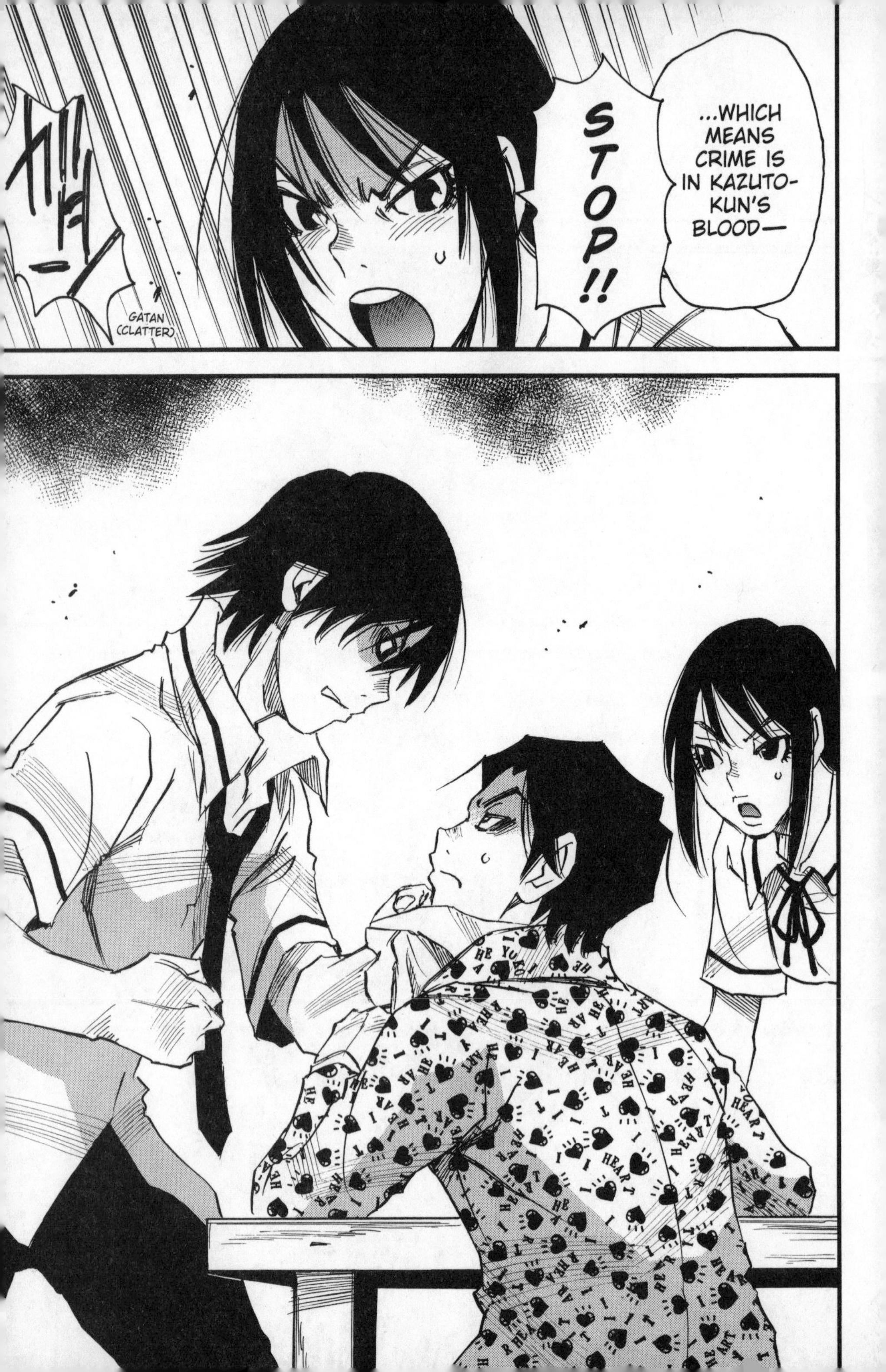
...WHICH MEANS CRIME IS IN KAZUTO-KUN'S BLOOD—
STOP!!
GATAN (CLATTER)

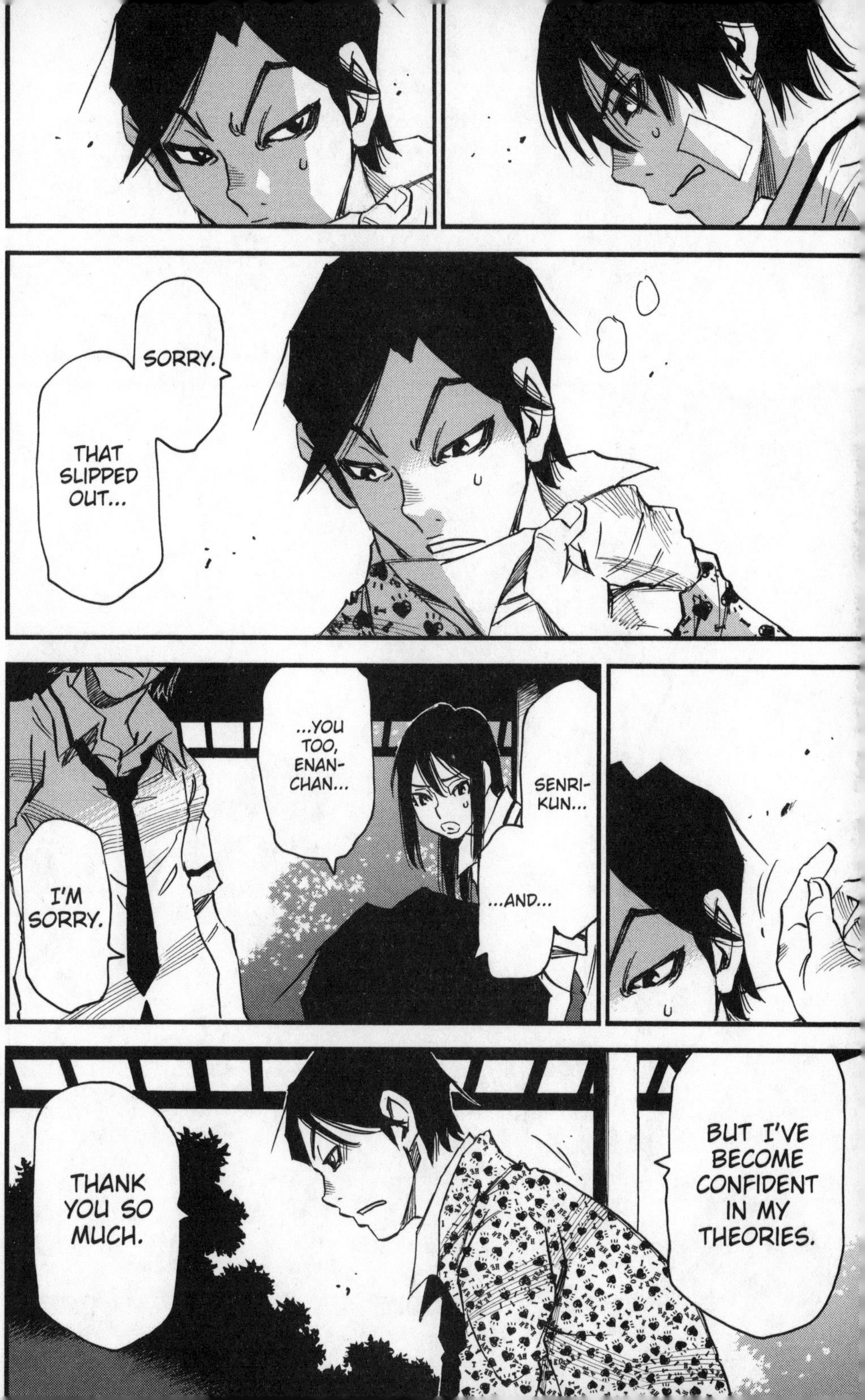
SORRY.
THAT SLIPPED OUT...
SENRI-KUN...
...AND...
...YOU TOO, ENAN-CHAN...
I'M SORRY.
BUT I'VE BECOME CONFIDENT IN MY THEORIES.
THANK YOU SO MUCH.

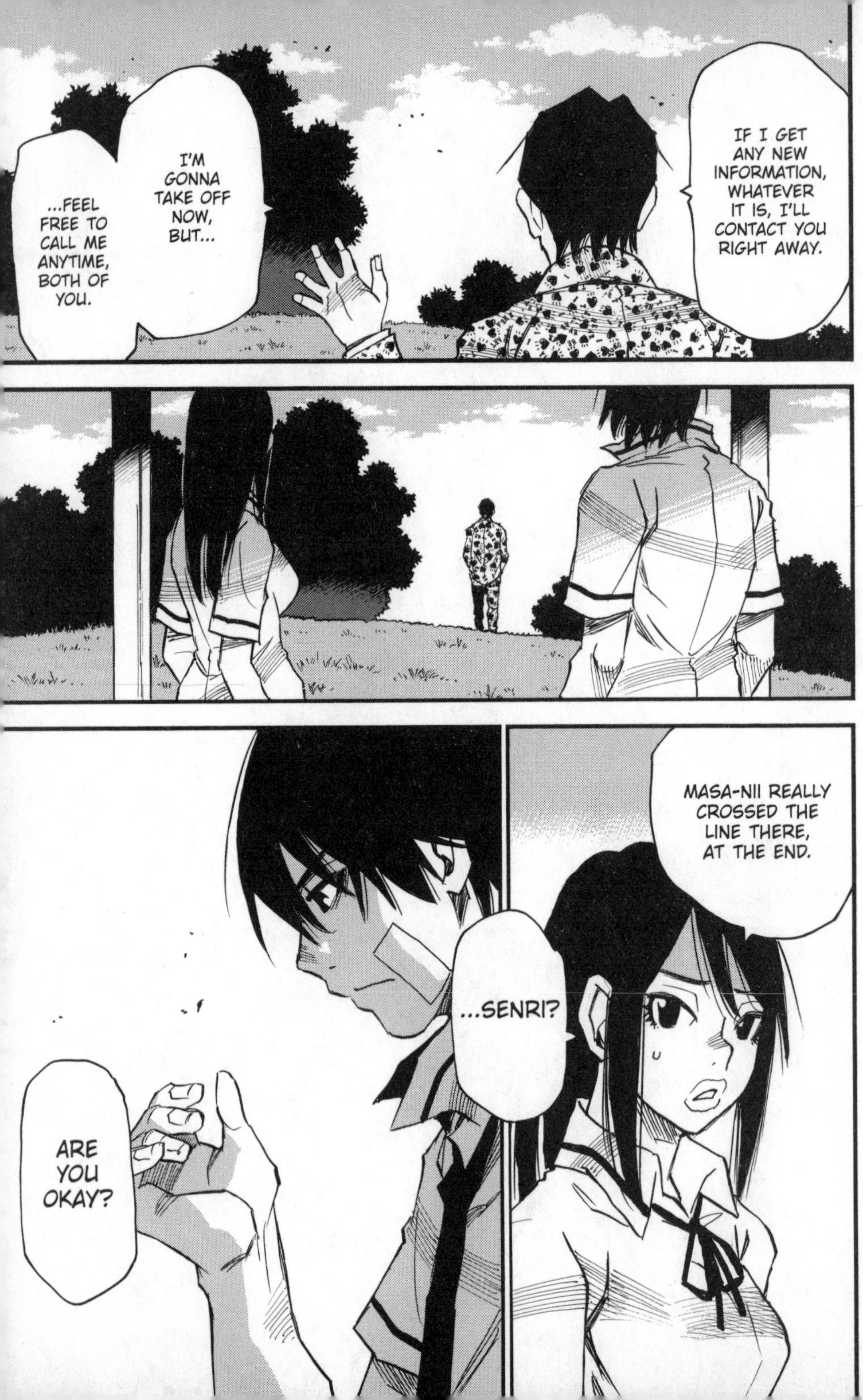
IF I GET ANY NEW INFORMATION, WHATEVER IT IS, I'LL CONTACT YOU RIGHT AWAY.
I'M GONNA TAKE OFF NOW, BUT...
...FEEL FREE TO CALL ME ANYTIME, BOTH OF YOU.
MASA-NII REALLY CROSSED THE LINE THERE, AT THE END.
...SENRI?
ARE YOU OKAY?

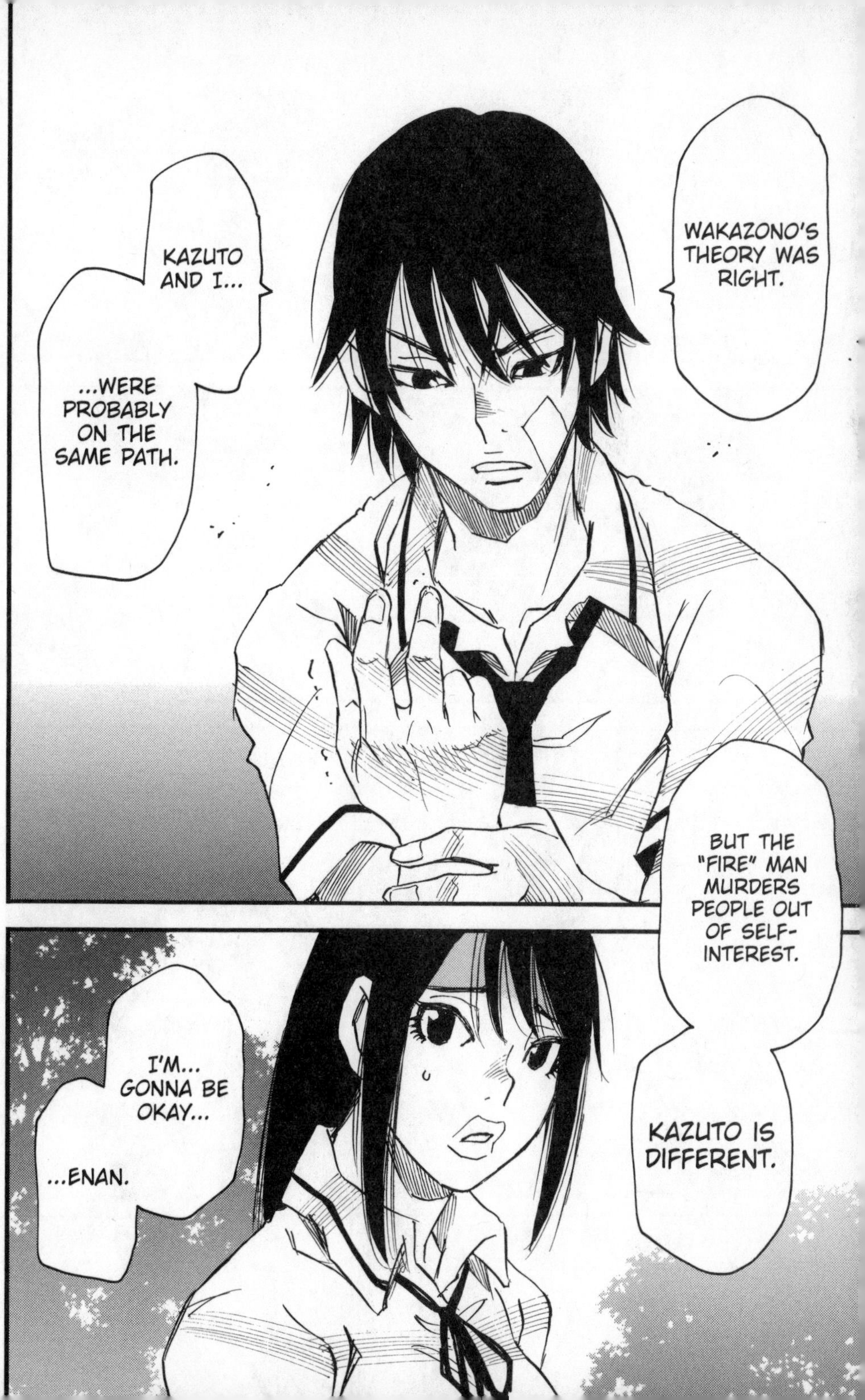
WAKAZONO'S THEORY WAS RIGHT.
KAZUTO AND I...
...WERE PROBABLY ON THE SAME PATH.
BUT THE "FIRE" MAN MURDERS PEOPLE OUT OF SELF-INTEREST.
KAZUTO IS DIFFERENT.
I'M... GONNA BE OKAY...
...ENAN.

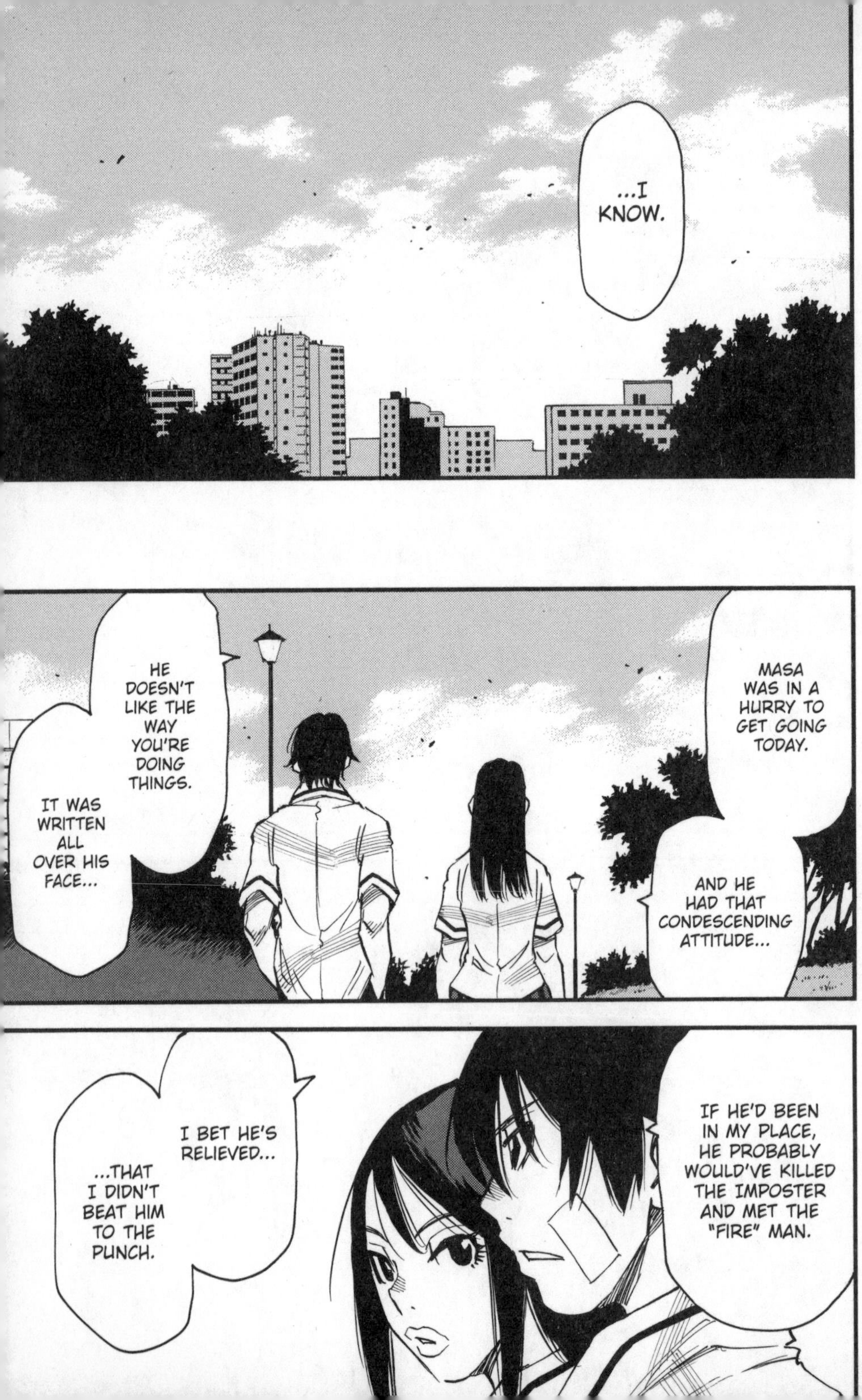
...I KNOW.
MASA WAS IN A HURRY TO GET GOING TODAY.
AND HE HAD THAT CONDESCENDING ATTITUDE...
HE DOESN'T LIKE THE WAY YOU'RE DOING THINGS.
IT WAS WRITTEN ALL OVER HIS FACE...
IF HE'D BEEN IN MY PLACE, HE PROBABLY WOULD'VE KILLED THE IMPOSTER AND MET THE "FIRE" MAN.
I BET HE'S RELIEVED...
...THAT I DIDN'T BEAT HIM TO THE PUNCH.

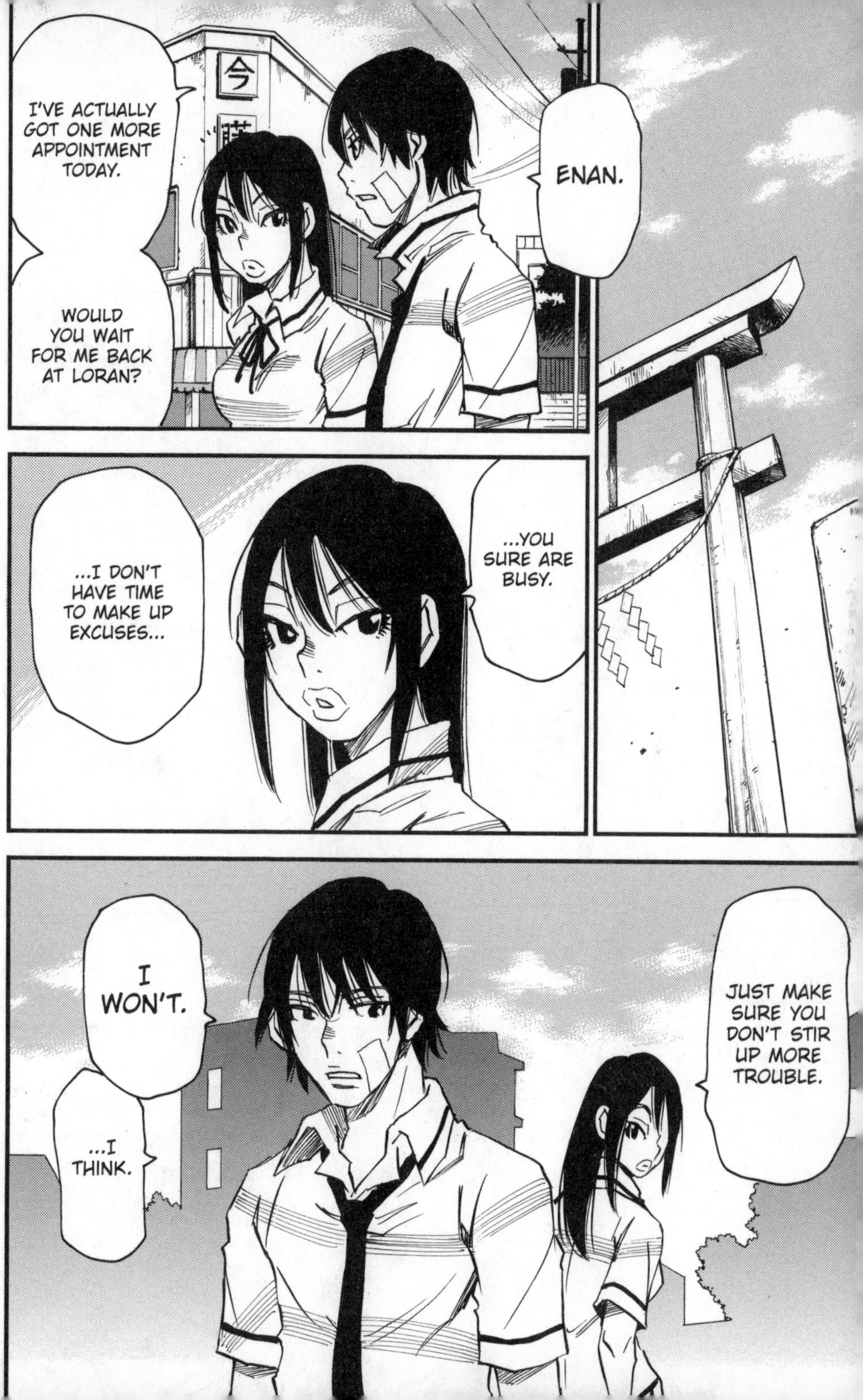
ENAN.
I'VE ACTUALLY GOT ONE MORE APPOINTMENT TODAY.
WOULD YOU WAIT FOR ME BACK AT LORAN?
...YOU SURE ARE BUSY.
...I DON'T HAVE TIME TO MAKE UP EXCUSES...
JUST MAKE SURE YOU DON'T STIR UP MORE TROUBLE.
I WON'T.
...I THINK.

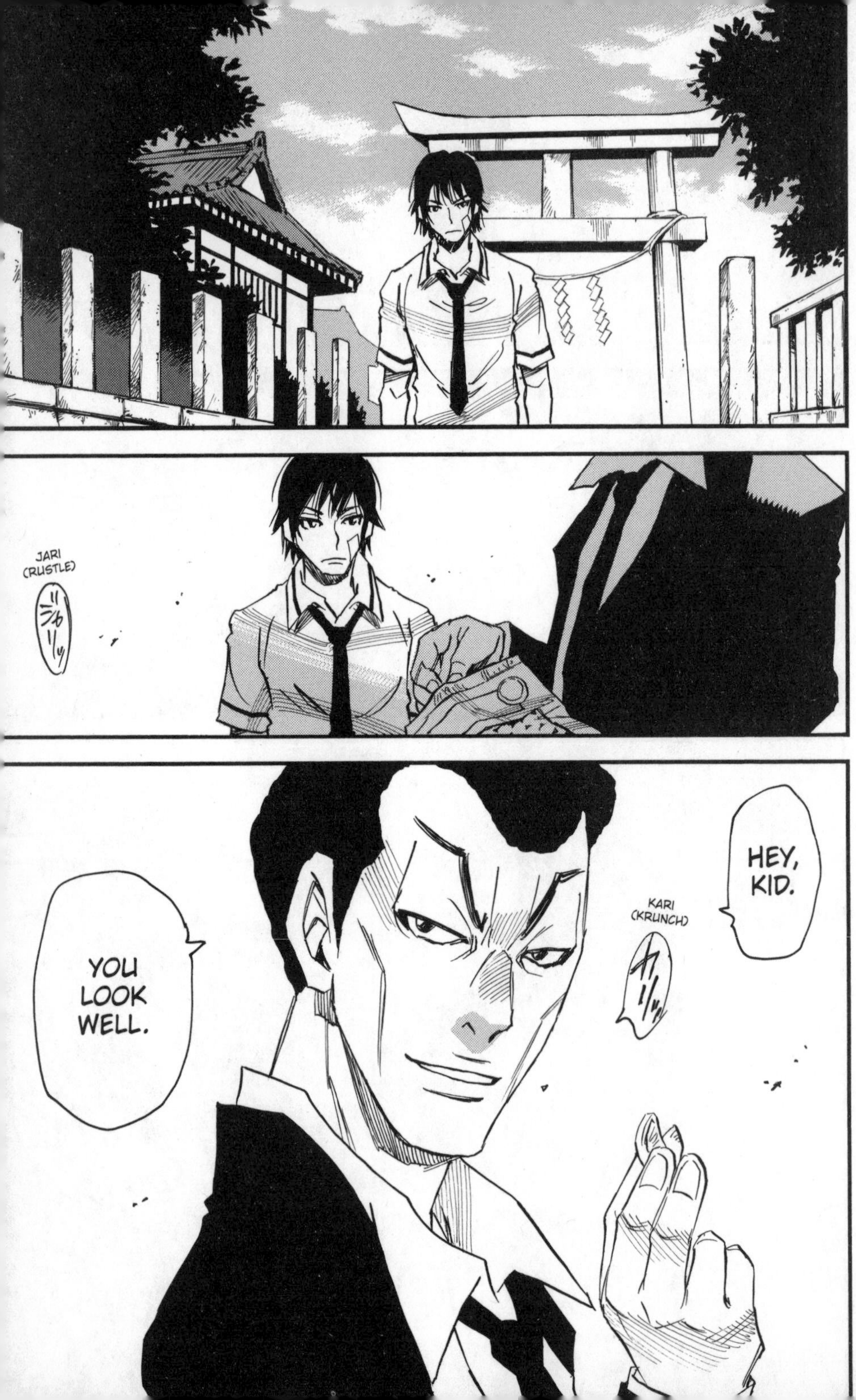
JARI (RUSTLE)
ジャリッ
HEY, KID.
KARI (KRUNCH)
カリッ
YOU LOOK WELL.

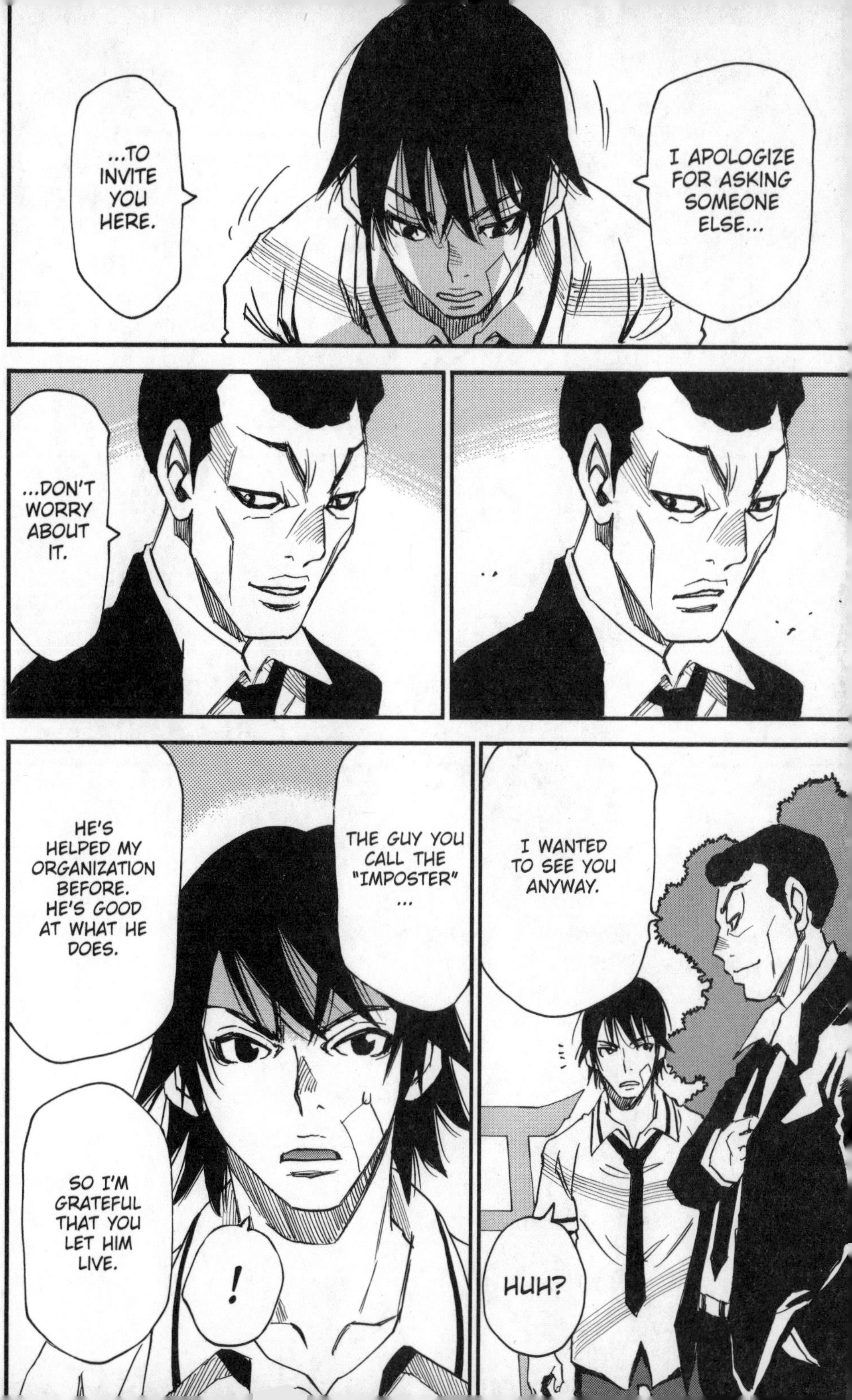

I APOLOGIZE FOR ASKING SOMEONE ELSE...
...TO INVITE YOU HERE.
...DON'T WORRY ABOUT IT.
I WANTED TO SEE YOU ANYWAY.
HUH?
THE GUY YOU CALL THE "IMPOSTER" ...
HE'S HELPED MY ORGANIZATION BEFORE. HE'S GOOD AT WHAT HE DOES.
SO I'M GRATEFUL THAT YOU LET HIM LIVE.
!

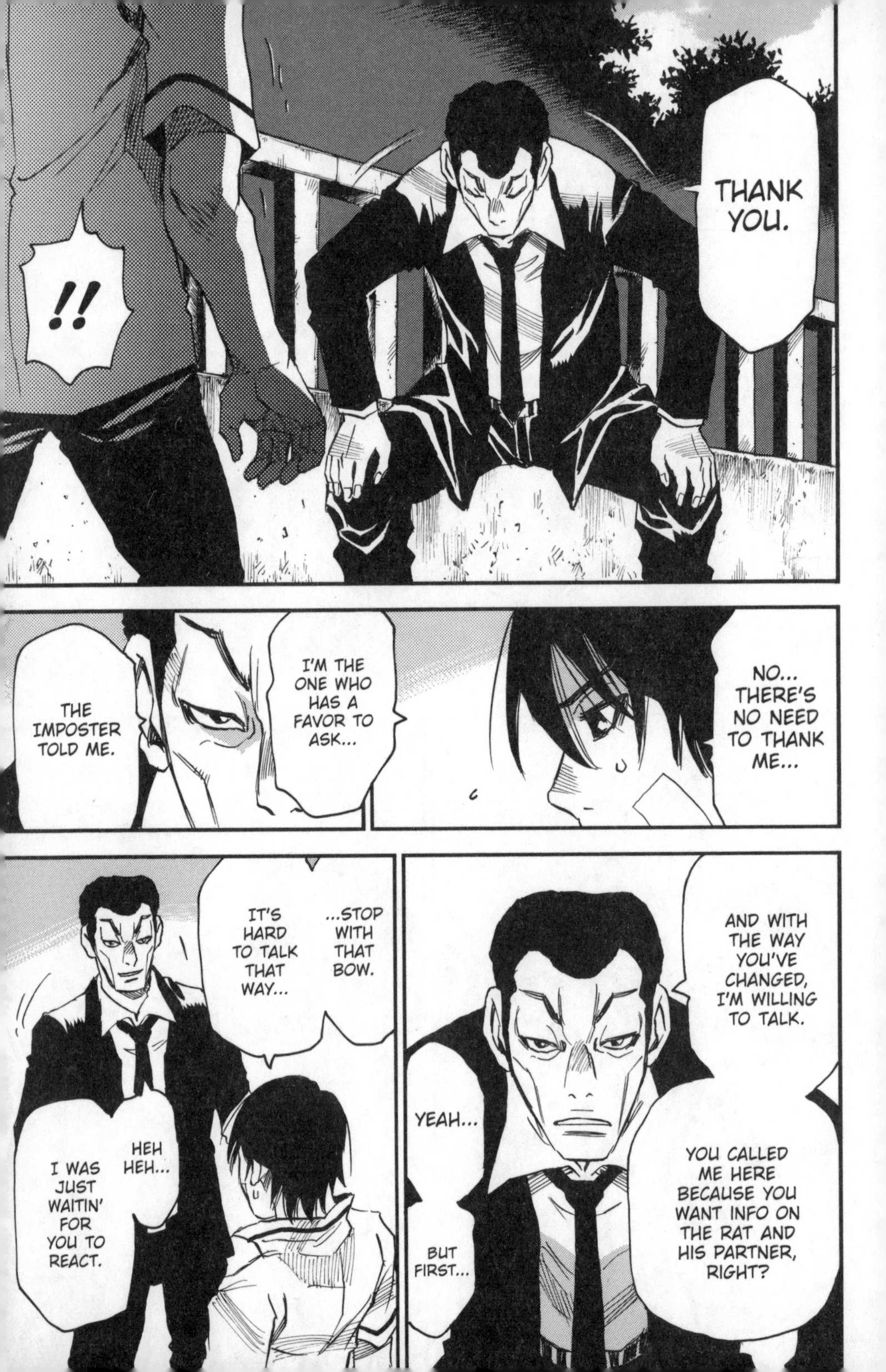
THANK YOU.
!!
NO... THERE'S NO NEED TO THANK ME...
I'M THE ONE WHO HAS A FAVOR TO ASK...
THE IMPOSTER TOLD ME.
AND WITH THE WAY YOU'VE CHANGED, I'M WILLING TO TALK.
YOU CALLED ME HERE BECAUSE YOU WANT INFO ON THE RAT AND HIS PARTNER, RIGHT?
YEAH...
BUT FIRST...
...STOP WITH THAT BOW.
IT'S HARD TO TALK THAT WAY...
HEH HEH...
I WAS JUST WAITIN' FOR YOU TO REACT.

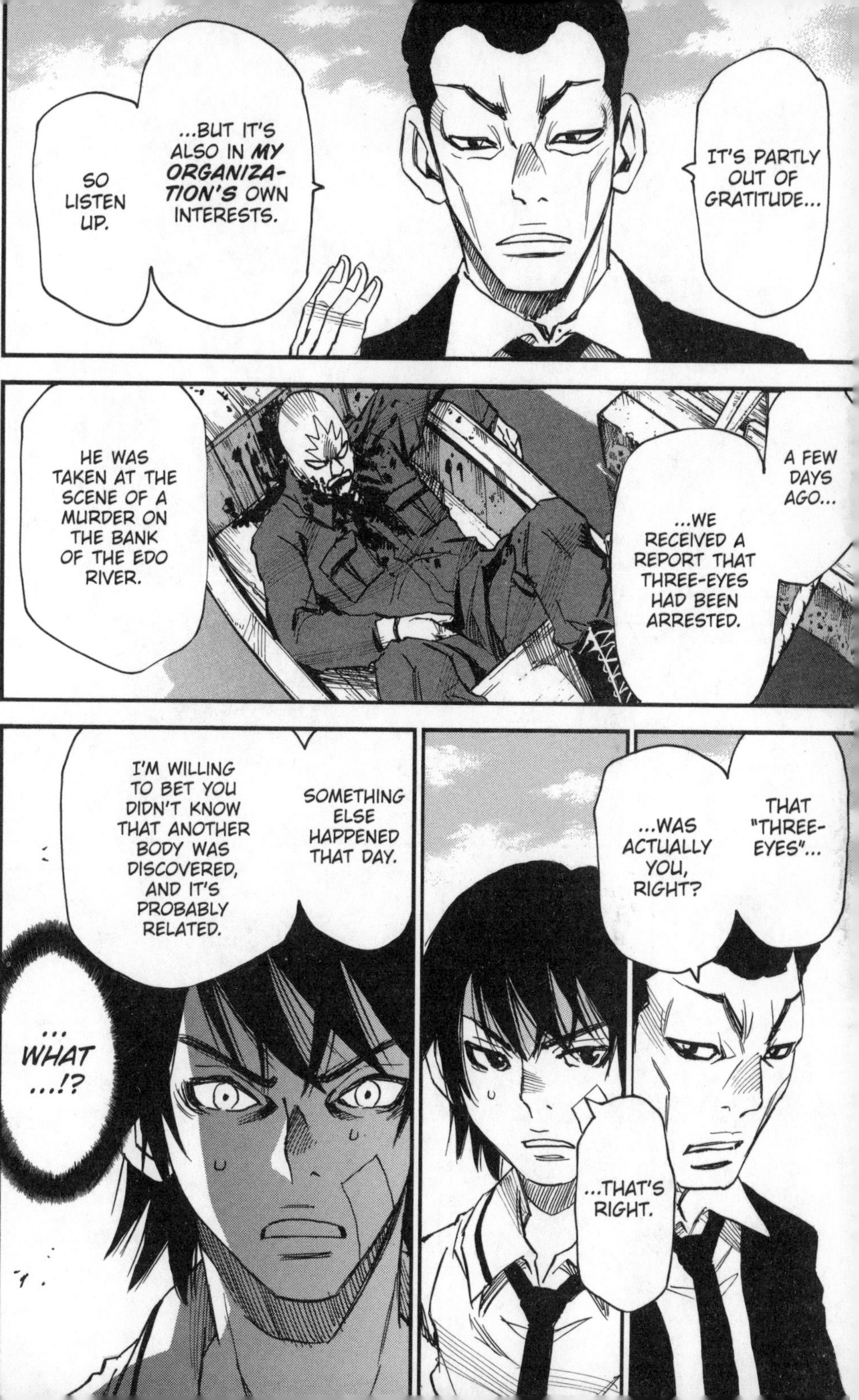
IT'S PARTLY OUT OF GRATITUDE...
...BUT IT'S ALSO IN MY ORGANIZATION'S OWN INTERESTS.
SO LISTEN UP.
A FEW DAYS AGO...
...WE RECEIVED A REPORT THAT THREE-EYES HAD BEEN ARRESTED.
HE WAS TAKEN AT THE SCENE OF A MURDER ON THE BANK OF THE EDO RIVER.
THAT "THREE-EYES"...
...WAS ACTUALLY YOU, RIGHT?
...THAT'S RIGHT.
SOMETHING ELSE HAPPENED THAT DAY.
I'M WILLING TO BET YOU DIDN'T KNOW THAT ANOTHER BODY WAS DISCOVERED, AND IT'S PROBABLY RELATED.
...WHAT...!?

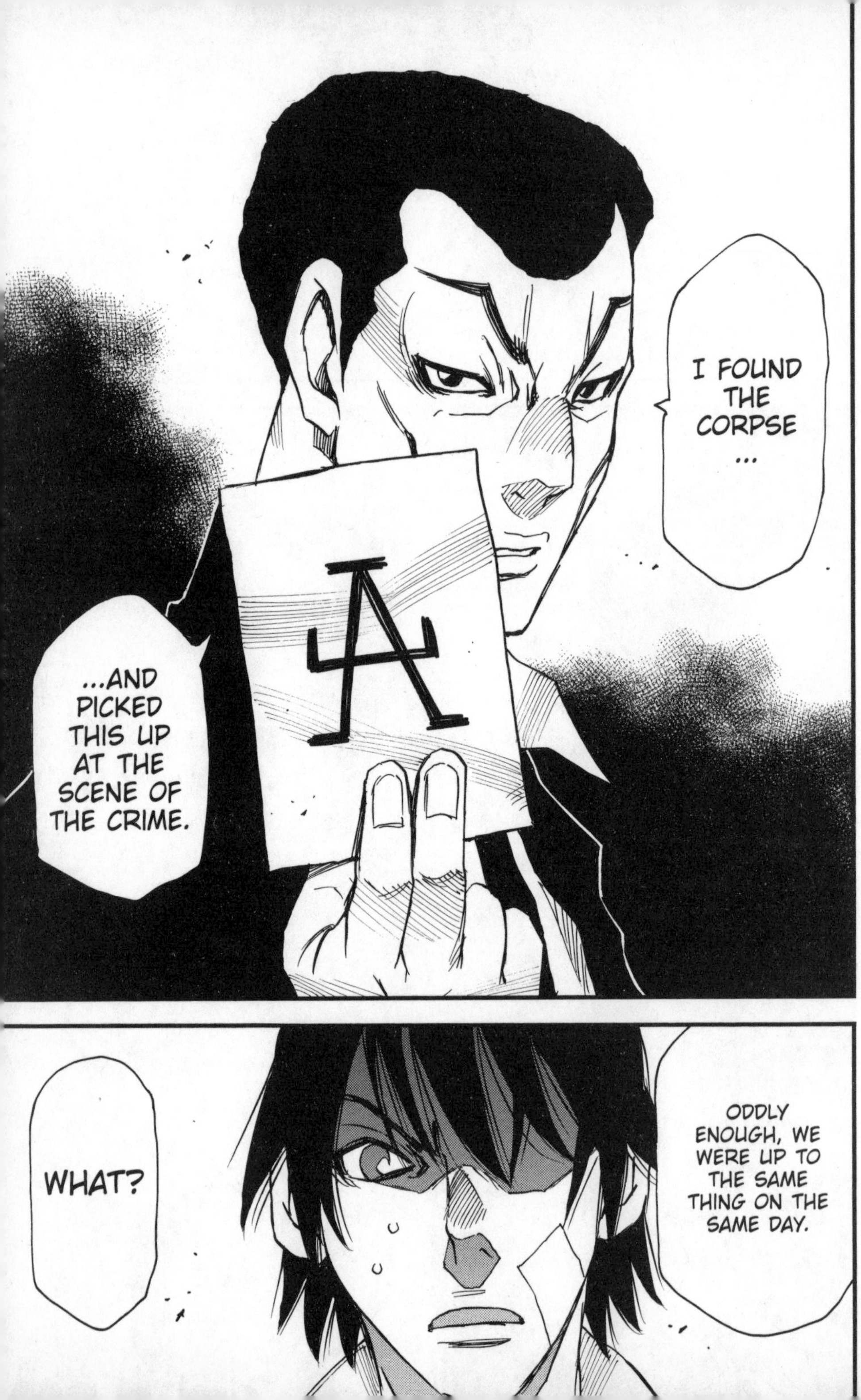
I FOUND THE CORPSE ...
...AND PICKED THIS UP AT THE SCENE OF THE CRIME.
ODDLY ENOUGH, WE WERE UP TO THE SAME THING ON THE SAME DAY.
WHAT?

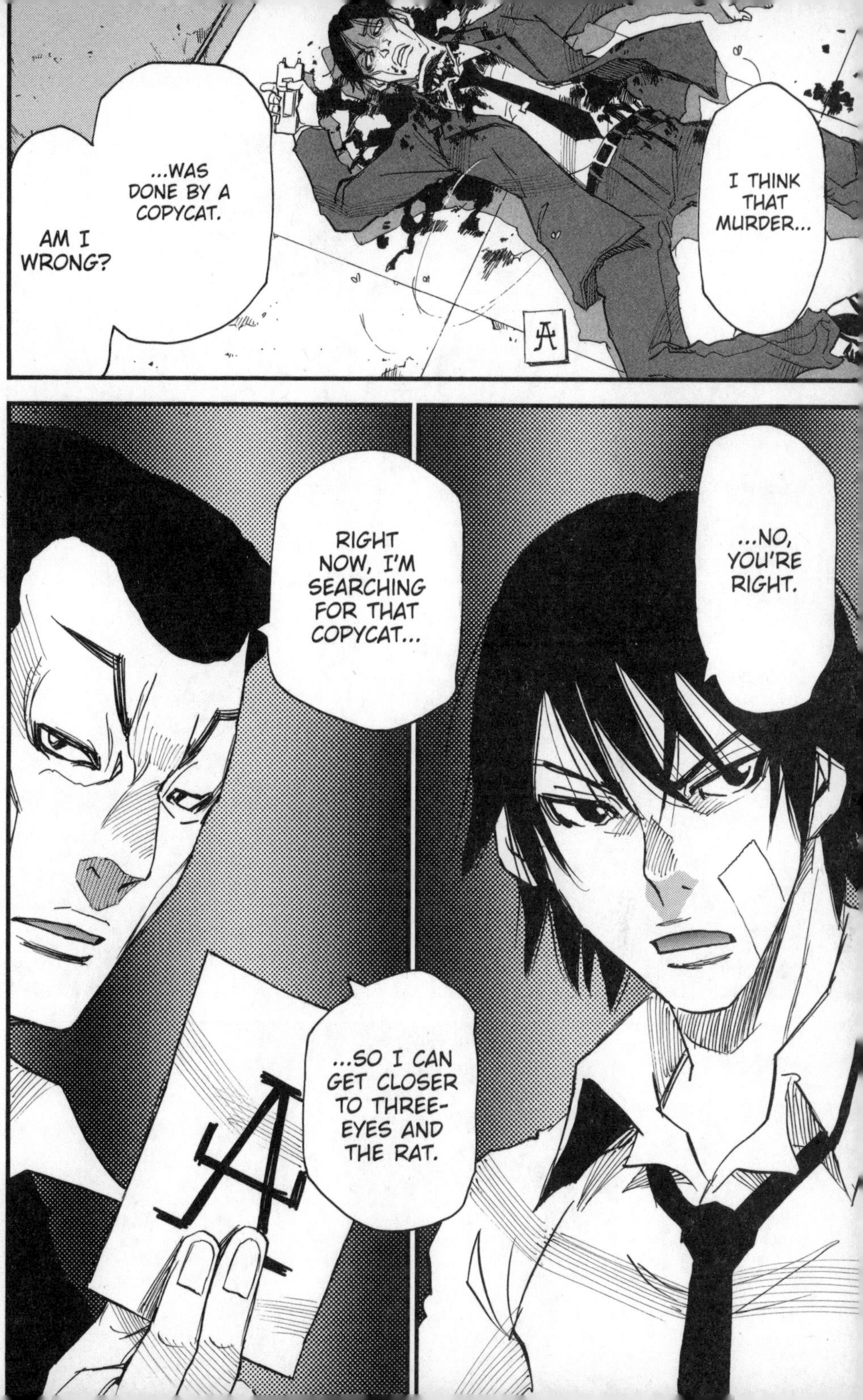
I THINK THAT MURDER...
...WAS DONE BY A COPYCAT.
AM I WRONG?
...NO, YOU'RE RIGHT.
RIGHT NOW, I'M SEARCHING FOR THAT COPYCAT...
...SO I CAN GET CLOSER TO THREE-EYES AND THE RAT.

#34 END

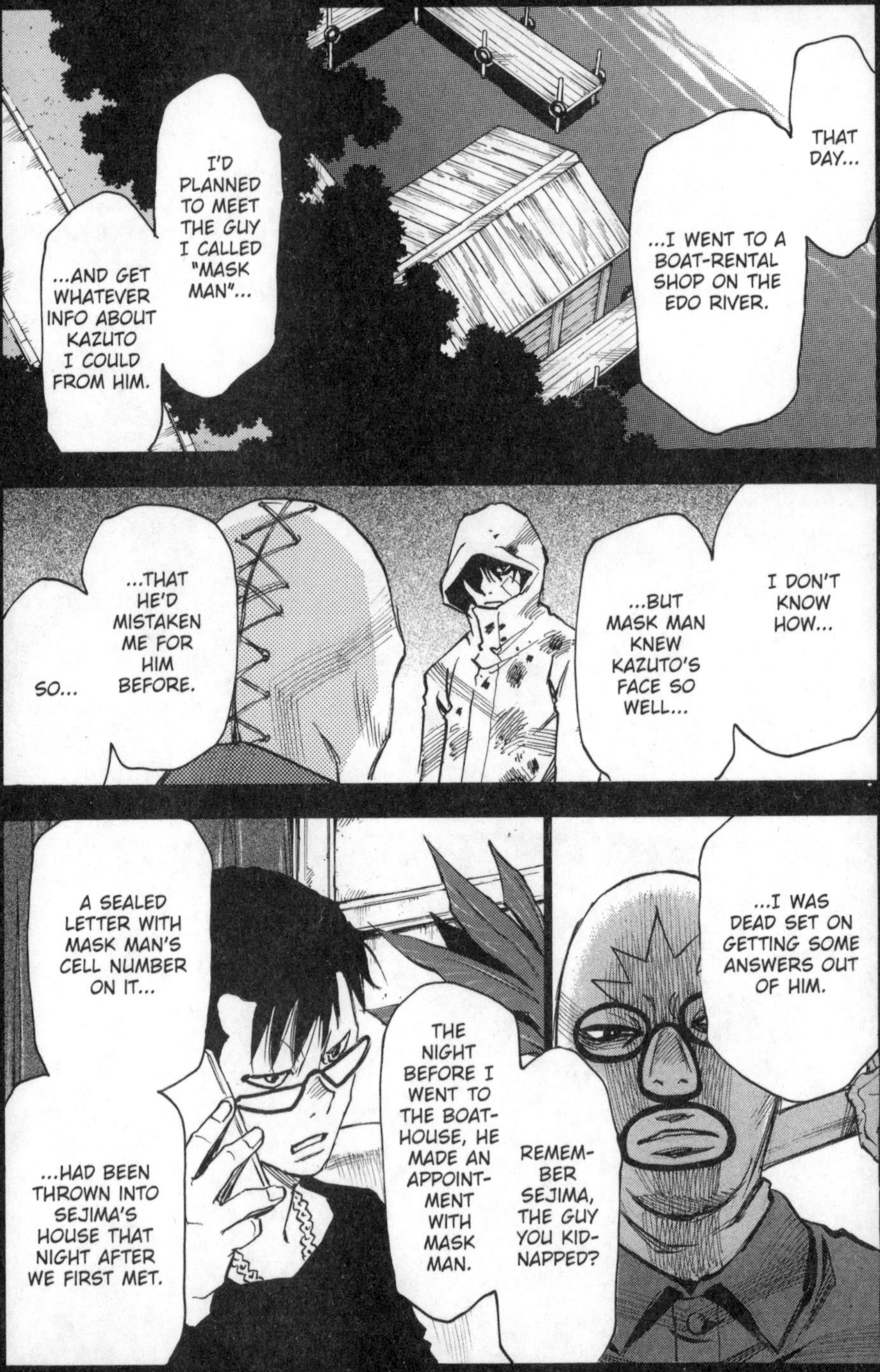
THAT DAY...
...I WENT TO A BOAT-RENTAL SHOP ON THE EDO RIVER.
I'D PLANNED TO MEET THE GUY I CALLED "MASK MAN"...
...AND GET WHATEVER INFO ABOUT KAZUTO I COULD FROM HIM.
I DON'T KNOW HOW...
...BUT MASK MAN KNEW KAZUTO'S FACE SO WELL...
...THAT HE'D MISTAKEN ME FOR HIM BEFORE.
SO...
...I WAS DEAD SET ON GETTING SOME ANSWERS OUT OF HIM.
REMEMBER SEJIMA, THE GUY YOU KIDNAPPED?
THE NIGHT BEFORE I WENT TO THE BOATHOUSE, HE MADE AN APPOINTMENT WITH MASK MAN.
A SEALED LETTER WITH MASK MAN'S CELL NUMBER ON IT...
...HAD BEEN THROWN INTO SEJIMA'S HOUSE THAT NIGHT AFTER WE FIRST MET.

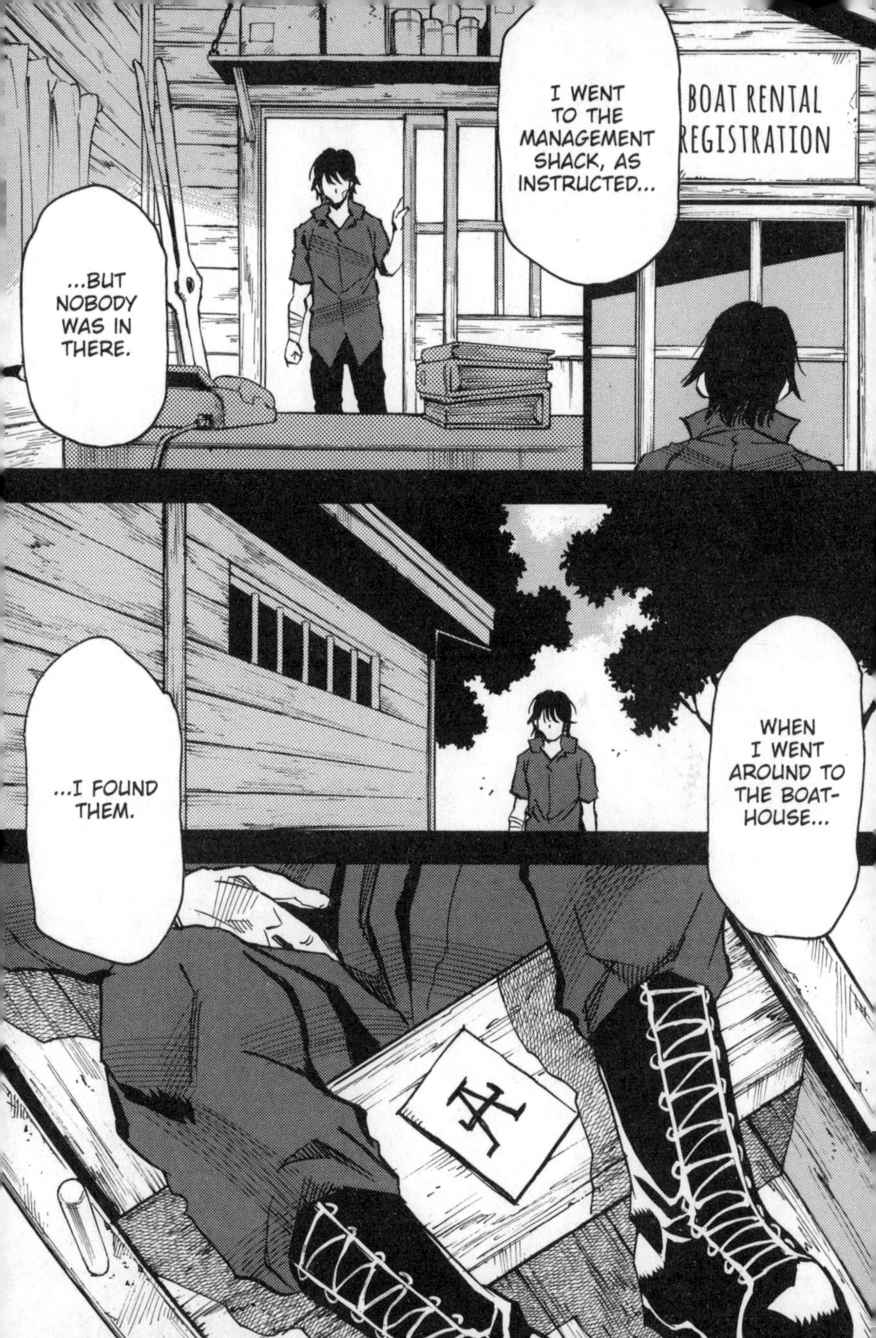
BOAT RENTAL REGISTRATION
I WENT TO THE MANAGEMENT SHACK, AS INSTRUCTED...
...BUT NOBODY WAS IN THERE.
WHEN I WENT AROUND TO THE BOAT-HOUSE...
...I FOUND THEM.

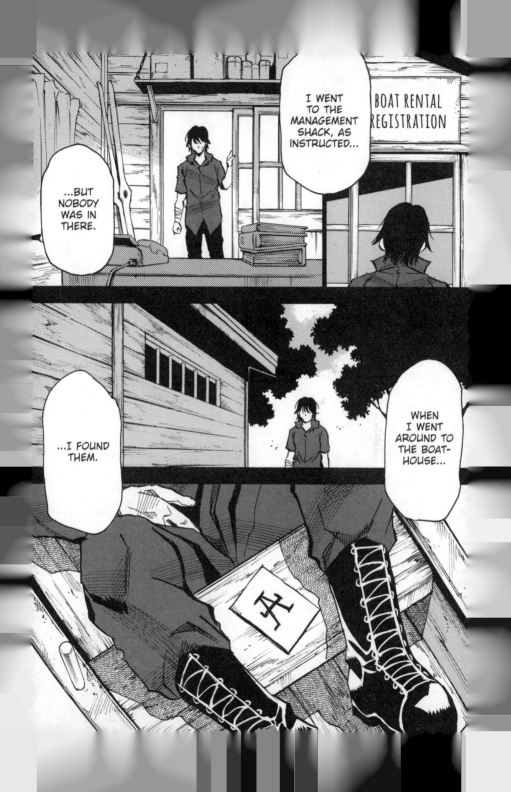

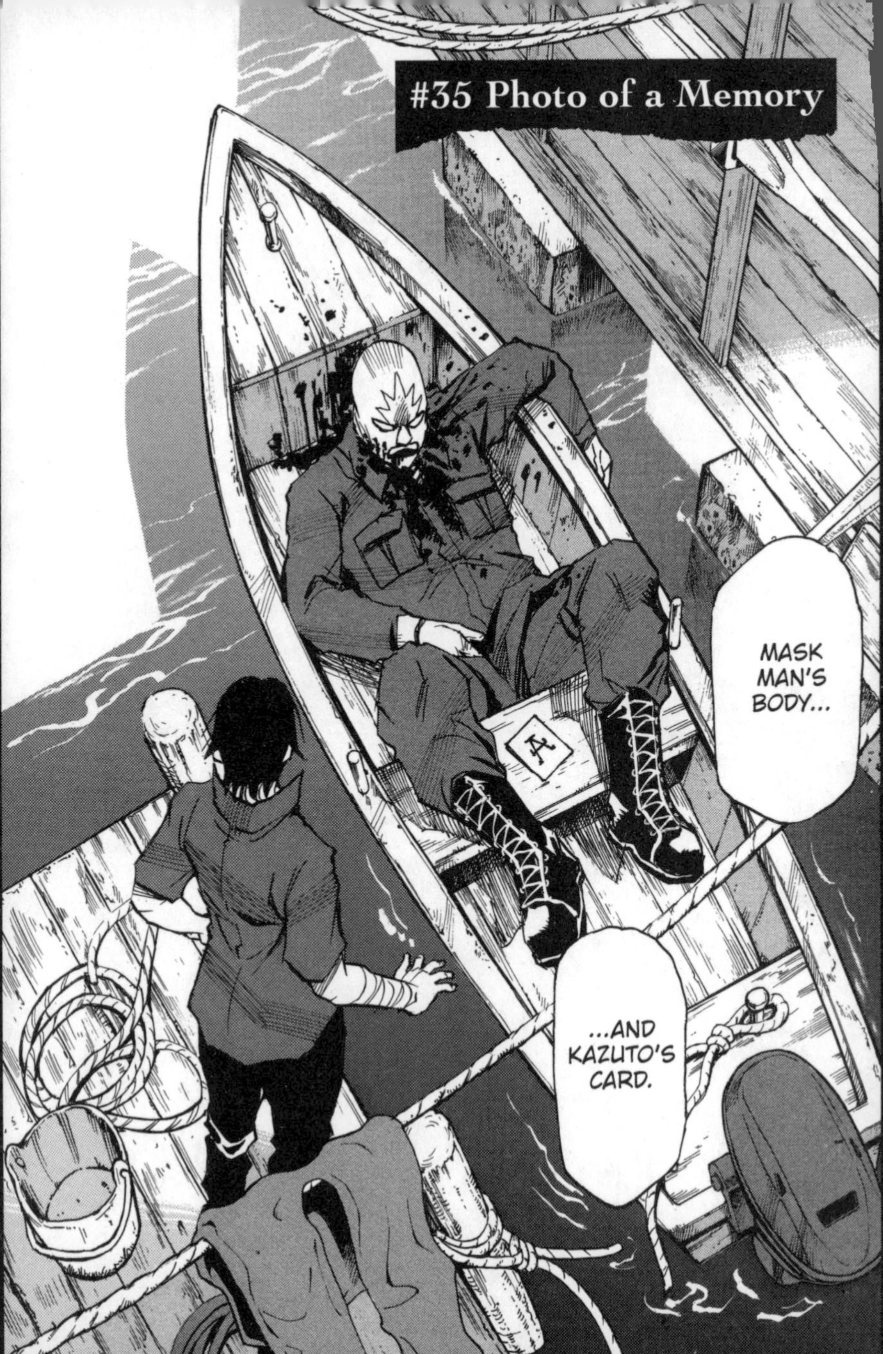
#35 Photo of a Memory
MASK MAN'S BODY...
...AND KAZUTO'S CARD.

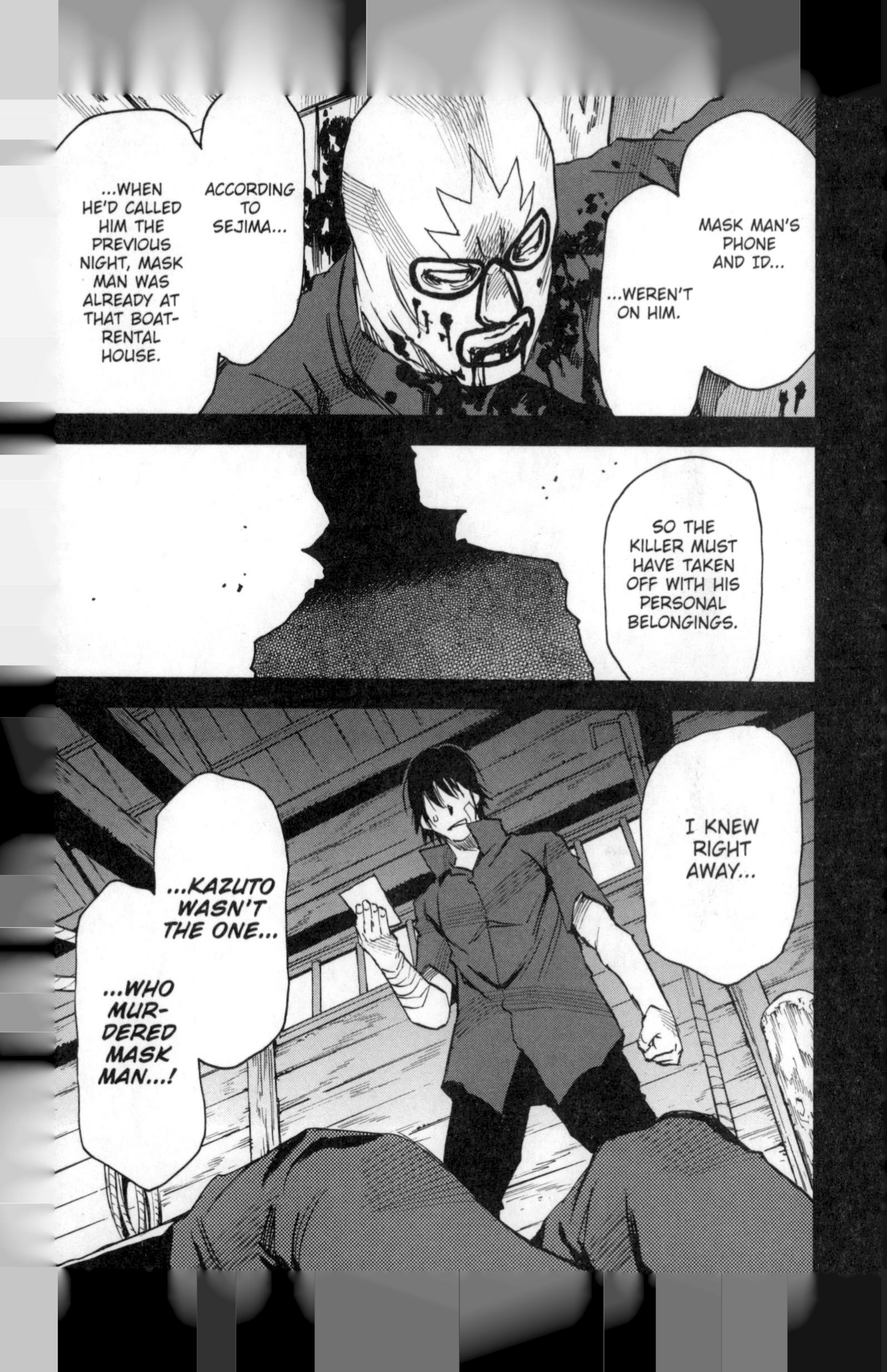
MASK MAN'S PHONE AND ID...
...WEREN'T ON HIM.
ACCORDING TO SEJIMA...
...WHEN HE'D CALLED HIM THE PREVIOUS NIGHT, MASK MAN WAS ALREADY AT THAT BOAT-RENTAL HOUSE.
SO THE KILLER MUST HAVE TAKEN OFF WITH HIS PERSONAL BELONGINGS.
I KNEW RIGHT AWAY...
...KAZUTO WASN'T THE ONE...
...WHO MURDERED MASK MAN...!

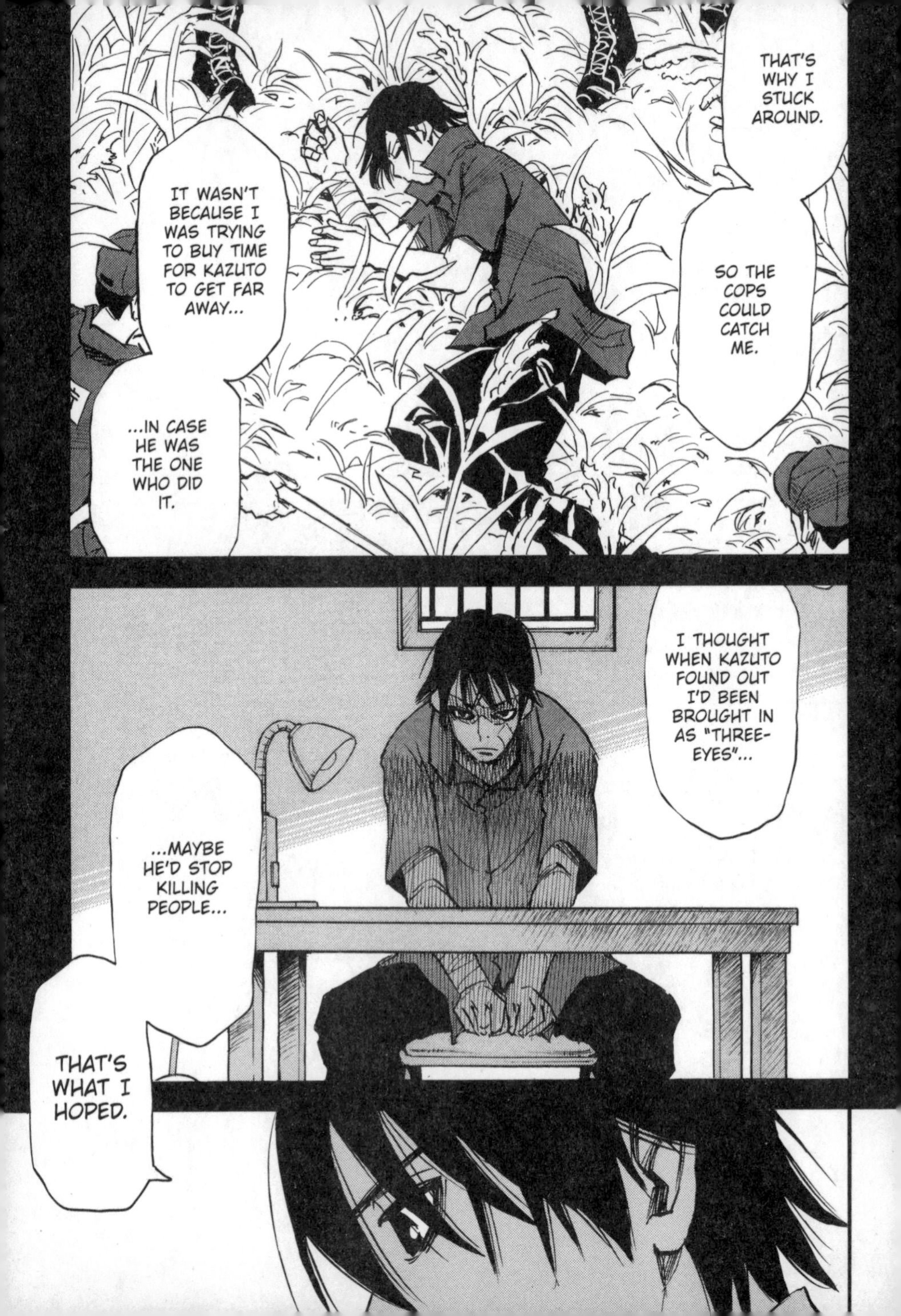
THAT'S WHY I STUCK AROUND.
SO THE COPS COULD CATCH ME.
IT WASN'T BECAUSE I WAS TRYING TO BUY TIME FOR KAZUTO TO GET FAR AWAY...
...IN CASE HE WAS THE ONE WHO DID IT.
I THOUGHT WHEN KAZUTO FOUND OUT I'D BEEN BROUGHT IN AS "THREE-EYES"...
...MAYBE HE'D STOP KILLING PEOPLE...
THAT'S WHAT I HOPED.

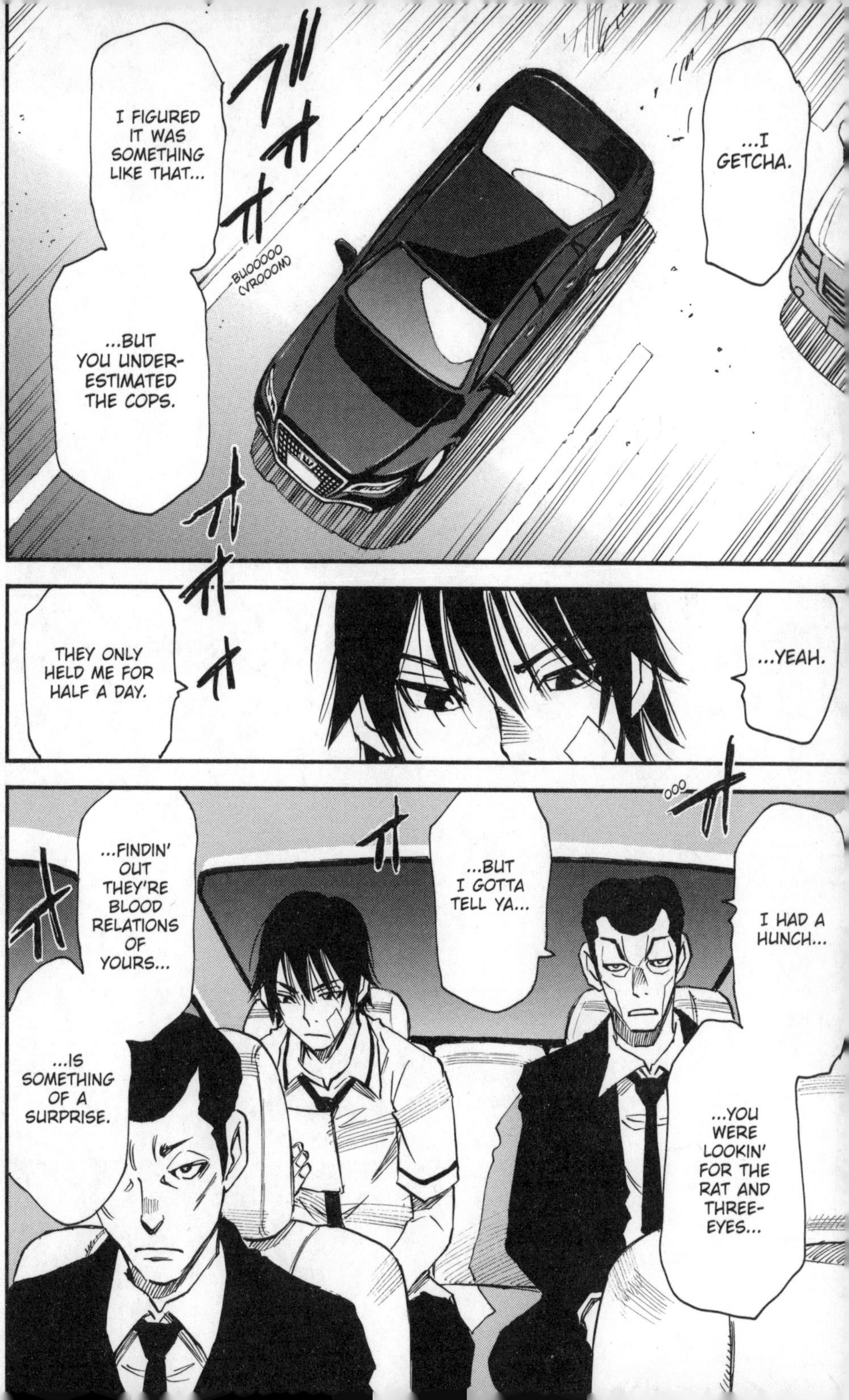
...I GETCHA.
I FIGURED IT WAS SOMETHING LIKE THAT...
BUOOOOO (VROOOM)
...BUT YOU UNDER-ESTIMATED THE COPS.
...YEAH.
THEY ONLY HELD ME FOR HALF A DAY.
OOO
I HAD A HUNCH...
...YOU WERE LOOKIN' FOR THE RAT AND THREE-EYES...
...BUT I GOTTA TELL YA...
...FINDIN' OUT THEY'RE BLOOD RELATIONS OF YOURS...
...IS SOMETHING OF A SURPRISE.

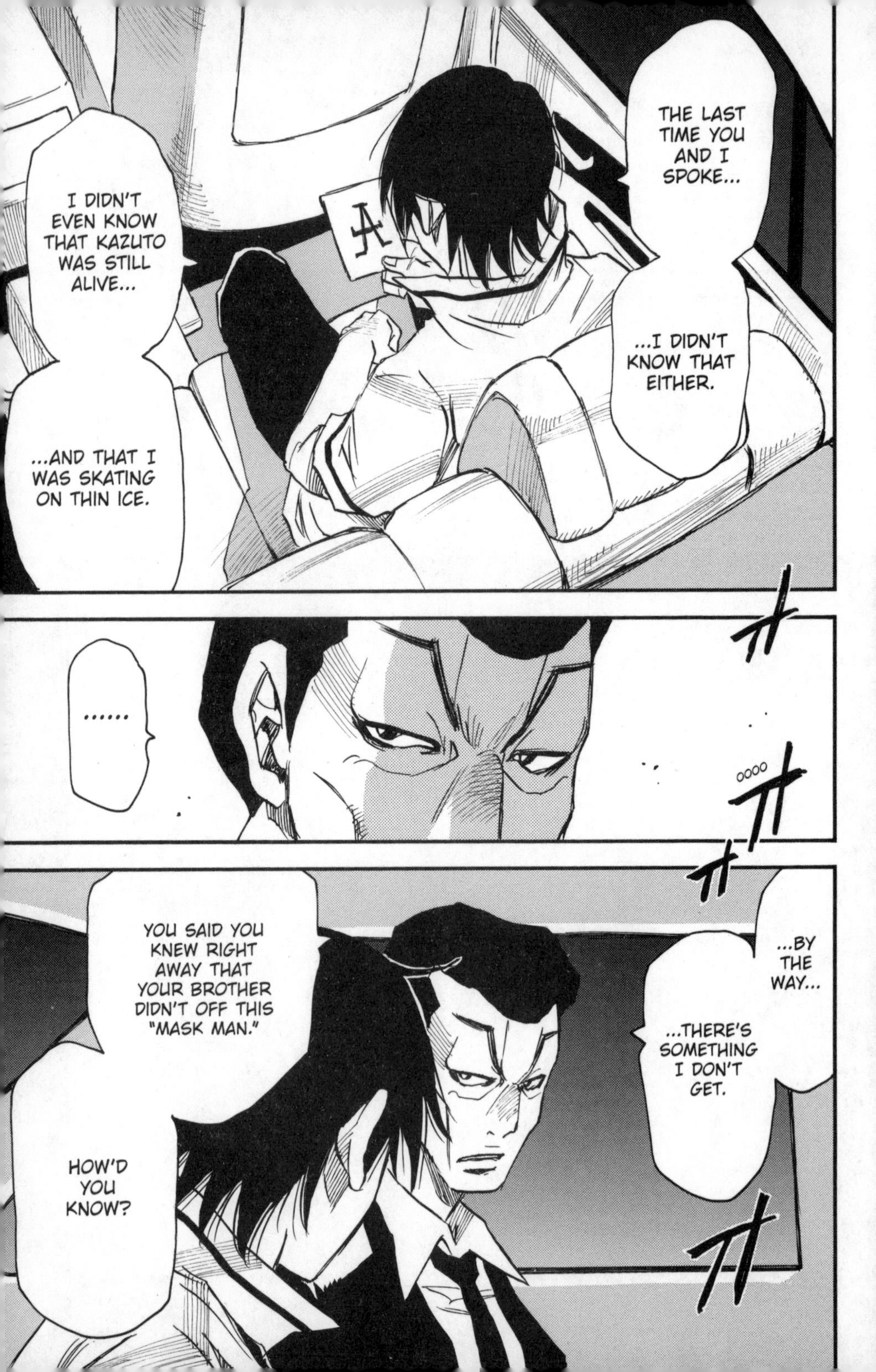
THE LAST TIME YOU AND I SPOKE...
...I DIDN'T KNOW THAT EITHER.
I DIDN'T EVEN KNOW THAT KAZUTO WAS STILL ALIVE...
...AND THAT I WAS SKATING ON THIN ICE.
oooo
......
...BY THE WAY...
...THERE'S SOMETHING I DON'T GET.
YOU SAID YOU KNEW RIGHT AWAY THAT YOUR BROTHER DIDN'T OFF THIS "MASK MAN."
HOW'D YOU KNOW?

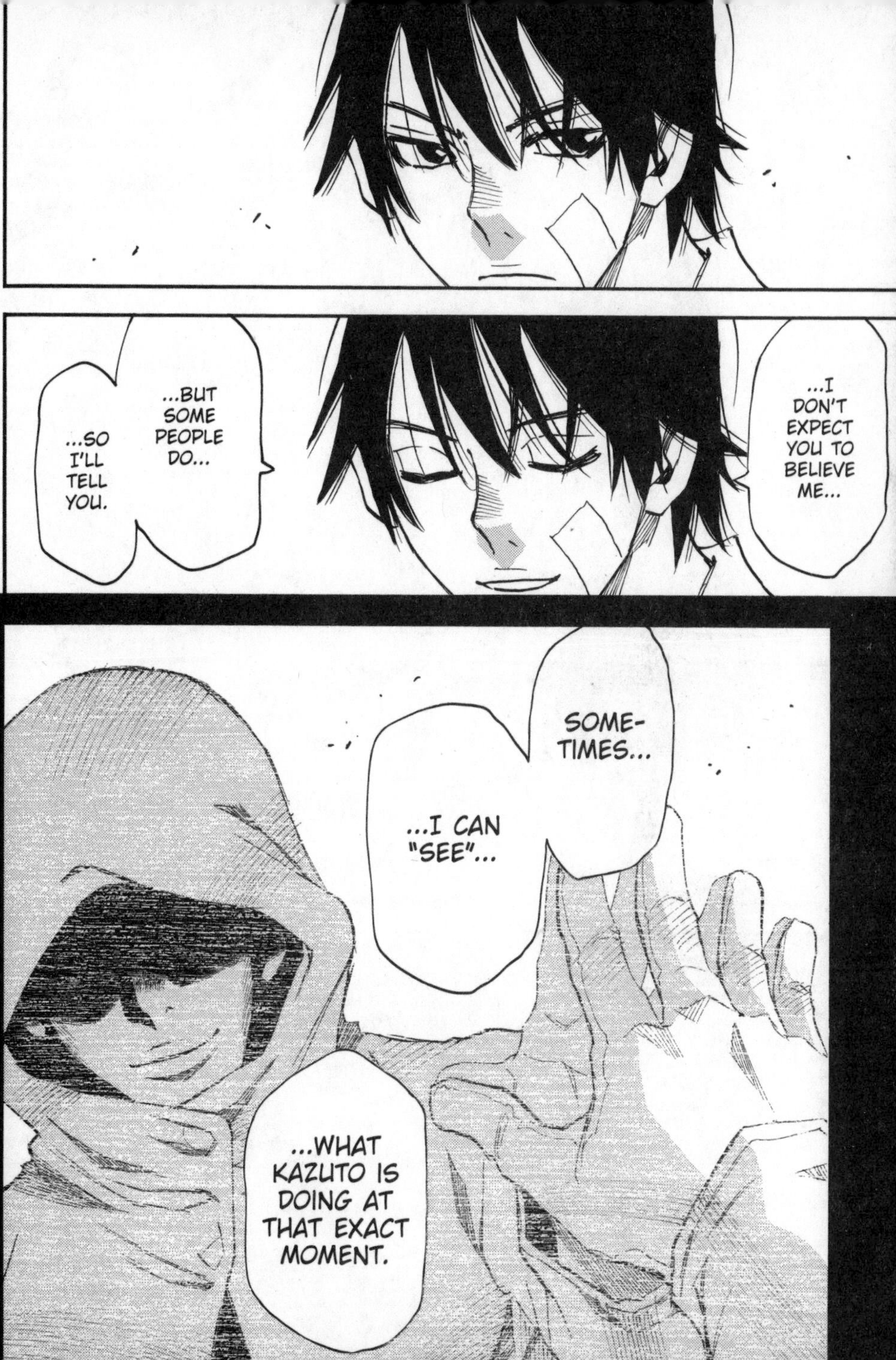
...I DON'T EXPECT YOU TO BELIEVE ME...
...BUT SOME PEOPLE DO...
...SO I'LL TELL YOU.
SOME-TIMES...
...I CAN "SEE"...
...WHAT KAZUTO IS DOING AT THAT EXACT MOMENT.

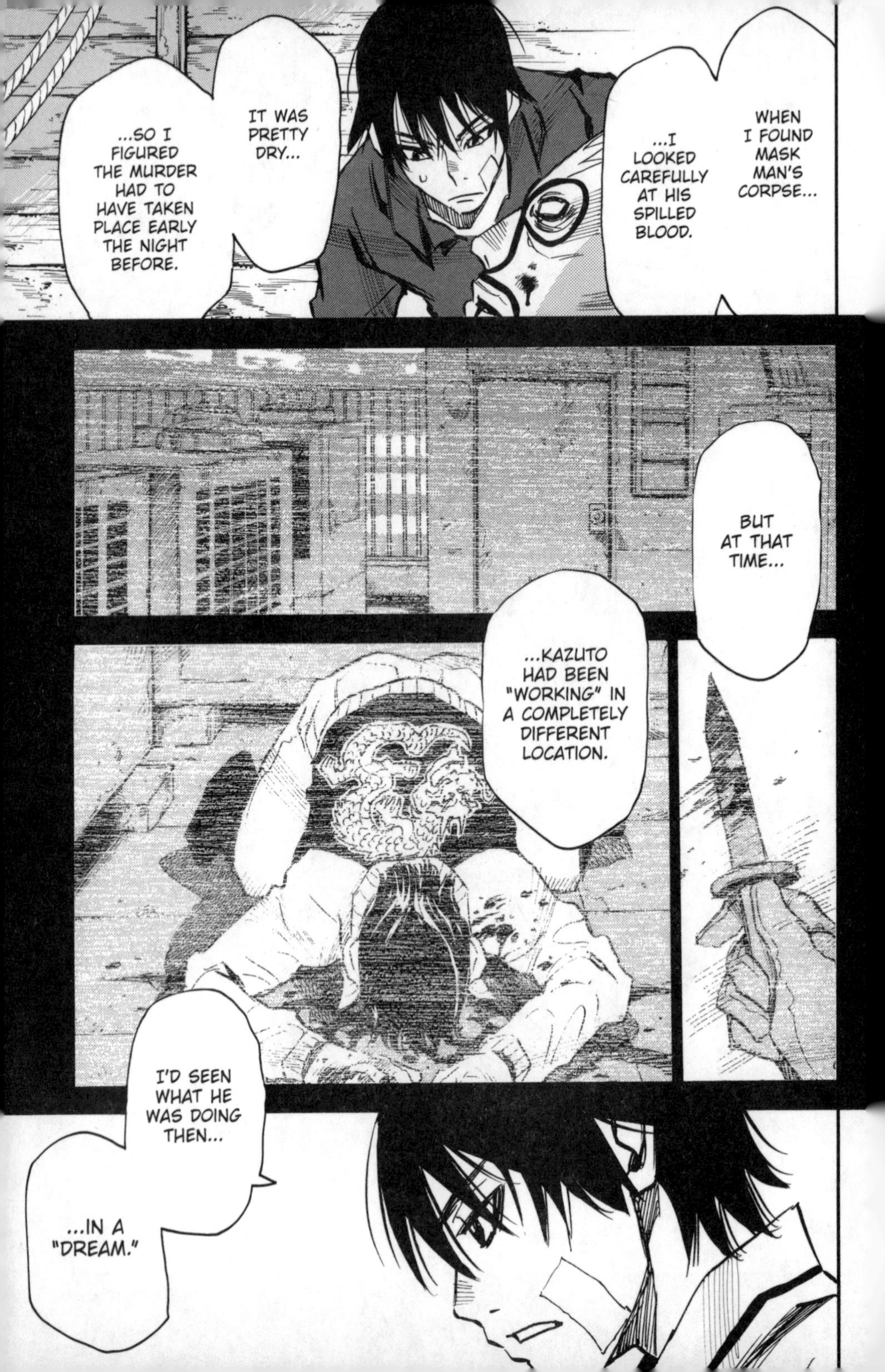
WHEN I FOUND MASK MAN'S CORPSE...
...I LOOKED CAREFULLY AT HIS SPILLED BLOOD.
IT WAS PRETTY DRY...
...SO I FIGURED THE MURDER HAD TO HAVE TAKEN PLACE EARLY THE NIGHT BEFORE.
BUT AT THAT TIME...
...KAZUTO HAD BEEN "WORKING" IN A COMPLETELY DIFFERENT LOCATION.
I'D SEEN WHAT HE WAS DOING THEN...
...IN A "DREAM."

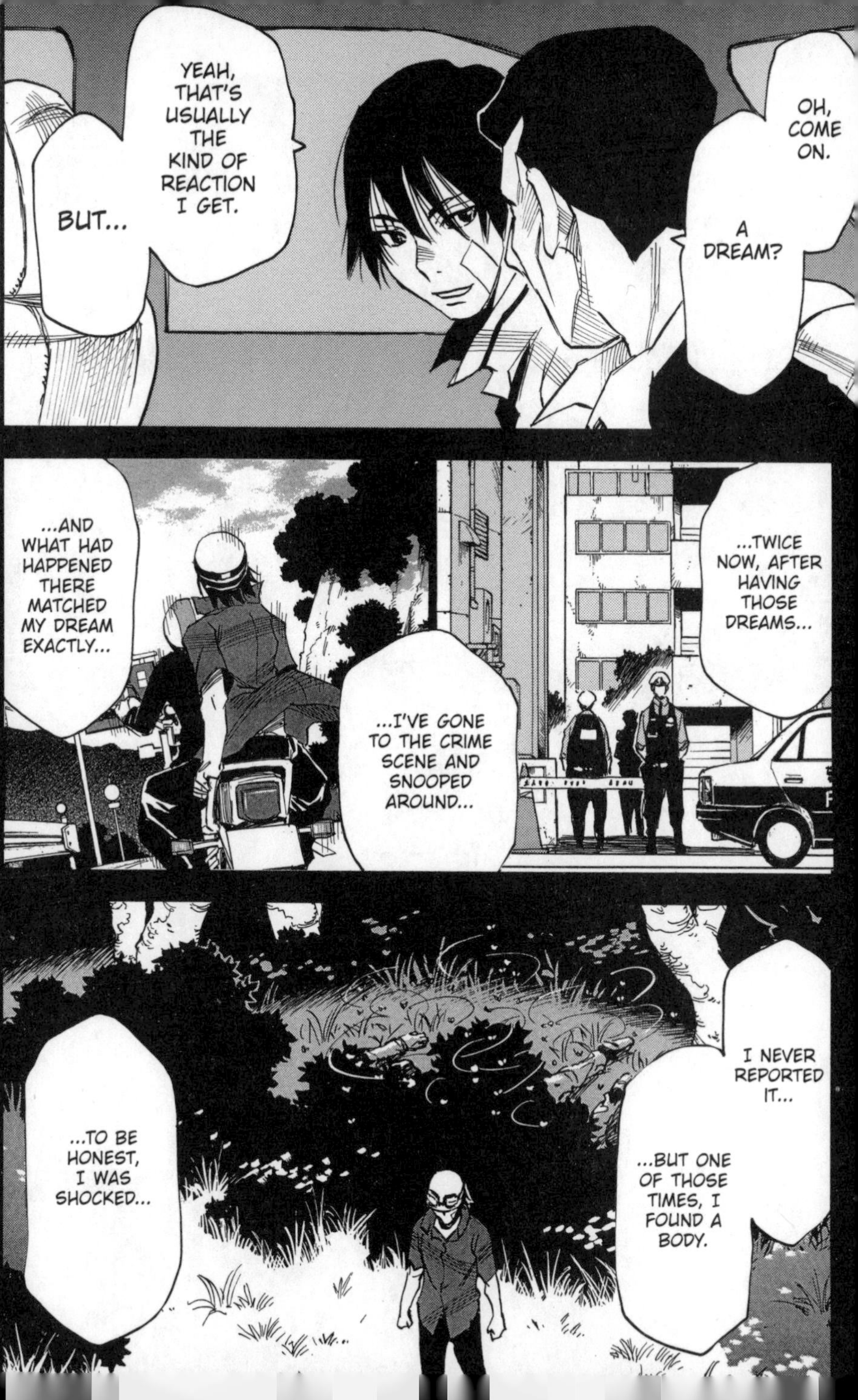
OH, COME ON.
A DREAM?
YEAH, THAT'S USUALLY THE KIND OF REACTION I GET.
BUT...
...TWICE NOW, AFTER HAVING THOSE DREAMS...
...I'VE GONE TO THE CRIME SCENE AND SNOOPED AROUND...
...AND WHAT HAD HAPPENED THERE MATCHED MY DREAM EXACTLY...
I NEVER REPORTED IT...
...BUT ONE OF THOSE TIMES, I FOUND A BODY.
...TO BE HONEST, I WAS SHOCKED...

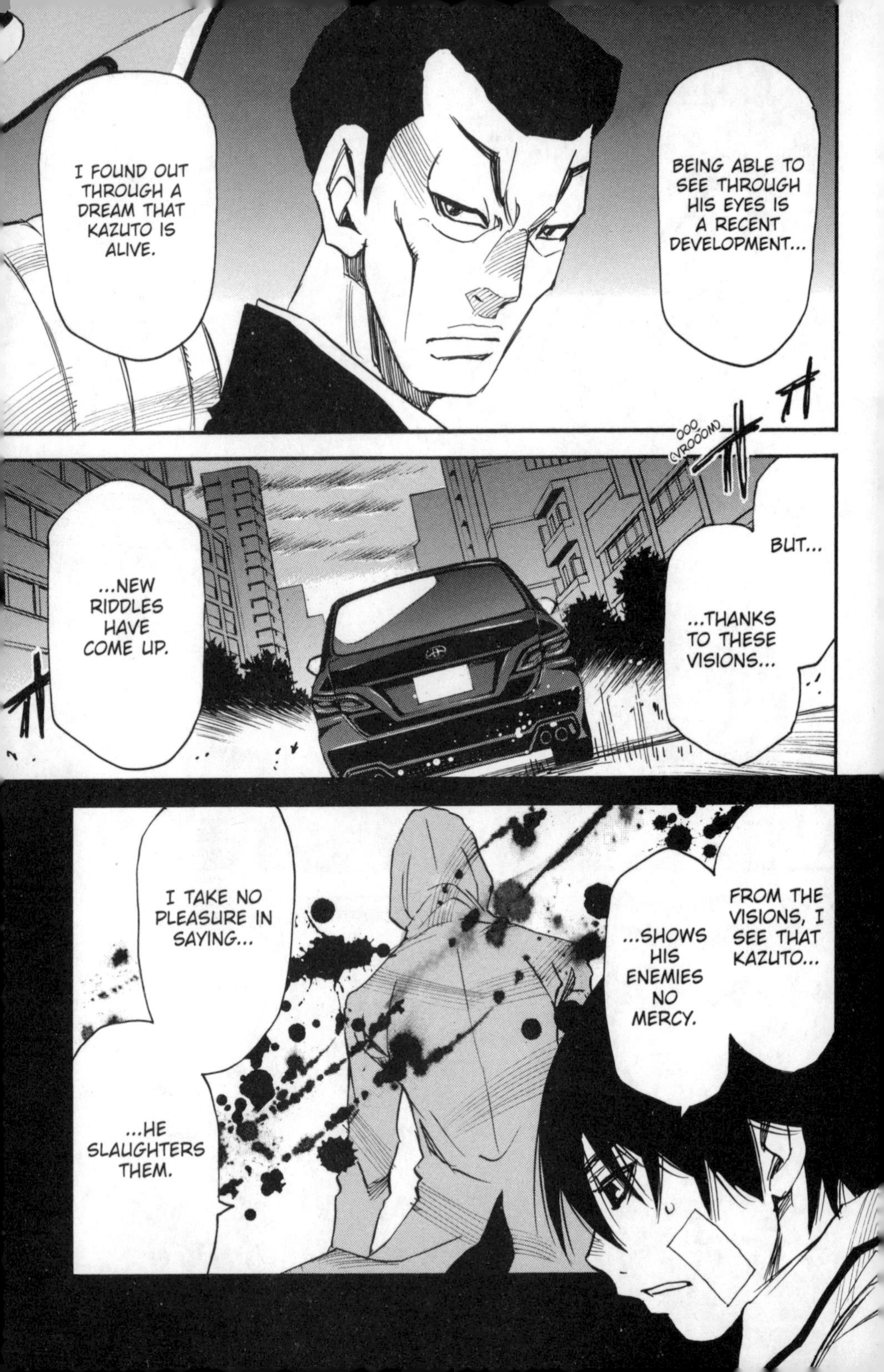
BEING ABLE TO SEE THROUGH HIS EYES IS A RECENT DEVELOPMENT...
I FOUND OUT THROUGH A DREAM THAT KAZUTO IS ALIVE.
OOO (VROOOM)
BUT...
...THANKS TO THESE VISIONS...
...NEW RIDDLES HAVE COME UP.
FROM THE VISIONS, I SEE THAT KAZUTO...
...SHOWS HIS ENEMIES NO MERCY.
I TAKE NO PLEASURE IN SAYING...
...HE SLAUGHTERS THEM.

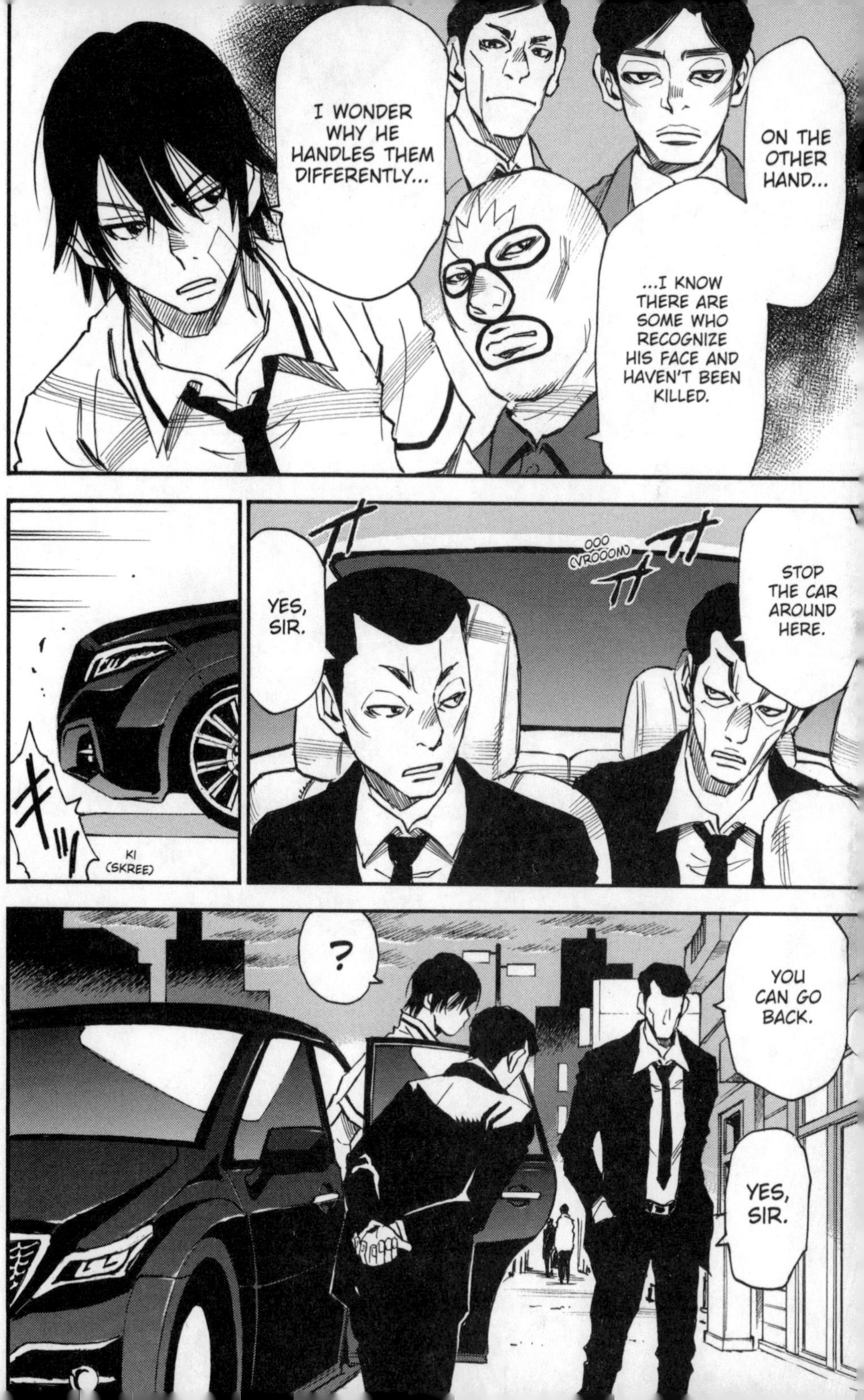
ON THE OTHER HAND...
...I KNOW THERE ARE SOME WHO RECOGNIZE HIS FACE AND HAVEN'T BEEN KILLED.
I WONDER WHY HE HANDLES THEM DIFFERENTLY...
STOP THE CAR AROUND HERE.
OOO (VROOOM)
YES, SIR.
KI (SKREE)
YOU CAN GO BACK.
?
YES, SIR.

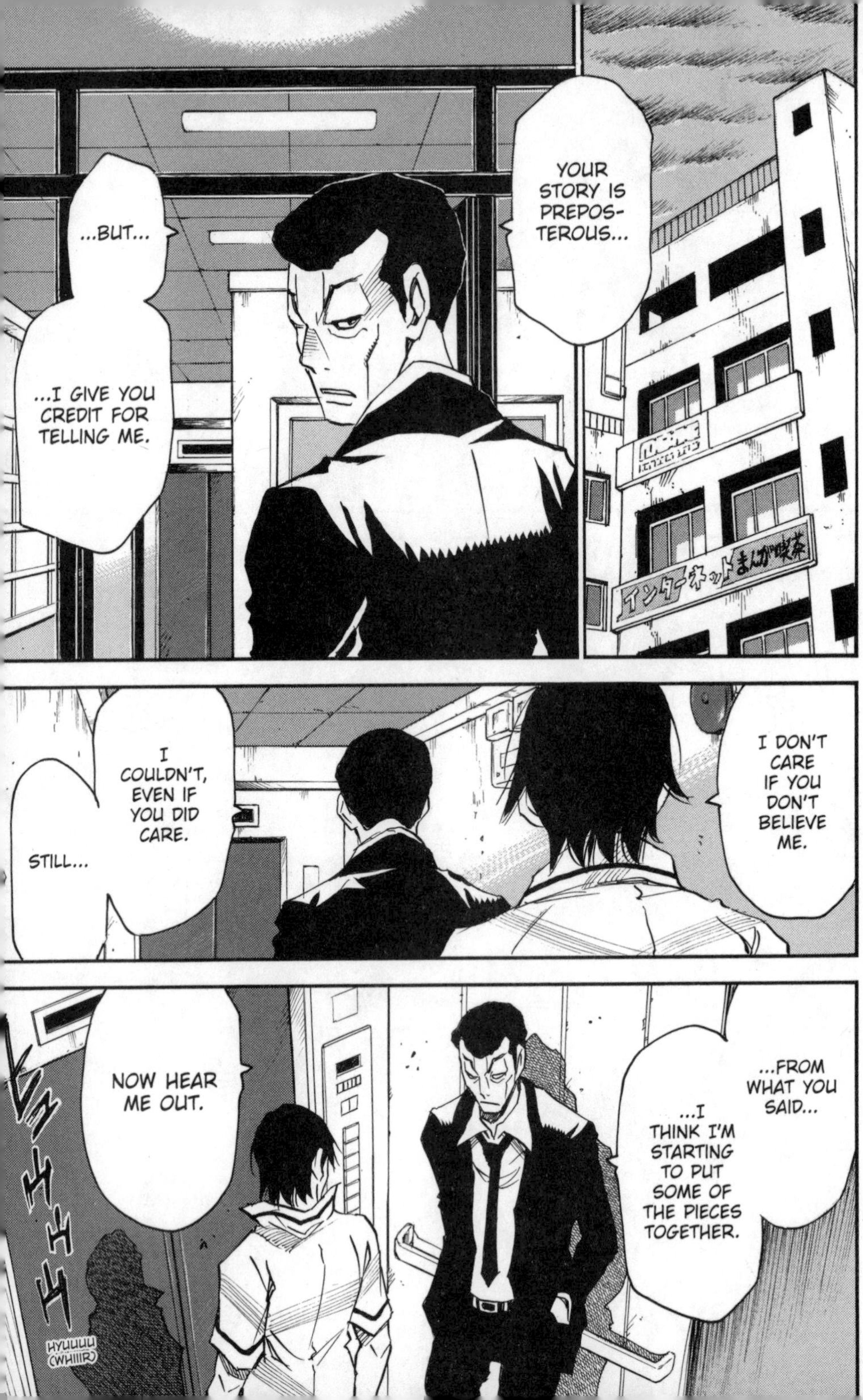
YOUR STORY IS PREPOS-TEROUS...
インターネットまんが喫茶
...BUT...
...I GIVE YOU CREDIT FOR TELLING ME.
I DON'T CARE IF YOU DON'T BELIEVE ME.
I COULDN'T, EVEN IF YOU DID CARE.
STILL...
...FROM WHAT YOU SAID...
...I THINK I'M STARTING TO PUT SOME OF THE PIECES TOGETHER.
NOW HEAR ME OUT.
HYUUUU (WHIIIR)

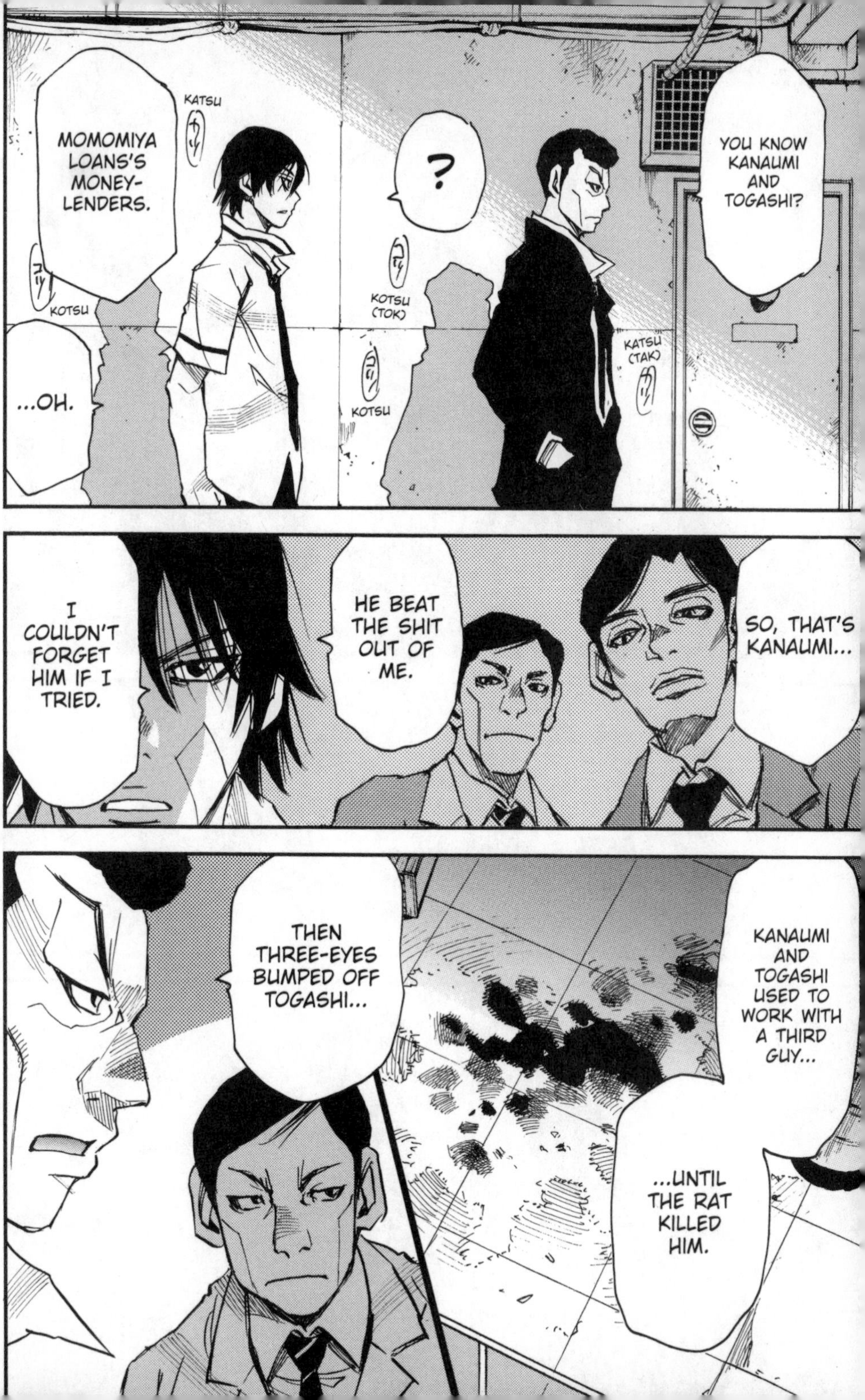
YOU KNOW KANAUMI AND TOGASHI?
KATSU (TAK)
?
KOTSU (TOK)
KOTSU
KATSU
MOMOMIYA LOANS'S MONEY-LENDERS.
KOTSU
...OH.
SO, THAT'S KANAUMI...
HE BEAT THE SHIT OUT OF ME.
I COULDN'T FORGET HIM IF I TRIED.
KANAUMI AND TOGASHI USED TO WORK WITH A THIRD GUY...
...UNTIL THE RAT KILLED HIM.
THEN THREE-EYES BUMPED OFF TOGASHI...

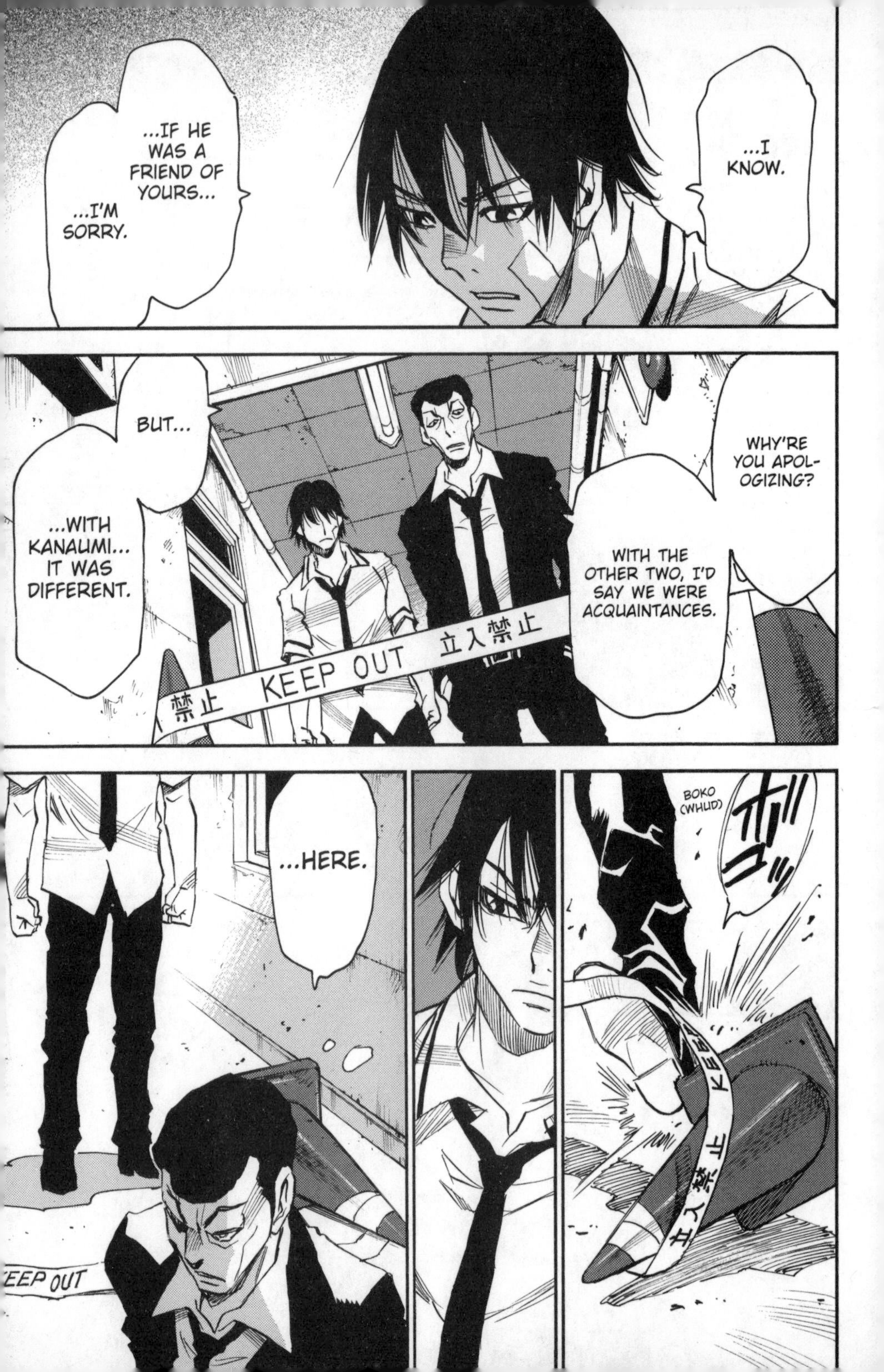
...I KNOW.
...IF HE WAS A FRIEND OF YOURS...
...I'M SORRY.
WHY'RE YOU APOLOGIZING?
WITH THE OTHER TWO, I'D SAY WE WERE ACQUAINTANCES.
BUT...
...WITH KANAUMI... IT WAS DIFFERENT.
禁止 KEEP OUT 立入禁止
BOKO (WHUD)
ボゴッ
KEEP
立入禁止
...HERE.
EEP OUT

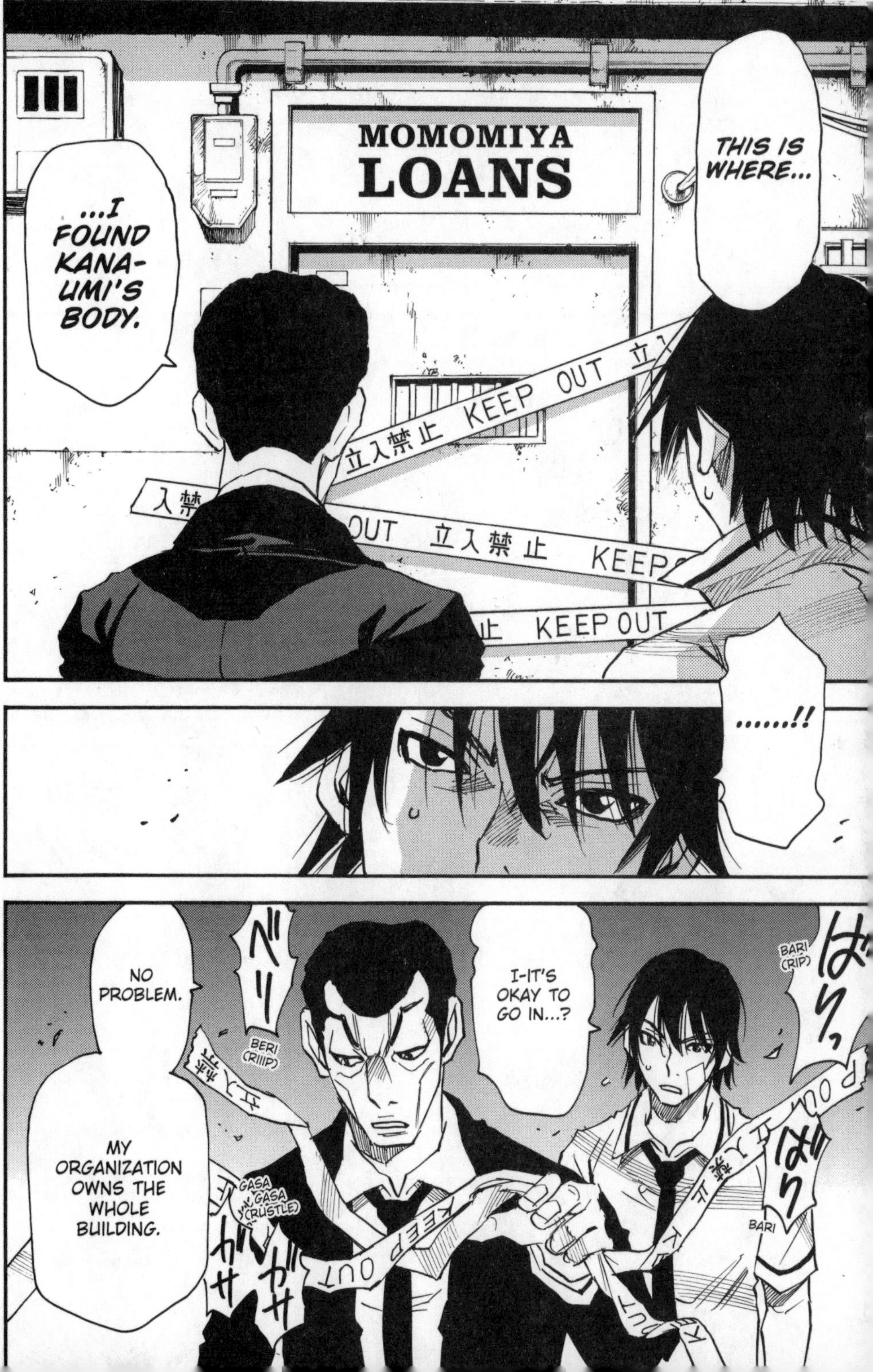
MOMOMIYA LOANS
THIS IS WHERE...
...I FOUND KANA-UMI'S BODY.
立入禁止 KEEP OUT
......!!
BARI (RIP)
I-IT'S OKAY TO GO IN...?
BERI (RIIIP)
NO PROBLEM.
MY ORGANIZATION OWNS THE WHOLE BUILDING.
GASA GASA (RUSTLE)
BARI

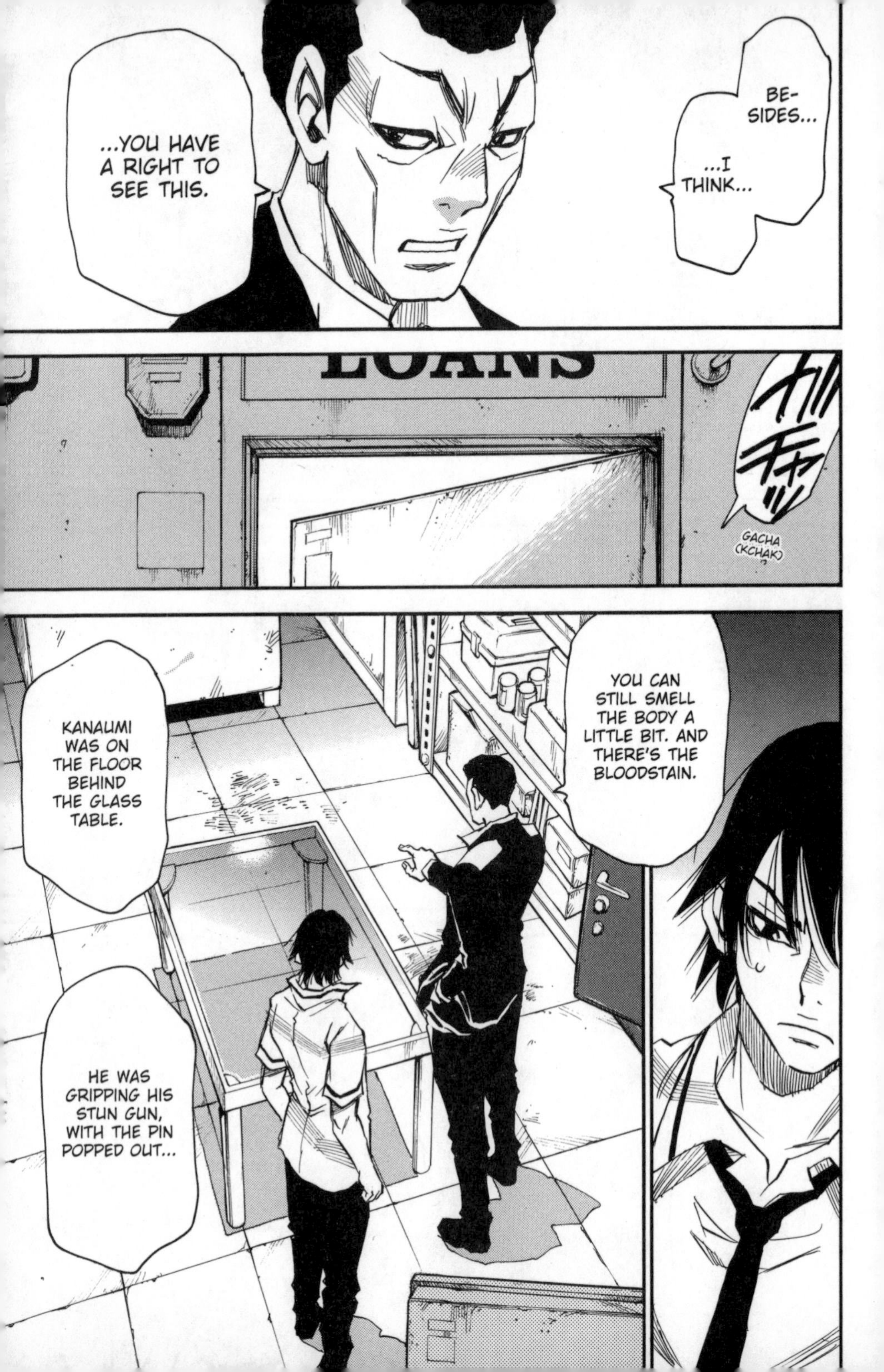
BE-SIDES...
...I THINK...
...YOU HAVE A RIGHT TO SEE THIS.
LOANS
ガチャッ
GACHA (KCHAK)
YOU CAN STILL SMELL THE BODY A LITTLE BIT. AND THERE'S THE BLOODSTAIN.
KANAUMI WAS ON THE FLOOR BEHIND THE GLASS TABLE.
HE WAS GRIPPING HIS STUN GUN, WITH THE PIN POPPED OUT...

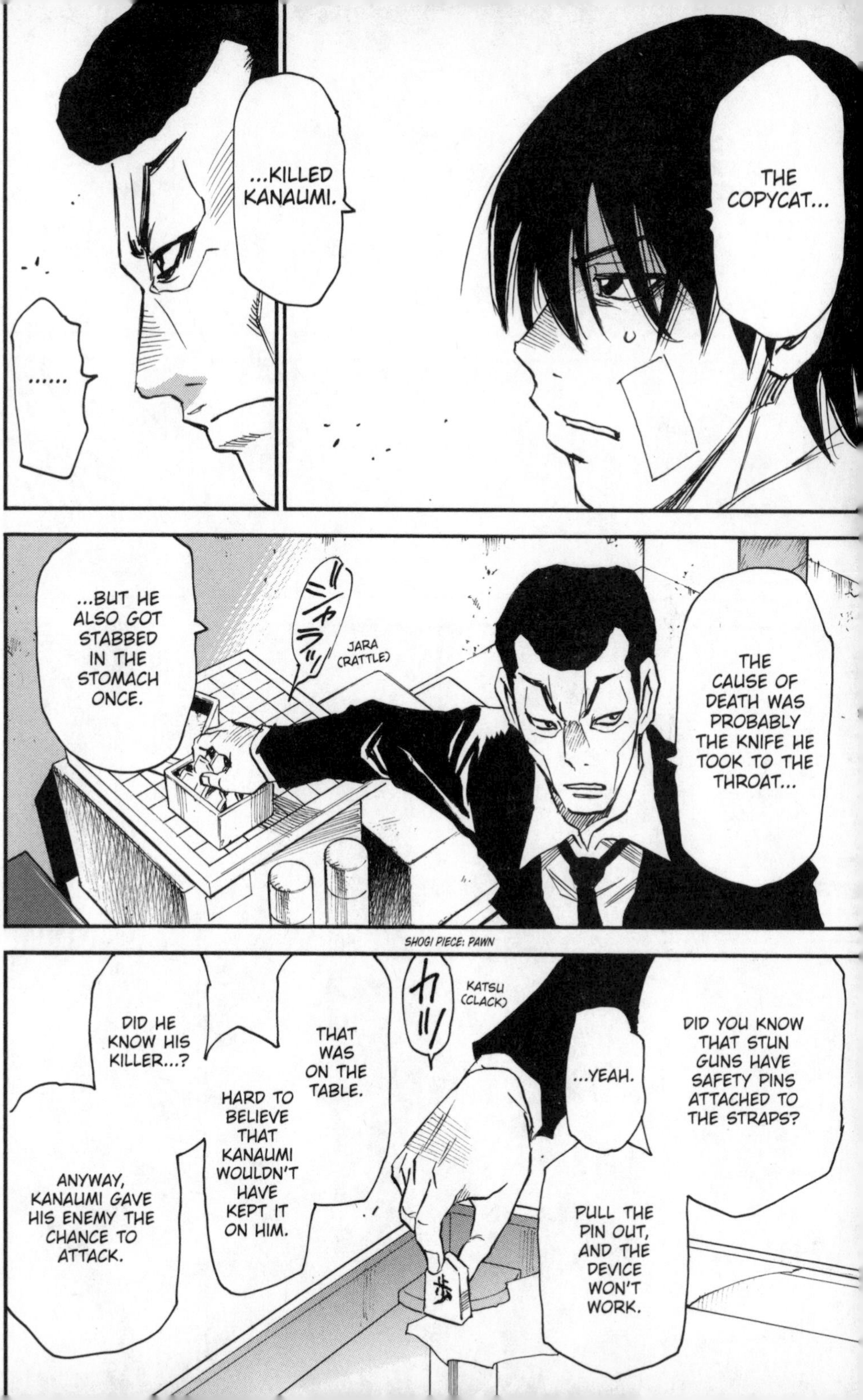
THE COPYCAT...
...KILLED KANAUMI.
......
THE CAUSE OF DEATH WAS PROBABLY THE KNIFE HE TOOK TO THE THROAT...
JARA (RATTLE)
...BUT HE ALSO GOT STABBED IN THE STOMACH ONCE.
SHOGI PIECE: PAWN
DID YOU KNOW THAT STUN GUNS HAVE SAFETY PINS ATTACHED TO THE STRAPS?
...YEAH.
PULL THE PIN OUT, AND THE DEVICE WON'T WORK.
KATSU (CLACK)
THAT WAS ON THE TABLE.
HARD TO BELIEVE THAT KANAUMI WOULDN'T HAVE KEPT IT ON HIM.
DID HE KNOW HIS KILLER...?
ANYWAY, KANAUMI GAVE HIS ENEMY THE CHANCE TO ATTACK.

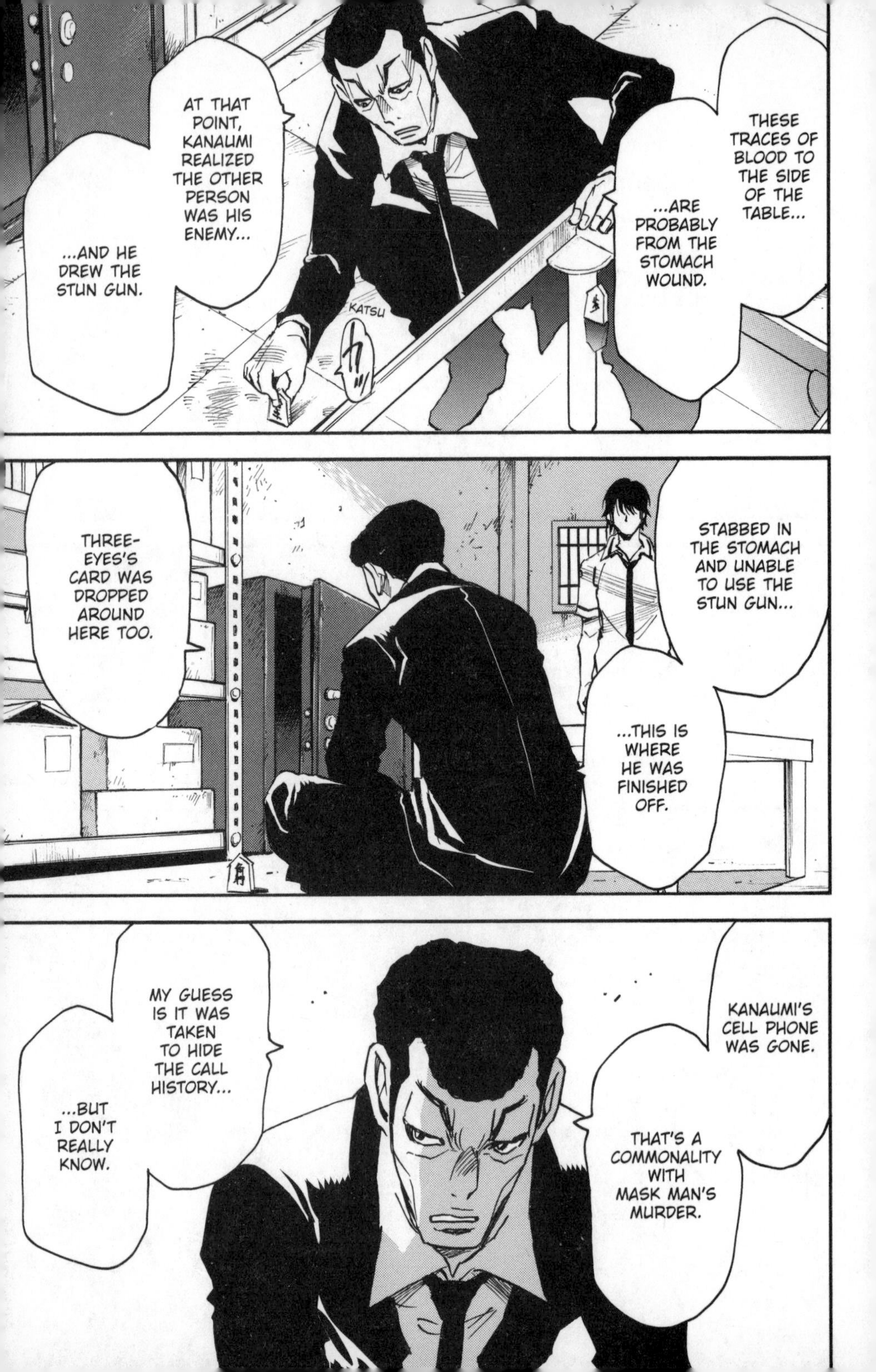
THESE TRACES OF BLOOD TO THE SIDE OF THE TABLE...
...ARE PROBABLY FROM THE STOMACH WOUND.
KATSU
AT THAT POINT, KANAUMI REALIZED THE OTHER PERSON WAS HIS ENEMY...
...AND HE DREW THE STUN GUN.
STABBED IN THE STOMACH AND UNABLE TO USE THE STUN GUN...
...THIS IS WHERE HE WAS FINISHED OFF.
THREE-EYES'S CARD WAS DROPPED AROUND HERE TOO.
KANAUMI'S CELL PHONE WAS GONE.
THAT'S A COMMONALITY WITH MASK MAN'S MURDER.
MY GUESS IS IT WAS TAKEN TO HIDE THE CALL HISTORY...
...BUT I DON'T REALLY KNOW.

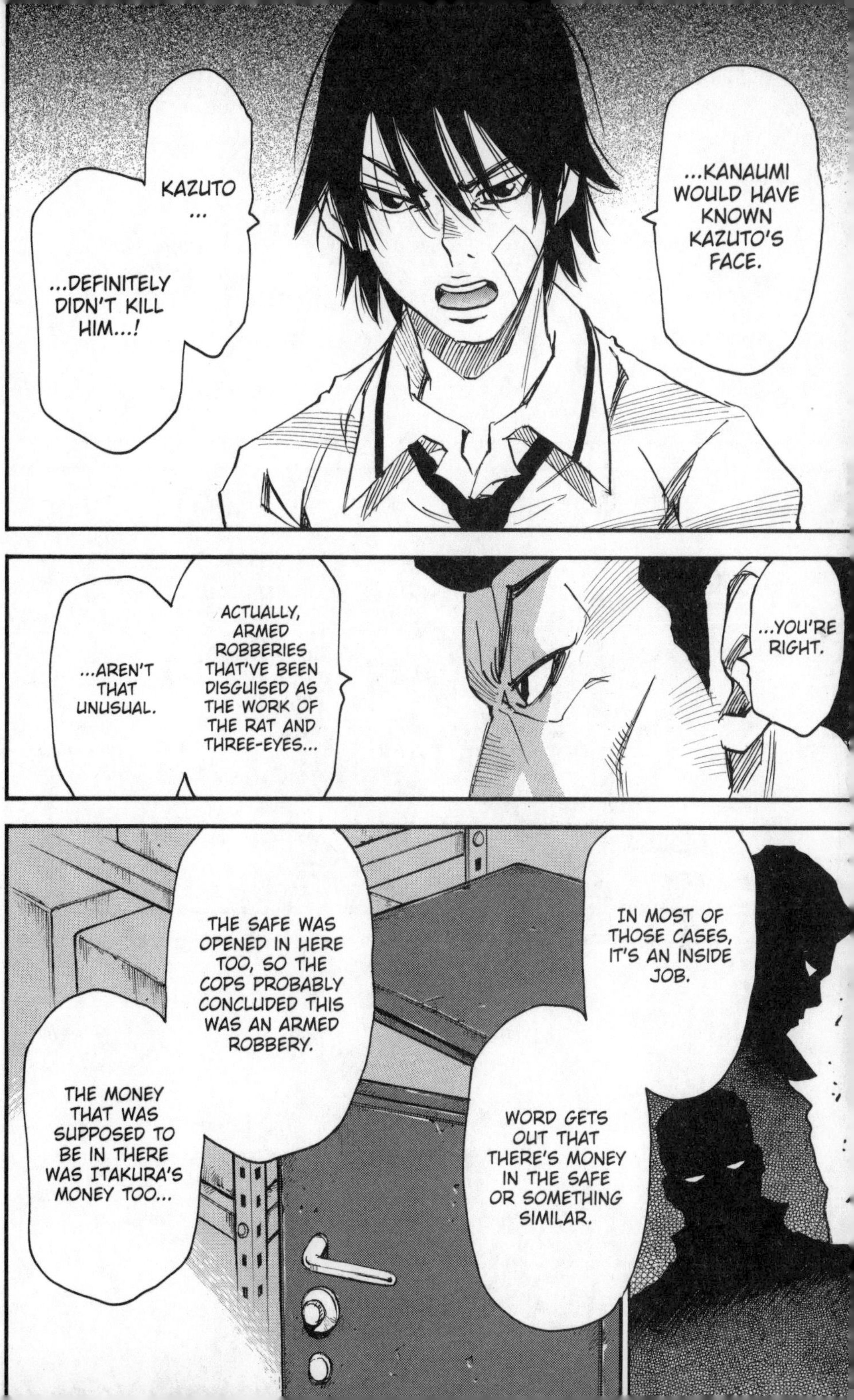
...KANAUMI WOULD HAVE KNOWN KAZUTO'S FACE.
KAZUTO ... ...DEFINITELY DIDN'T KILL HIM...!
...YOU'RE RIGHT.
ACTUALLY, ARMED ROBBERIES THAT'VE BEEN DISGUISED AS THE WORK OF THE RAT AND THREE-EYES...
...AREN'T THAT UNUSUAL.
IN MOST OF THOSE CASES, IT'S AN INSIDE JOB.
THE SAFE WAS OPENED IN HERE TOO, SO THE COPS PROBABLY CONCLUDED THIS WAS AN ARMED ROBBERY.
WORD GETS OUT THAT THERE'S MONEY IN THE SAFE OR SOMETHING SIMILAR.
THE MONEY THAT WAS SUPPOSED TO BE IN THERE WAS ITAKURA'S MONEY TOO...

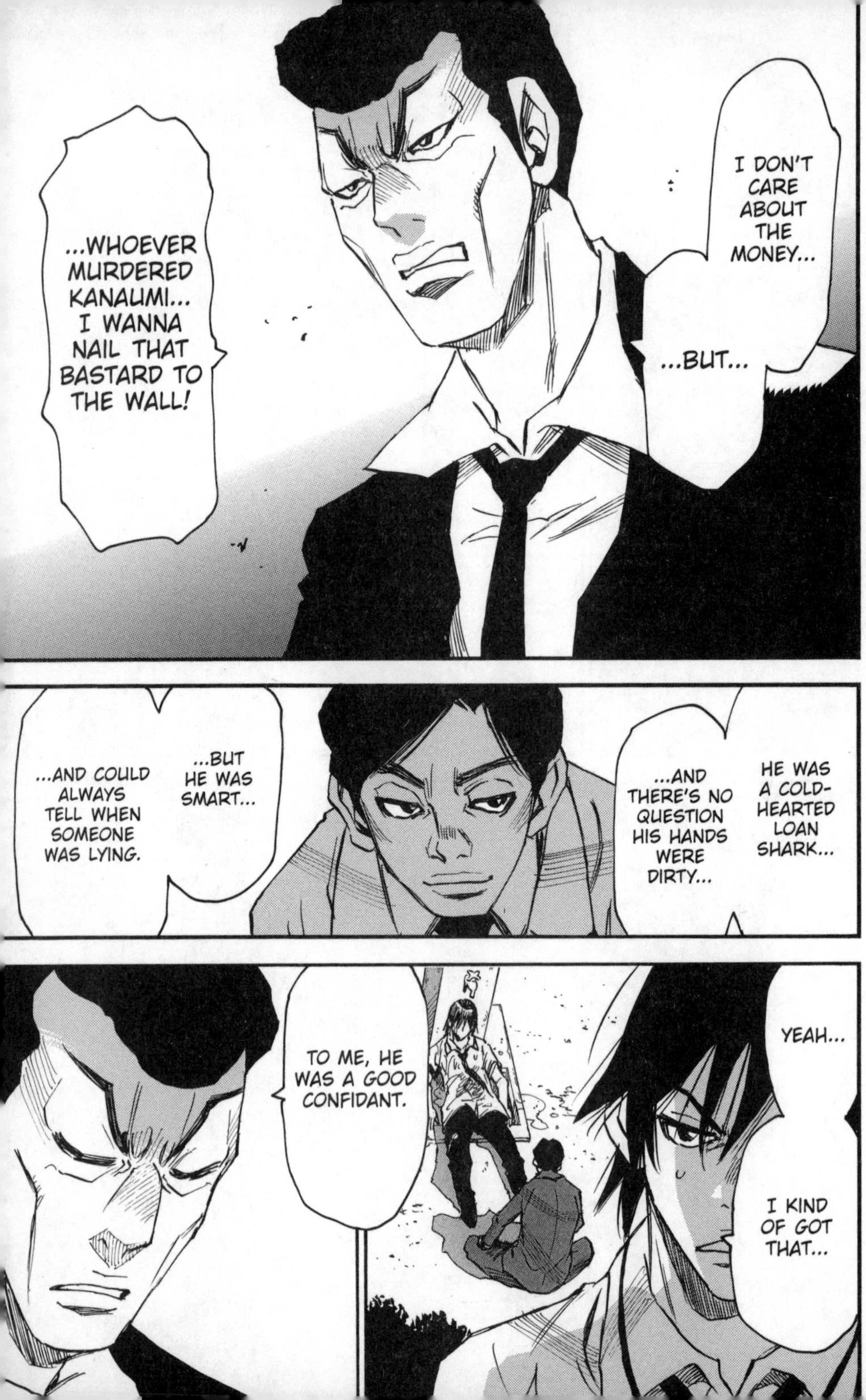
I DON'T CARE ABOUT THE MONEY...
...BUT...
...WHOEVER MURDERED KANAUMI... I WANNA NAIL THAT BASTARD TO THE WALL!
HE WAS A COLD-HEARTED LOAN SHARK...
...AND THERE'S NO QUESTION HIS HANDS WERE DIRTY...
...BUT HE WAS SMART...
...AND COULD ALWAYS TELL WHEN SOMEONE WAS LYING.
TO ME, HE WAS A GOOD CONFIDANT.
YEAH...
I KIND OF GOT THAT...

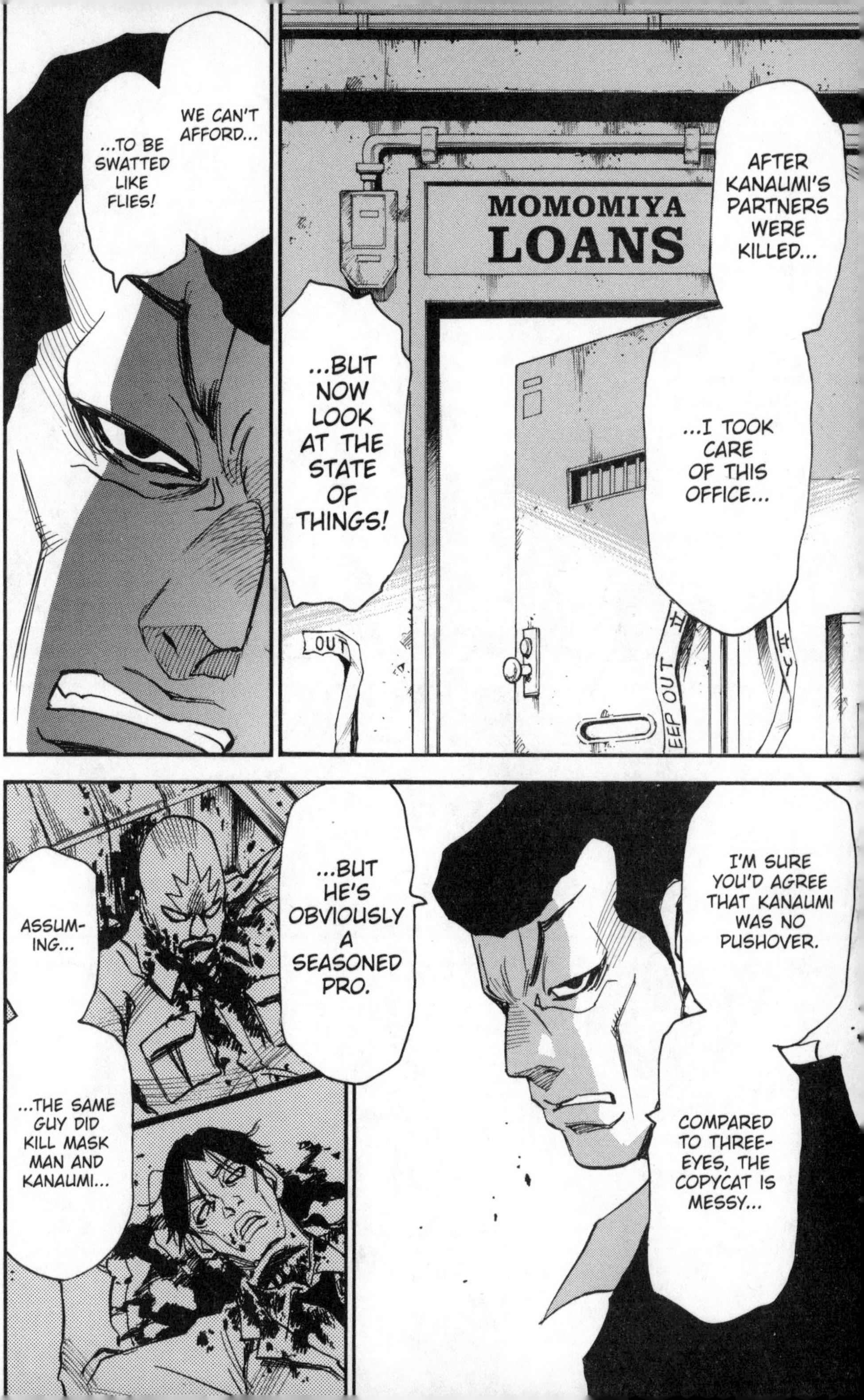
AFTER KANAUMI'S PARTNERS WERE KILLED...
MOMOMIYA LOANS
...I TOOK CARE OF THIS OFFICE...
...BUT NOW LOOK AT THE STATE OF THINGS!
WE CAN'T AFFORD...
...TO BE SWATTED LIKE FLIES!
I'M SURE YOU'D AGREE THAT KANAUMI WAS NO PUSHOVER.
...BUT HE'S OBVIOUSLY A SEASONED PRO.
COMPARED TO THREE-EYES, THE COPYCAT IS MESSY...
ASSUM-ING...
...THE SAME GUY DID KILL MASK MAN AND KANAUMI...

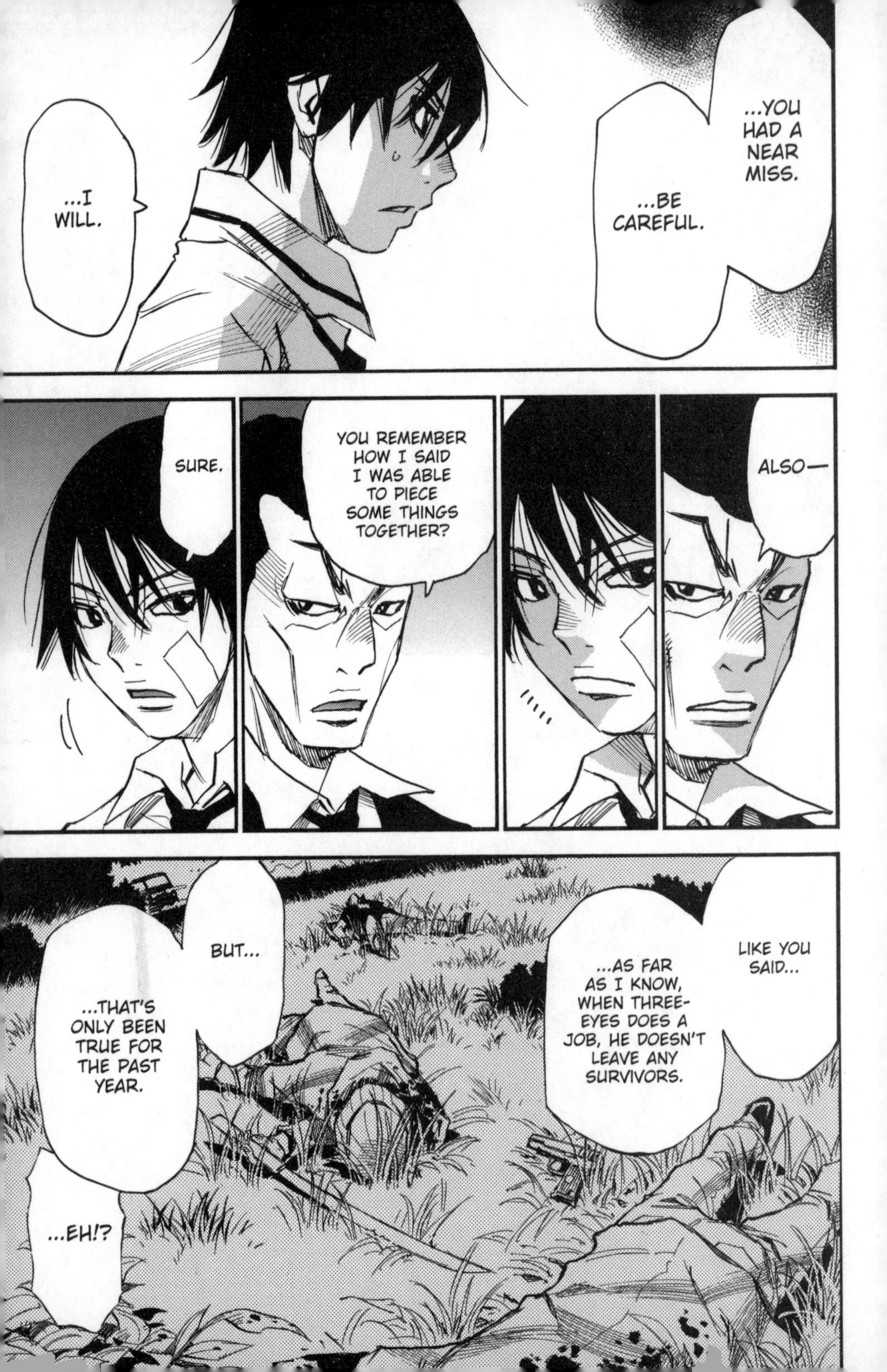
...YOU HAD A NEAR MISS.
...BE CAREFUL.
...I WILL.
ALSO—
YOU REMEMBER HOW I SAID I WAS ABLE TO PIECE SOME THINGS TOGETHER?
SURE.
LIKE YOU SAID...
...AS FAR AS I KNOW, WHEN THREE-EYES DOES A JOB, HE DOESN'T LEAVE ANY SURVIVORS.
BUT...
...THAT'S ONLY BEEN TRUE FOR THE PAST YEAR.
...EH!?

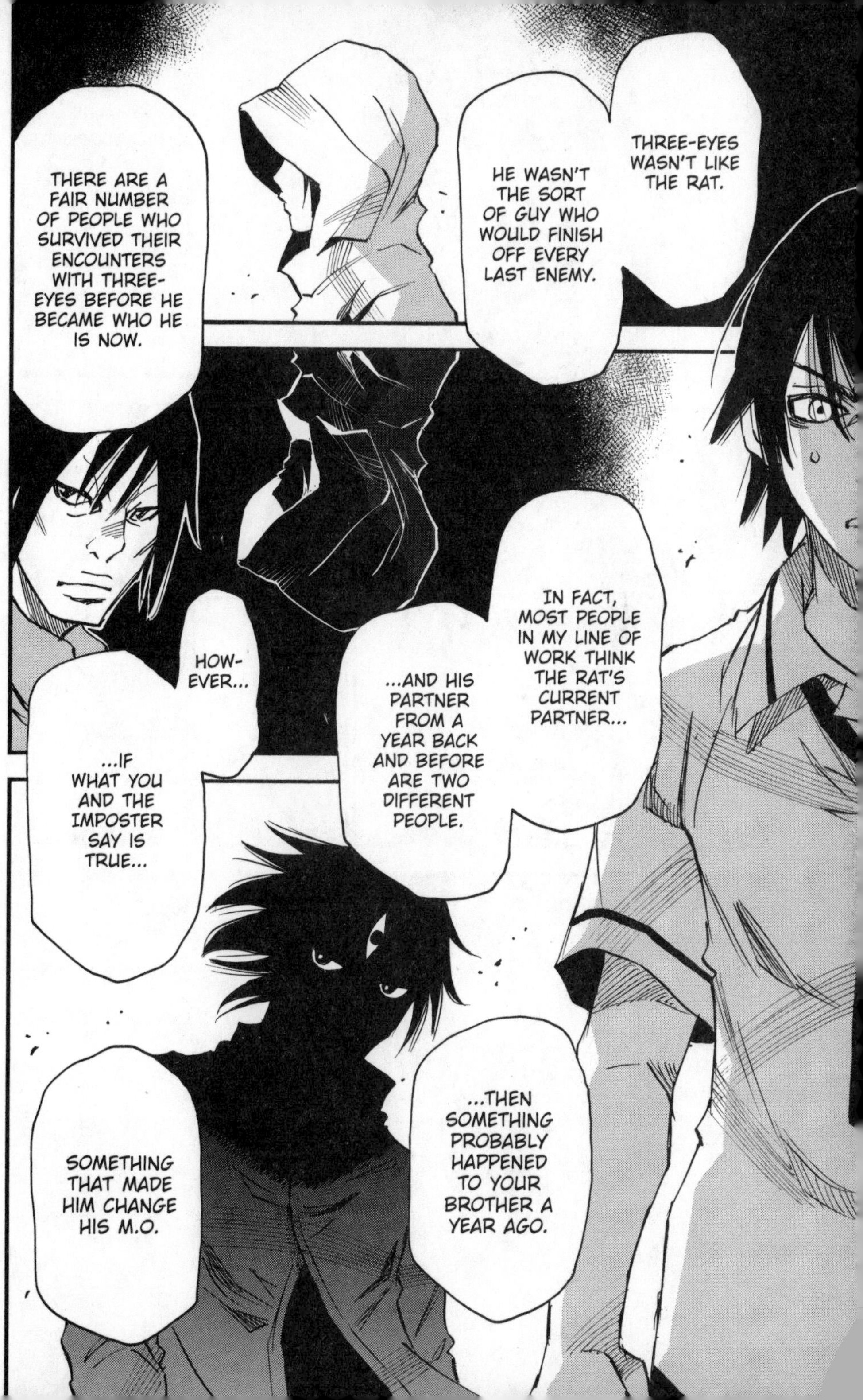
THREE-EYES WASN'T LIKE THE RAT.
HE WASN'T THE SORT OF GUY WHO WOULD FINISH OFF EVERY LAST ENEMY.
THERE ARE A FAIR NUMBER OF PEOPLE WHO SURVIVED THEIR ENCOUNTERS WITH THREE-EYES BEFORE HE BECAME WHO HE IS NOW.
IN FACT, MOST PEOPLE IN MY LINE OF WORK THINK THE RAT'S CURRENT PARTNER...
...AND HIS PARTNER FROM A YEAR BACK AND BEFORE ARE TWO DIFFERENT PEOPLE.
HOW-EVER...
...IF WHAT YOU AND THE IMPOSTER SAY IS TRUE...
...THEN SOMETHING PROBABLY HAPPENED TO YOUR BROTHER A YEAR AGO.
SOMETHING THAT MADE HIM CHANGE HIS M.O.

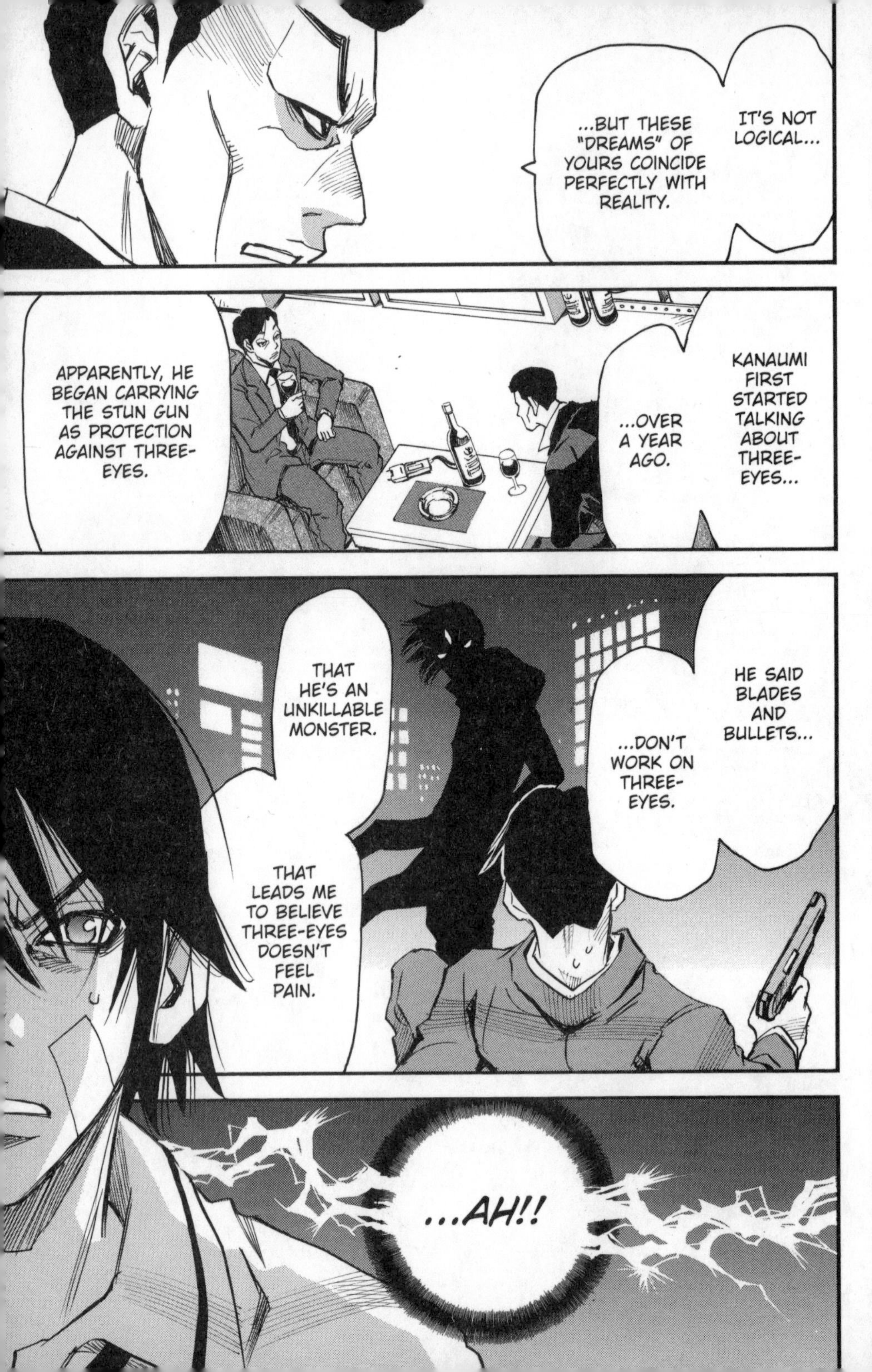
IT'S NOT LOGICAL...
...BUT THESE "DREAMS" OF YOURS COINCIDE PERFECTLY WITH REALITY.
KANAUMI FIRST STARTED TALKING ABOUT THREE-EYES...
...OVER A YEAR AGO.
APPARENTLY, HE BEGAN CARRYING THE STUN GUN AS PROTECTION AGAINST THREE-EYES.
HE SAID BLADES AND BULLETS...
...DON'T WORK ON THREE-EYES.
THAT HE'S AN UNKILLABLE MONSTER.
THAT LEADS ME TO BELIEVE THREE-EYES DOESN'T FEEL PAIN.
...AH!!

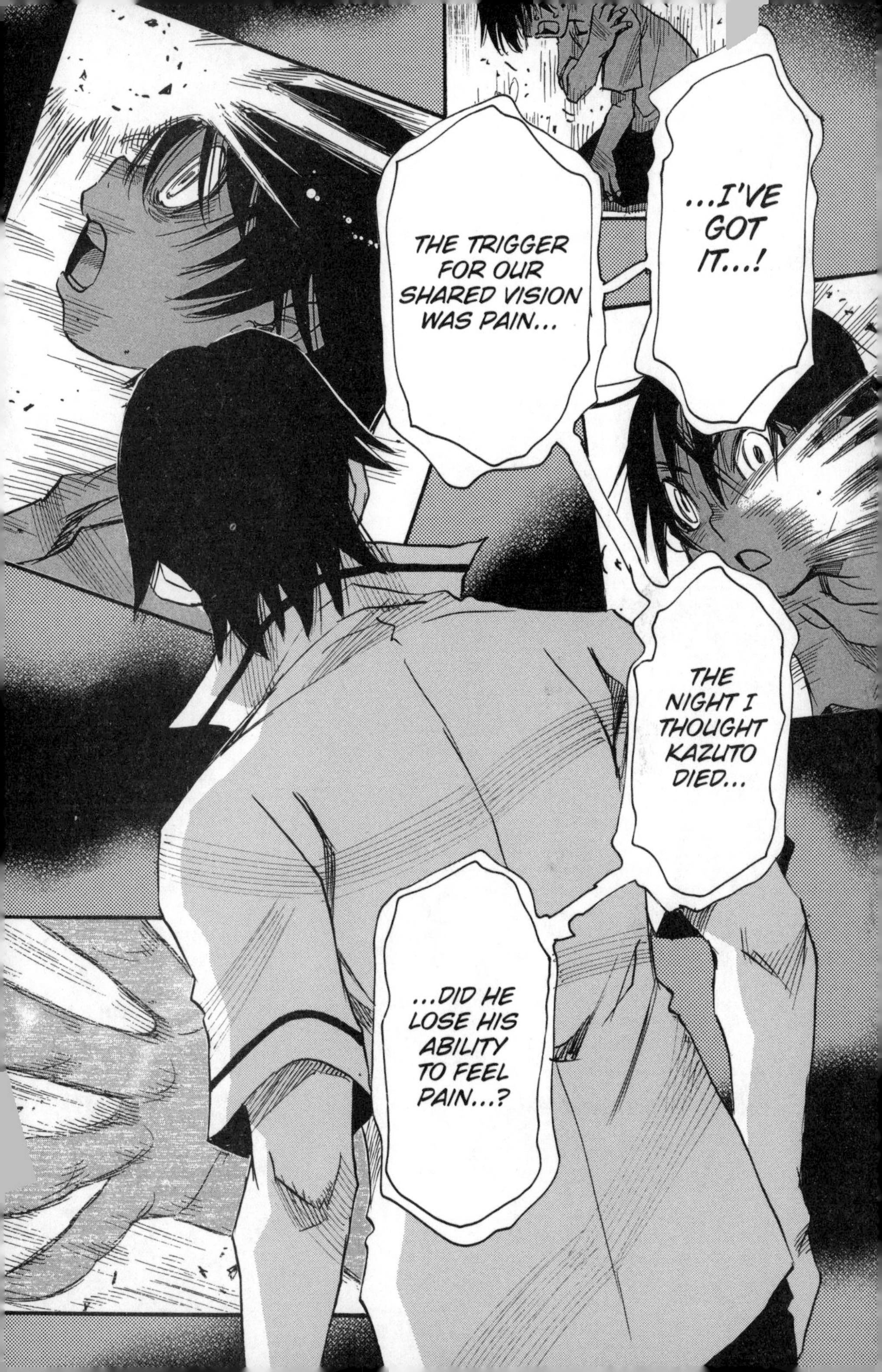
...I'VE GOT IT...!
THE TRIGGER FOR OUR SHARED VISION WAS PAIN...
THE NIGHT I THOUGHT KAZUTO DIED...
...DID HE LOSE HIS ABILITY TO FEEL PAIN...?

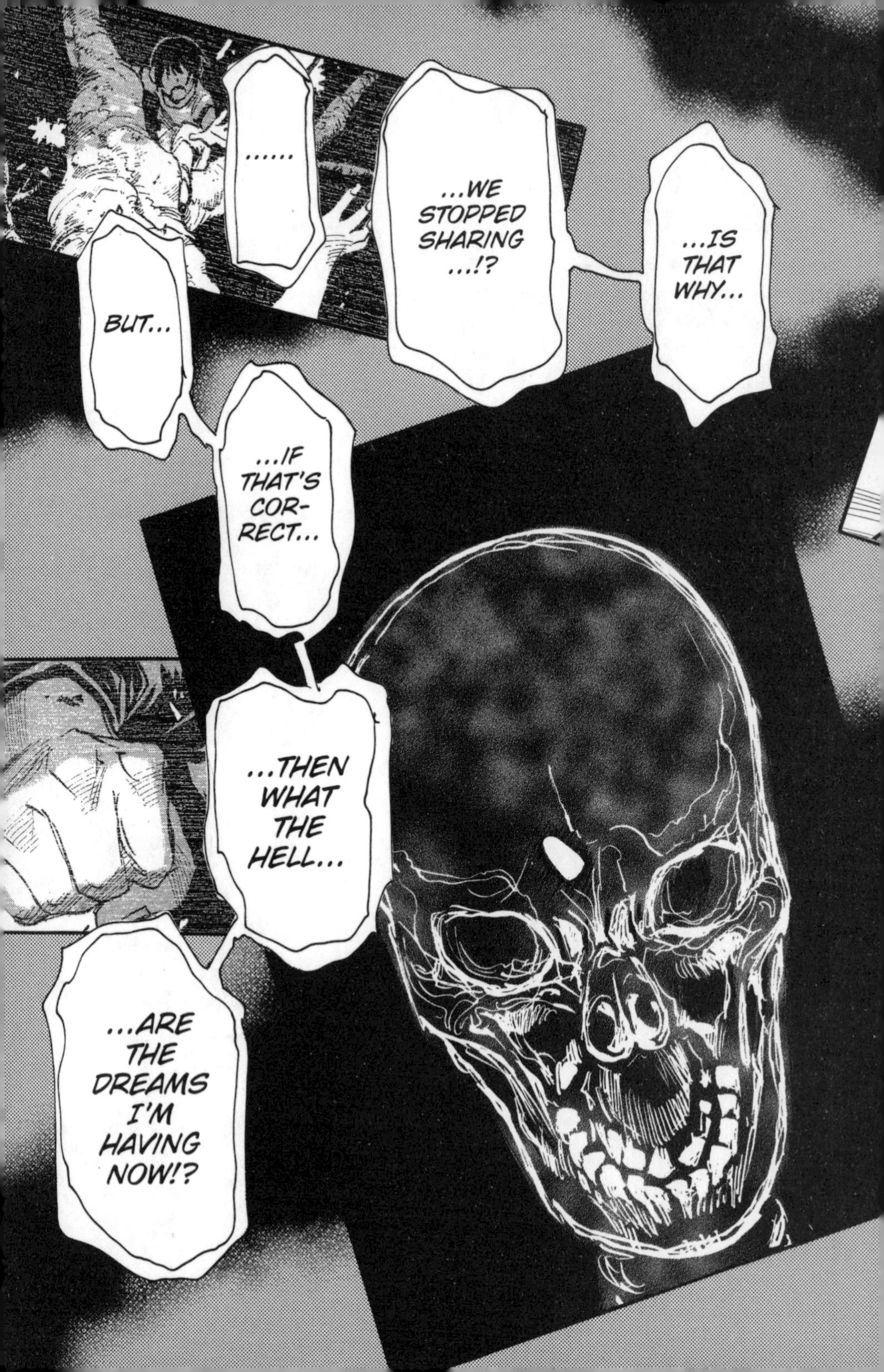
...IS THAT WHY...
...WE STOPPED SHARING ...!?
......
BUT...
...IF THAT'S COR-RECT...
...THEN WHAT THE HELL...
...ARE THE DREAMS I'M HAVING NOW!?

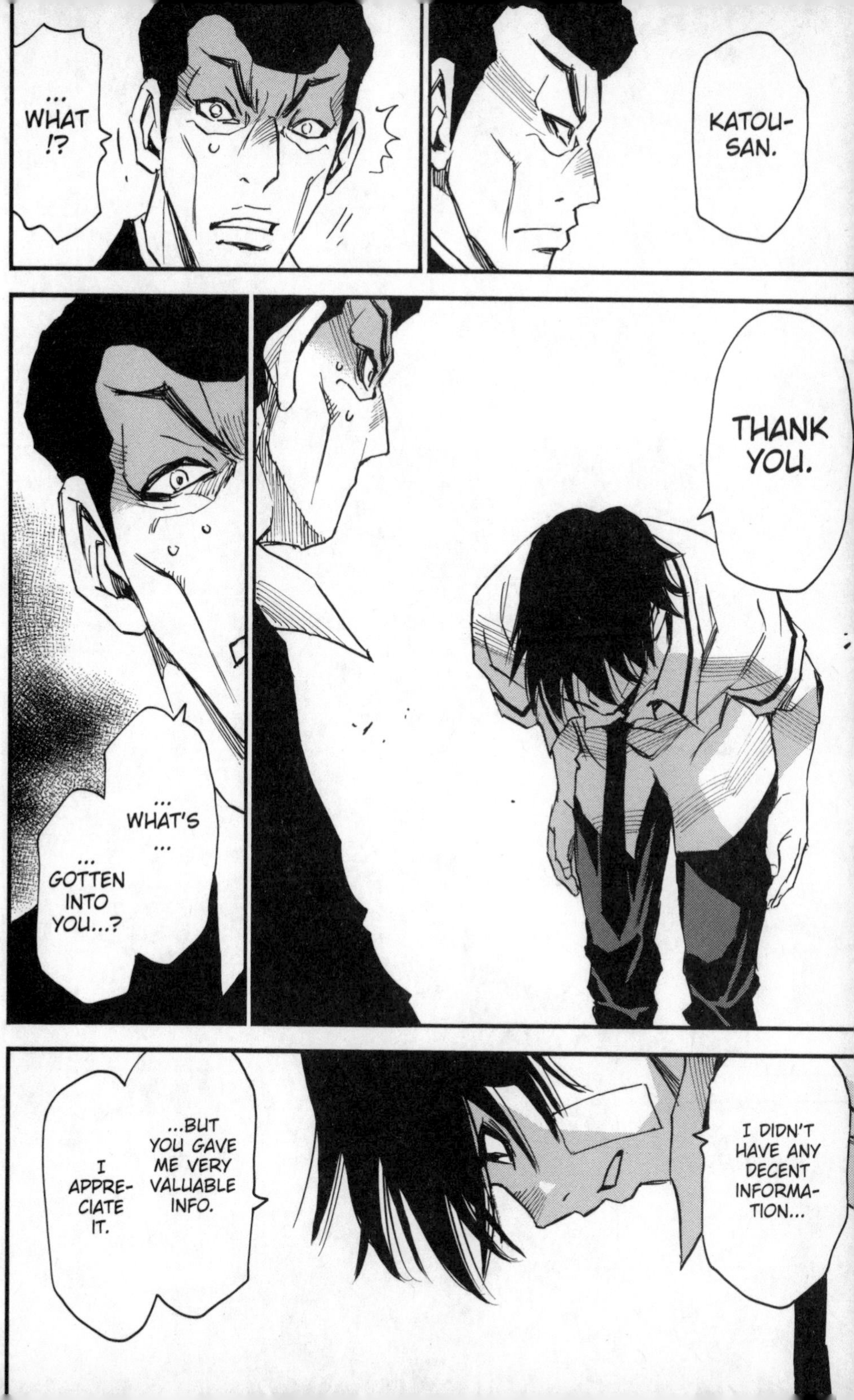
KATOU-SAN.
...WHAT!?
THANK YOU.
...WHAT'S... ...GOTTEN INTO YOU...?
I DIDN'T HAVE ANY DECENT INFORMATION...
...BUT YOU GAVE ME VERY VALUABLE INFO.
I APPRECIATE IT.

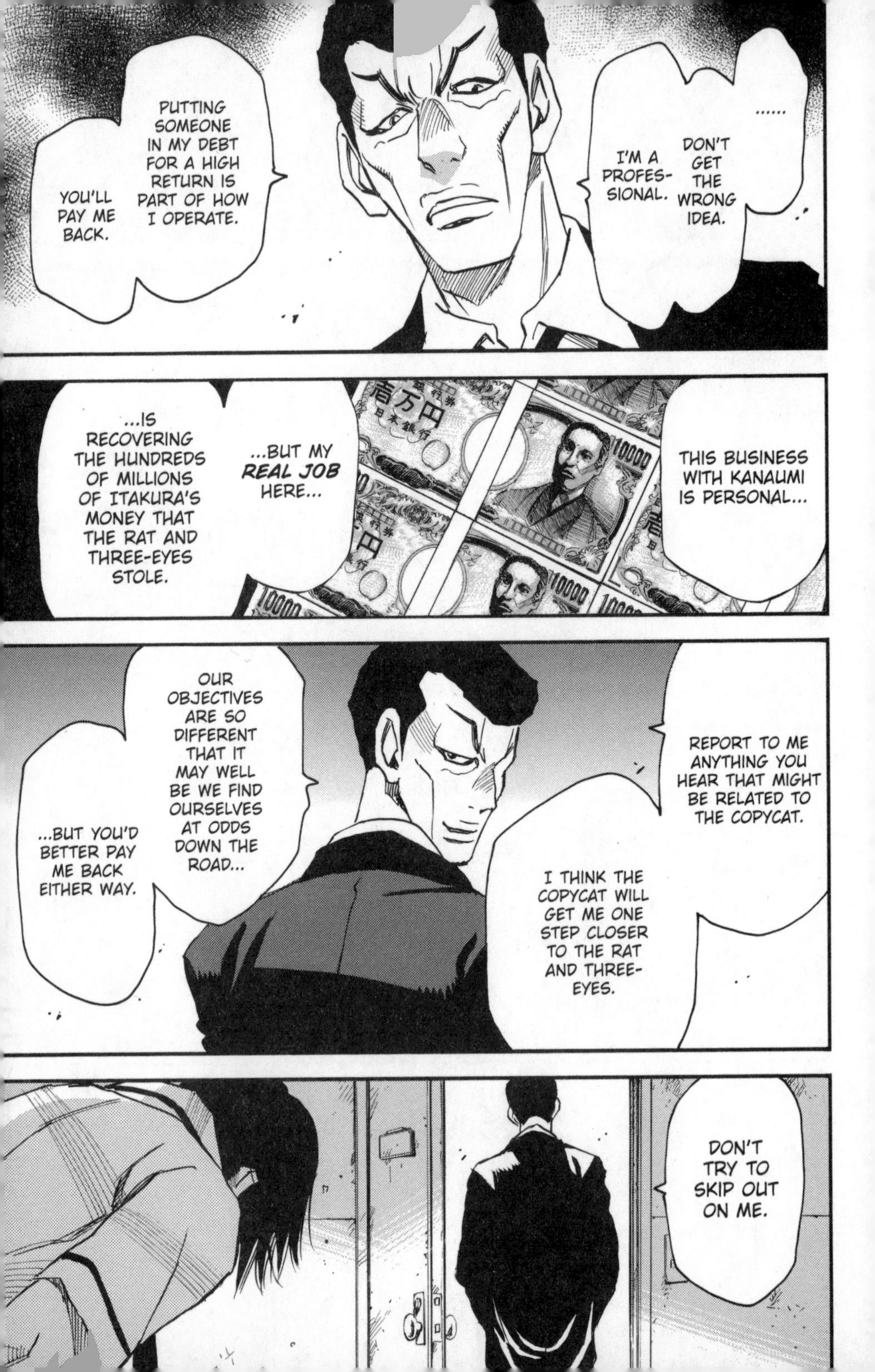
......
DON'T GET THE WRONG IDEA.
I'M A PROFESSIONAL.
PUTTING SOMEONE IN MY DEBT FOR A HIGH RETURN IS PART OF HOW I OPERATE.
YOU'LL PAY ME BACK.
THIS BUSINESS WITH KANAUMI IS PERSONAL...
...BUT MY *REAL JOB* HERE...
...IS RECOVERING THE HUNDREDS OF MILLIONS OF ITAKURA'S MONEY THAT THE RAT AND THREE-EYES STOLE.
REPORT TO ME ANYTHING YOU HEAR THAT MIGHT BE RELATED TO THE COPYCAT.
I THINK THE COPYCAT WILL GET ME ONE STEP CLOSER TO THE RAT AND THREE-EYES.
OUR OBJECTIVES ARE SO DIFFERENT THAT IT MAY WELL BE WE FIND OURSELVES AT ODDS DOWN THE ROAD...
...BUT YOU'D BETTER PAY ME BACK EITHER WAY.
DON'T TRY TO SKIP OUT ON ME.

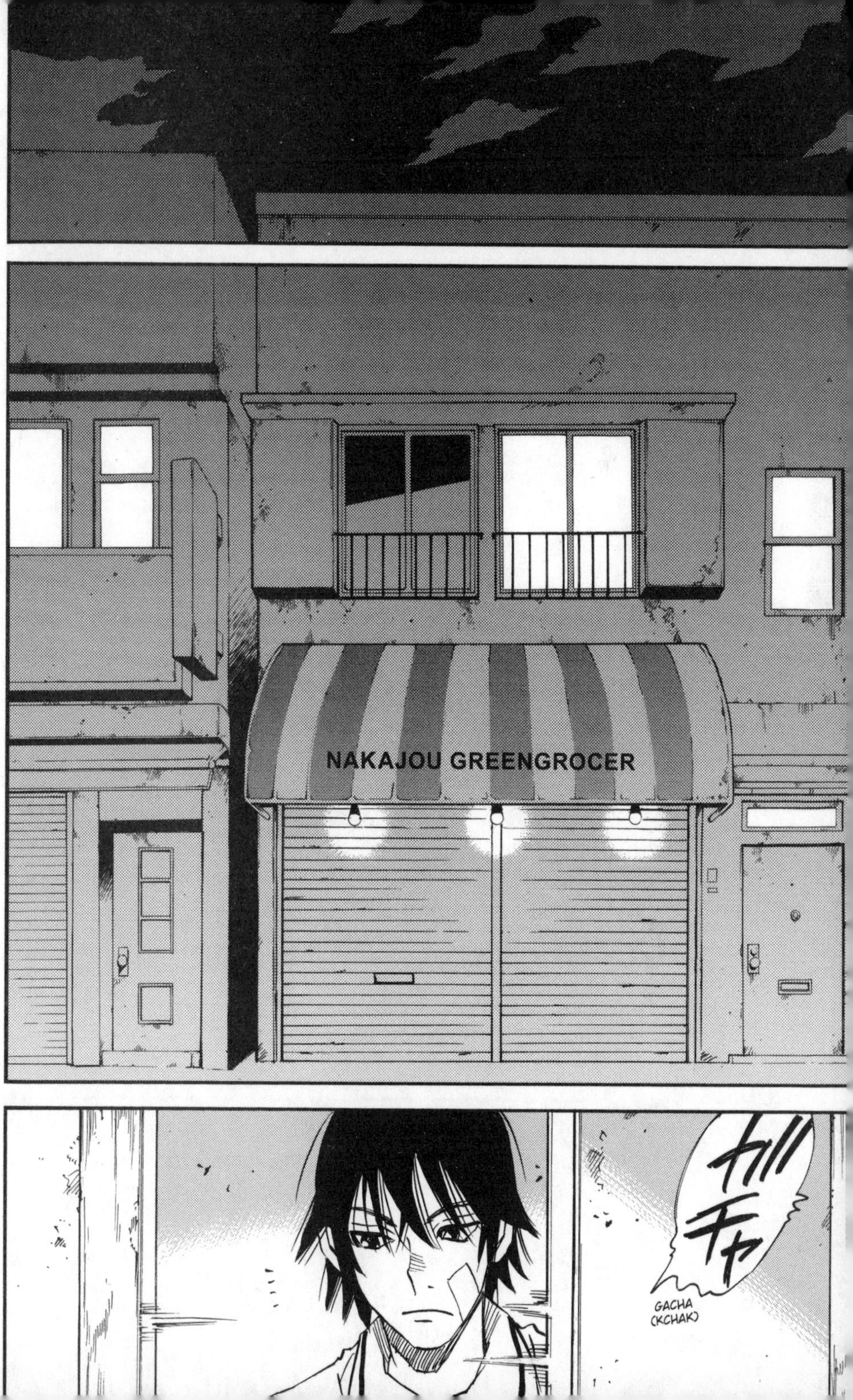
NAKAJOU GREENGROCER
ガチャ
GACHA (KCHAK)

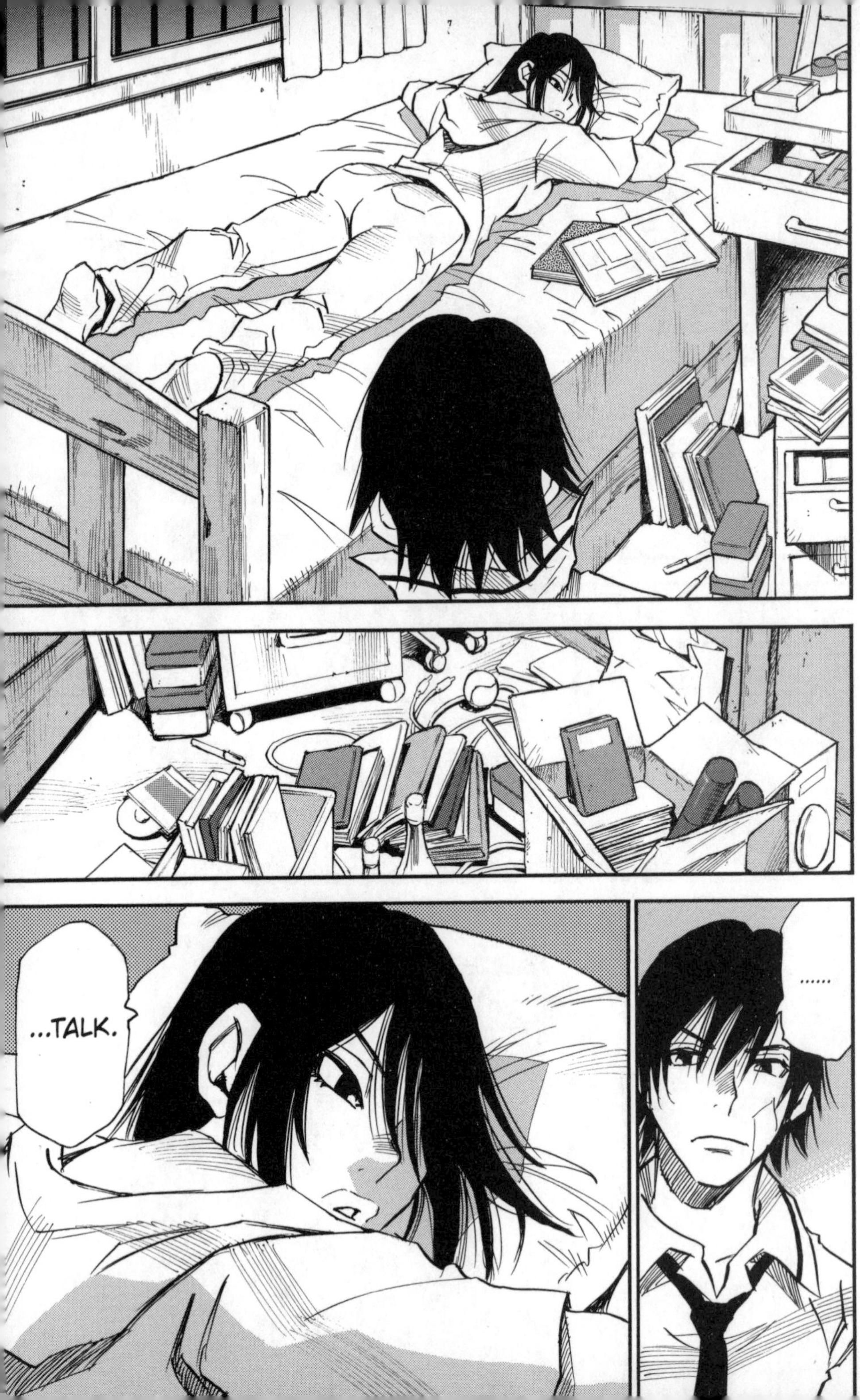
......
...TALK.

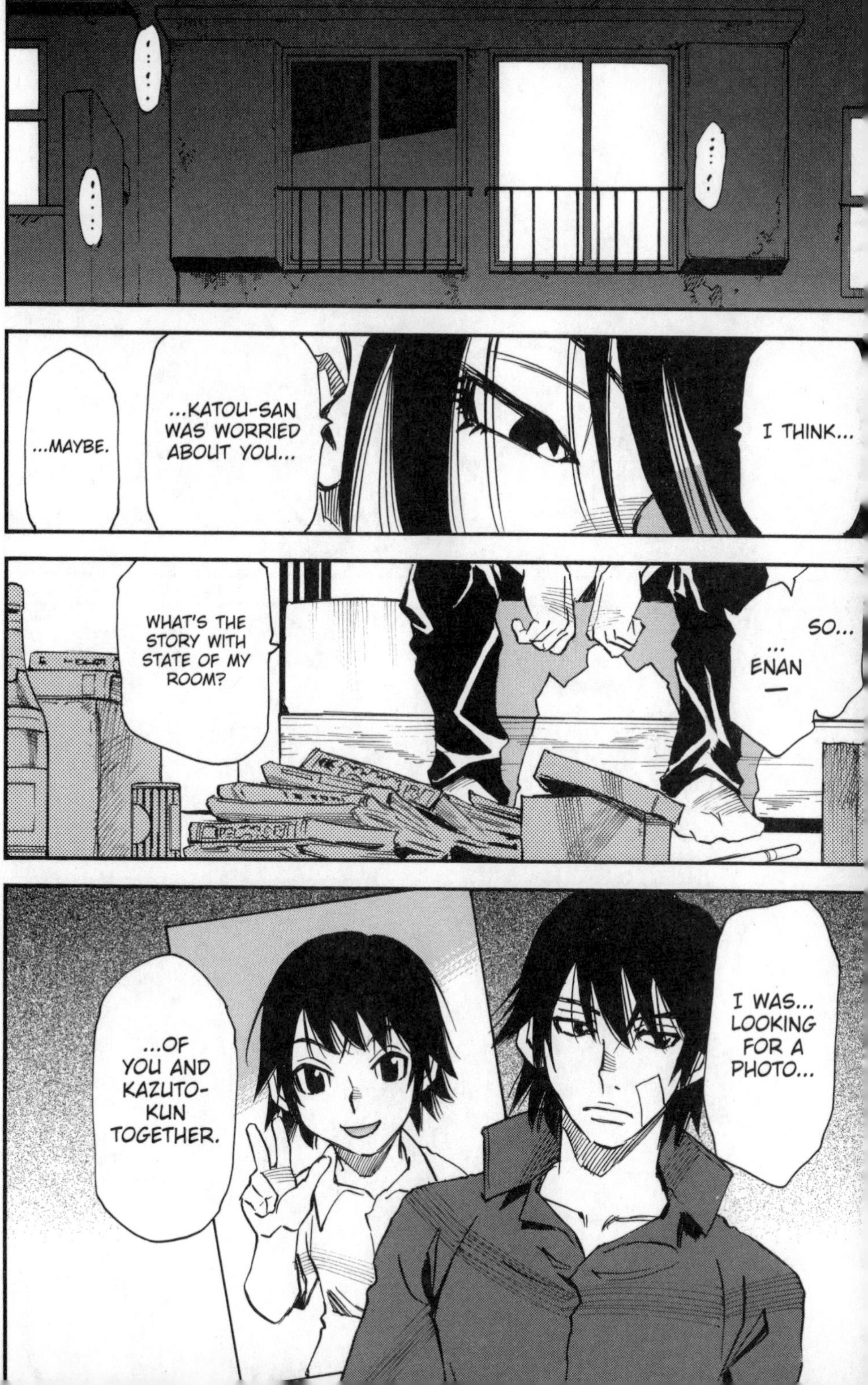
....
....
....
I THINK...
...KATOU-SAN WAS WORRIED ABOUT YOU...
...MAYBE.
SO... ...ENAN—
WHAT'S THE STORY WITH STATE OF MY ROOM?
I WAS... LOOKING FOR A PHOTO...
...OF YOU AND KAZUTO-KUN TOGETHER.

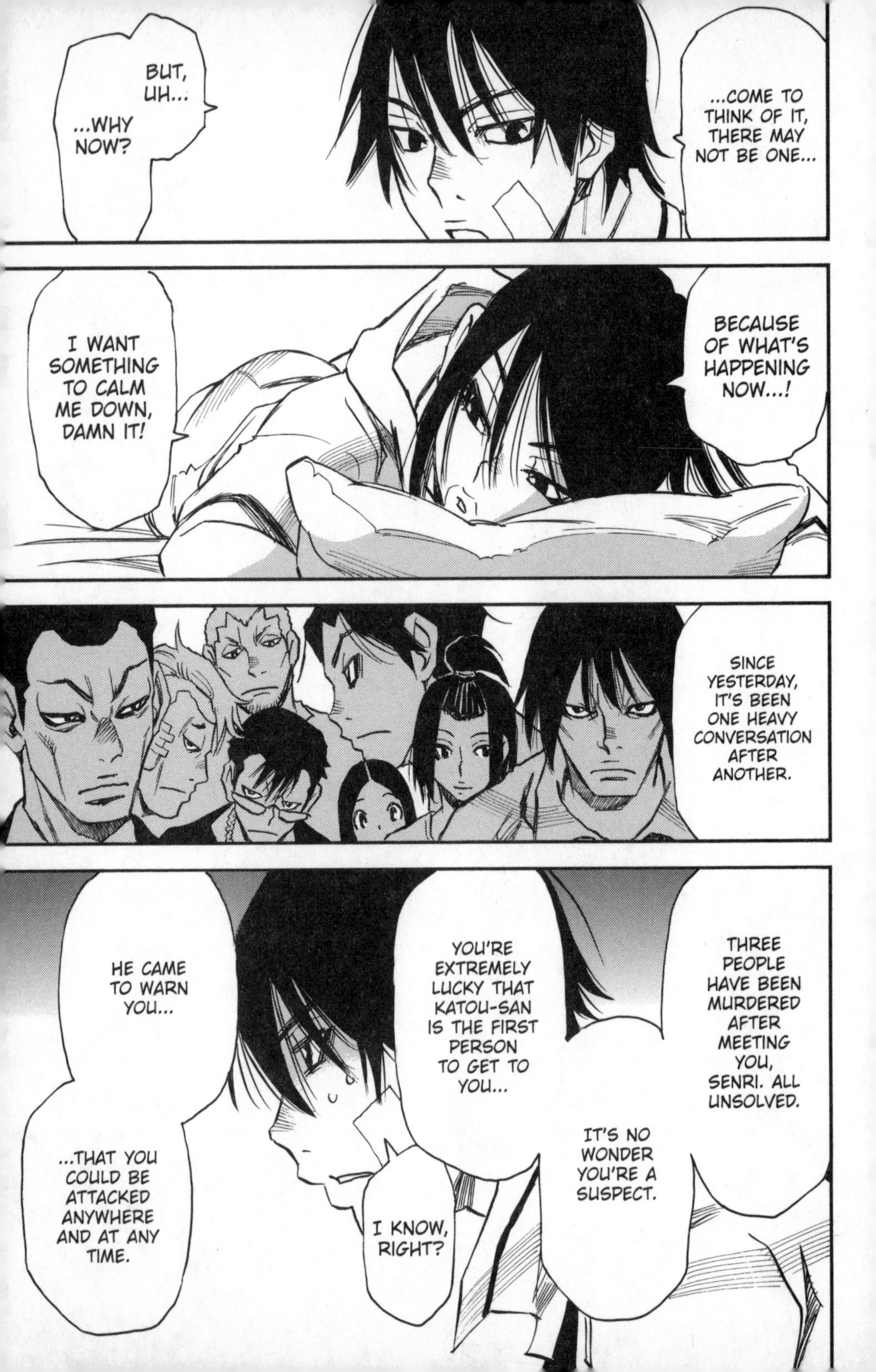
...COME TO THINK OF IT, THERE MAY NOT BE ONE...
BUT, UH... ...WHY NOW?
BECAUSE OF WHAT'S HAPPENING NOW...!
I WANT SOMETHING TO CALM ME DOWN, DAMN IT!
SINCE YESTERDAY, IT'S BEEN ONE HEAVY CONVERSATION AFTER ANOTHER.
THREE PEOPLE HAVE BEEN MURDERED AFTER MEETING YOU, SENRI. ALL UNSOLVED.
IT'S NO WONDER YOU'RE A SUSPECT.
YOU'RE EXTREMELY LUCKY THAT KATOU-SAN IS THE FIRST PERSON TO GET TO YOU...
I KNOW, RIGHT?
HE CAME TO WARN YOU...
...THAT YOU COULD BE ATTACKED ANYWHERE AND AT ANY TIME.

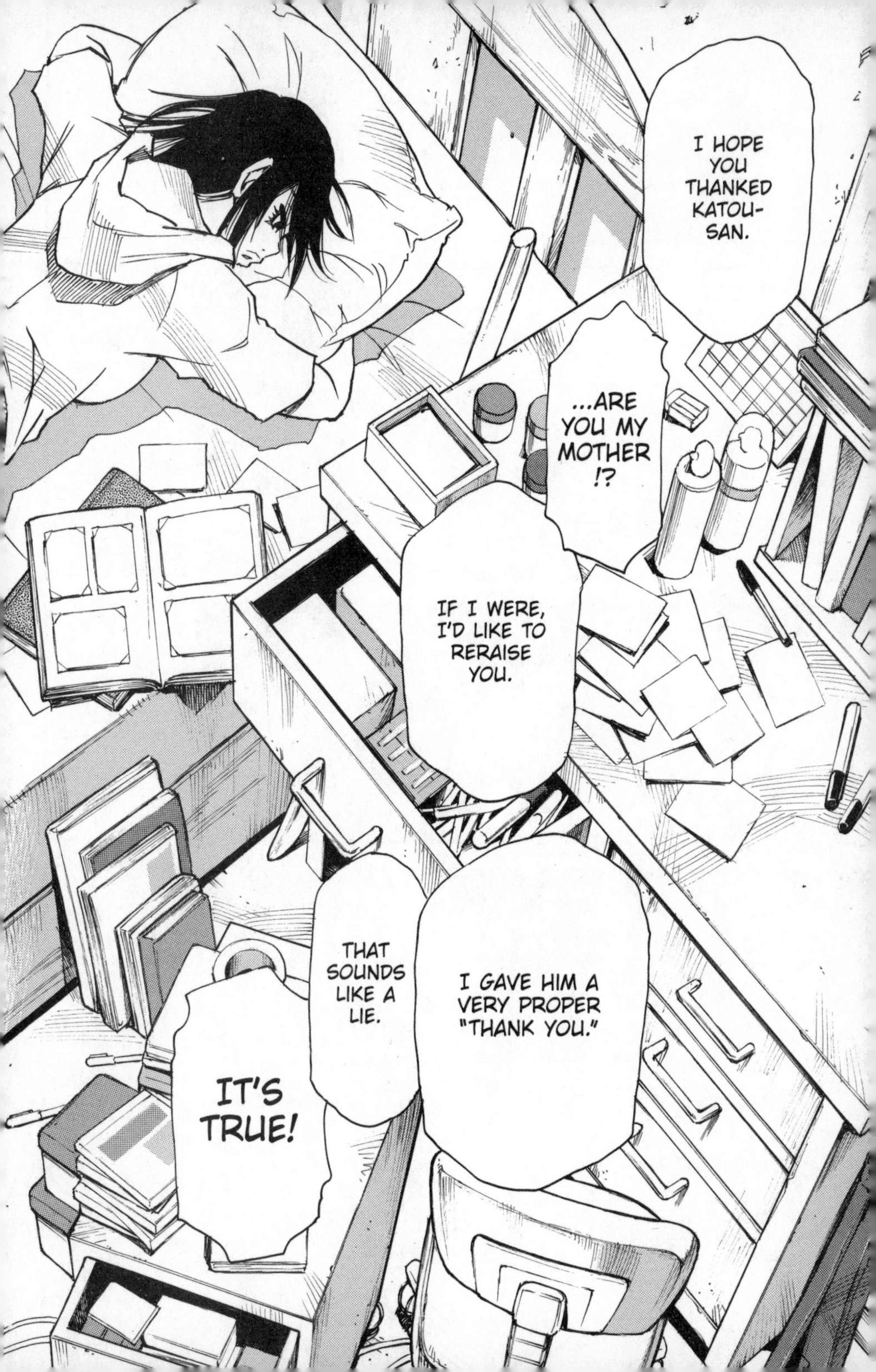
I HOPE YOU THANKED KATOU-SAN.
...ARE YOU MY MOTHER !?
IF I WERE, I'D LIKE TO RERAISE YOU.
I GAVE HIM A VERY PROPER "THANK YOU."
THAT SOUNDS LIKE A LIE.
IT'S TRUE!

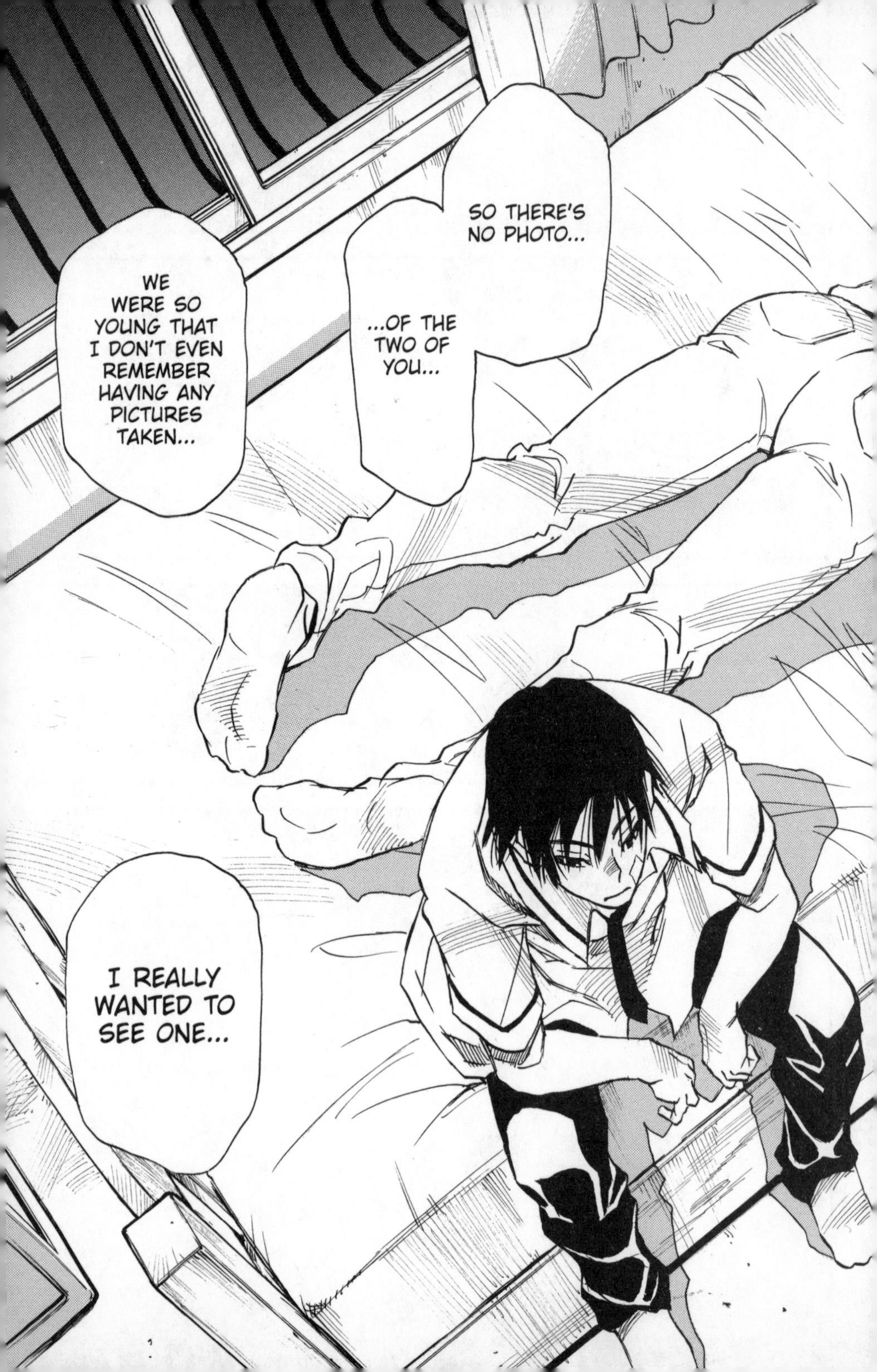
SO THERE'S NO PHOTO...
...OF THE TWO OF YOU...
WE WERE SO YOUNG THAT I DON'T EVEN REMEMBER HAVING ANY PICTURES TAKEN...
I REALLY WANTED TO SEE ONE...

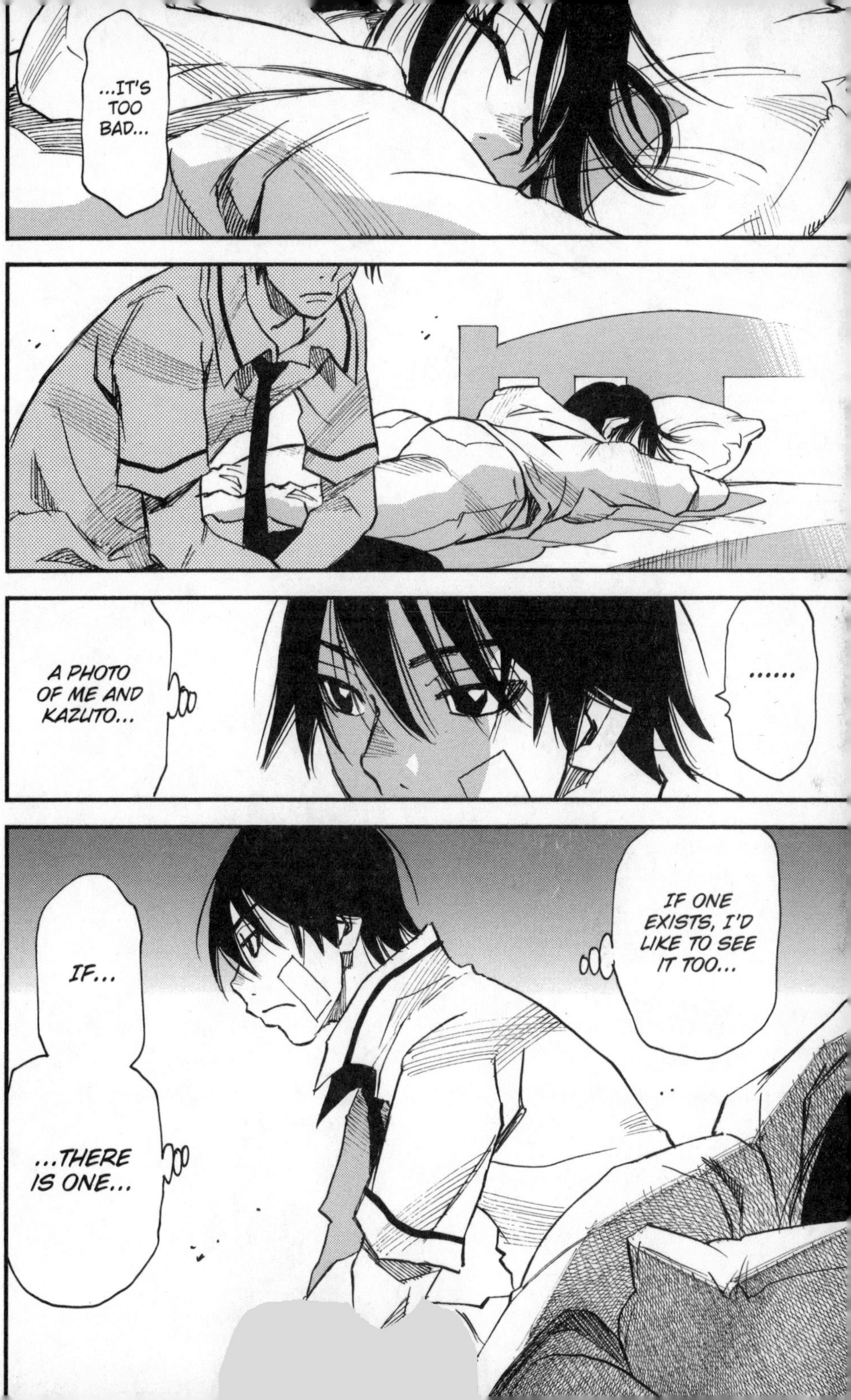
...IT'S TOO BAD...
......
A PHOTO OF ME AND KAZUTO...
IF ONE EXISTS, I'D LIKE TO SEE IT TOO...
IF...
...THERE IS ONE...

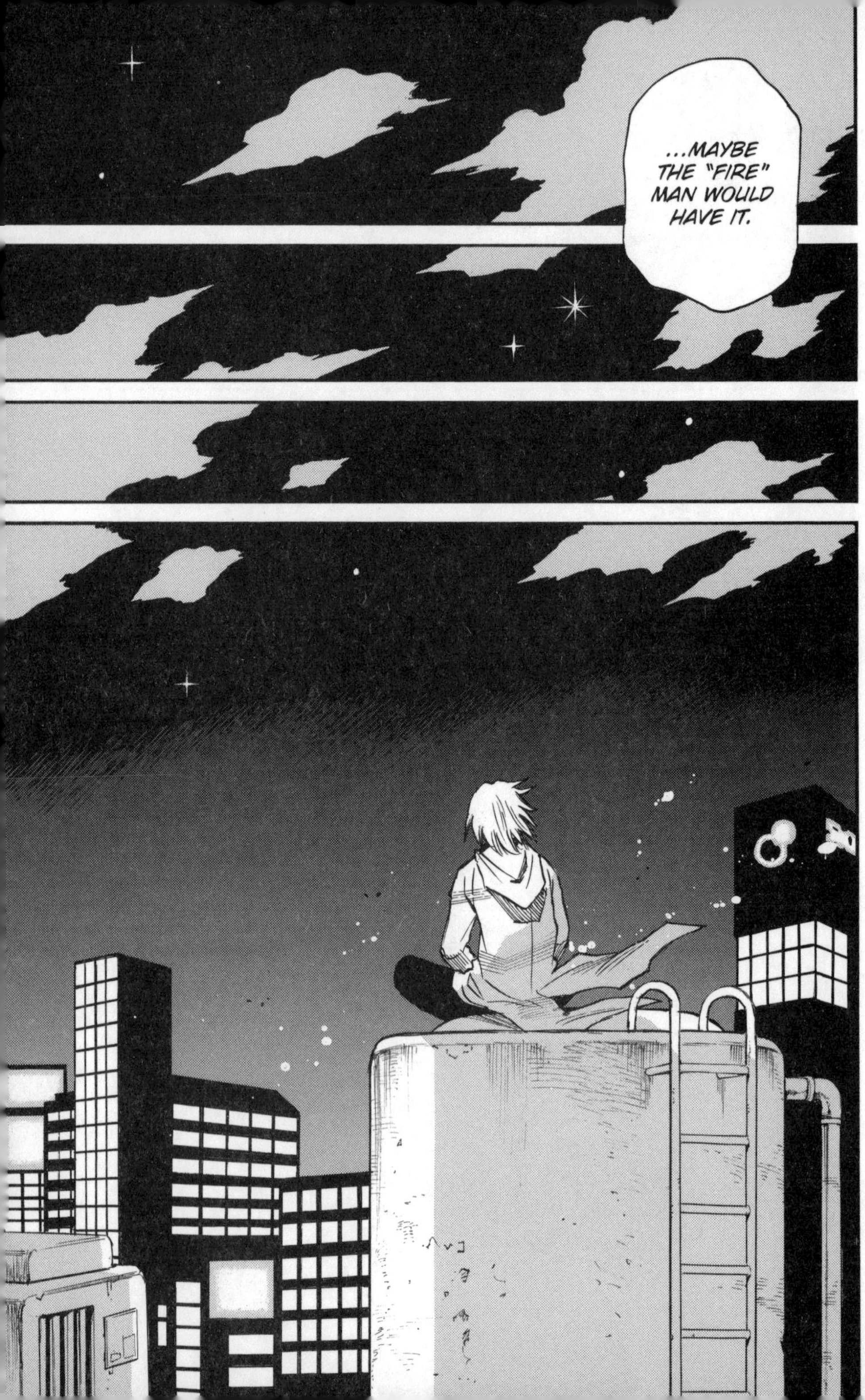
...MAYBE THE "FIRE" MAN WOULD HAVE IT.

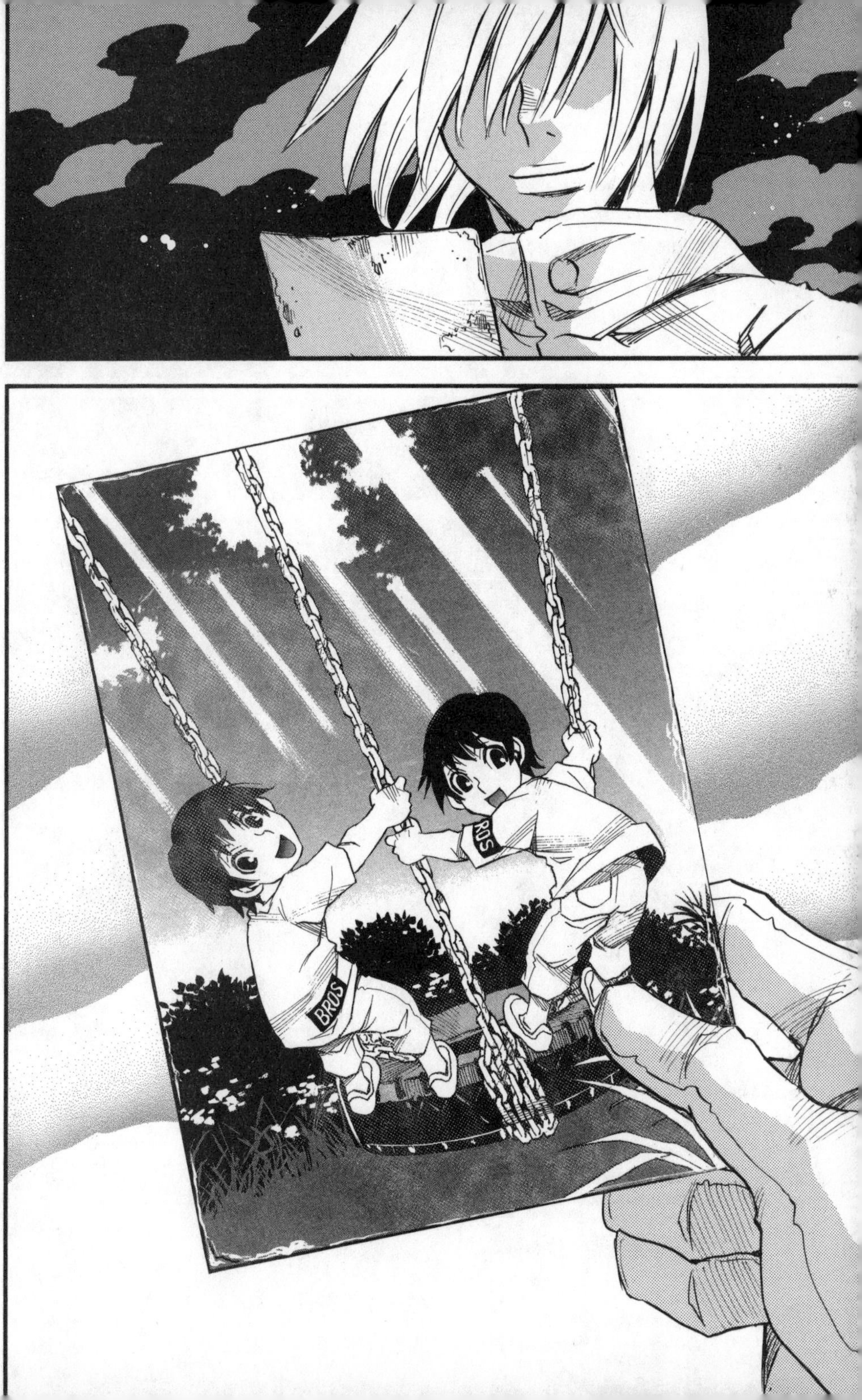
ROS
BROS

#35 END

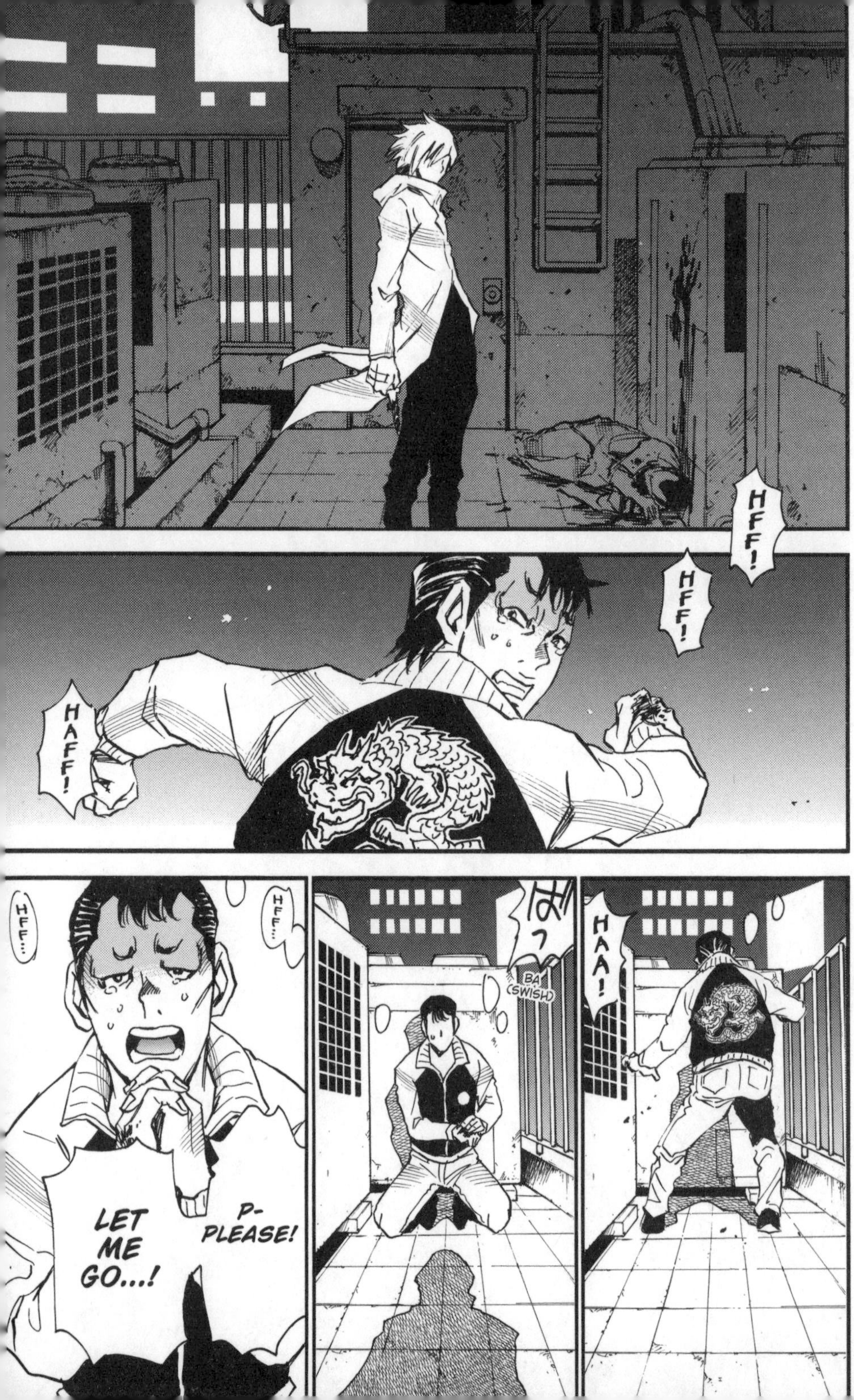
HFF!
HFF!
HAFF!
HAAA!
ぱっ
BA (SWISH)
HFF...
HFF...
P-PLEASE!
LET ME GO...!

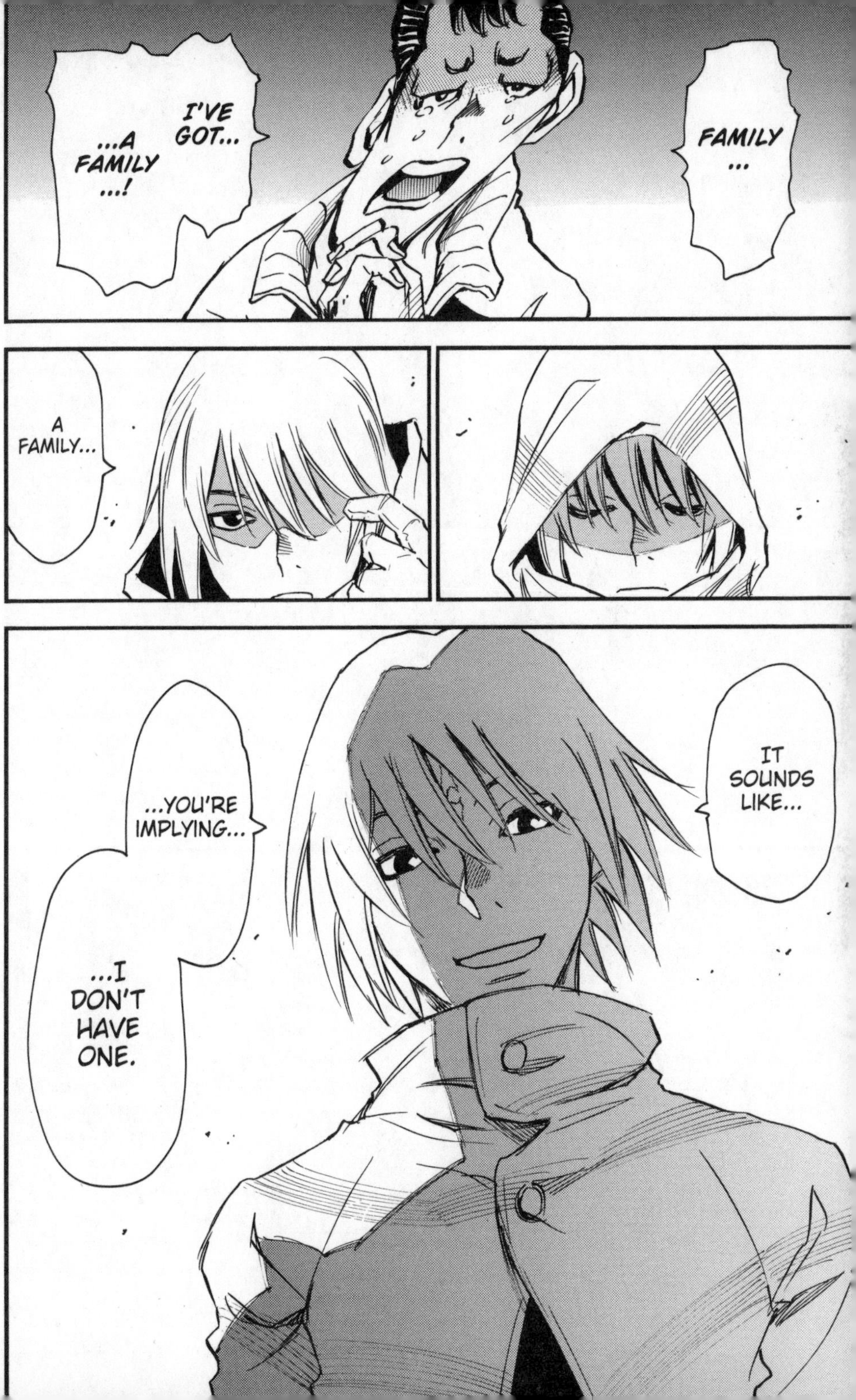
FAMILY...
I'VE GOT... ...A FAMILY ...!
A FAMILY...
IT SOUNDS LIKE...
...YOU'RE IMPLYING...
...I DON'T HAVE ONE.

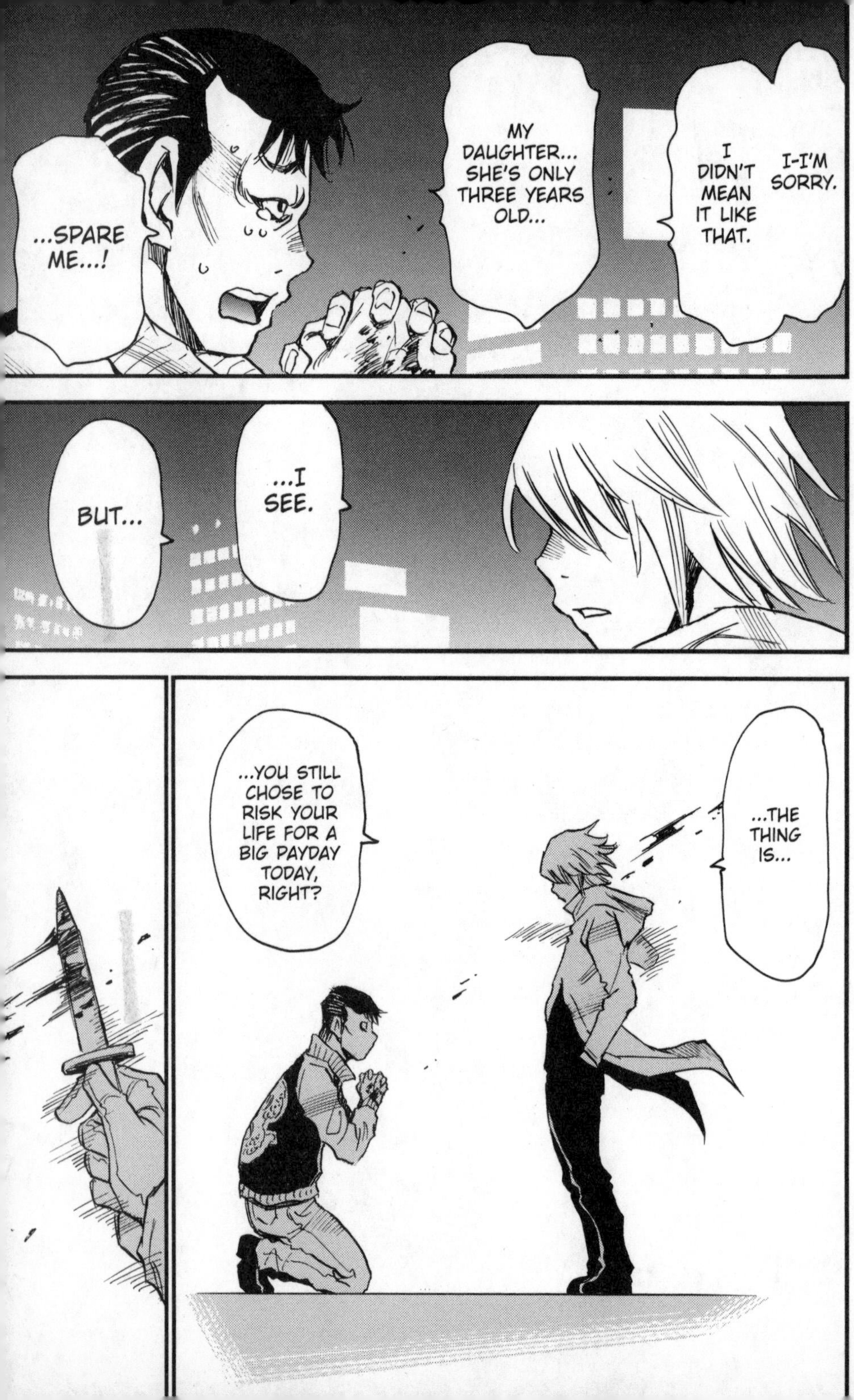
I-I'M SORRY.
I DIDN'T MEAN IT LIKE THAT.
MY DAUGHTER... SHE'S ONLY THREE YEARS OLD...
...SPARE ME...!
...I SEE.
BUT...
...THE THING IS...
...YOU STILL CHOSE TO RISK YOUR LIFE FOR A BIG PAYDAY TODAY, RIGHT?

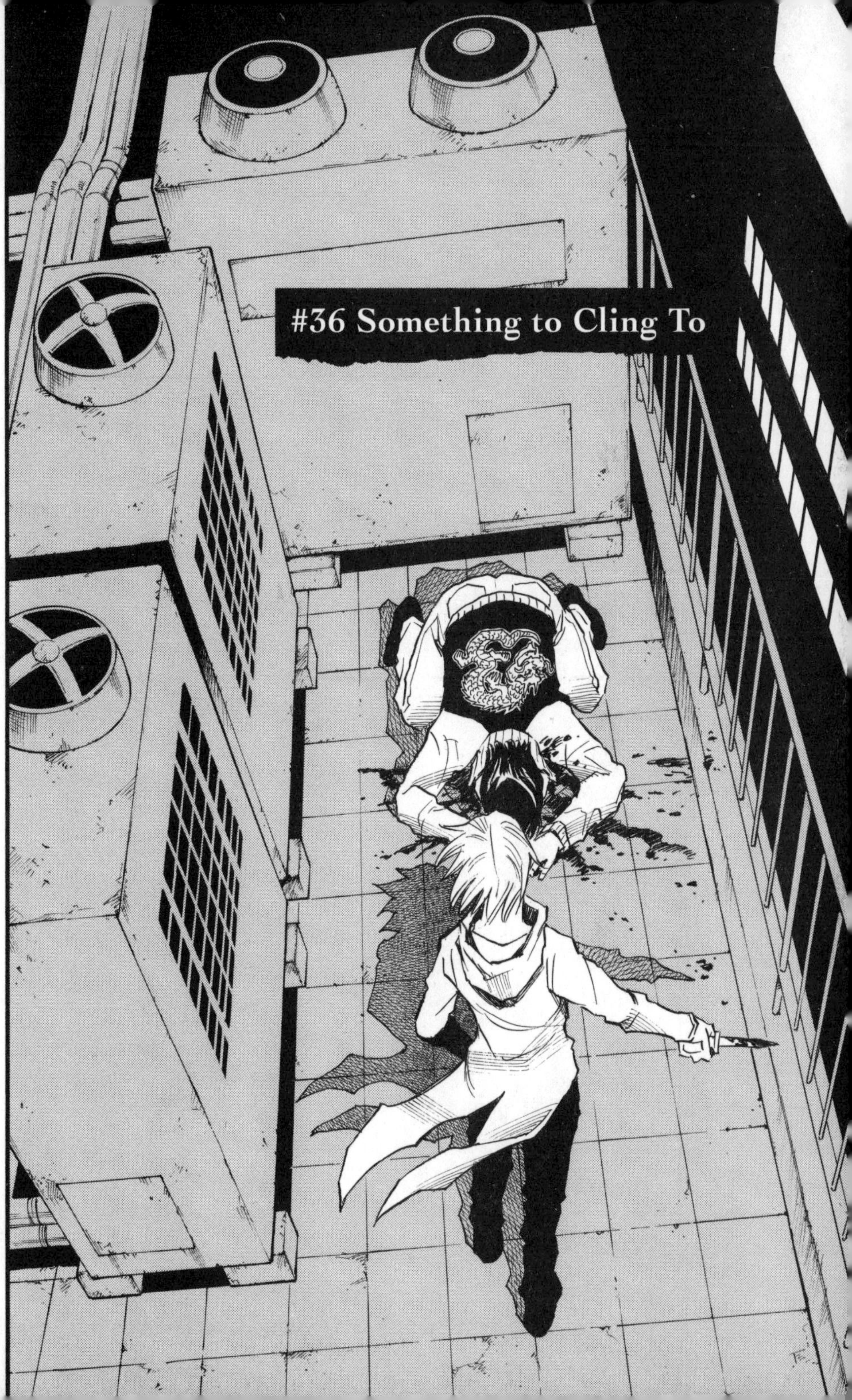
#36 Something to Cling To

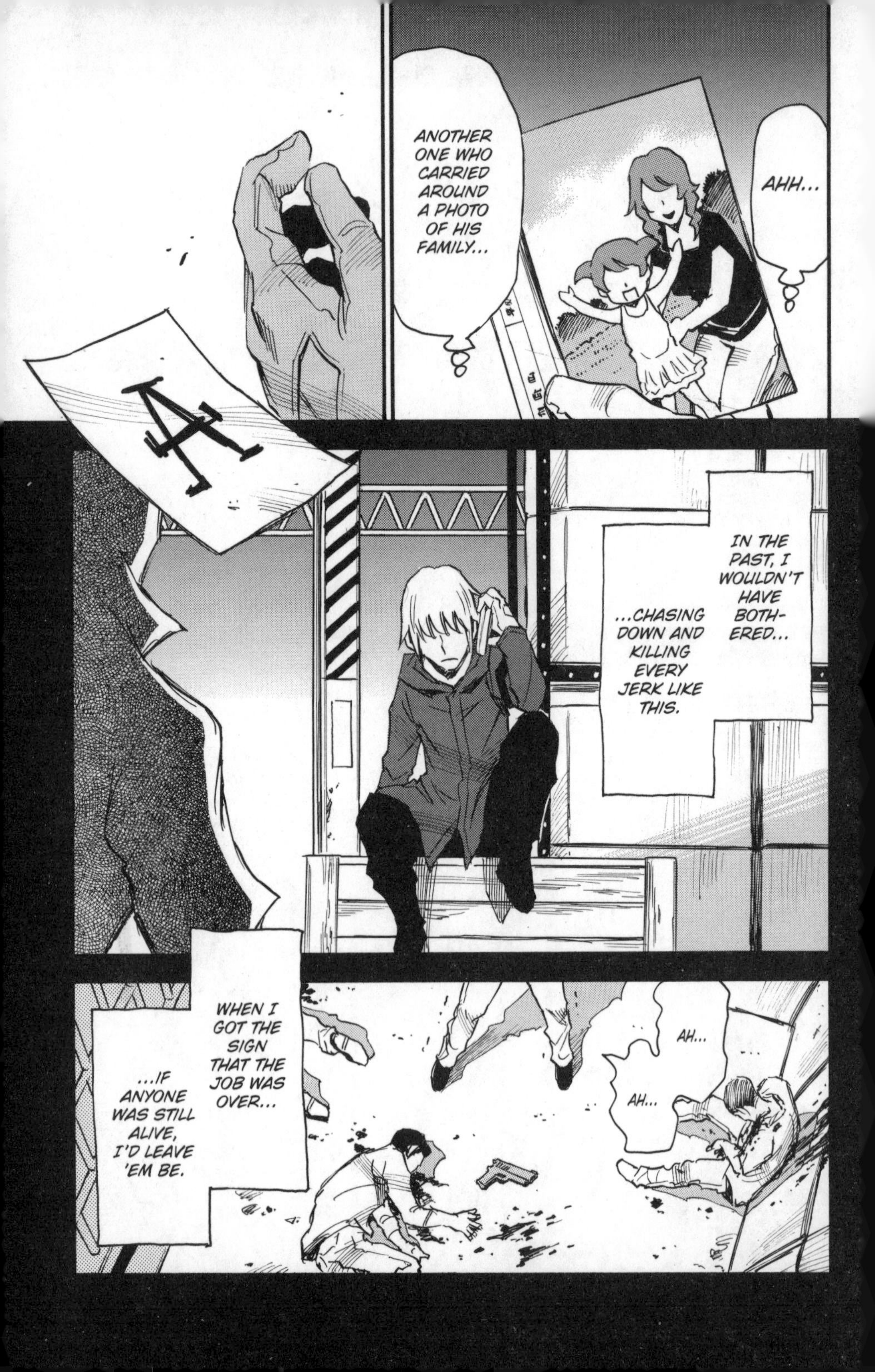
AHH...
ANOTHER ONE WHO CARRIED AROUND A PHOTO OF HIS FAMILY...
IN THE PAST, I WOULDN'T HAVE BOTH-ERED...
...CHASING DOWN AND KILLING EVERY JERK LIKE THIS.
AH...
AH...
WHEN I GOT THE SIGN THAT THE JOB WAS OVER...
...IF ANYONE WAS STILL ALIVE, I'D LEAVE 'EM BE.

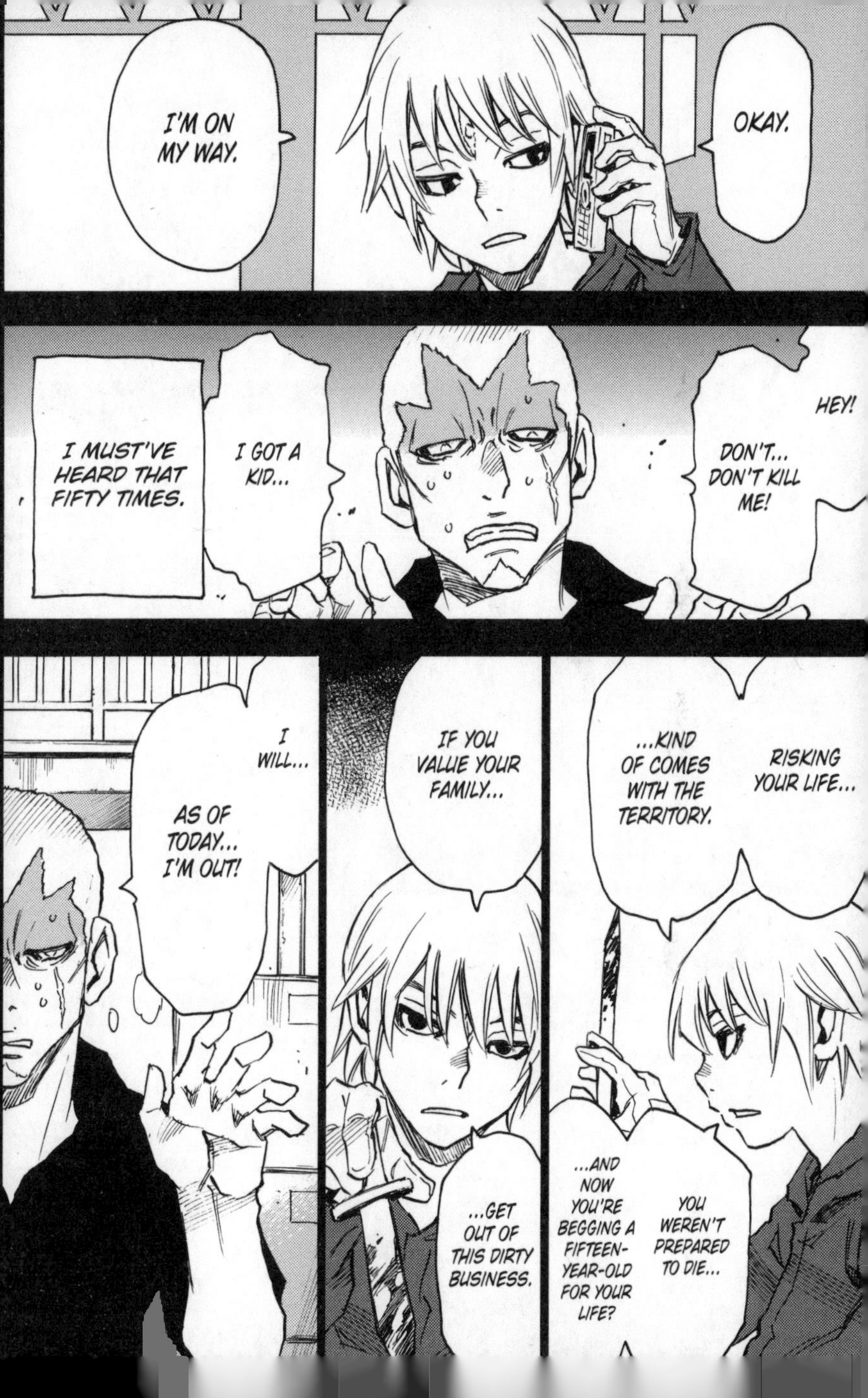
OKAY.
I'M ON MY WAY.
HEY!
DON'T... DON'T KILL ME!
I GOT A KID...
I MUST'VE HEARD THAT FIFTY TIMES.
RISKING YOUR LIFE...
...KIND OF COMES WITH THE TERRITORY.
YOU WEREN'T PREPARED TO DIE...
...AND NOW YOU'RE BEGGING A FIFTEEN-YEAR-OLD FOR YOUR LIFE?
IF YOU VALUE YOUR FAMILY...
...GET OUT OF THIS DIRTY BUSINESS.
I WILL...
AS OF TODAY... I'M OUT!

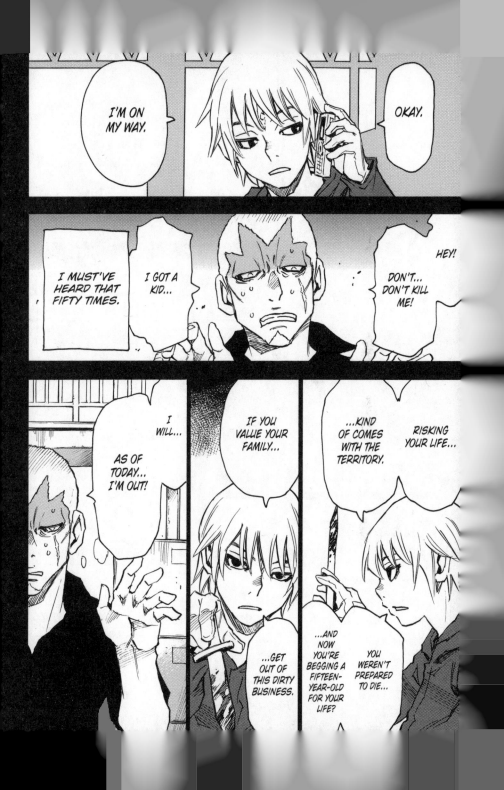

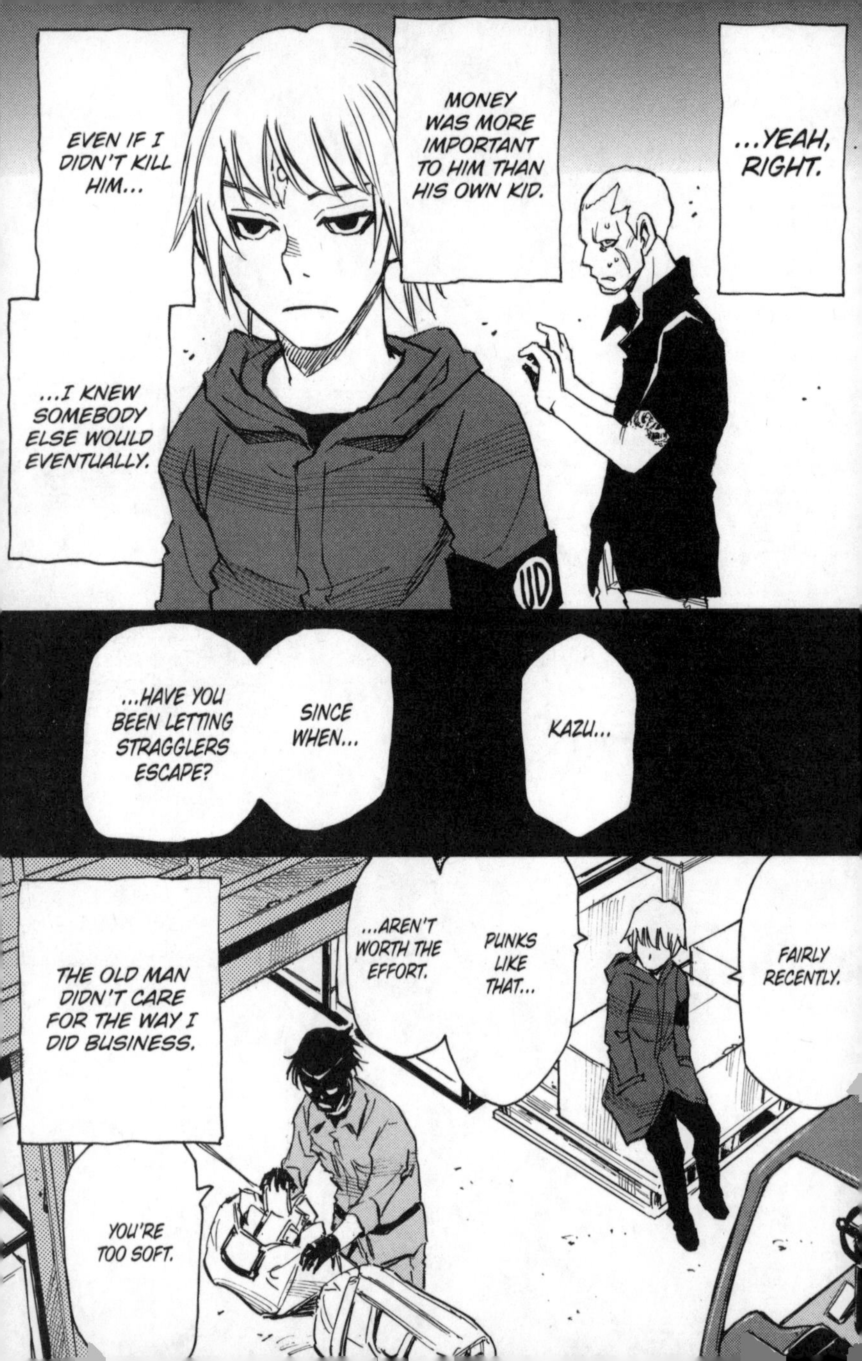
...YEAH, RIGHT.
MONEY WAS MORE IMPORTANT TO HIM THAN HIS OWN KID.
EVEN IF I DIDN'T KILL HIM...
...I KNEW SOMEBODY ELSE WOULD EVENTUALLY.
KAZU...
SINCE WHEN...
...HAVE YOU BEEN LETTING STRAGGLERS ESCAPE?
FAIRLY RECENTLY.
PUNKS LIKE THAT...
...AREN'T WORTH THE EFFORT.
THE OLD MAN DIDN'T CARE FOR THE WAY I DID BUSINESS.
YOU'RE TOO SOFT.

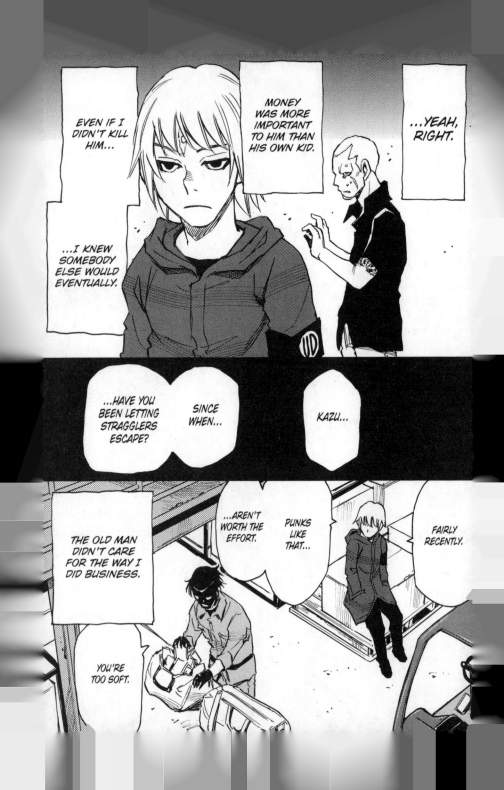

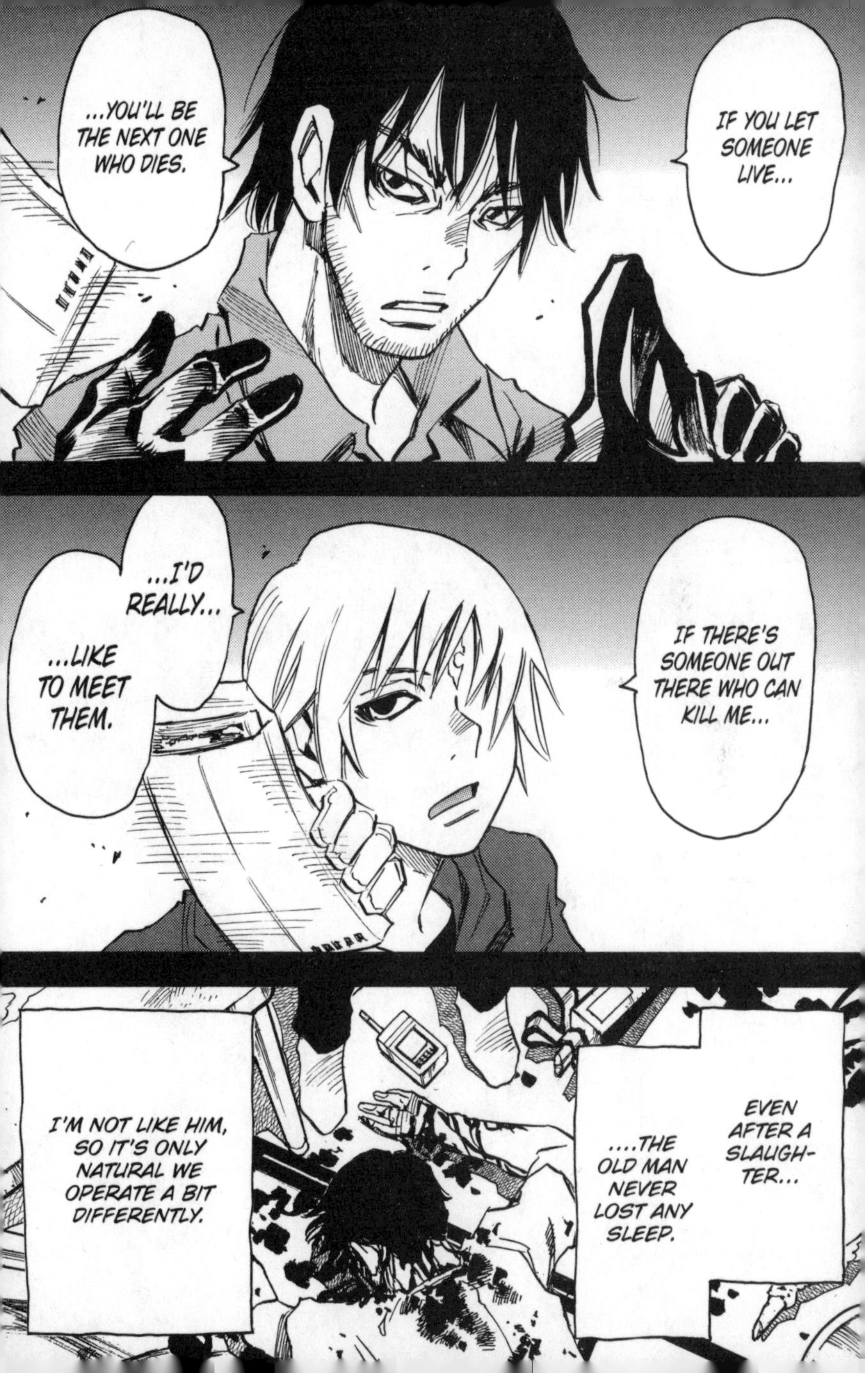
IF YOU LET SOMEONE LIVE...
...YOU'LL BE THE NEXT ONE WHO DIES.
IF THERE'S SOMEONE OUT THERE WHO CAN KILL ME...
...I'D REALLY...
...LIKE TO MEET THEM.
EVEN AFTER A SLAUGH-TER...
....THE OLD MAN NEVER LOST ANY SLEEP.
I'M NOT LIKE HIM, SO IT'S ONLY NATURAL WE OPERATE A BIT DIFFERENTLY.

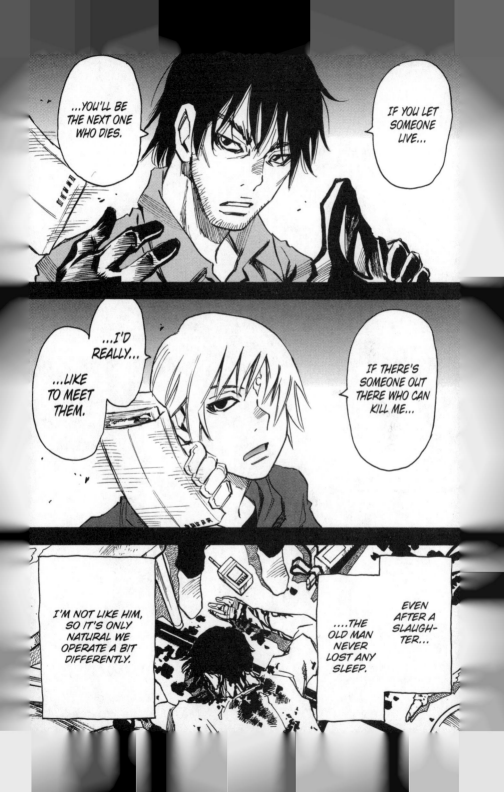

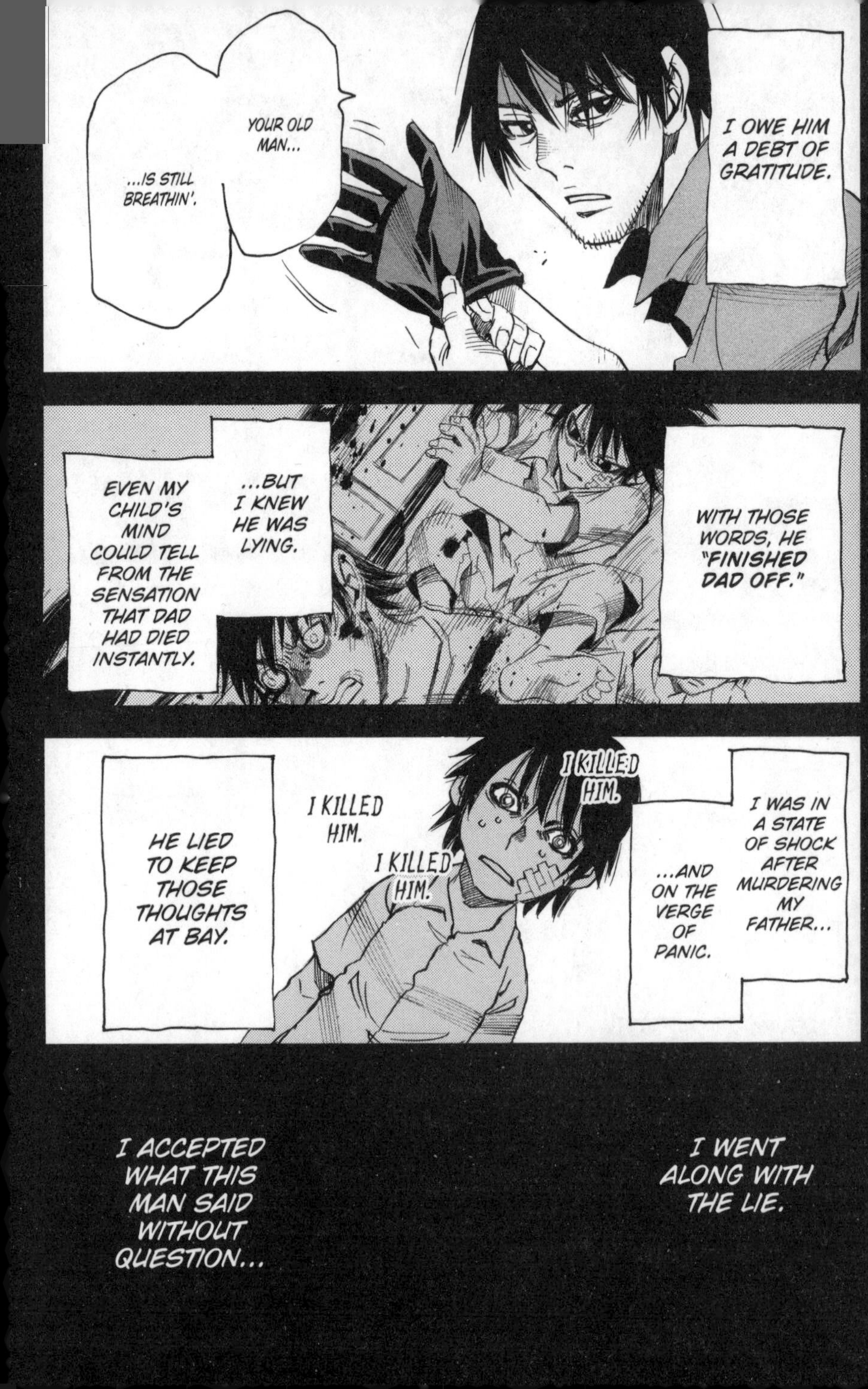
I OWE HIM A DEBT OF GRATITUDE.
YOUR OLD MAN...
...IS STILL BREATHIN'.
WITH THOSE WORDS, HE "FINISHED DAD OFF."
...BUT I KNEW HE WAS LYING.
EVEN MY CHILD'S MIND COULD TELL FROM THE SENSATION THAT DAD HAD DIED INSTANTLY.
I WAS IN A STATE OF SHOCK AFTER MURDERING MY FATHER...
...AND ON THE VERGE OF PANIC.
I KILLED HIM.
I KILLED HIM.
I KILLED HIM.
HE LIED TO KEEP THOSE THOUGHTS AT BAY.
I WENT ALONG WITH THE LIE.
I ACCEPTED WHAT THIS MAN SAID WITHOUT QUESTION...

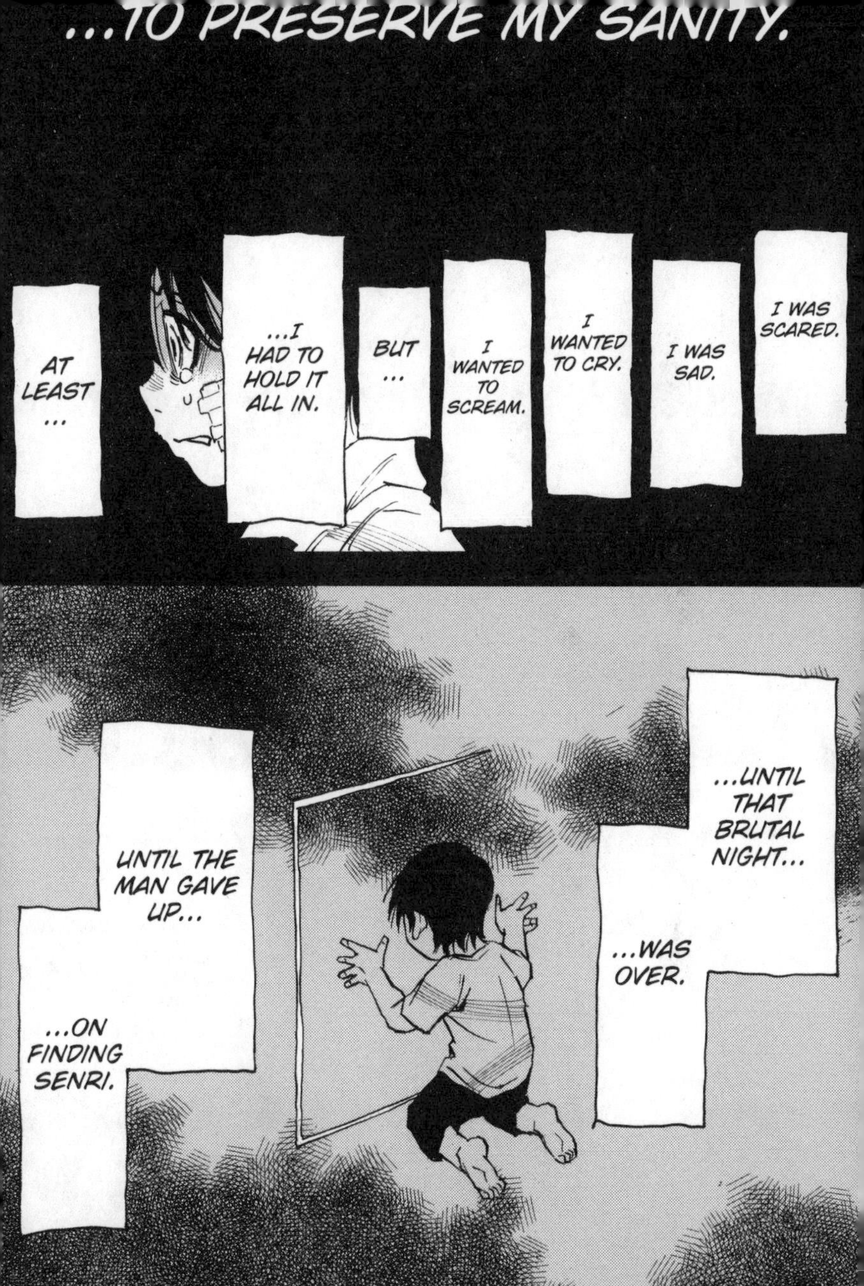
...TO PRESERVE MY SANITY.
I WAS SCARED.
I WAS SAD.
I WANTED TO CRY.
I WANTED TO SCREAM.
BUT...
...I HAD TO HOLD IT ALL IN.
AT LEAST...
...UNTIL THAT BRUTAL NIGHT...
...WAS OVER.
UNTIL THE MAN GAVE UP...
...ON FINDING SENRI.

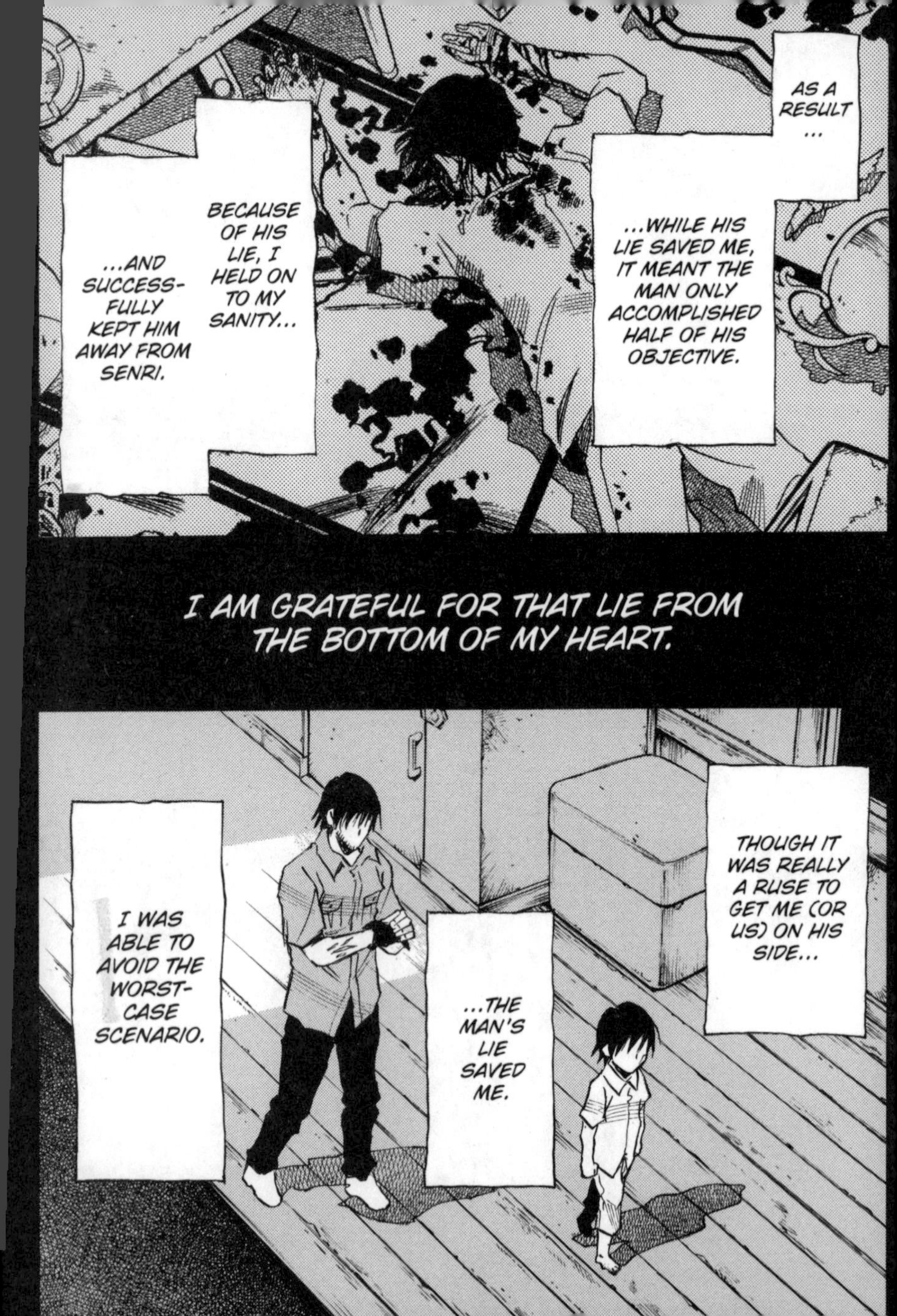
AS A RESULT...
...WHILE HIS LIE SAVED ME, IT MEANT THE MAN ONLY ACCOMPLISHED HALF OF HIS OBJECTIVE.
BECAUSE OF HIS LIE, I HELD ON TO MY SANITY...
...AND SUCCESSFULLY KEPT HIM AWAY FROM SENRI.
I AM GRATEFUL FOR THAT LIE FROM THE BOTTOM OF MY HEART.
THOUGH IT WAS REALLY A RUSE TO GET ME (OR US) ON HIS SIDE...
...THE MAN'S LIE SAVED ME.
I WAS ABLE TO AVOID THE WORST-CASE SCENARIO.

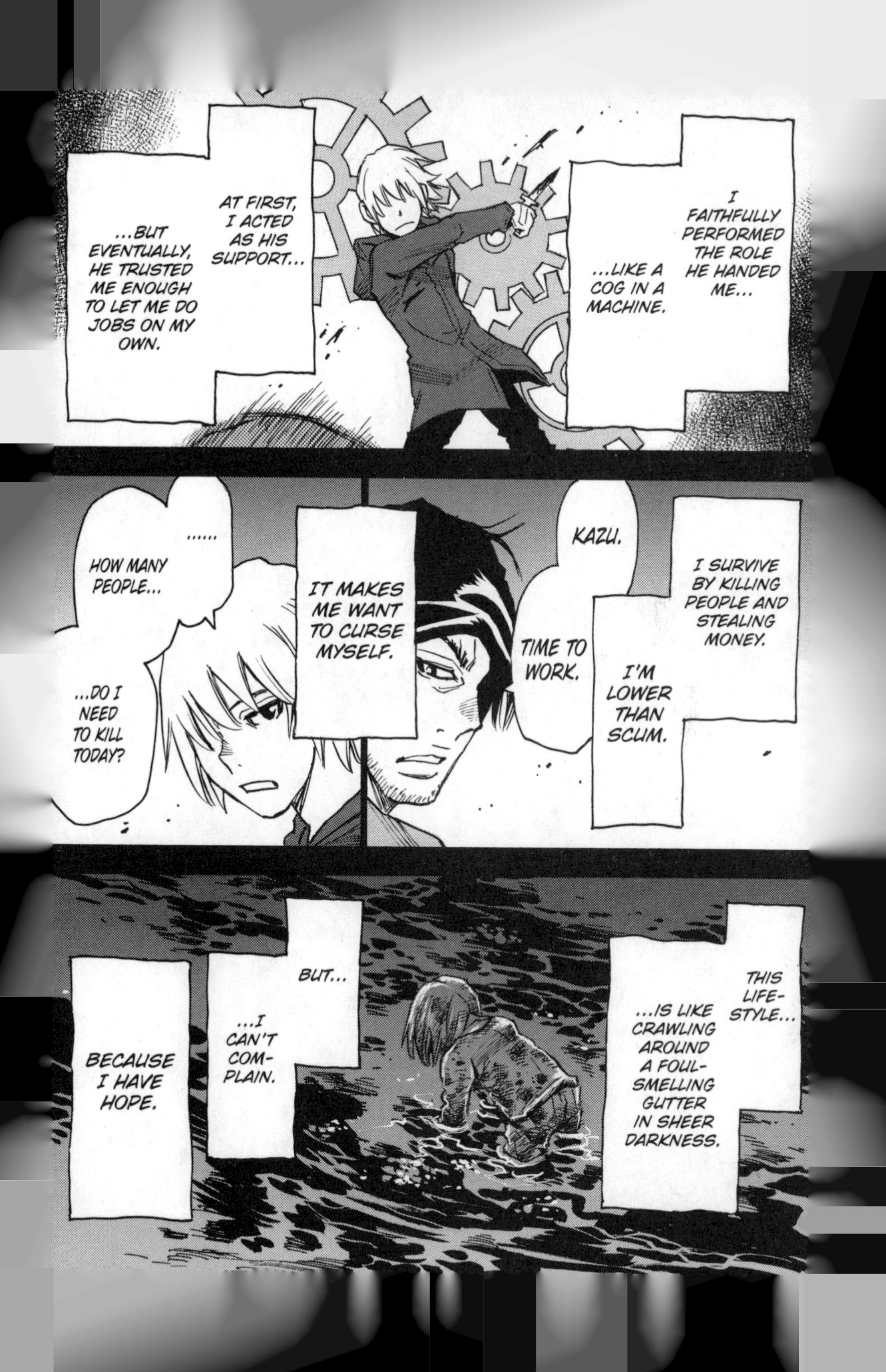
I FAITHFULLY PERFORMED THE ROLE HE HANDED ME...
...LIKE A COG IN A MACHINE.
AT FIRST, I ACTED AS HIS SUPPORT...
...BUT EVENTUALLY, HE TRUSTED ME ENOUGH TO LET ME DO JOBS ON MY OWN.
I SURVIVE BY KILLING PEOPLE AND STEALING MONEY.
I'M LOWER THAN SCUM.
KAZU.
TIME TO WORK.
IT MAKES ME WANT TO CURSE MYSELF.
......
HOW MANY PEOPLE...
...DO I NEED TO KILL TODAY?
THIS LIFE-STYLE...
...IS LIKE CRAWLING AROUND A FOUL-SMELLING GUTTER IN SHEER DARKNESS.
BUT...
...I CAN'T COM-PLAIN.
BECAUSE I HAVE HOPE.

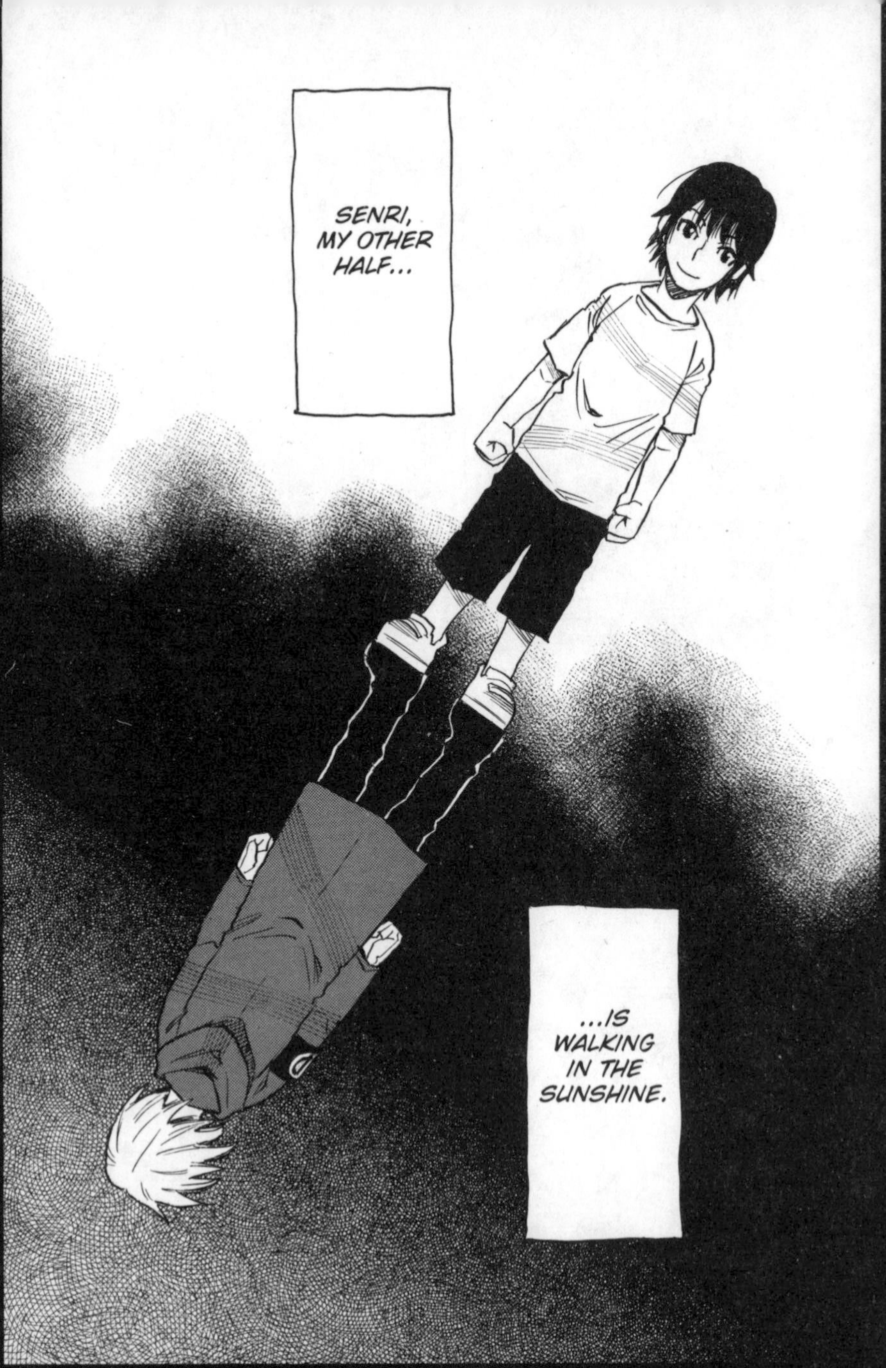
SENRI, MY OTHER HALF...
...IS WALKING IN THE SUNSHINE.

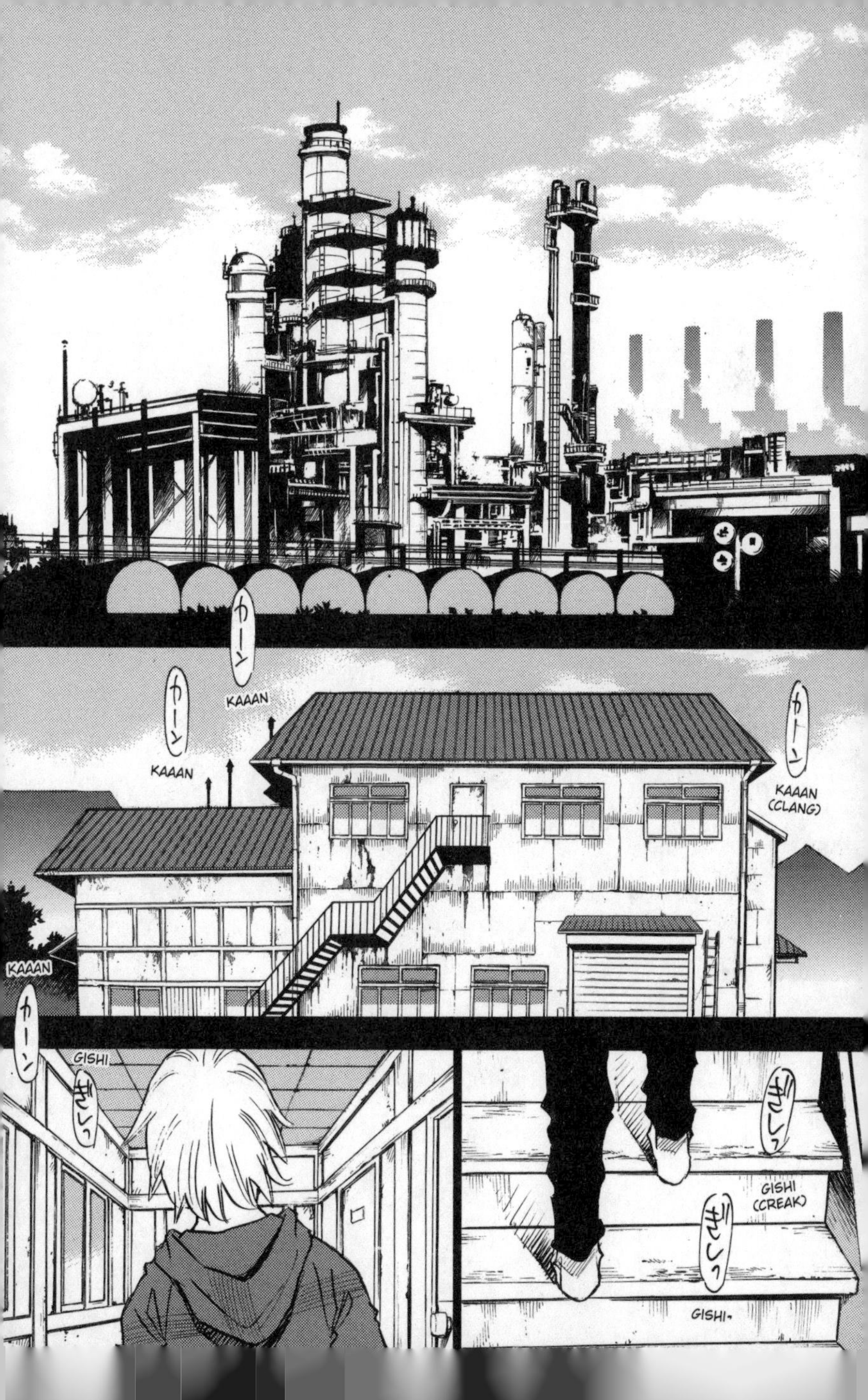
かーン
KAAAN (CLANG)
かーン
KAAAN
かーン
KAAAN
KAAAN
かーン
ぎしっ
GISHI (CREAK)
ぎしっ
GISHI
GISHI
ぎしっ

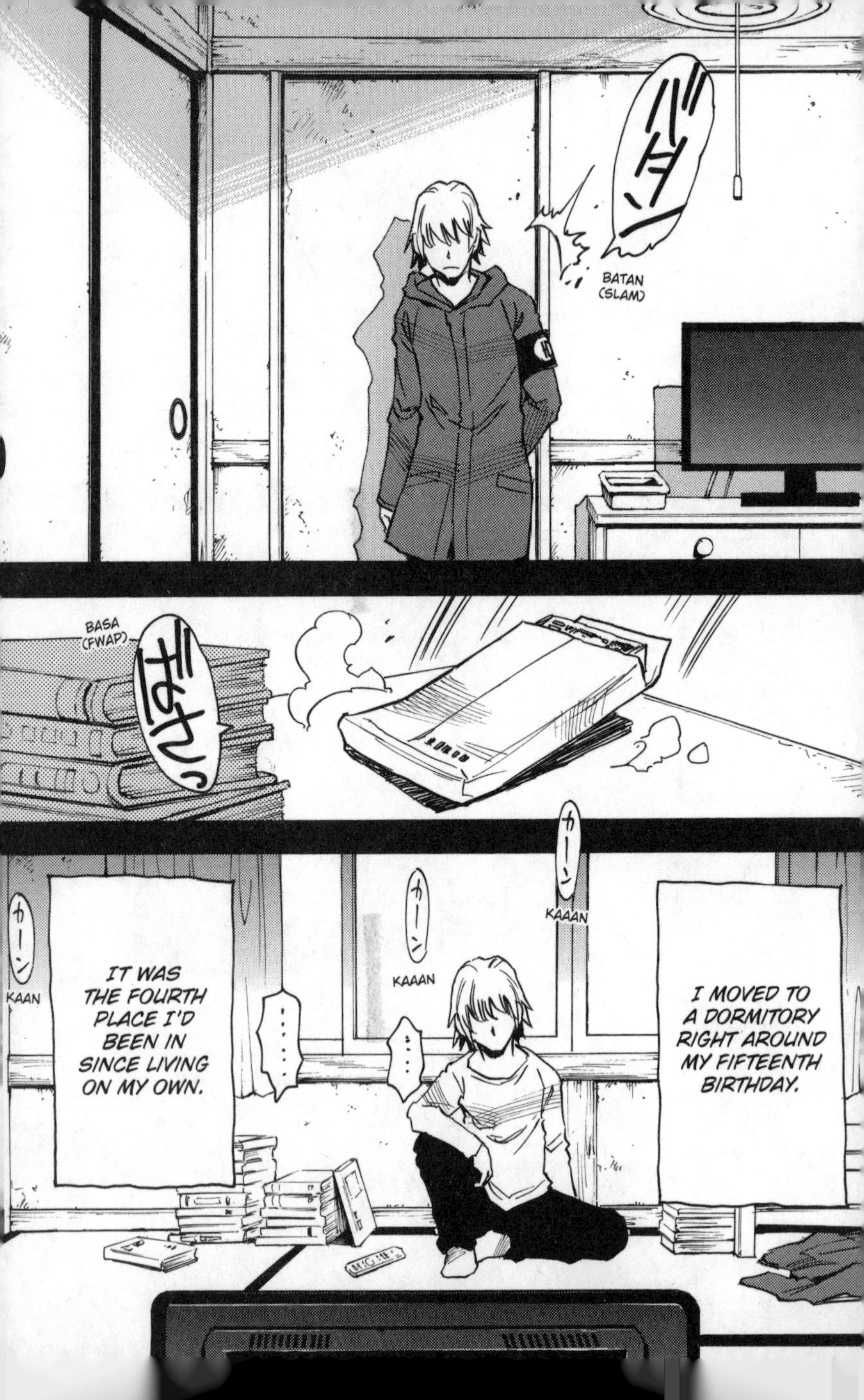
バタン
BATAN (SLAM)
ばさっ
BASA (FWAP)
I MOVED TO A DORMITORY RIGHT AROUND MY FIFTEENTH BIRTHDAY.
カーン
KAAAN
……
カーン
KAAAN
……
カーン
KAAN
IT WAS THE FOURTH PLACE I'D BEEN IN SINCE LIVING ON MY OWN.

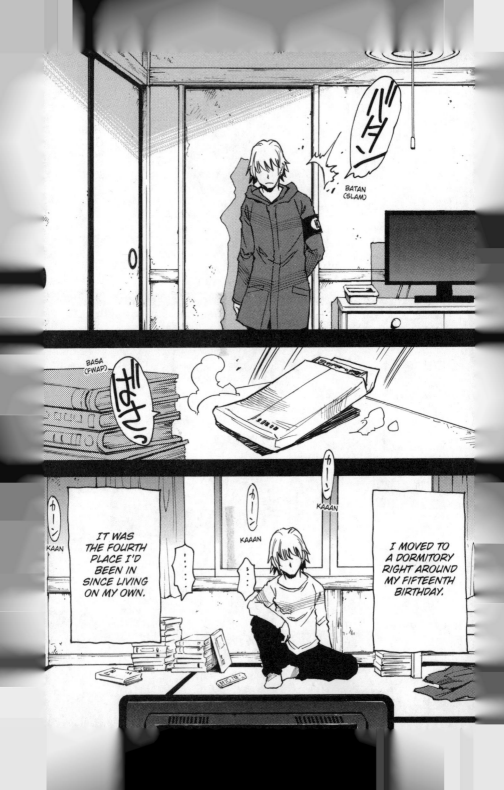

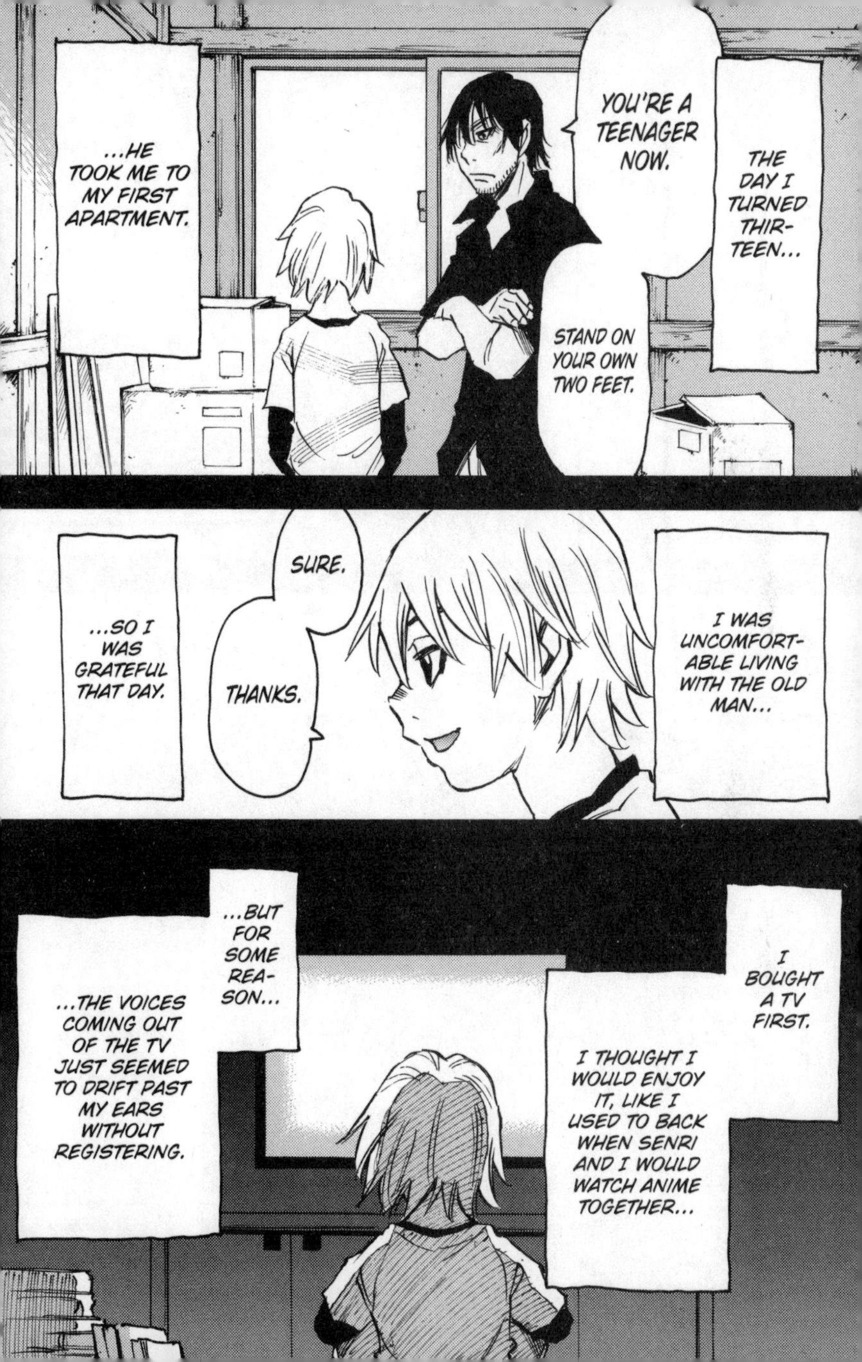
THE DAY I TURNED THIRTEEN...
YOU'RE A TEENAGER NOW.
STAND ON YOUR OWN TWO FEET.
...HE TOOK ME TO MY FIRST APARTMENT.
I WAS UNCOMFORTABLE LIVING WITH THE OLD MAN...
SURE.
THANKS.
...SO I WAS GRATEFUL THAT DAY.
I BOUGHT A TV FIRST.
I THOUGHT I WOULD ENJOY IT, LIKE I USED TO BACK WHEN SENRI AND I WOULD WATCH ANIME TOGETHER...
...BUT FOR SOME REASON...
...THE VOICES COMING OUT OF THE TV JUST SEEMED TO DRIFT PAST MY EARS WITHOUT REGISTERING.

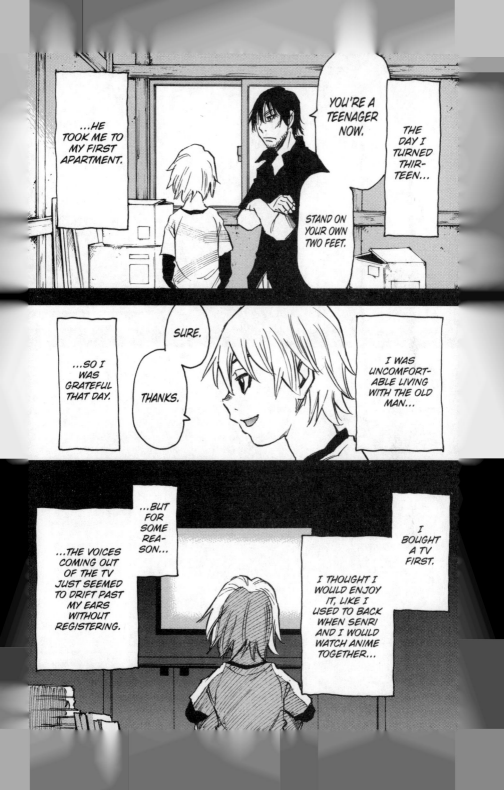

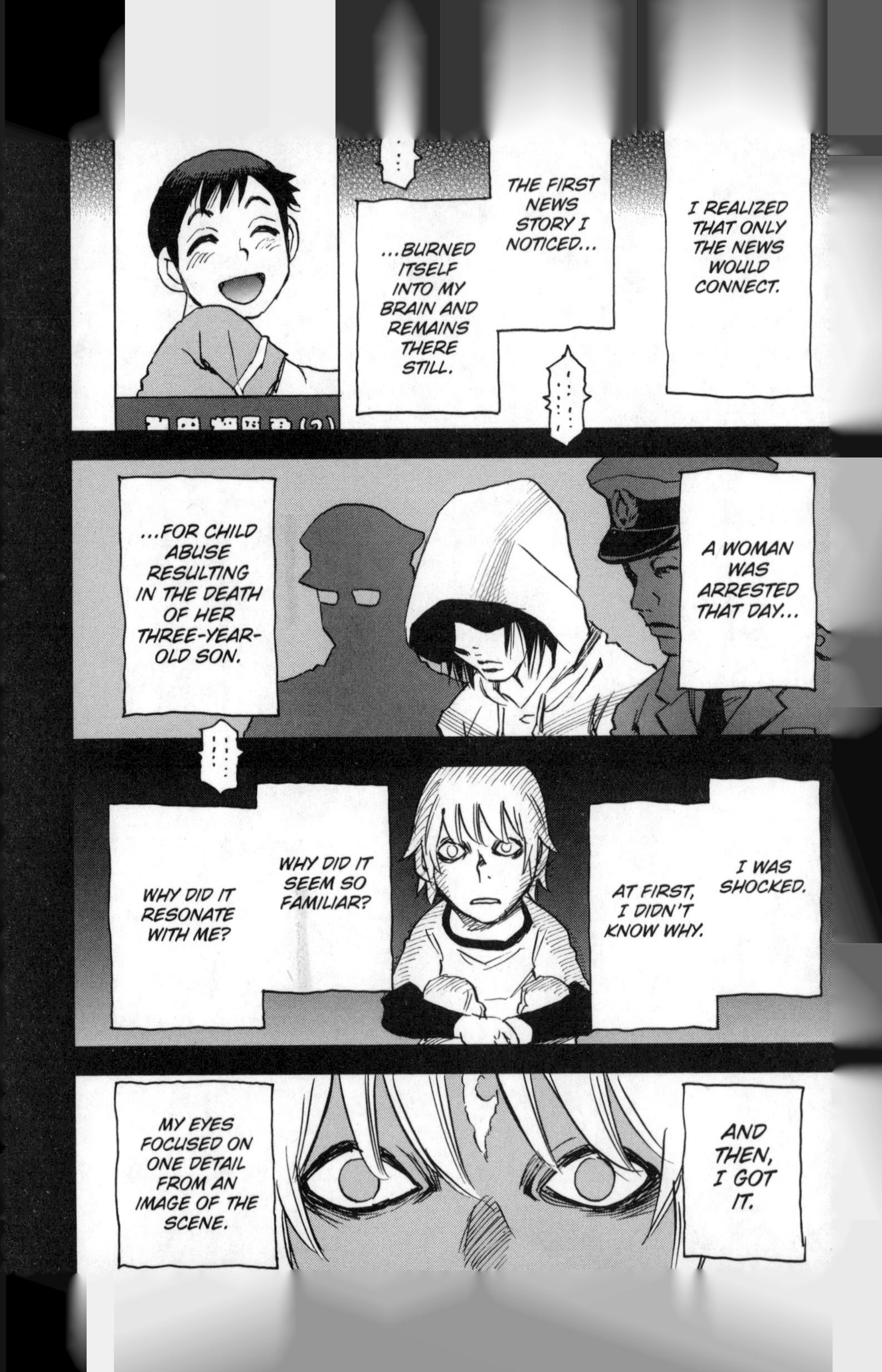
I REALIZED THAT ONLY THE NEWS WOULD CONNECT.
THE FIRST NEWS STORY I NOTICED...
...BURNED ITSELF INTO MY BRAIN AND REMAINS THERE STILL.
A WOMAN WAS ARRESTED THAT DAY...
...FOR CHILD ABUSE RESULTING IN THE DEATH OF HER THREE-YEAR-OLD SON.
I WAS SHOCKED.
AT FIRST, I DIDN'T KNOW WHY.
WHY DID IT SEEM SO FAMILIAR?
WHY DID IT RESONATE WITH ME?
AND THEN, I GOT IT.
MY EYES FOCUSED ON ONE DETAIL FROM AN IMAGE OF THE SCENE.

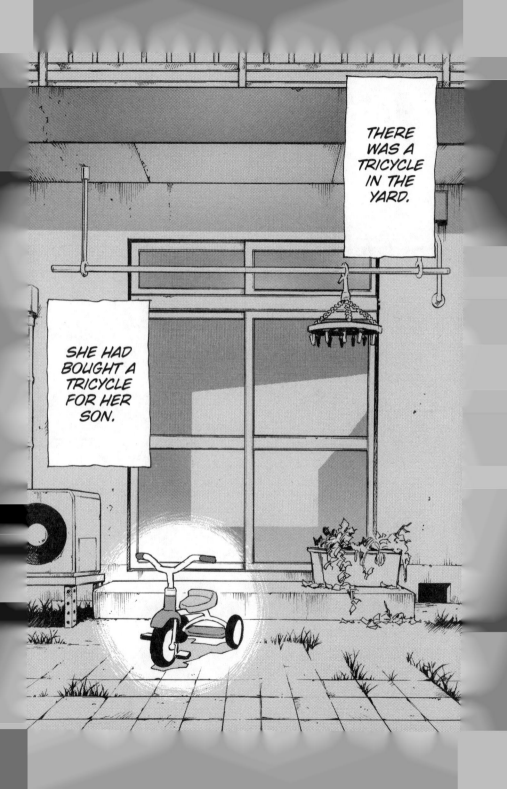

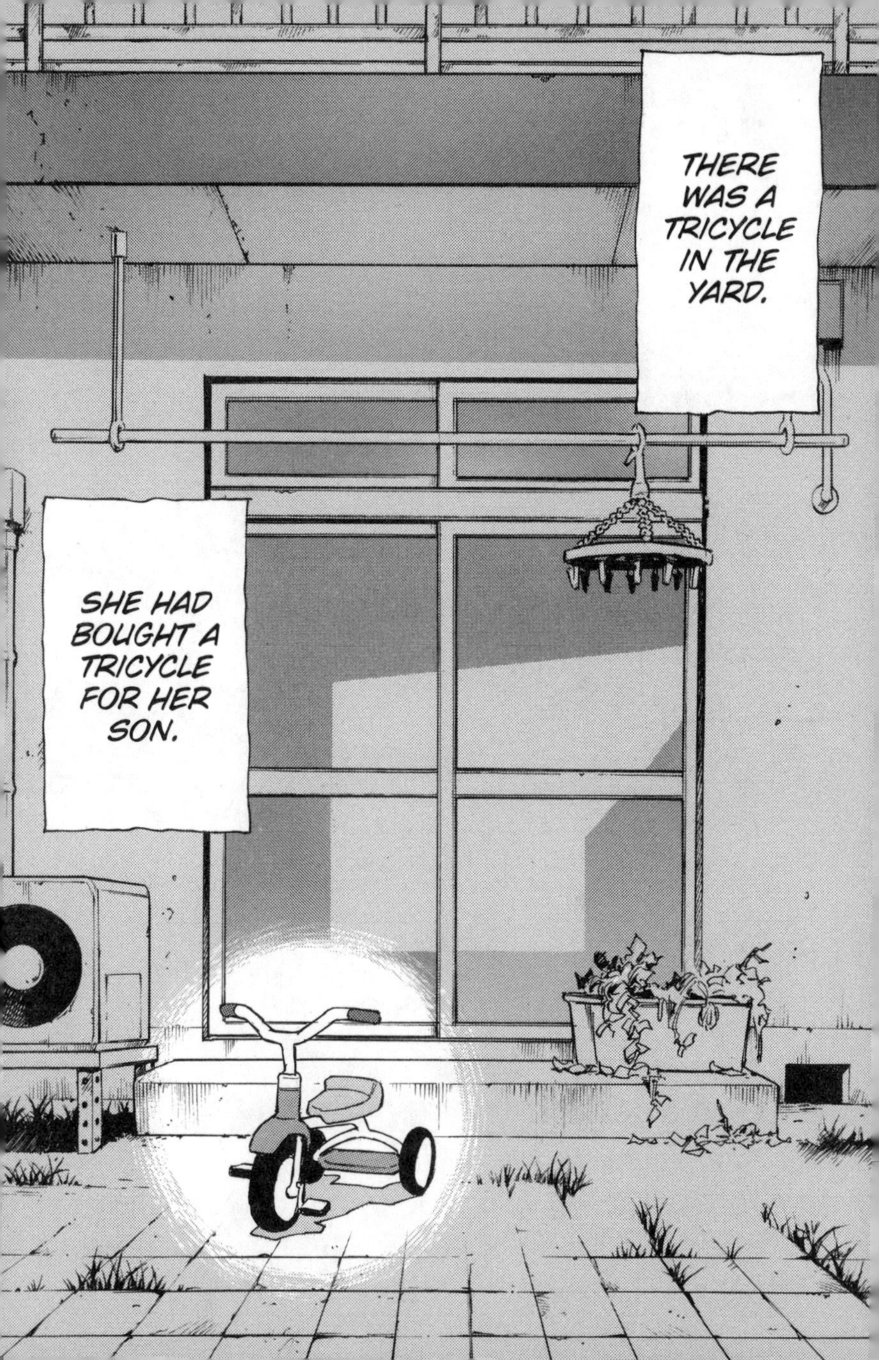
THERE WAS A TRICYCLE IN THE YARD.
SHE HAD BOUGHT A TRICYCLE FOR HER SON.

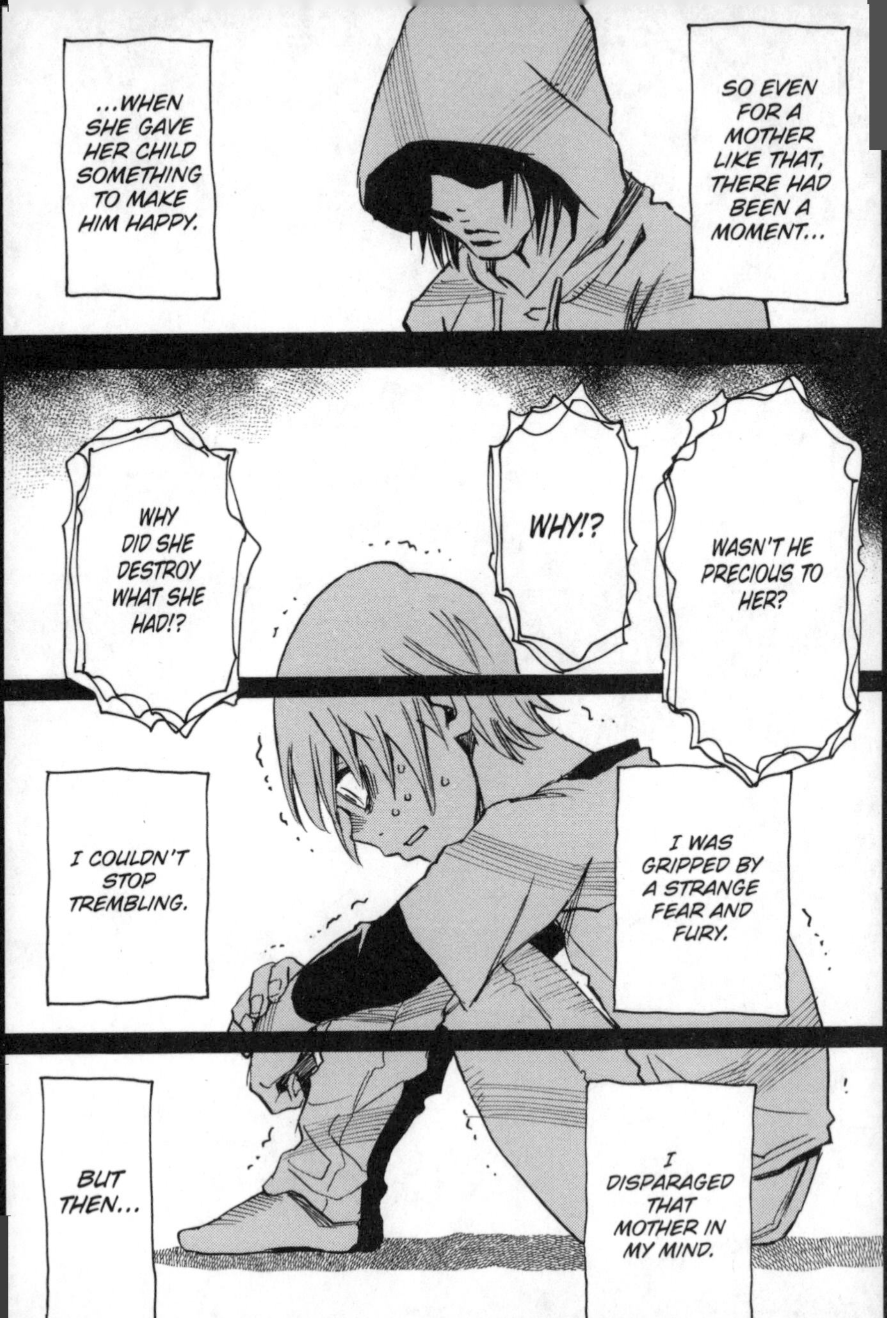
SO EVEN FOR A MOTHER LIKE THAT, THERE HAD BEEN A MOMENT...
...WHEN SHE GAVE HER CHILD SOMETHING TO MAKE HIM HAPPY.
WASN'T HE PRECIOUS TO HER?
WHY!?
WHY DID SHE DESTROY WHAT SHE HAD!?
I WAS GRIPPED BY A STRANGE FEAR AND FURY.
I COULDN'T STOP TREMBLING.
I DISPARAGED THAT MOTHER IN MY MIND.
BUT THEN...

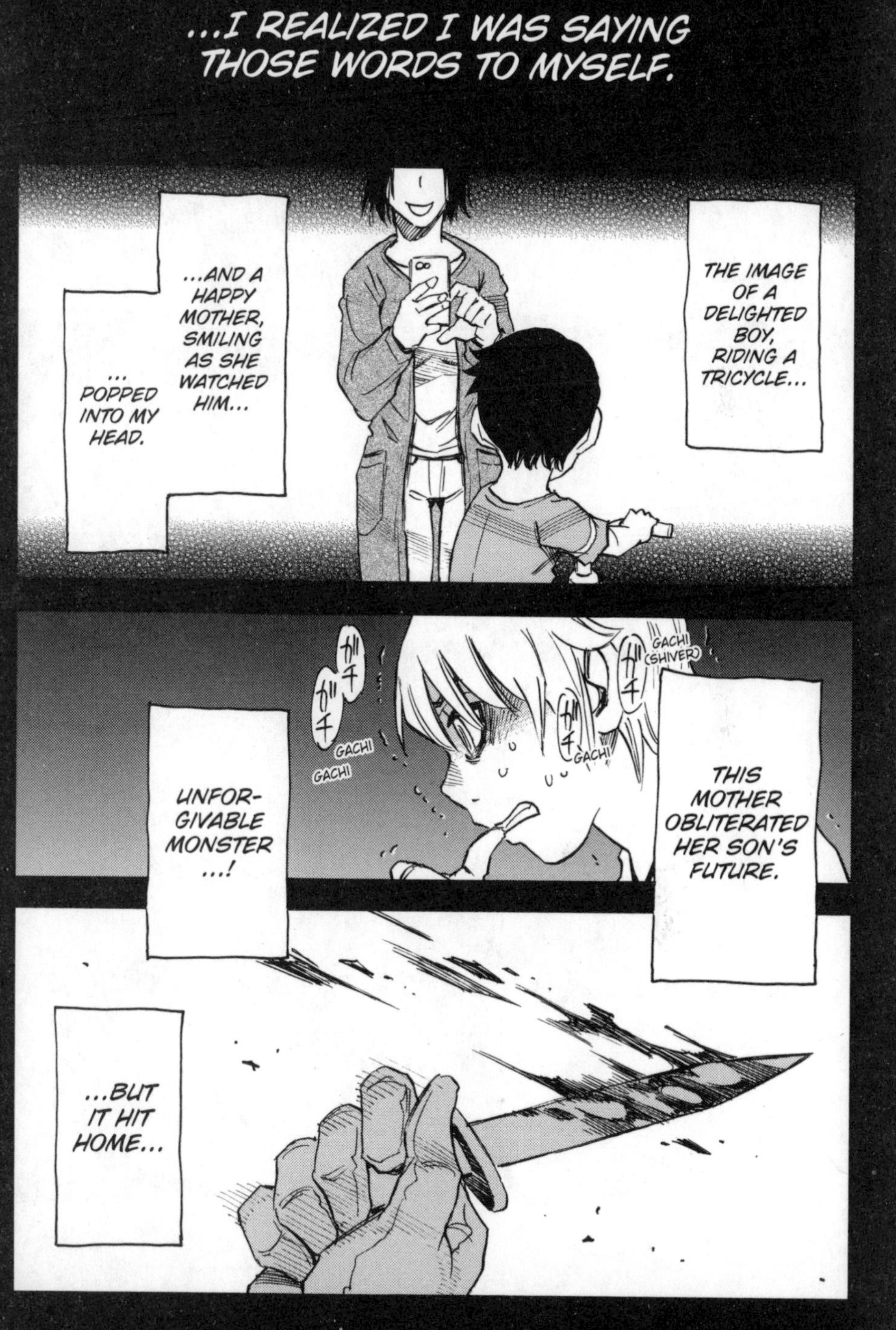
...I REALIZED I WAS SAYING THOSE WORDS TO MYSELF.
THE IMAGE OF A DELIGHTED BOY, RIDING A TRICYCLE...
...AND A HAPPY MOTHER, SMILING AS SHE WATCHED HIM...
...POPPED INTO MY HEAD.
ガチ GACHI (SHIVER)
ガチ GACHI
THIS MOTHER OBLITERATED HER SON'S FUTURE.
ガチガチ GACHI GACHI
UNFORGIVABLE MONSTER...!
...BUT IT HIT HOME...

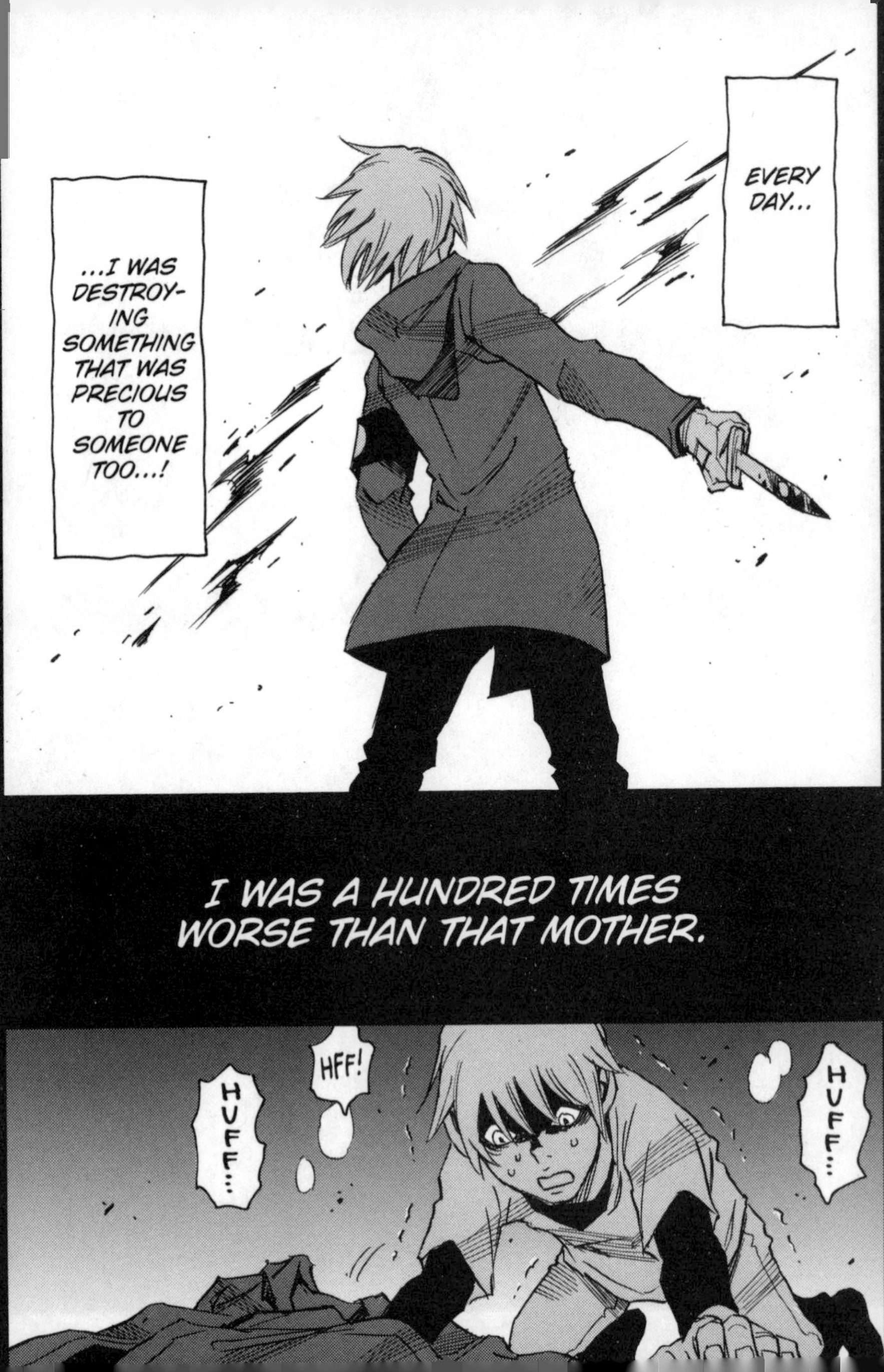
EVERY DAY...
...I WAS DESTROYING SOMETHING THAT WAS PRECIOUS TO SOMEONE TOO...!
I WAS A HUNDRED TIMES WORSE THAN THAT MOTHER.
HUFF...
HFF!
HUFF...

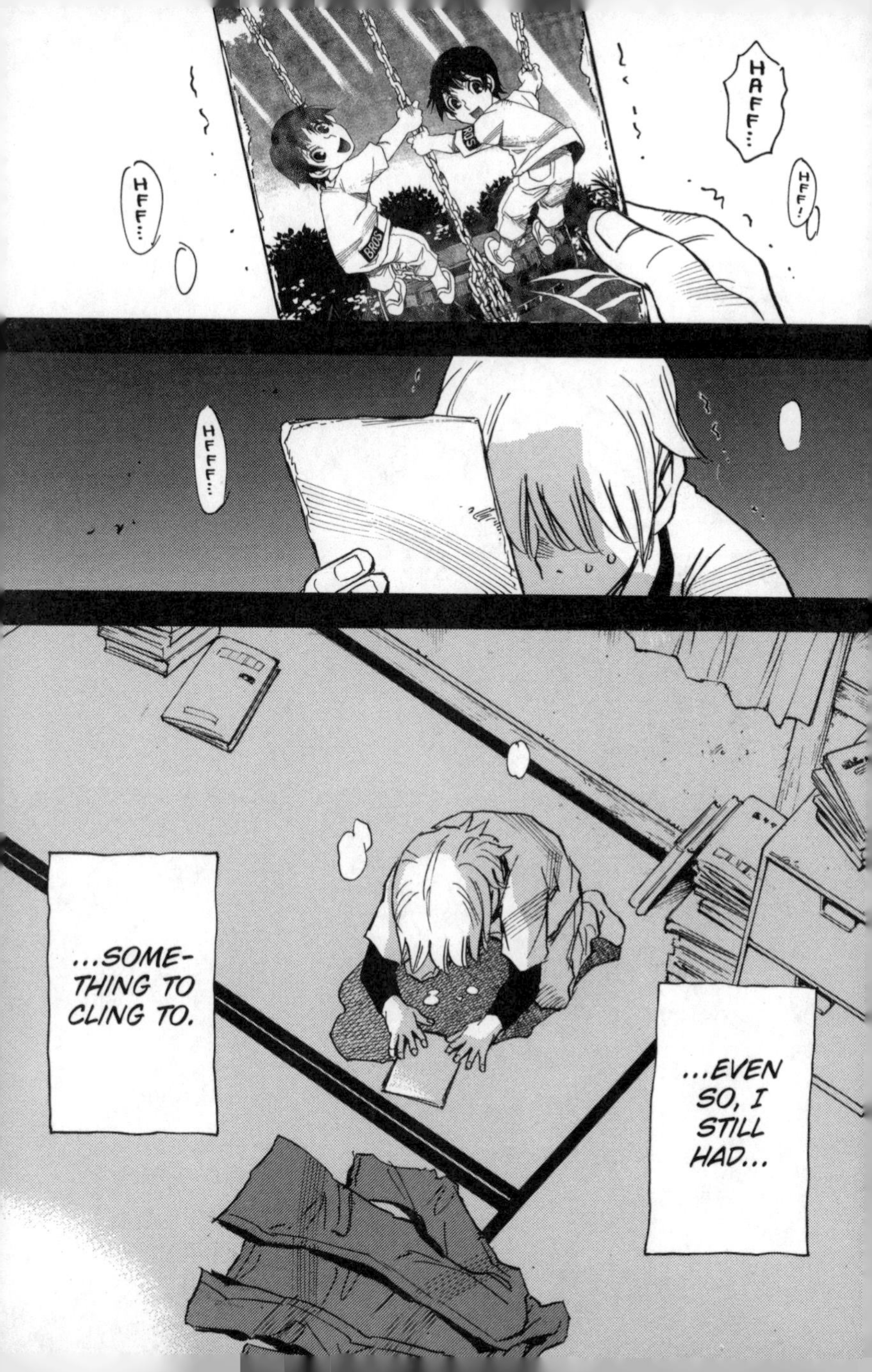
HAFF...
HFF!
HFF...
HFFF...
...EVEN SO, I STILL HAD...
...SOME-THING TO CLING TO.

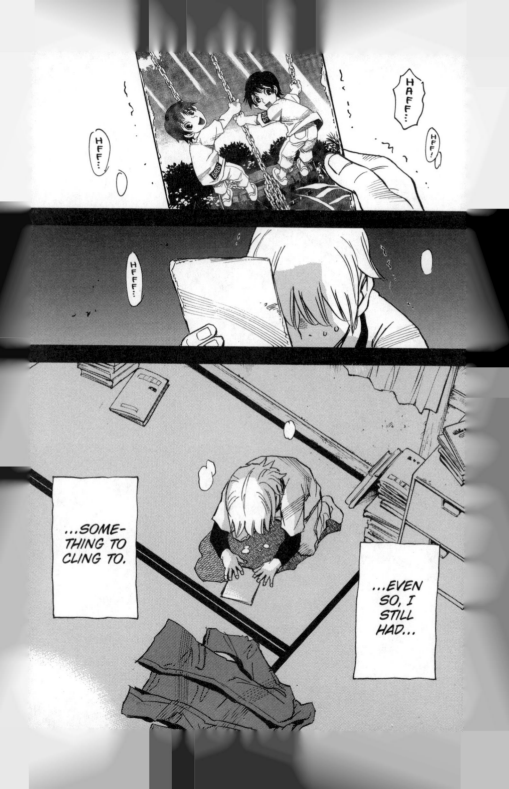

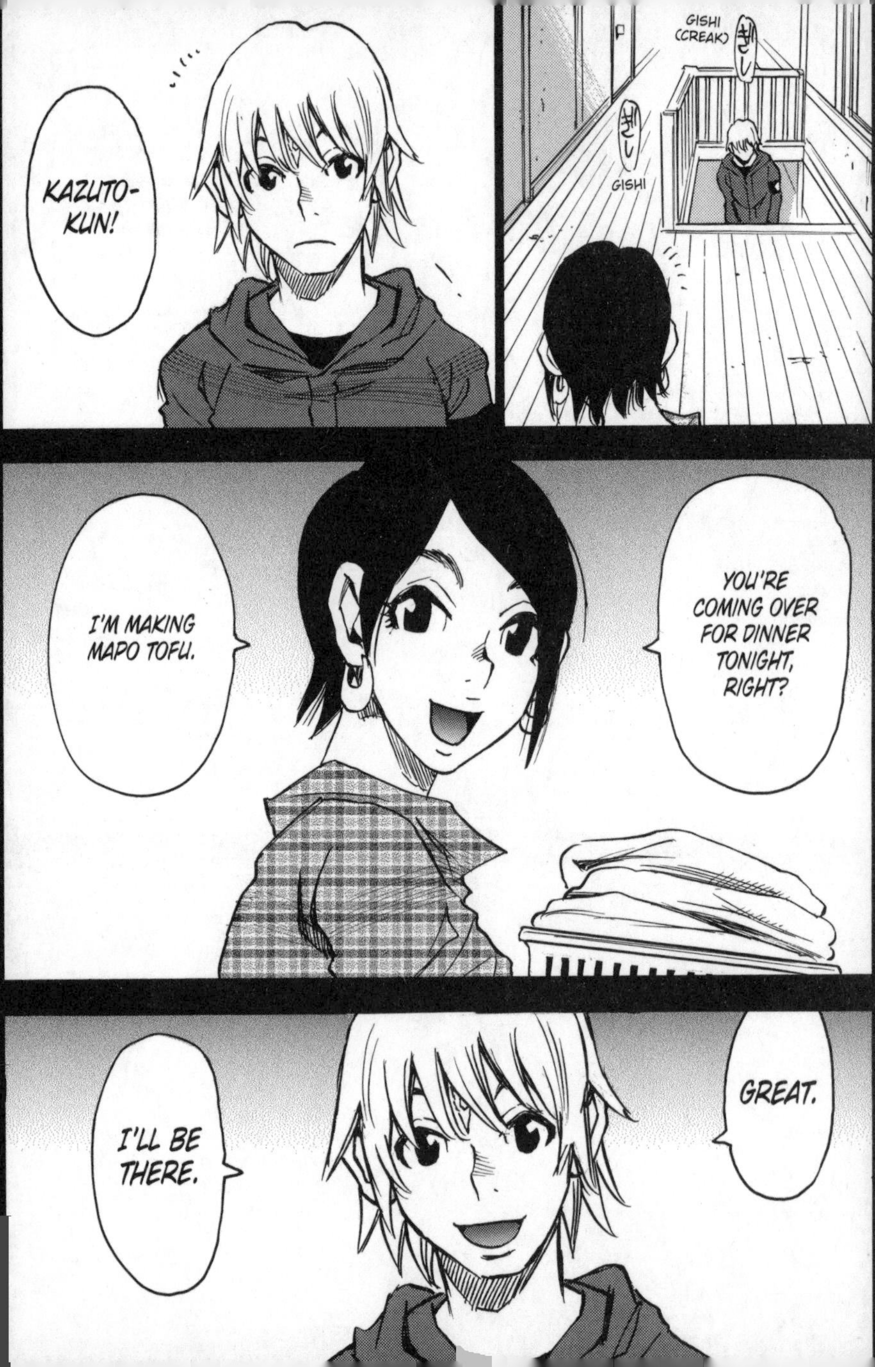
GISHI (CREAK)
きし
きし
GISHI
KAZUTO-KUN!
YOU'RE COMING OVER FOR DINNER TONIGHT, RIGHT?
I'M MAKING MAPO TOFU.
GREAT.
I'LL BE THERE.

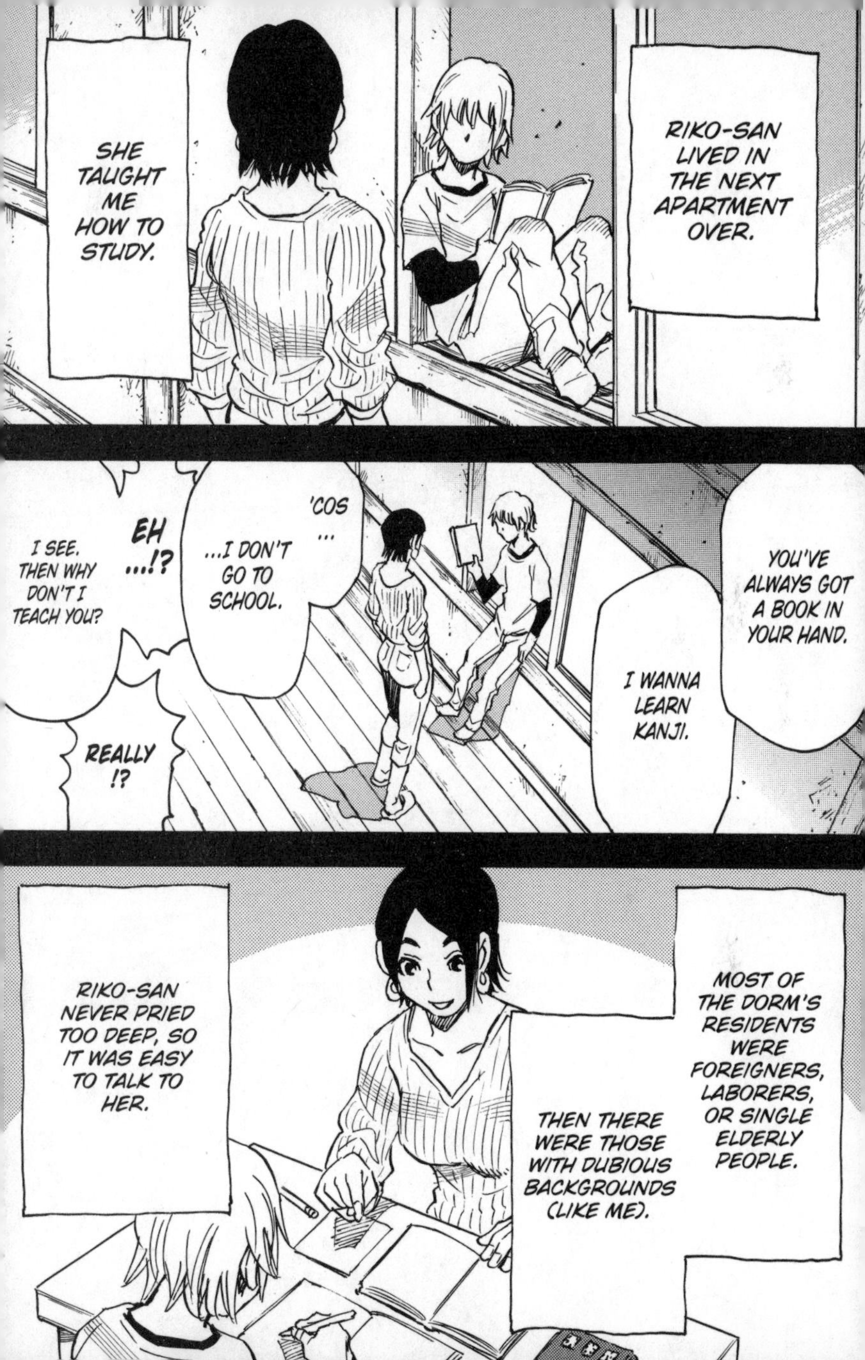
RIKO-SAN LIVED IN THE NEXT APARTMENT OVER.
SHE TAUGHT ME HOW TO STUDY.
YOU'VE ALWAYS GOT A BOOK IN YOUR HAND.
I WANNA LEARN KANJI.
'COS ...
...I DON'T GO TO SCHOOL.
EH ...!?
I SEE. THEN WHY DON'T I TEACH YOU?
REALLY !?
MOST OF THE DORM'S RESIDENTS WERE FOREIGNERS, LABORERS, OR SINGLE ELDERLY PEOPLE.
THEN THERE WERE THOSE WITH DUBIOUS BACKGROUNDS (LIKE ME).
RIKO-SAN NEVER PRIED TOO DEEP, SO IT WAS EASY TO TALK TO HER.

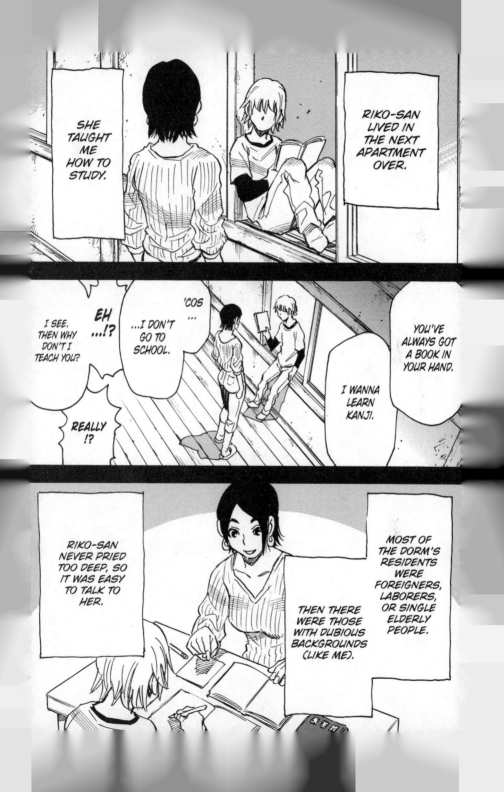

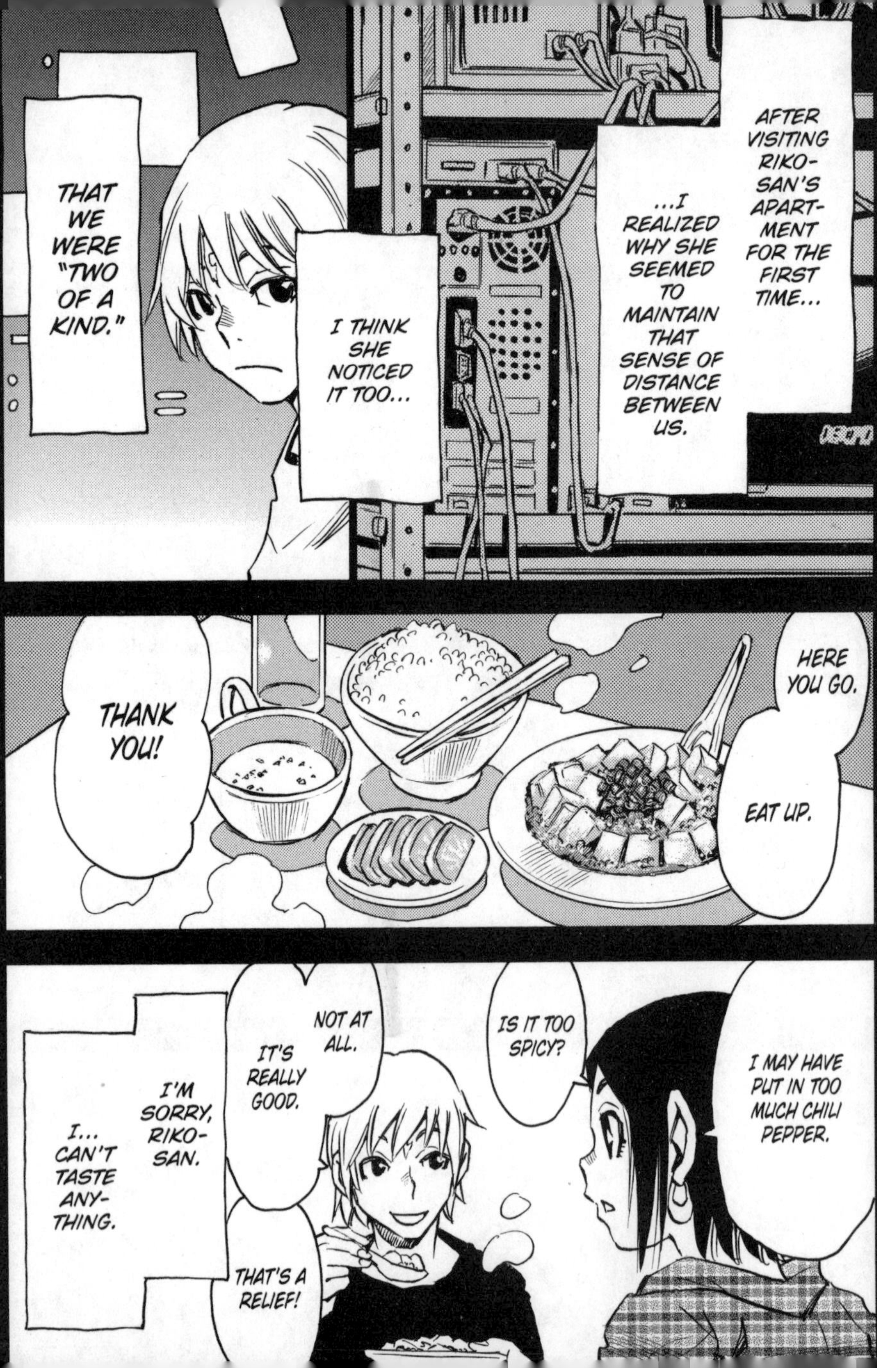
AFTER VISITING RIKO-SAN'S APARTMENT FOR THE FIRST TIME...
...I REALIZED WHY SHE SEEMED TO MAINTAIN THAT SENSE OF DISTANCE BETWEEN US.
I THINK SHE NOTICED IT TOO...
THAT WE WERE "TWO OF A KIND."
HERE YOU GO.
EAT UP.
THANK YOU!
I MAY HAVE PUT IN TOO MUCH CHILI PEPPER.
IS IT TOO SPICY?
NOT AT ALL.
IT'S REALLY GOOD.
THAT'S A RELIEF!
I'M SORRY, RIKO-SAN.
I... CAN'T TASTE ANY-THING.

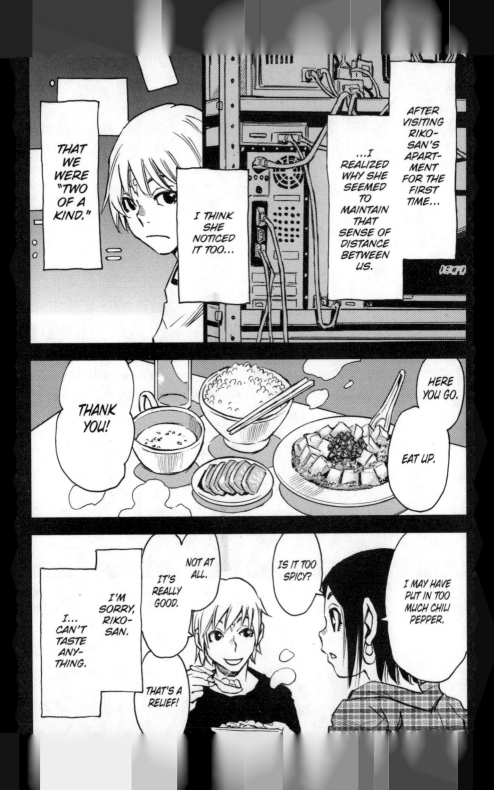

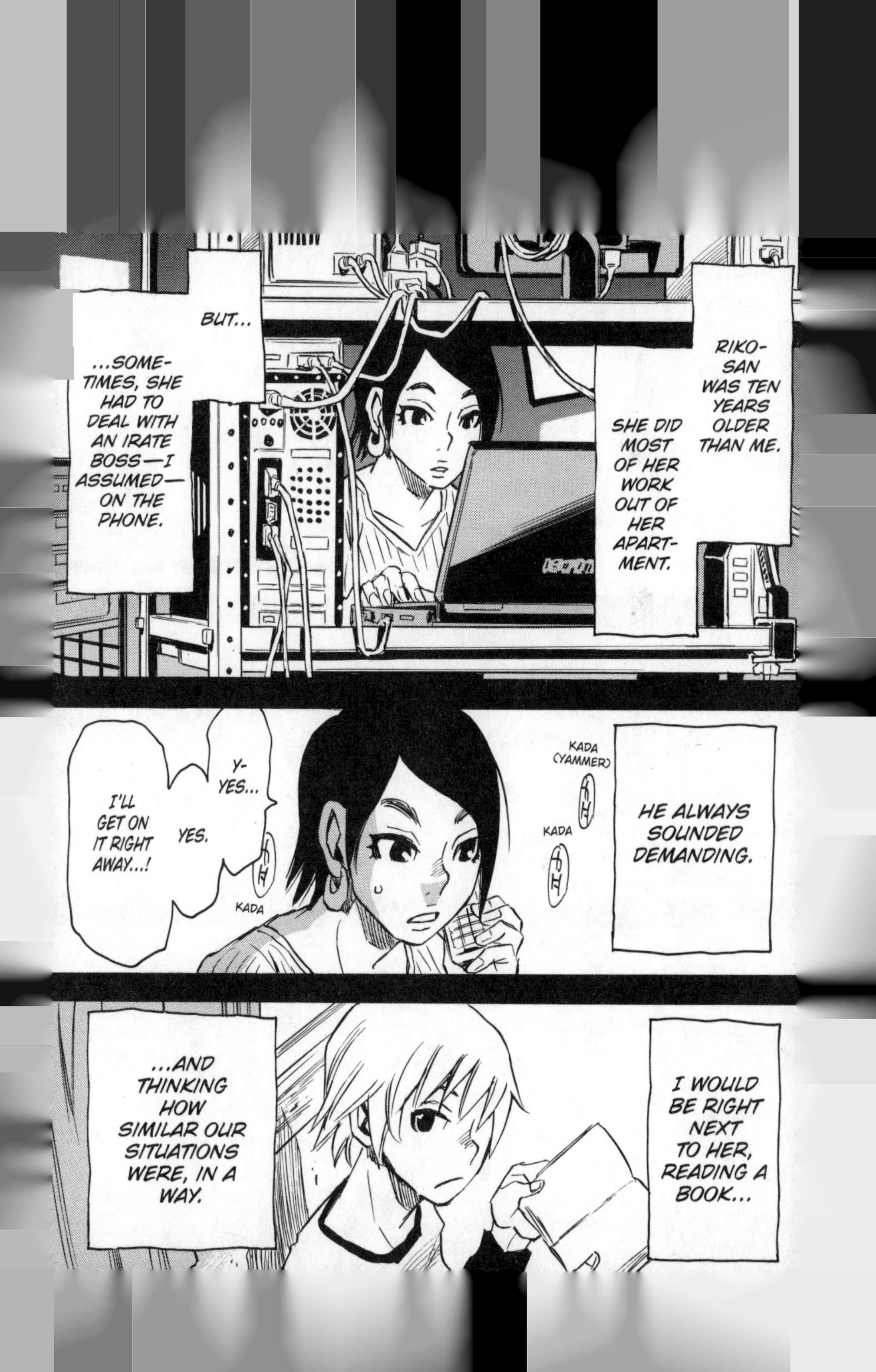
RIKO-SAN WAS TEN YEARS OLDER THAN ME.
SHE DID MOST OF HER WORK OUT OF HER APARTMENT.
BUT...
...SOMETIMES, SHE HAD TO DEAL WITH AN IRATE BOSS—I ASSUMED—ON THE PHONE.
HE ALWAYS SOUNDED DEMANDING.
KADA (YAMMER)
KADA
Y-YES...
YES.
I'LL GET ON IT RIGHT AWAY...!
KADA
I WOULD BE RIGHT NEXT TO HER, READING A BOOK...
...AND THINKING HOW SIMILAR OUR SITUATIONS WERE, IN A WAY.

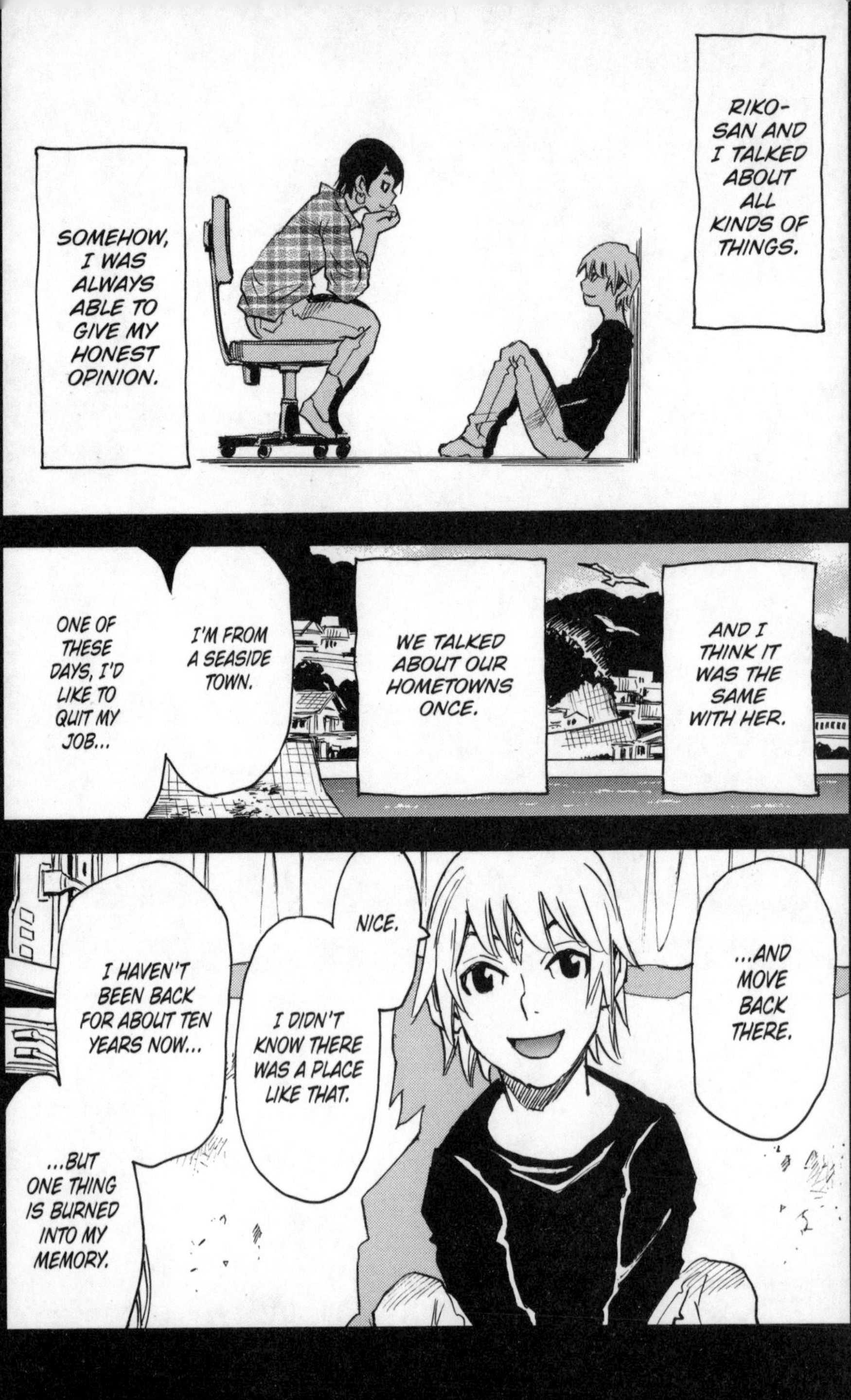
RIKO-SAN AND I TALKED ABOUT ALL KINDS OF THINGS.
SOMEHOW, I WAS ALWAYS ABLE TO GIVE MY HONEST OPINION.
AND I THINK IT WAS THE SAME WITH HER.
WE TALKED ABOUT OUR HOMETOWNS ONCE.
I'M FROM A SEASIDE TOWN.
ONE OF THESE DAYS, I'D LIKE TO QUIT MY JOB...
...AND MOVE BACK THERE.
NICE.
I DIDN'T KNOW THERE WAS A PLACE LIKE THAT.
I HAVEN'T BEEN BACK FOR ABOUT TEN YEARS NOW...
...BUT ONE THING IS BURNED INTO MY MEMORY.

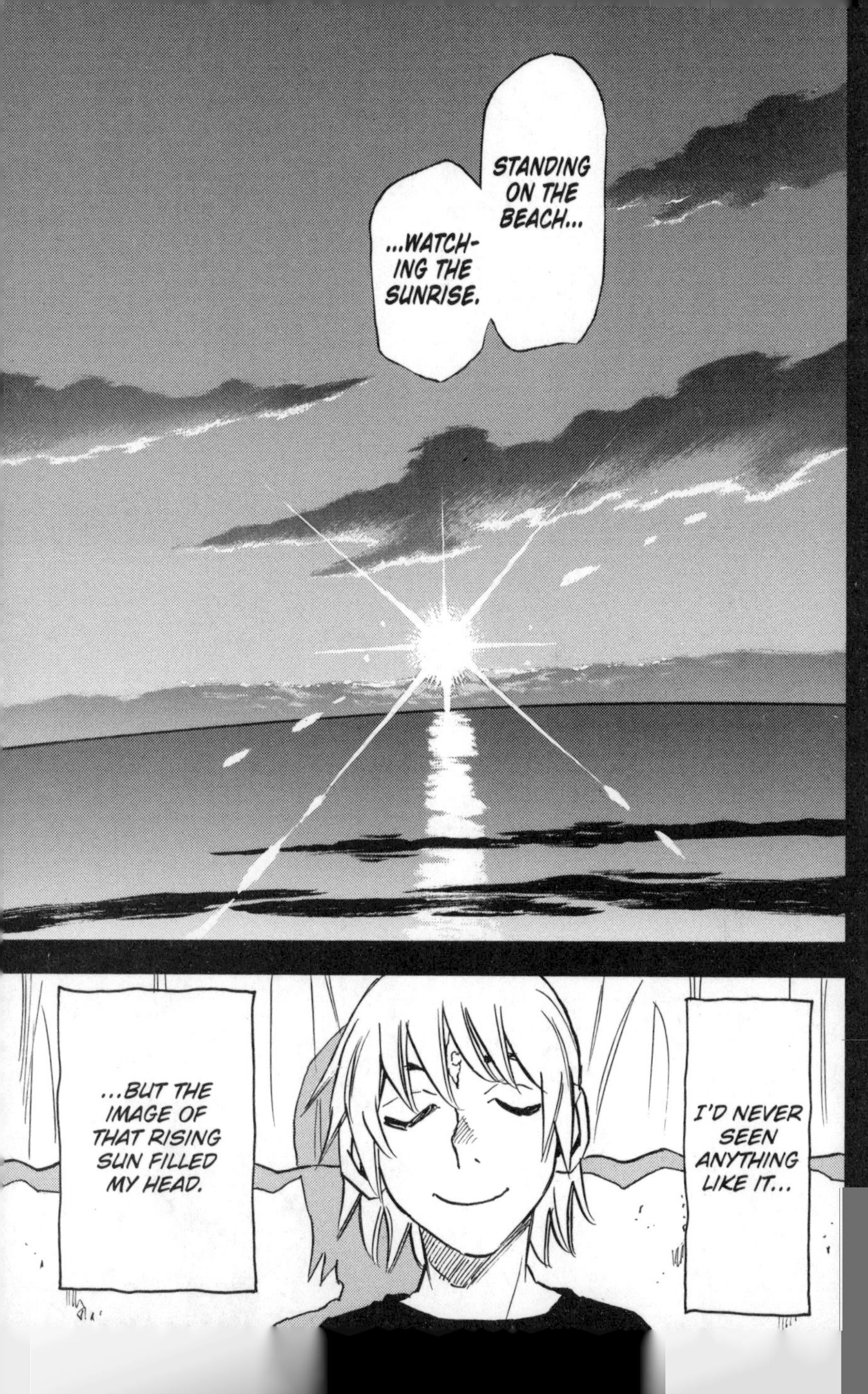
STANDING ON THE BEACH...
...WATCHING THE SUNRISE.
I'D NEVER SEEN ANYTHING LIKE IT...
...BUT THE IMAGE OF THAT RISING SUN FILLED MY HEAD.

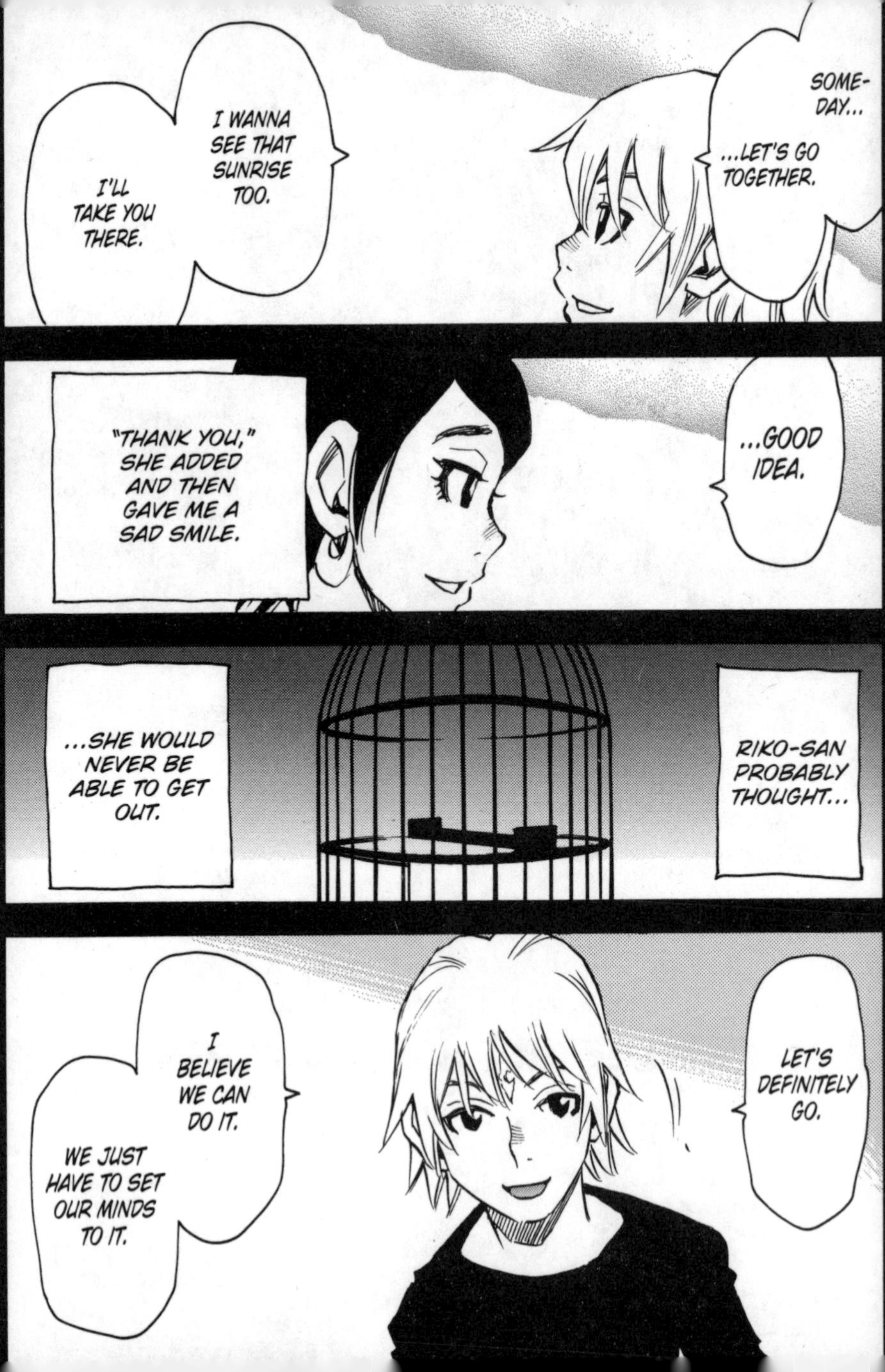
SOME-DAY...
...LET'S GO TOGETHER.
I WANNA SEE THAT SUNRISE TOO.
I'LL TAKE YOU THERE.
...GOOD IDEA.
"THANK YOU," SHE ADDED AND THEN GAVE ME A SAD SMILE.
RIKO-SAN PROBABLY THOUGHT...
...SHE WOULD NEVER BE ABLE TO GET OUT.
LET'S DEFINITELY GO.
I BELIEVE WE CAN DO IT.
WE JUST HAVE TO SET OUR MINDS TO IT.

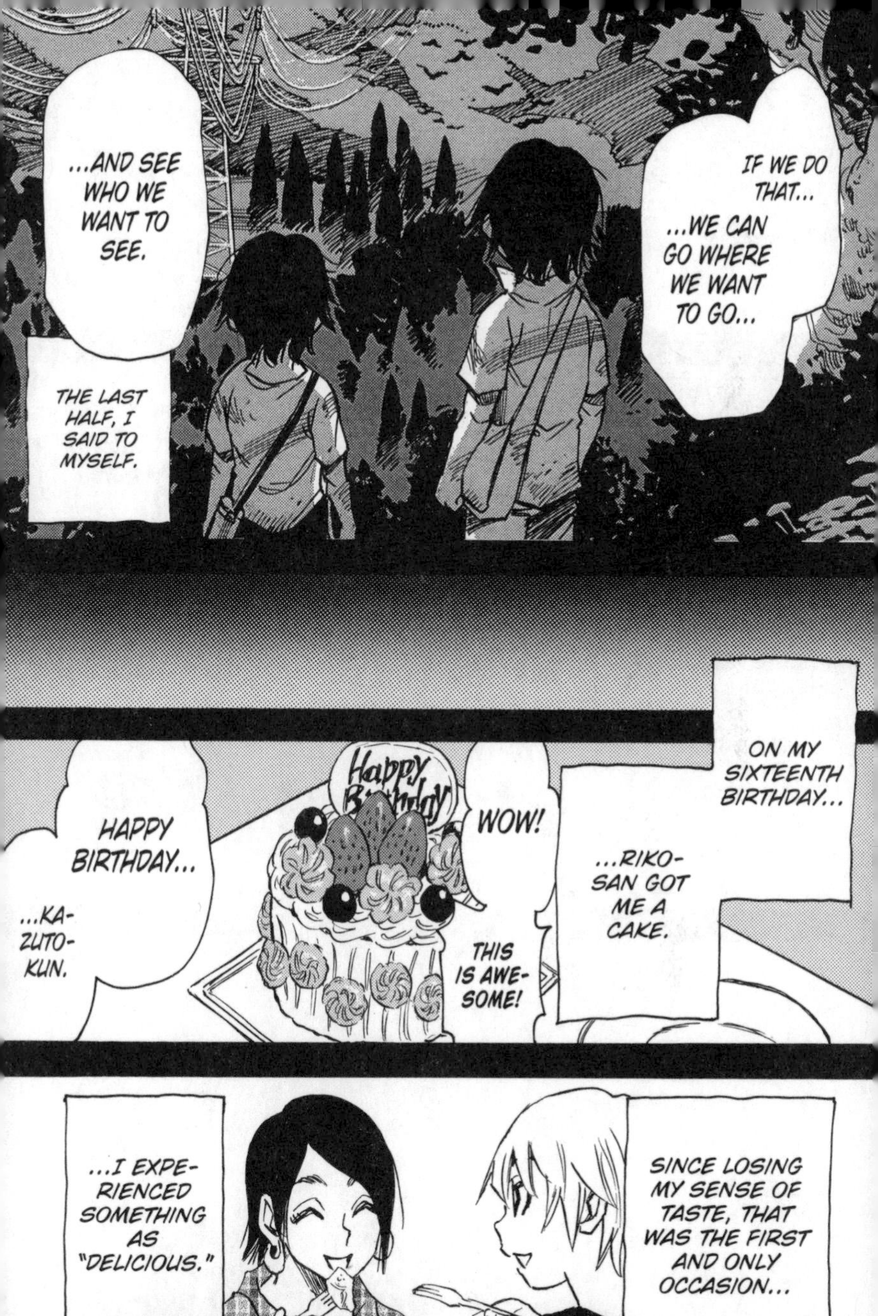
IF WE DO THAT...
...WE CAN GO WHERE WE WANT TO GO...
...AND SEE WHO WE WANT TO SEE.
THE LAST HALF, I SAID TO MYSELF.
ON MY SIXTEENTH BIRTHDAY...
...RIKO-SAN GOT ME A CAKE.
WOW!
THIS IS AWESOME!
Happy Birthday
HAPPY BIRTHDAY...
...KAZUTO-KUN.
SINCE LOSING MY SENSE OF TASTE, THAT WAS THE FIRST AND ONLY OCCASION...
...I EXPERIENCED SOMETHING AS "DELICIOUS."

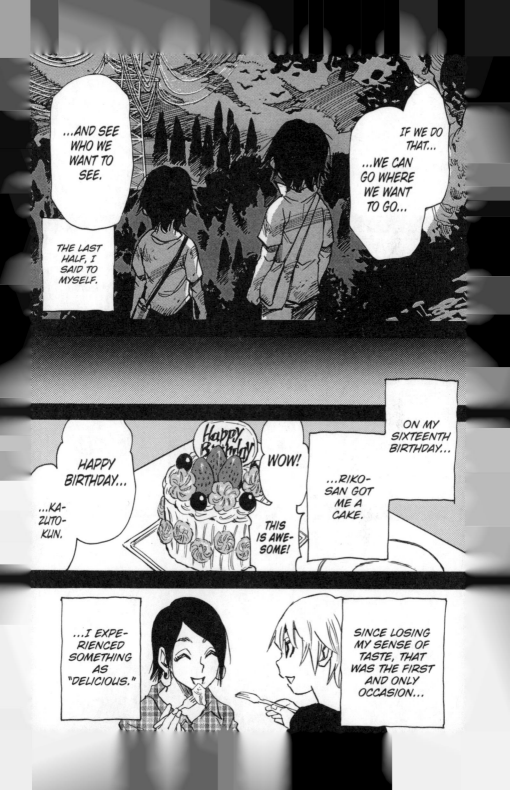

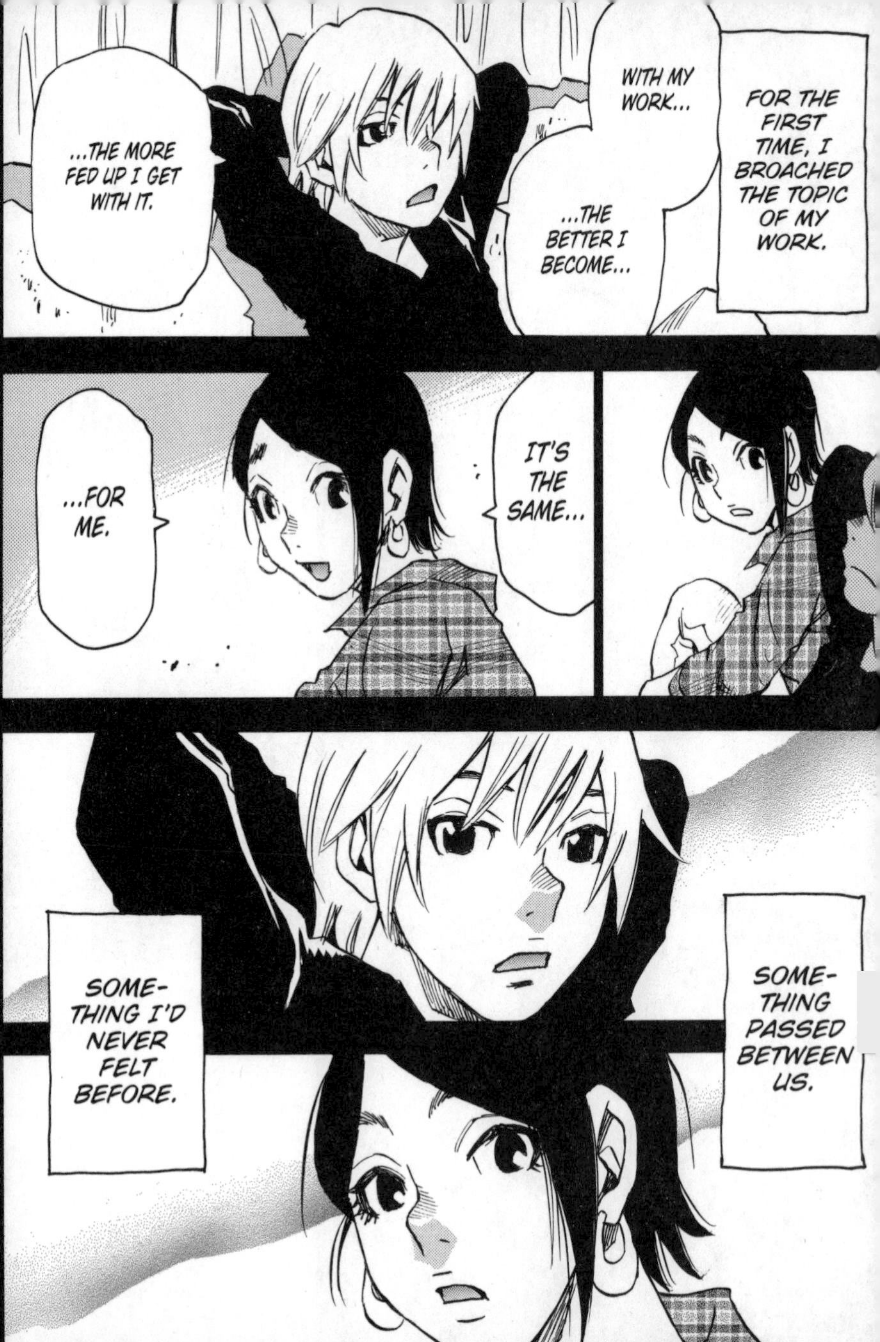
FOR THE FIRST TIME, I BROACHED THE TOPIC OF MY WORK.
WITH MY WORK...
...THE BETTER I BECOME...
...THE MORE FED UP I GET WITH IT.
IT'S THE SAME...
...FOR ME.
SOME-THING PASSED BETWEEN US.
SOME-THING I'D NEVER FELT BEFORE.

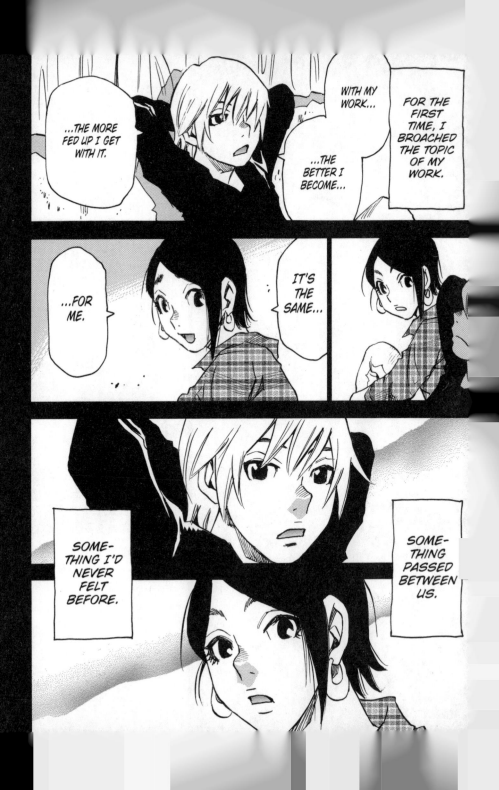

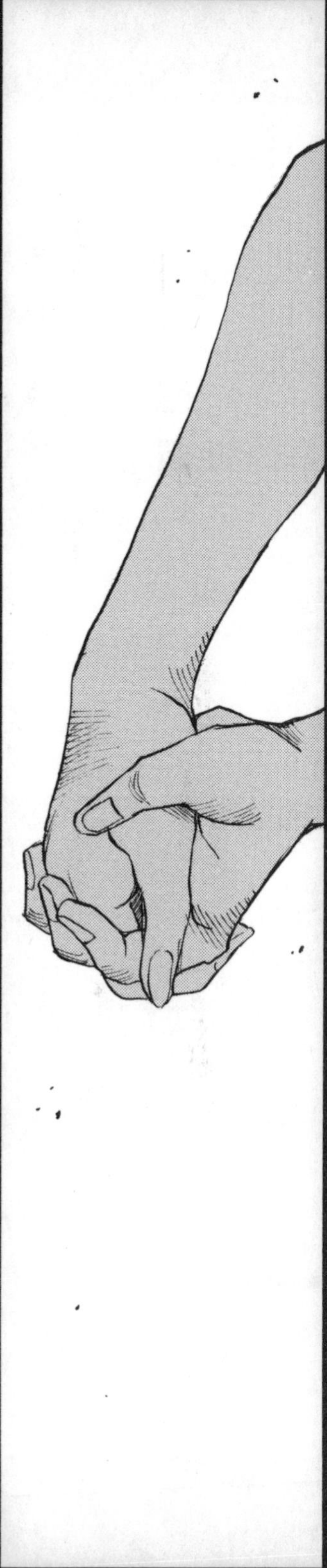

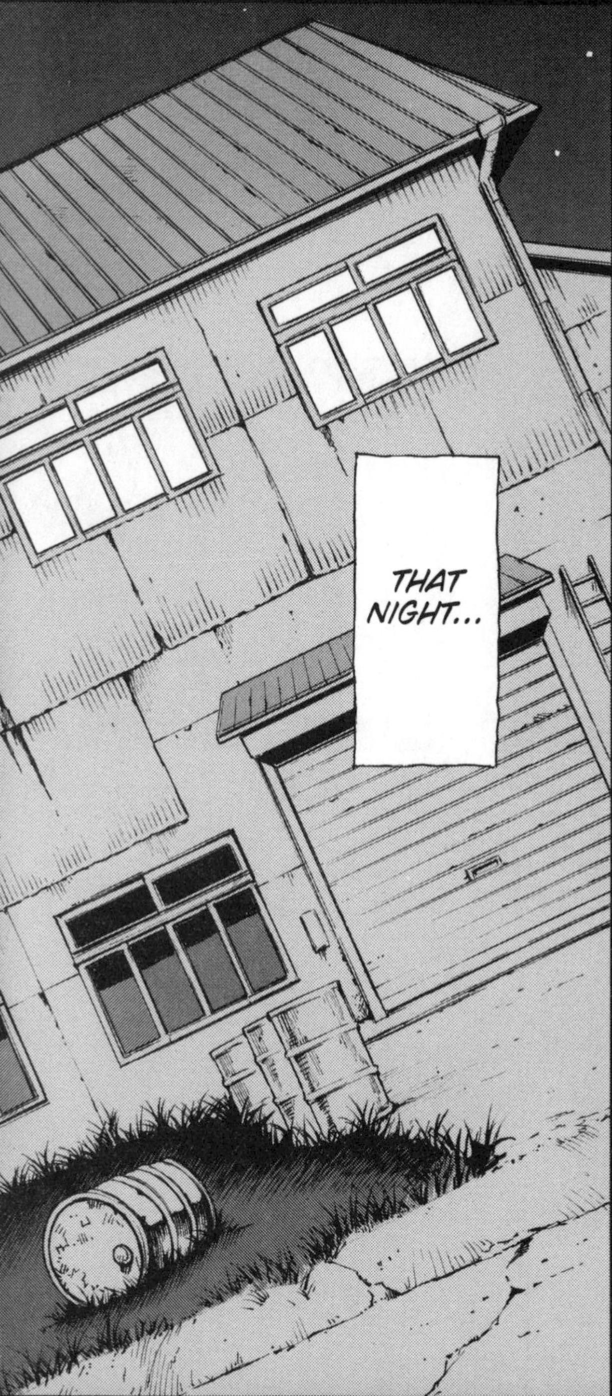
THAT NIGHT...

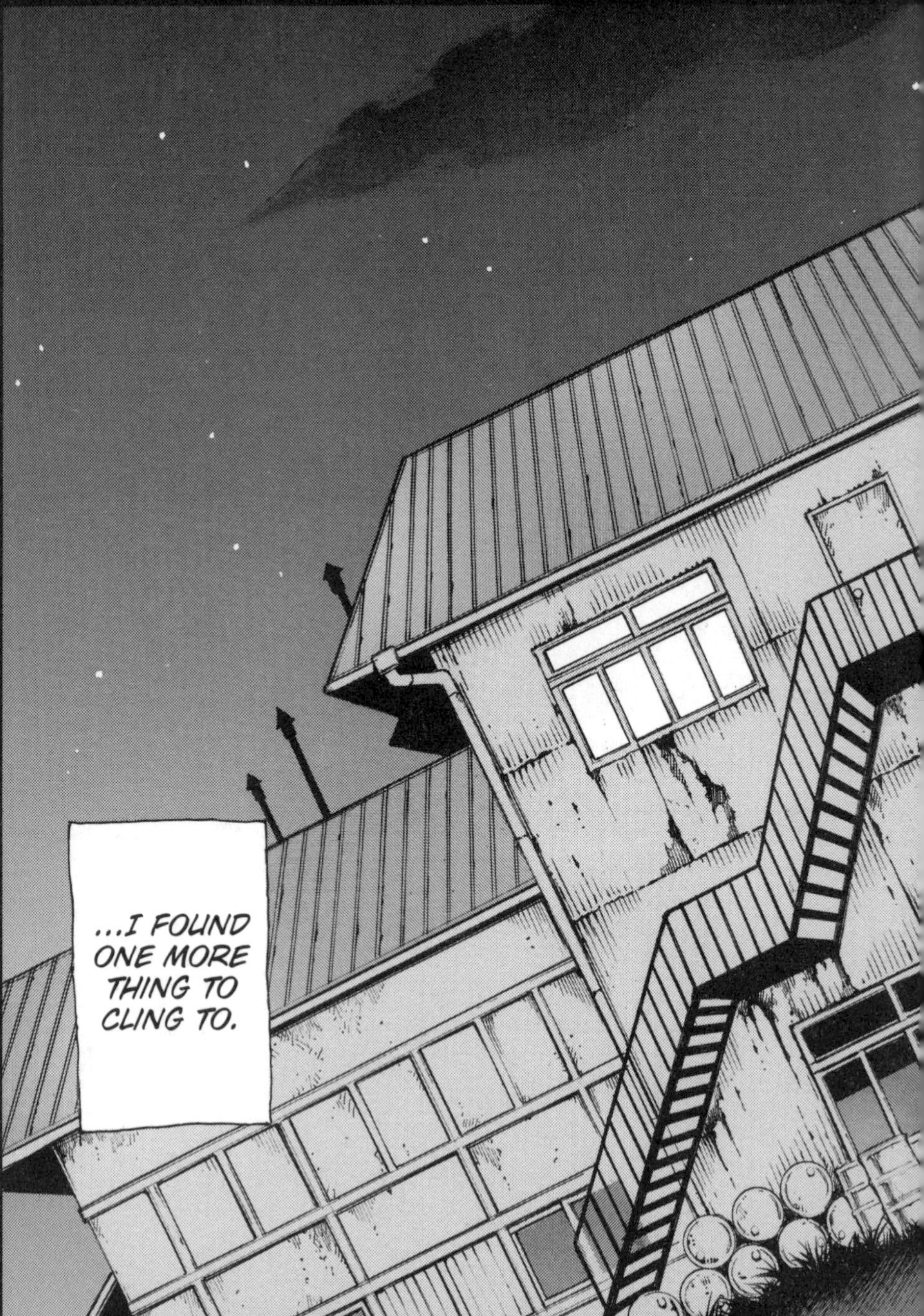
...I FOUND ONE MORE THING TO CLING TO.

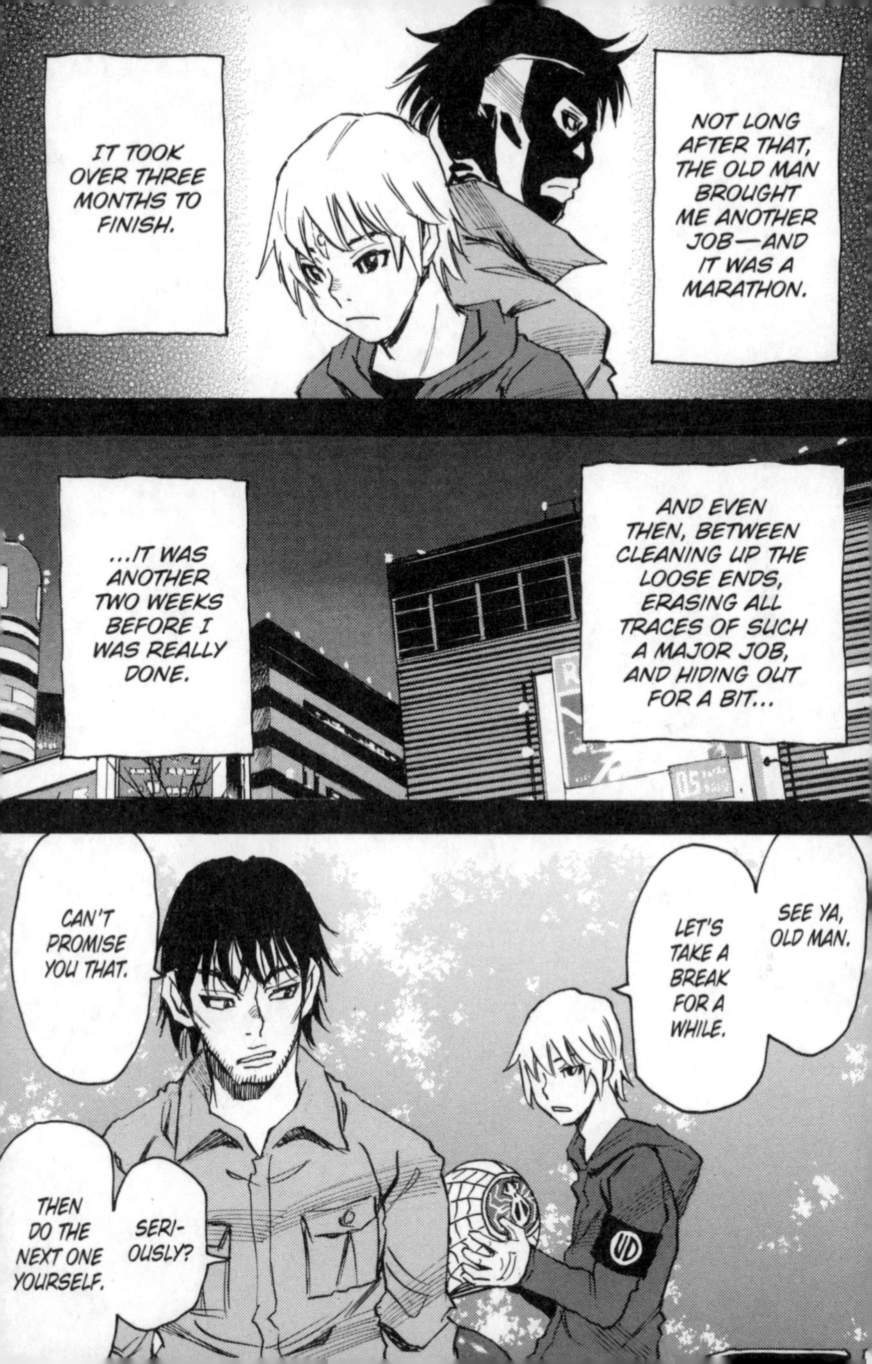
NOT LONG AFTER THAT, THE OLD MAN BROUGHT ME ANOTHER JOB—AND IT WAS A MARATHON.
IT TOOK OVER THREE MONTHS TO FINISH.
AND EVEN THEN, BETWEEN CLEANING UP THE LOOSE ENDS, ERASING ALL TRACES OF SUCH A MAJOR JOB, AND HIDING OUT FOR A BIT...
...IT WAS ANOTHER TWO WEEKS BEFORE I WAS REALLY DONE.
SEE YA, OLD MAN.
LET'S TAKE A BREAK FOR A WHILE.
CAN'T PROMISE YOU THAT.
SERI-OUSLY?
THEN DO THE NEXT ONE YOURSELF.

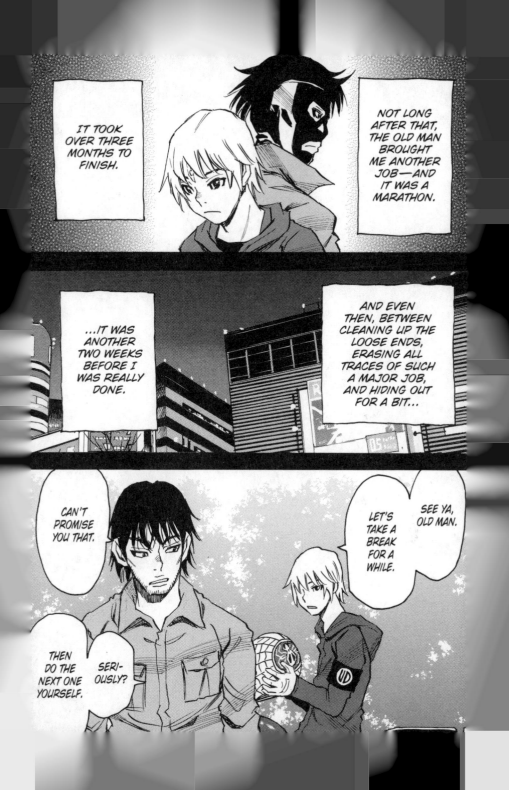

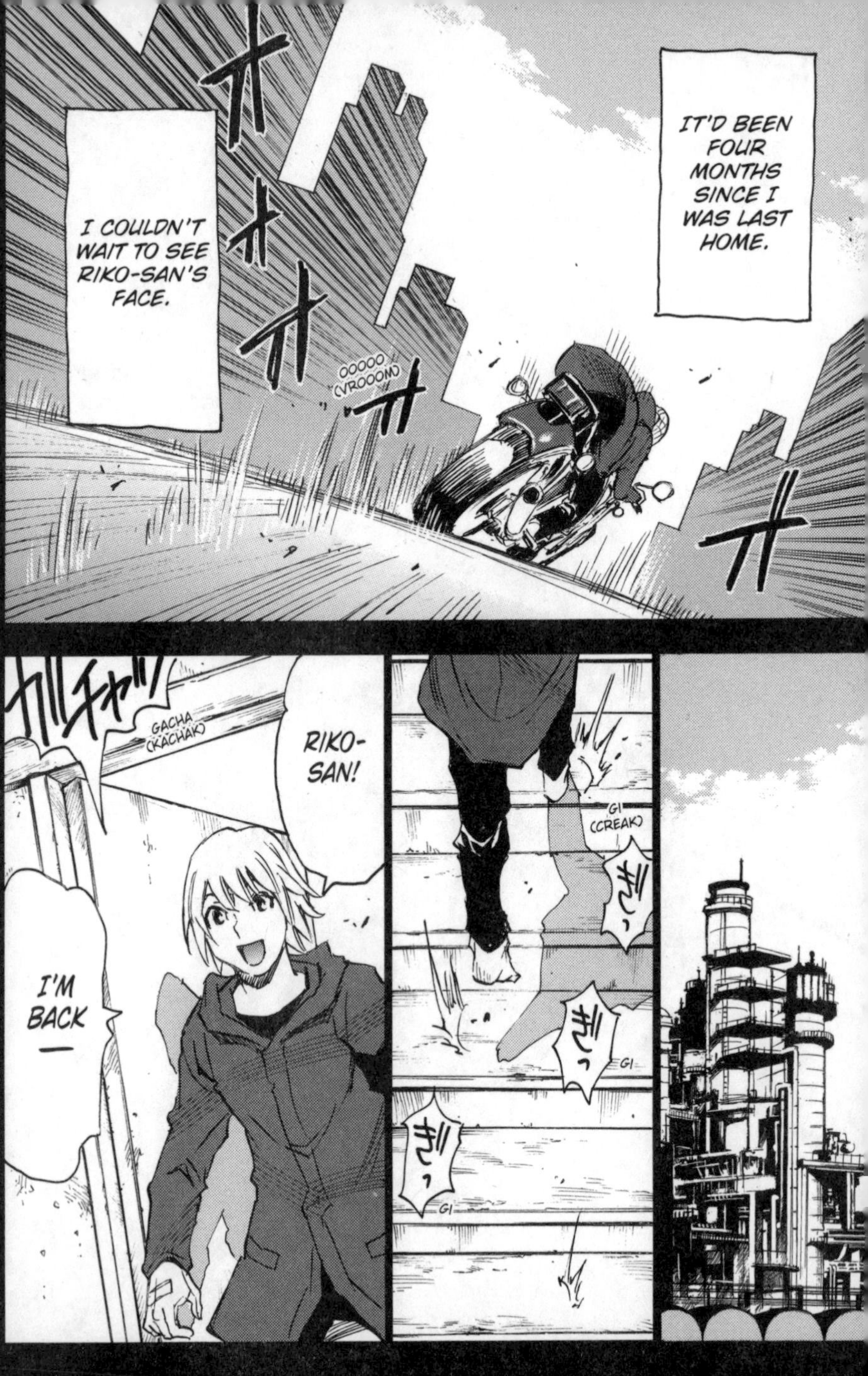
IT'D BEEN FOUR MONTHS SINCE I WAS LAST HOME.
I COULDN'T WAIT TO SEE RIKO-SAN'S FACE.
OOOOO (VROOOM)
GI (CREAK)
GI
GI
GACHA (KACHAK)
RIKO-SAN!
I'M BACK —

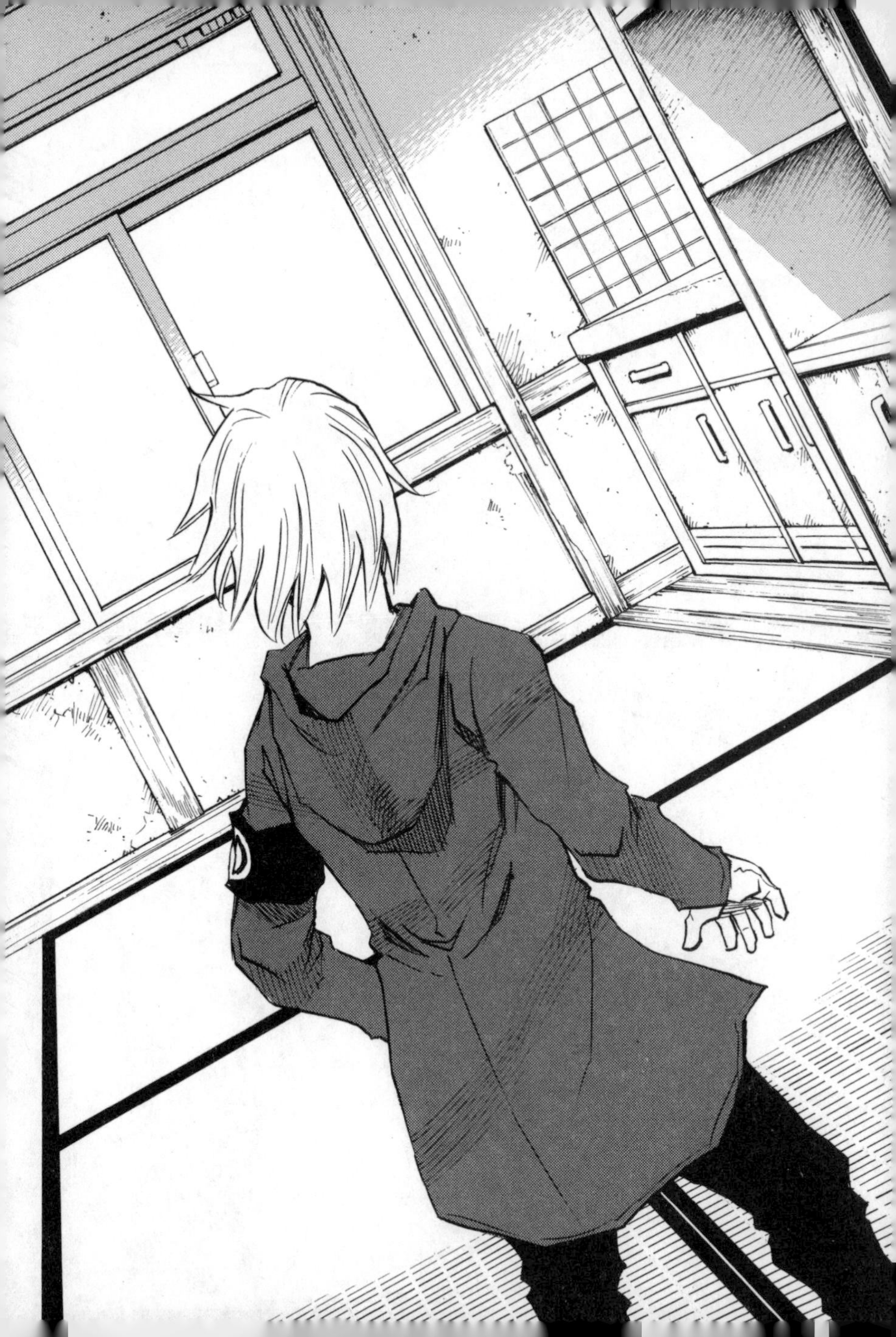

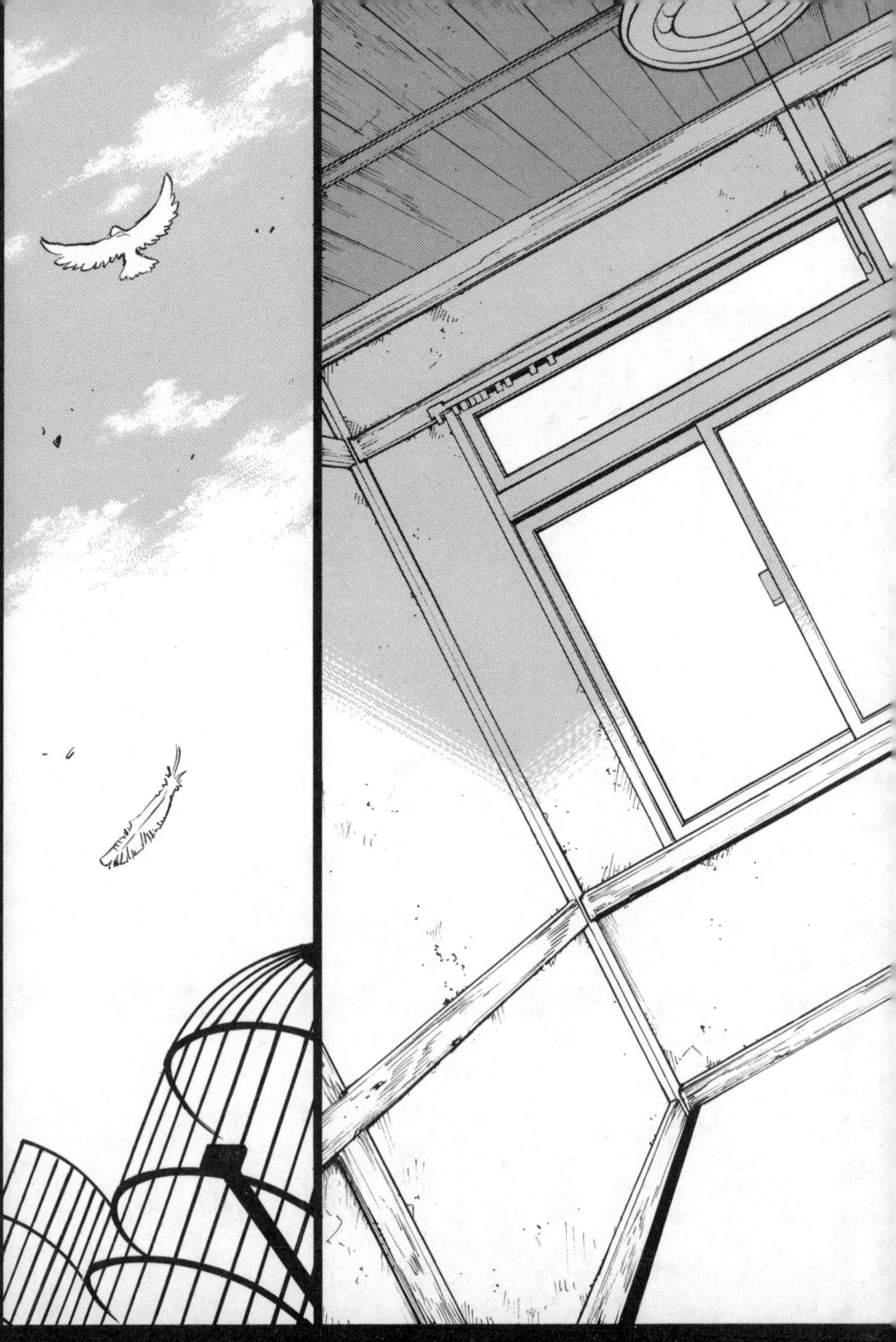

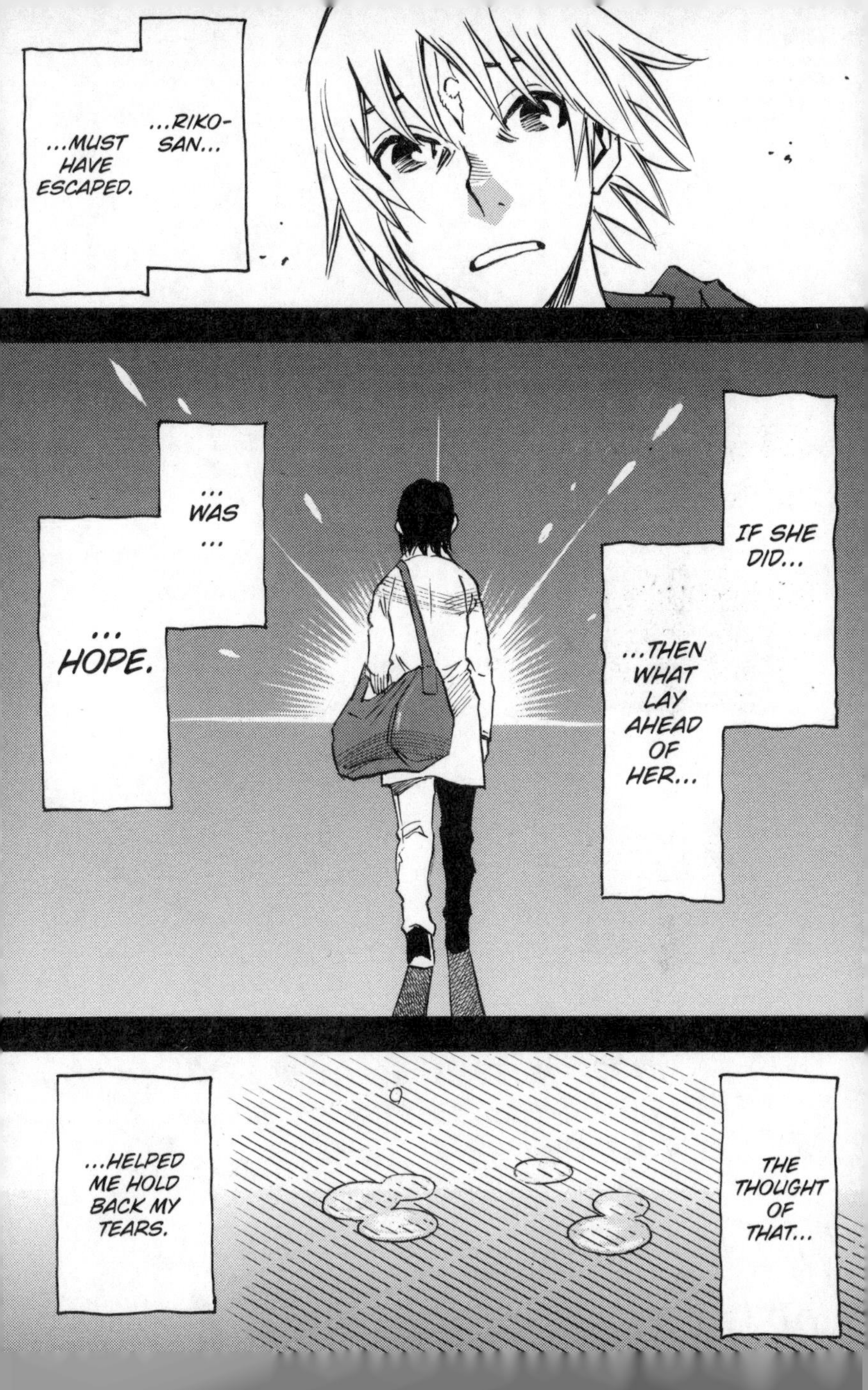
...RIKO-SAN...
...MUST HAVE ESCAPED.
IF SHE DID...
...THEN WHAT LAY AHEAD OF HER...
...WAS...
...HOPE.
THE THOUGHT OF THAT...
...HELPED ME HOLD BACK MY TEARS.

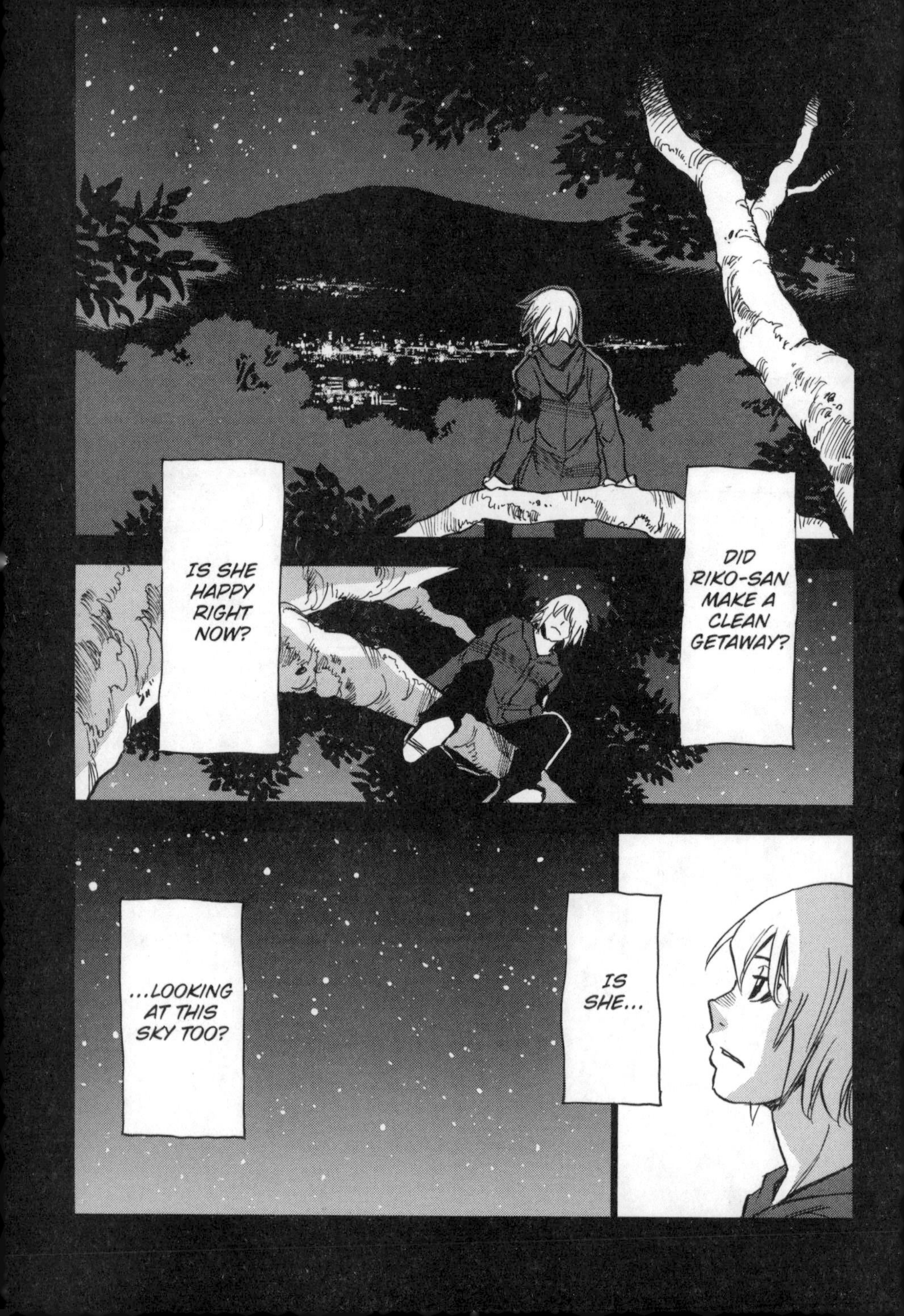
DID RIKO-SAN MAKE A CLEAN GETAWAY?
IS SHE HAPPY RIGHT NOW?
IS SHE...
...LOOKING AT THIS SKY TOO?

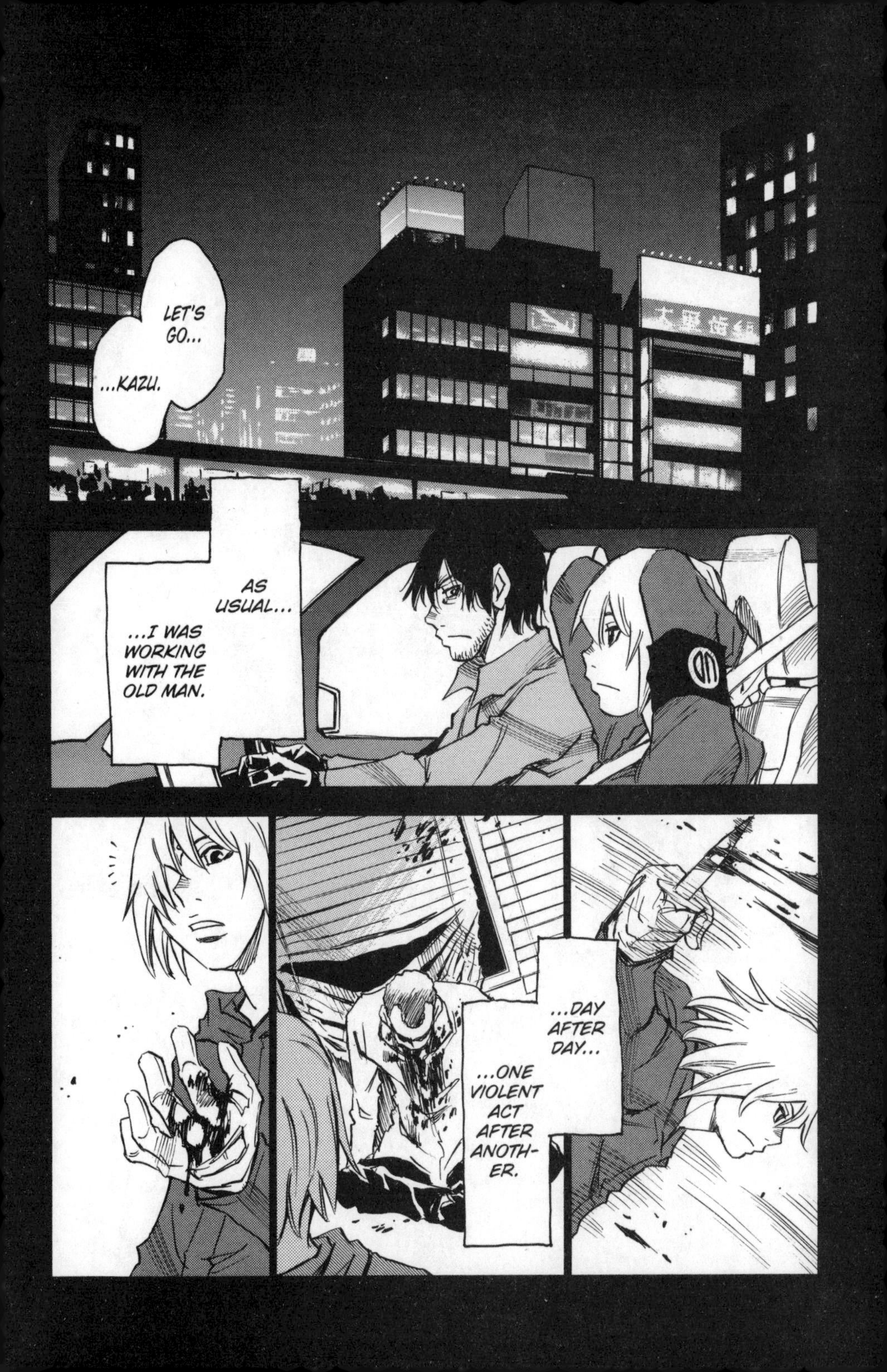
LET'S GO...
...KAZU.
AS USUAL...
...I WAS WORKING WITH THE OLD MAN.
...DAY AFTER DAY...
...ONE VIOLENT ACT AFTER ANOTHER.

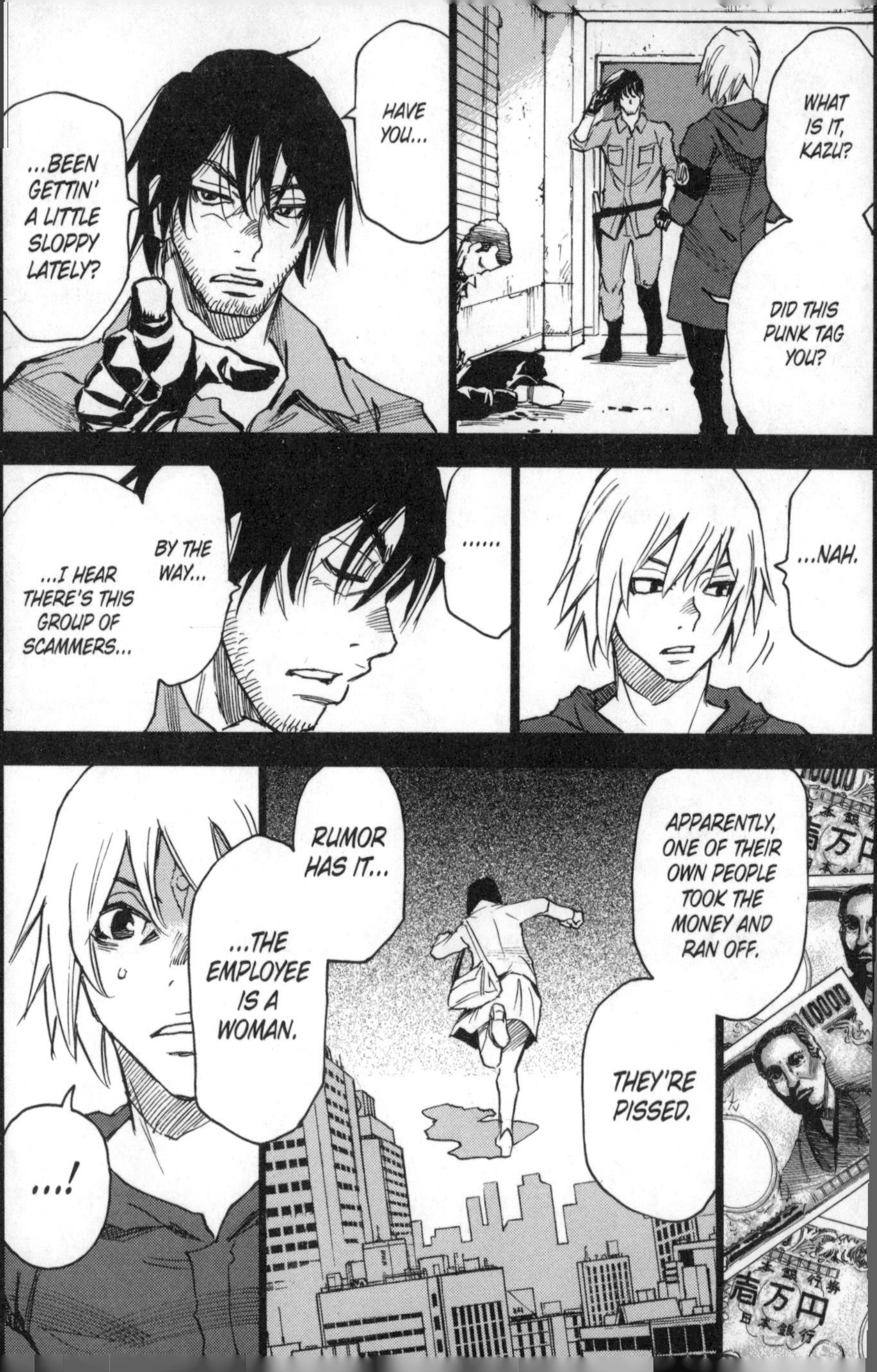
WHAT IS IT, KAZU?
DID THIS PUNK TAG YOU?
HAVE YOU...
...BEEN GETTIN' A LITTLE SLOPPY LATELY?
...NAH.
......
BY THE WAY...
...I HEAR THERE'S THIS GROUP OF SCAMMERS...
APPARENTLY, ONE OF THEIR OWN PEOPLE TOOK THE MONEY AND RAN OFF.
THEY'RE PISSED.
RUMOR HAS IT...
...THE EMPLOYEE IS A WOMAN.
...!

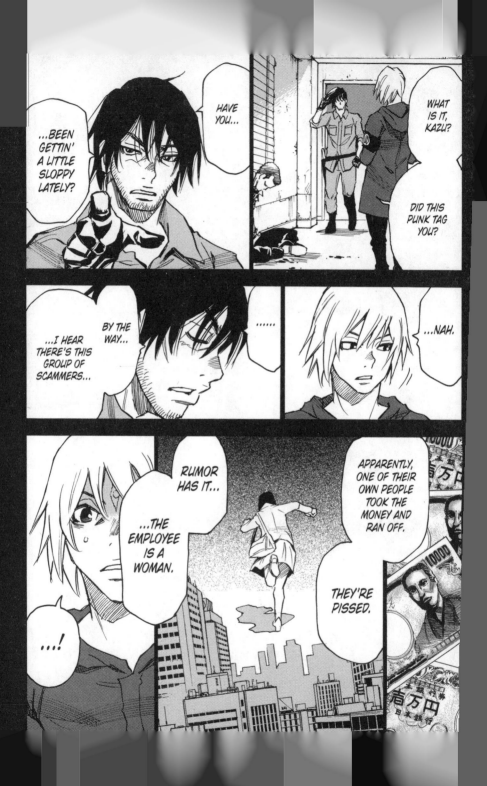

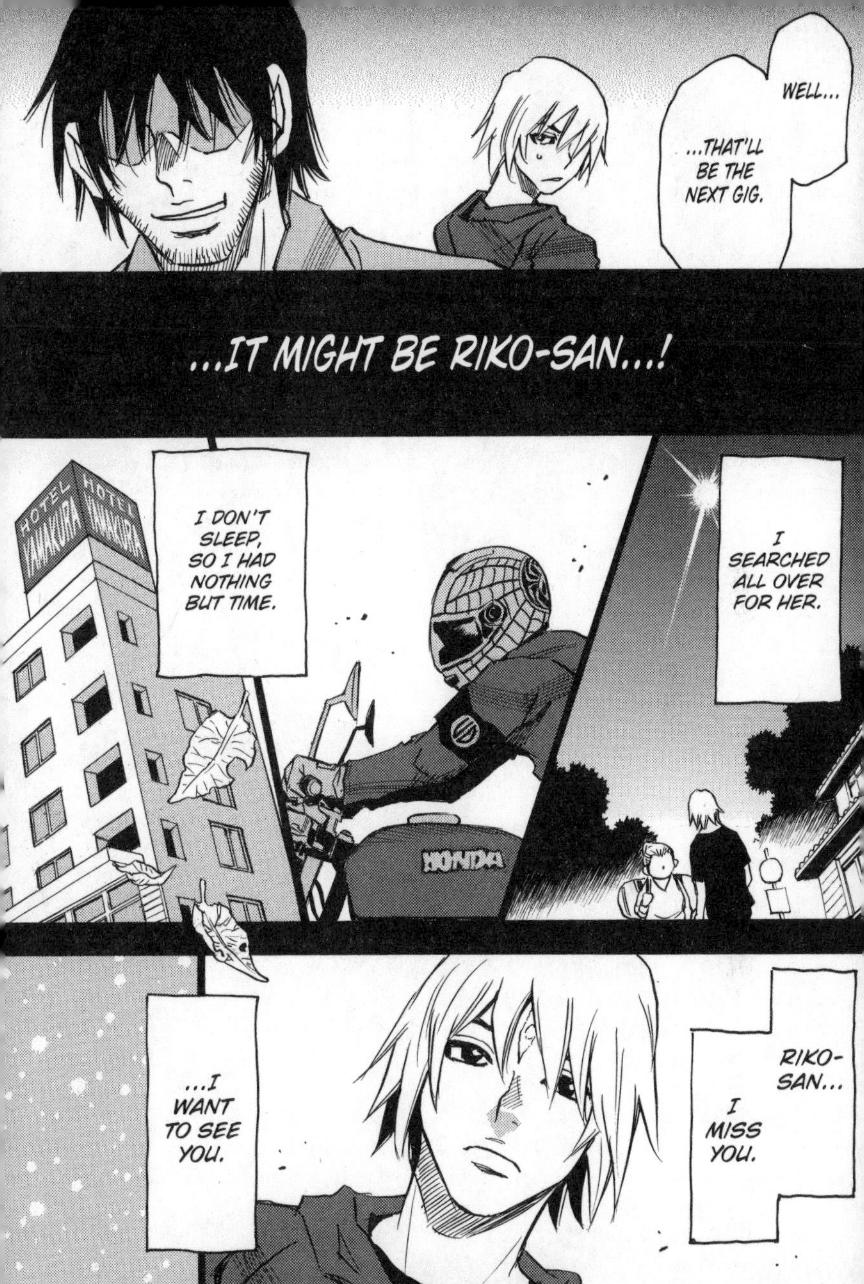
WELL...
...THAT'LL BE THE NEXT GIG.
...IT MIGHT BE RIKO-SAN...!
I SEARCHED ALL OVER FOR HER.
I DON'T SLEEP, SO I HAD NOTHING BUT TIME.
HOTEL YAMAKURA
HOTEL YAMAKURA
HONDA
RIKO-SAN...
I MISS YOU.
...I WANT TO SEE YOU.

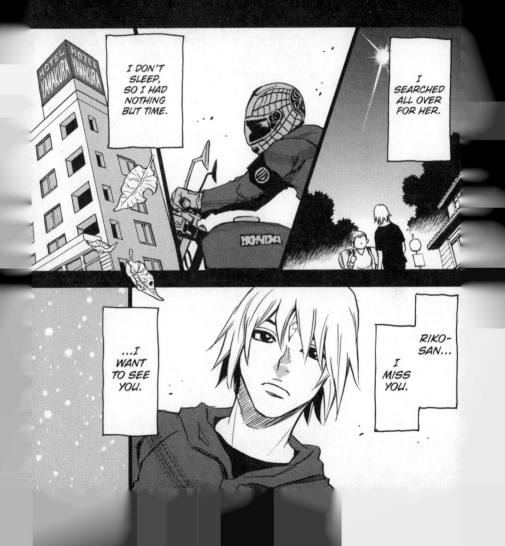

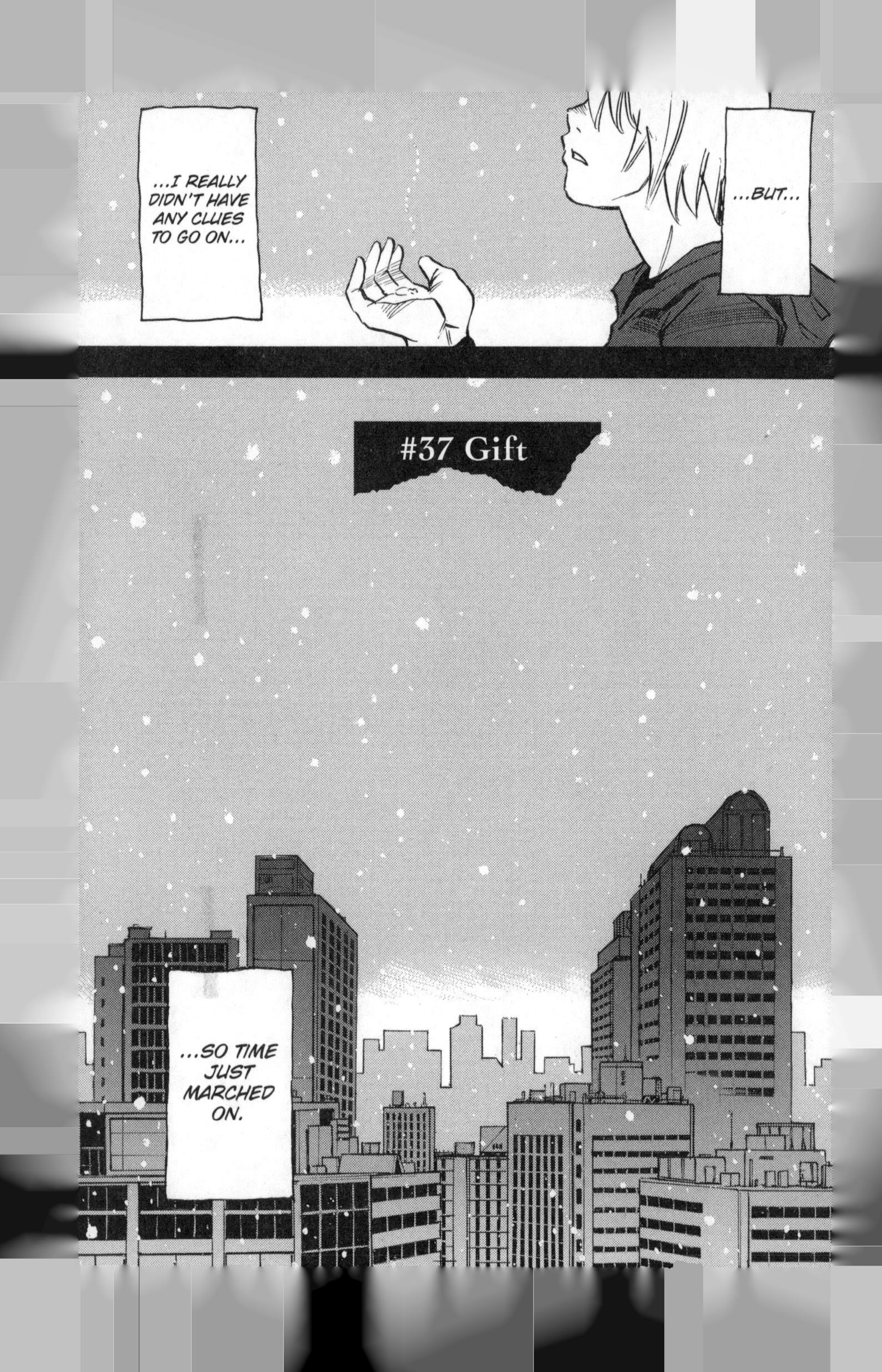
...BUT...
...I REALLY DIDN'T HAVE ANY CLUES TO GO ON...
#37 Gift
...SO TIME JUST MARCHED ON.

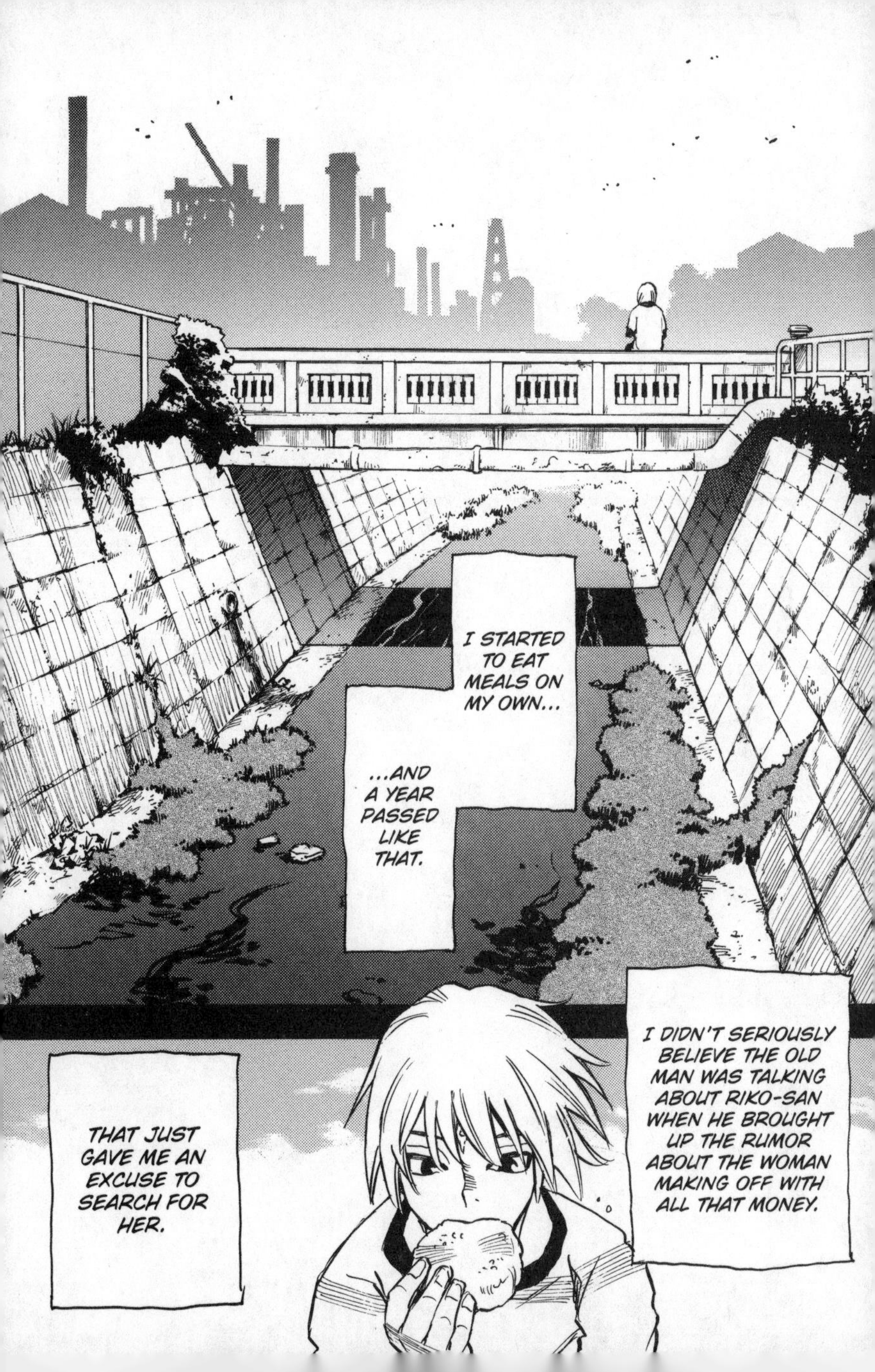
I STARTED TO EAT MEALS ON MY OWN...
...AND A YEAR PASSED LIKE THAT.
I DIDN'T SERIOUSLY BELIEVE THE OLD MAN WAS TALKING ABOUT RIKO-SAN WHEN HE BROUGHT UP THE RUMOR ABOUT THE WOMAN MAKING OFF WITH ALL THAT MONEY.
THAT JUST GAVE ME AN EXCUSE TO SEARCH FOR HER.

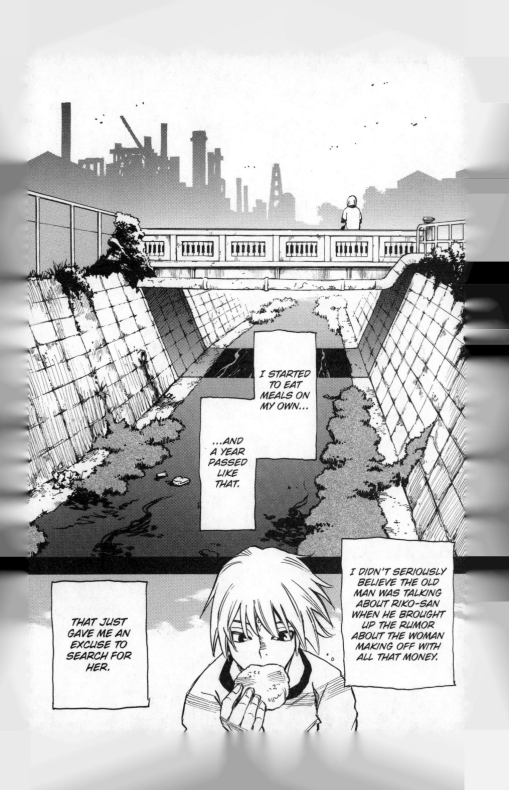

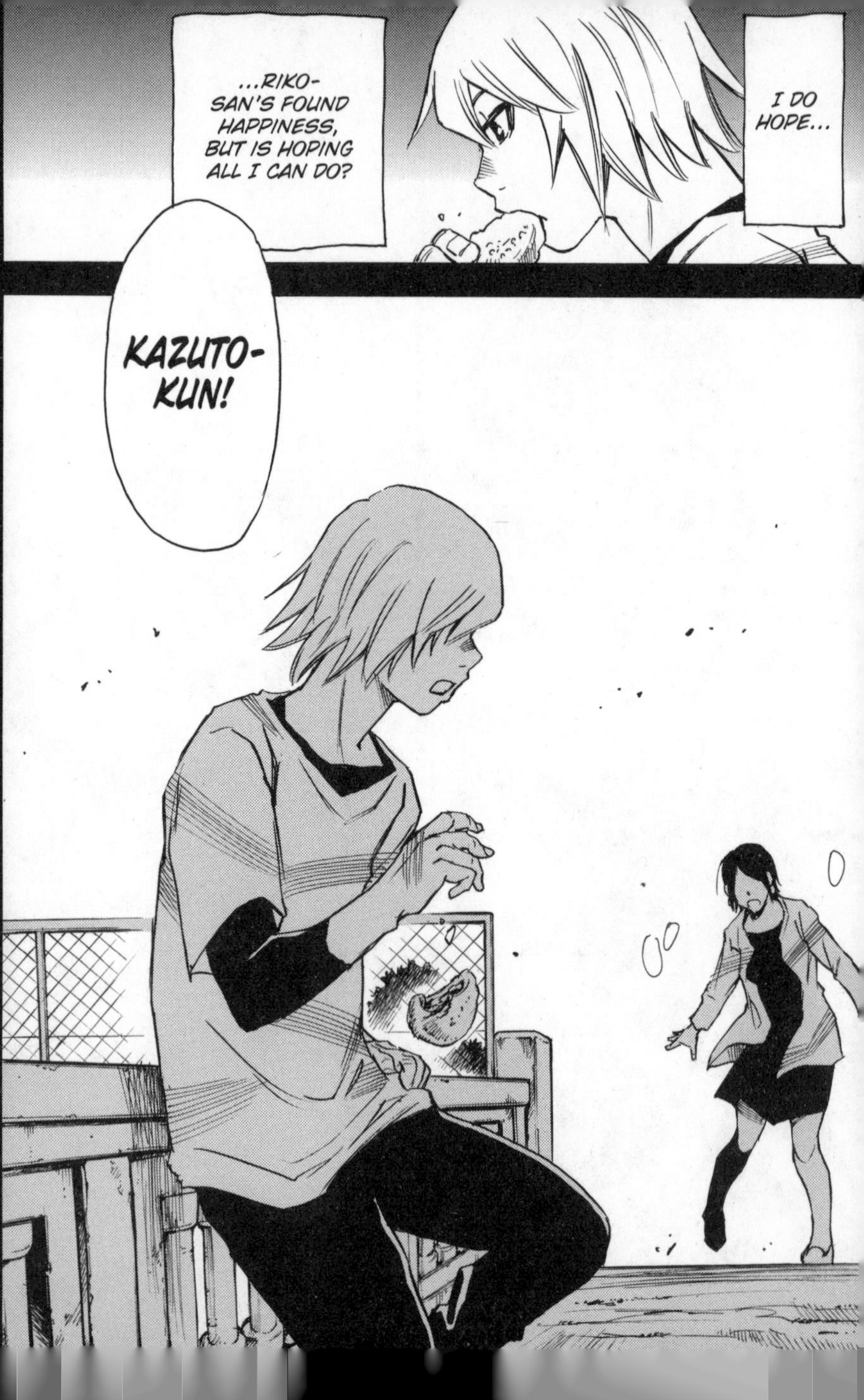
I DO HOPE...
...RIKO-SAN'S FOUND HAPPINESS, BUT IS HOPING ALL I CAN DO?
KAZUTO-KUN!

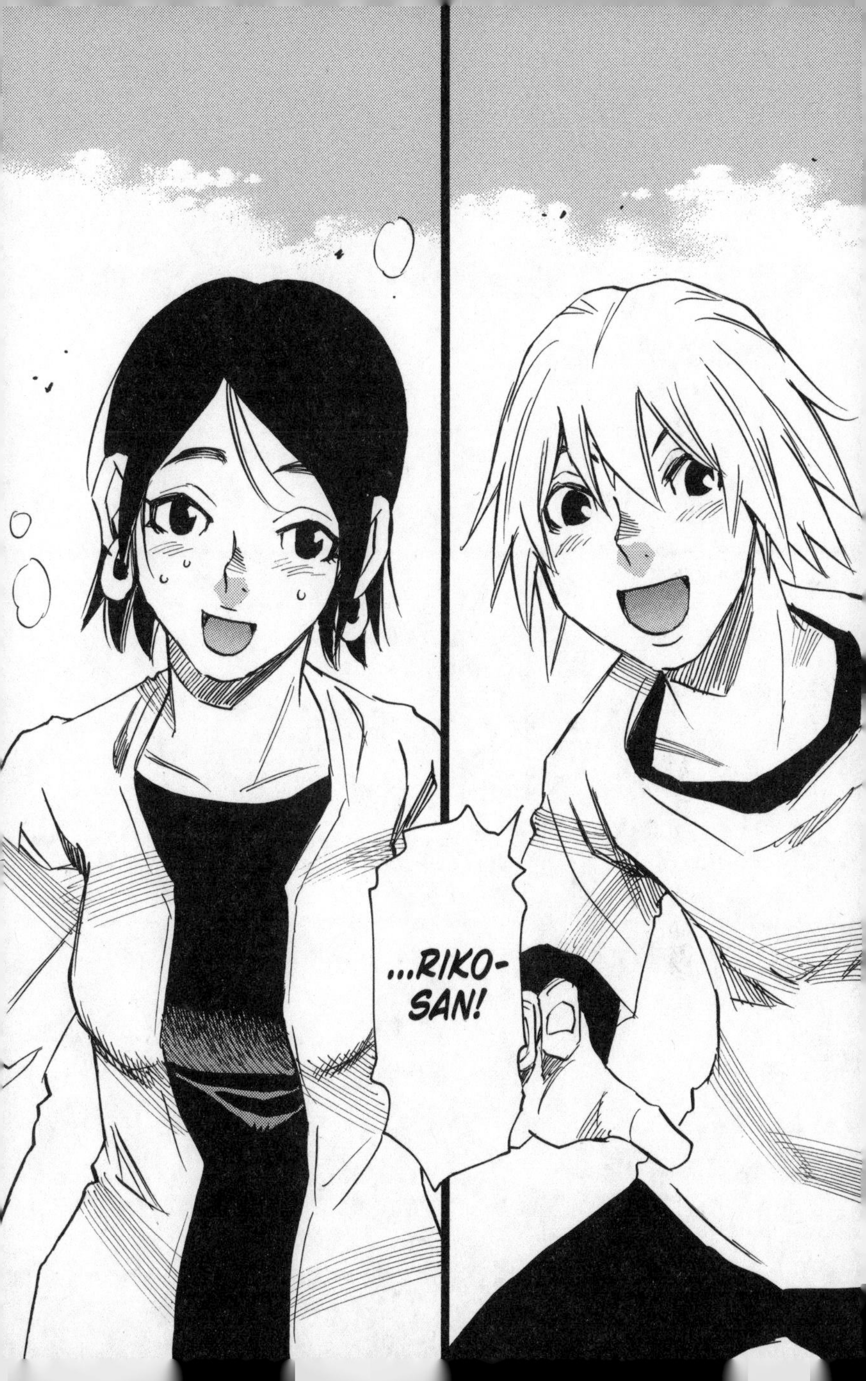
...RIKO-SAN!

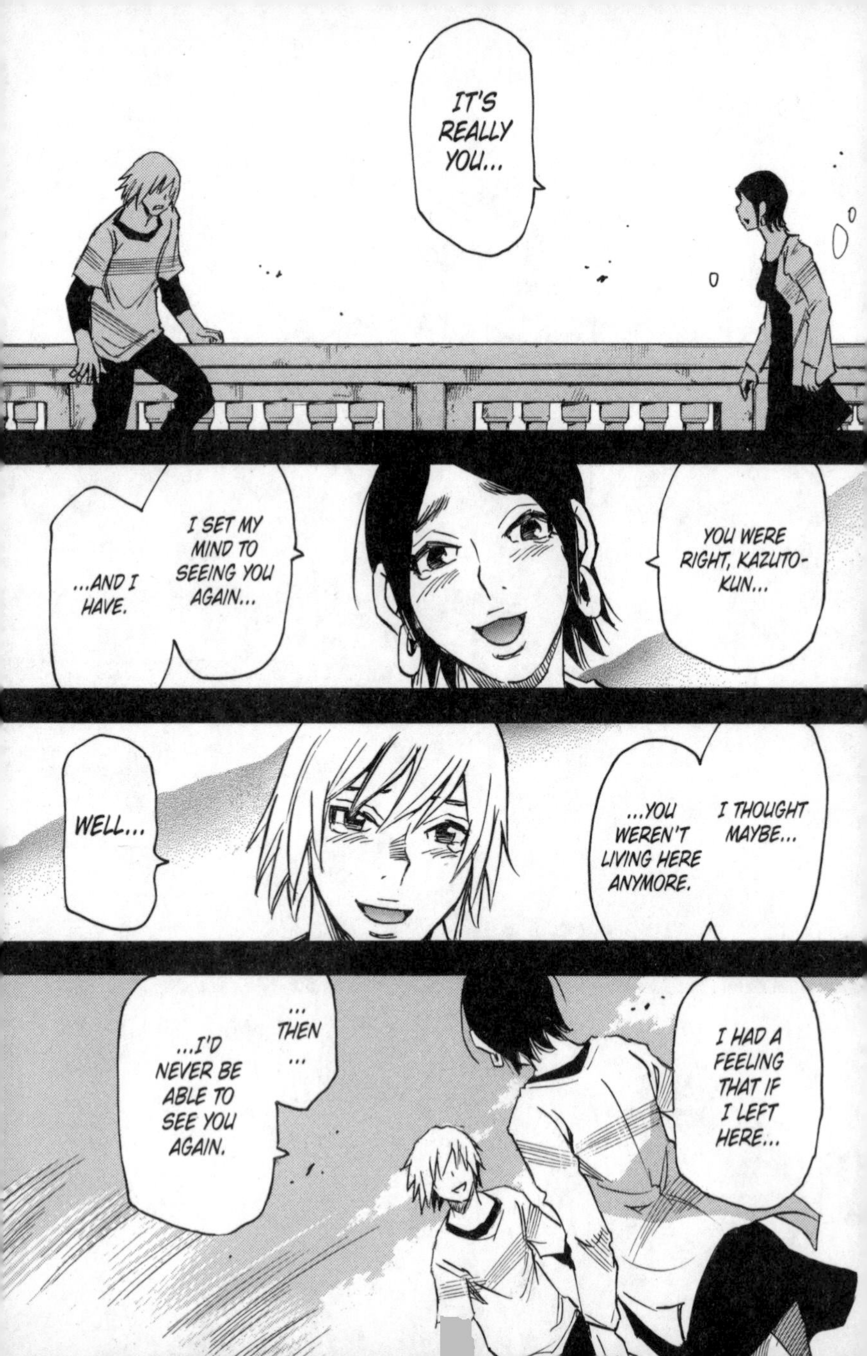
IT'S REALLY YOU...
YOU WERE RIGHT, KAZUTO-KUN...
I SET MY MIND TO SEEING YOU AGAIN...
...AND I HAVE.
I THOUGHT MAYBE...
...YOU WEREN'T LIVING HERE ANYMORE.
WELL...
I HAD A FEELING THAT IF I LEFT HERE...
...THEN...
...I'D NEVER BE ABLE TO SEE YOU AGAIN.

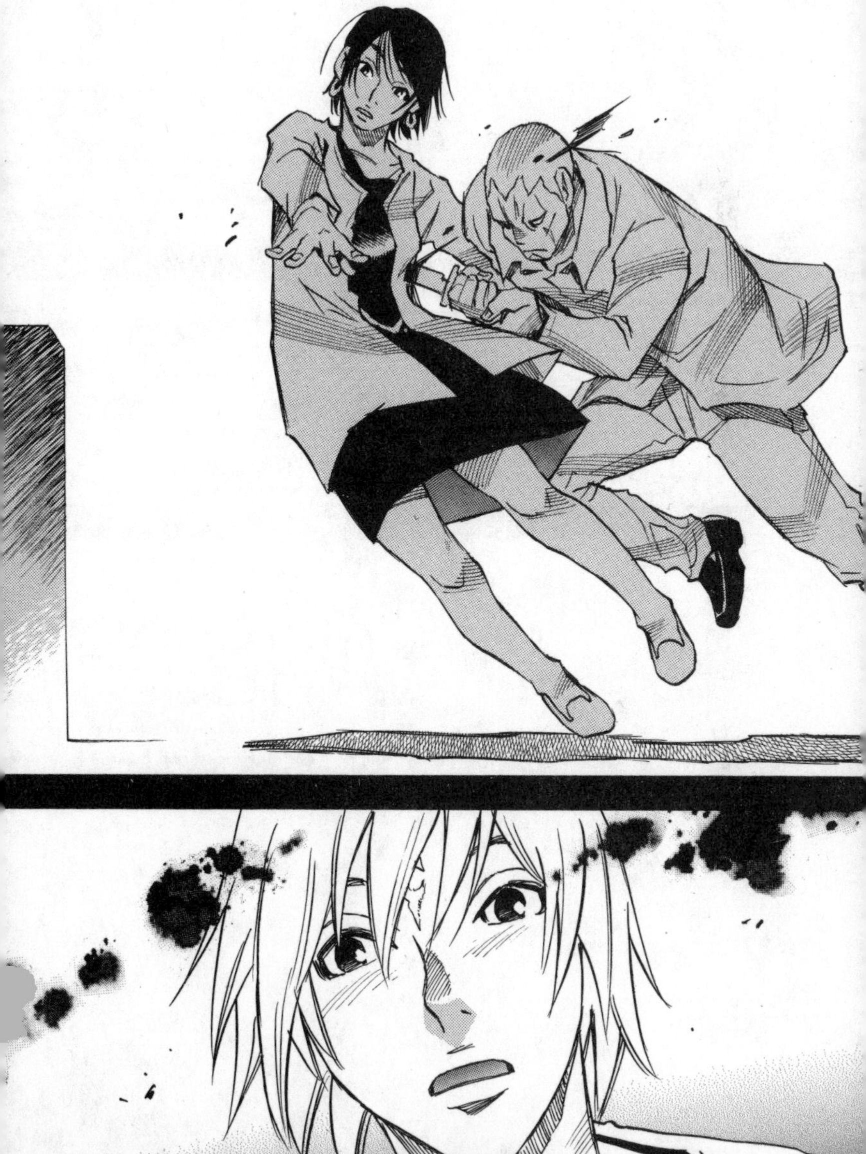

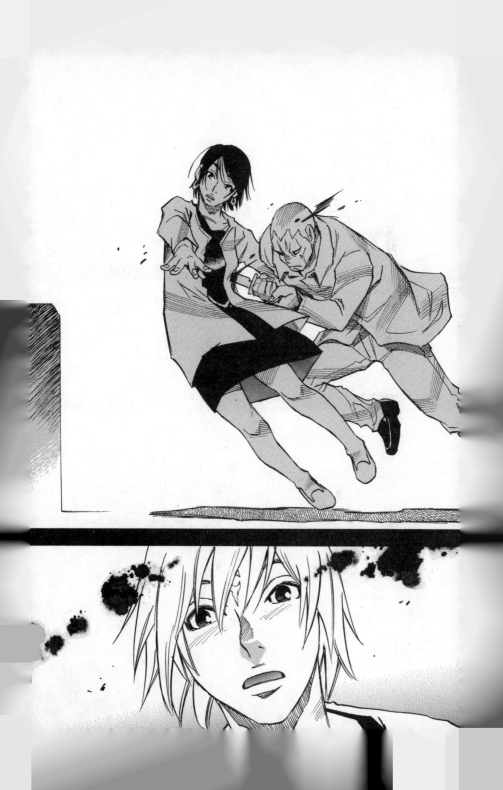

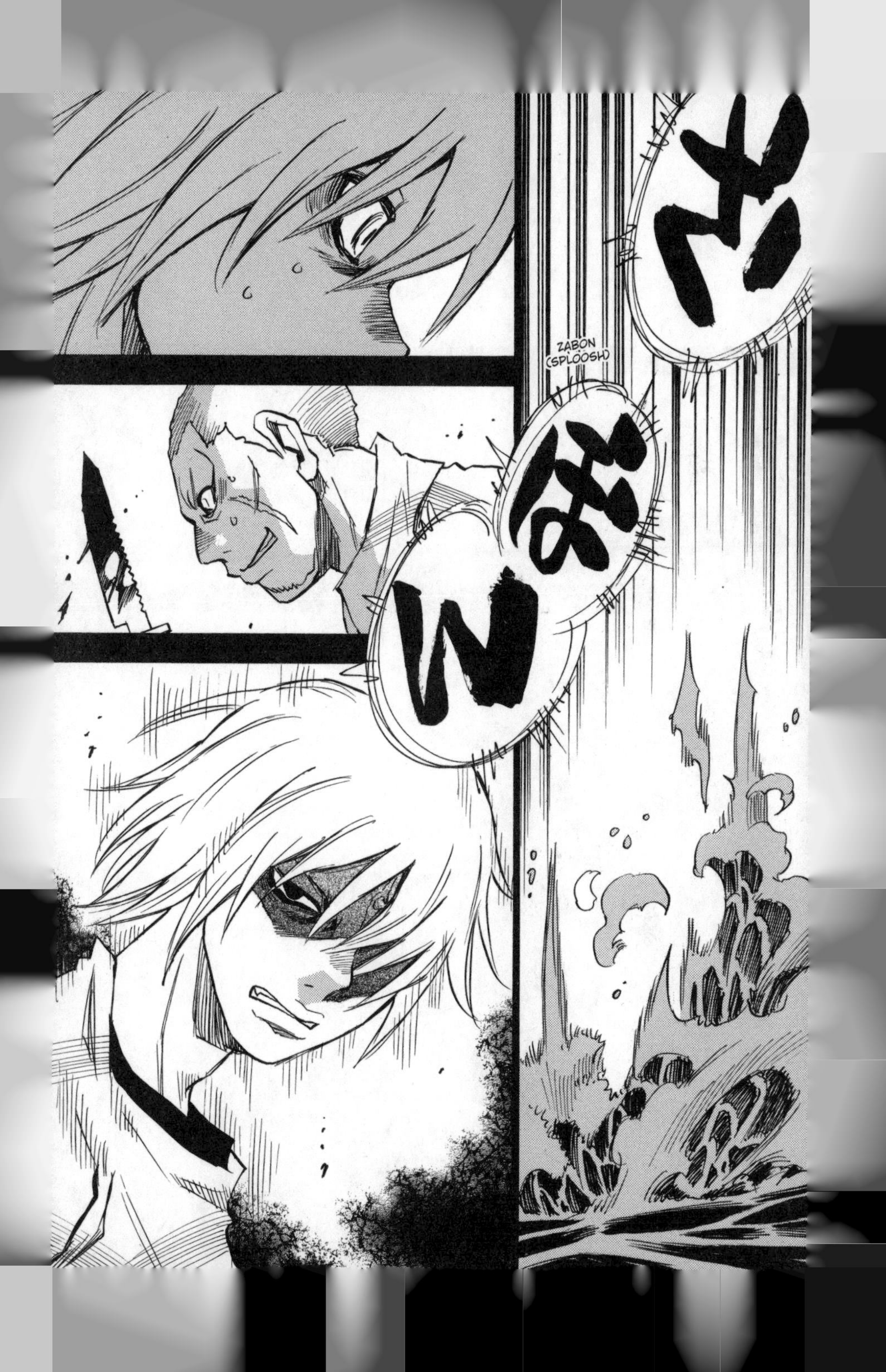
ざぼん
ZABON (SPLÖÖSH)

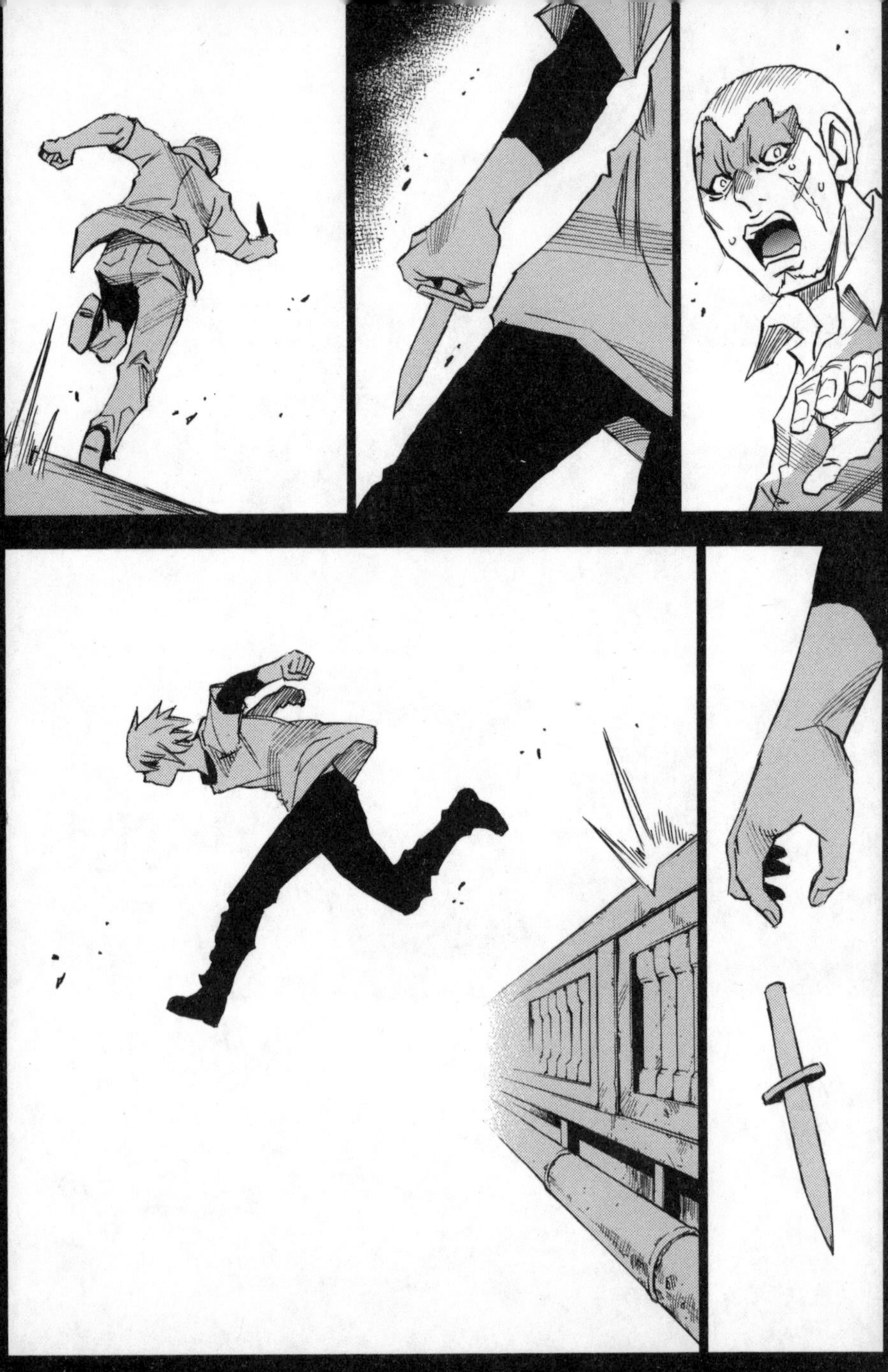

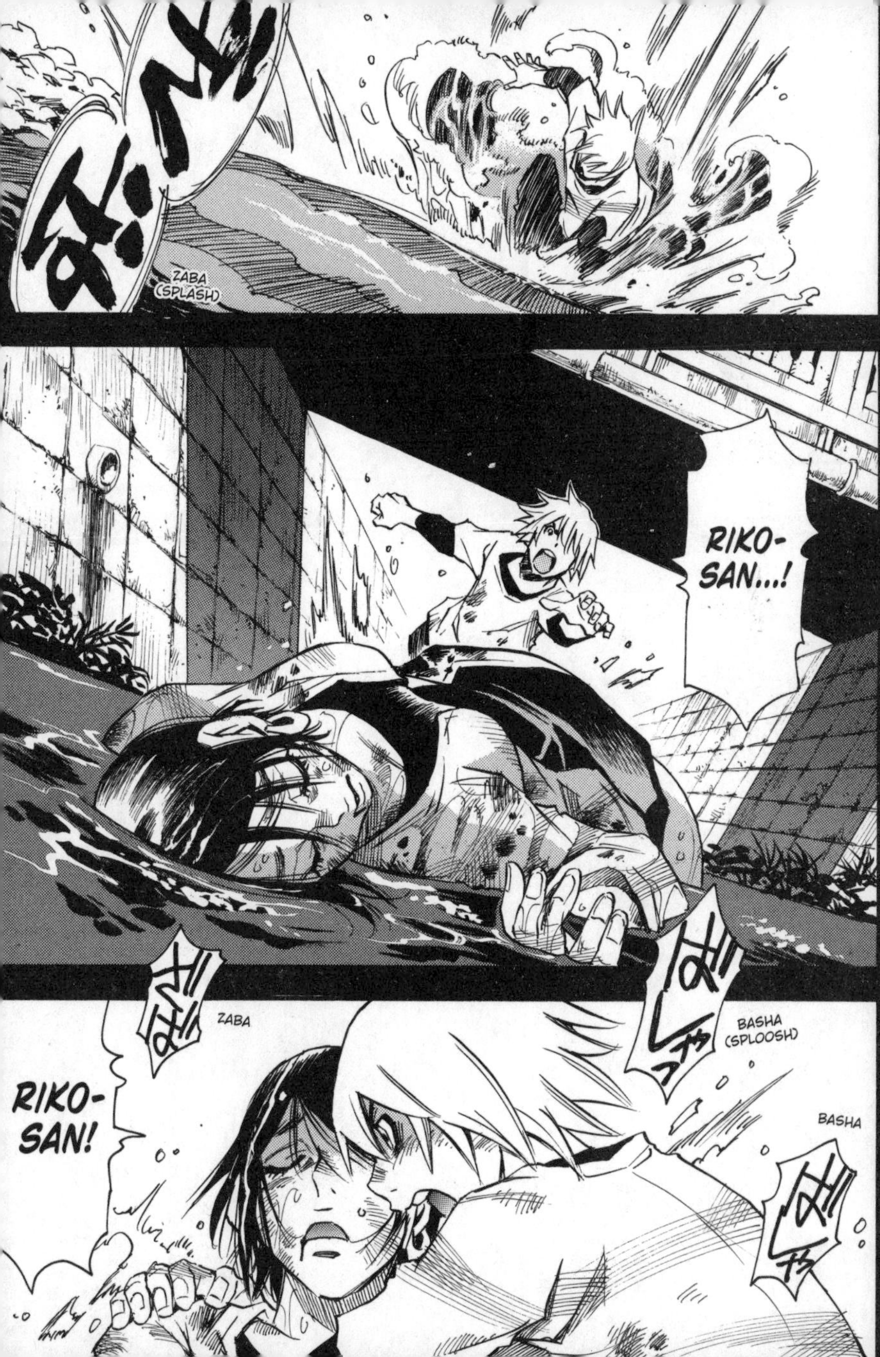
ZABA
(SPLASH)
RIKO-
SAN...!
BASHA
(SPLOOSH)
BASHA
ZABA
RIKO-
SAN!

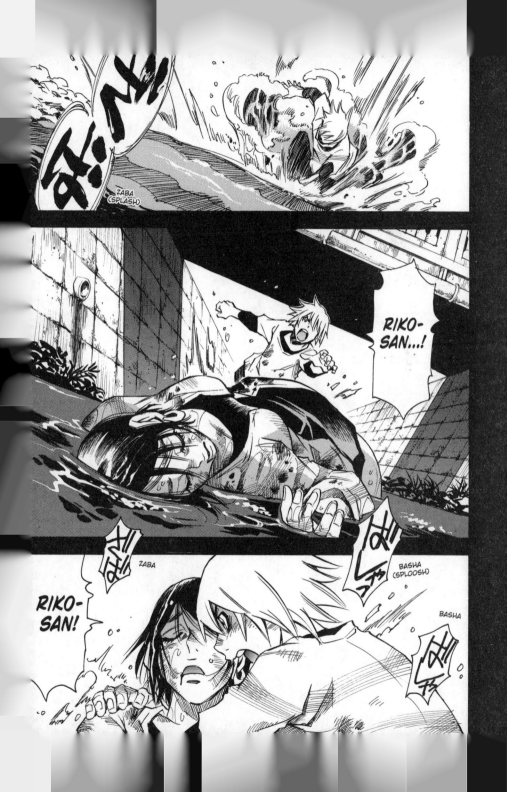

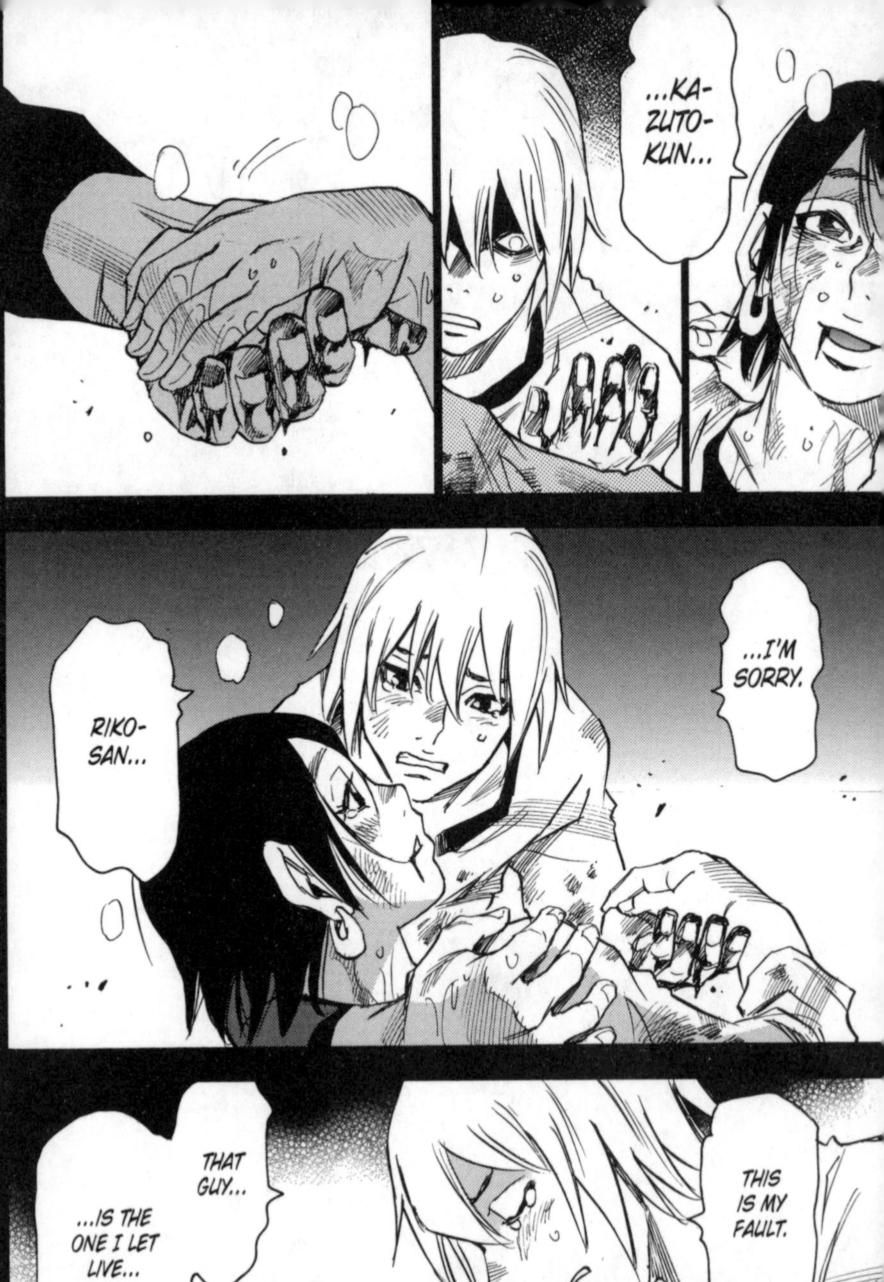
...KA-ZUTO-KUN...
...I'M SORRY.
RIKO-SAN...
THIS IS MY FAULT.
THAT GUY...
...IS THE ONE I LET LIVE...

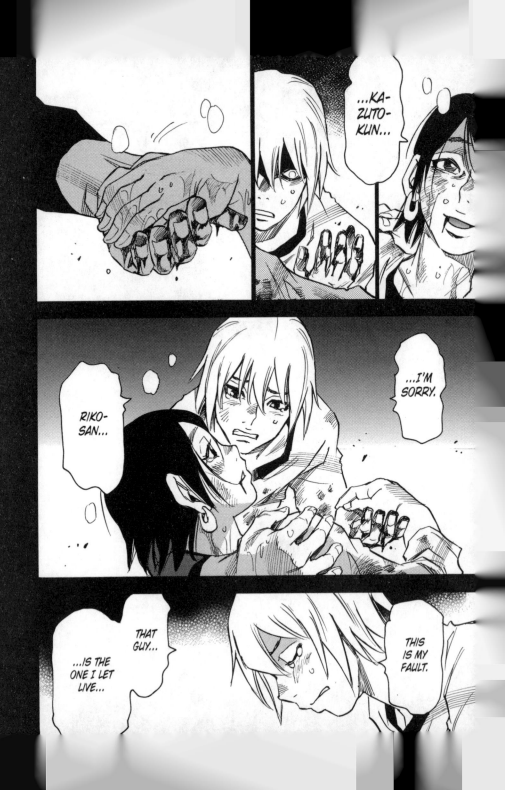

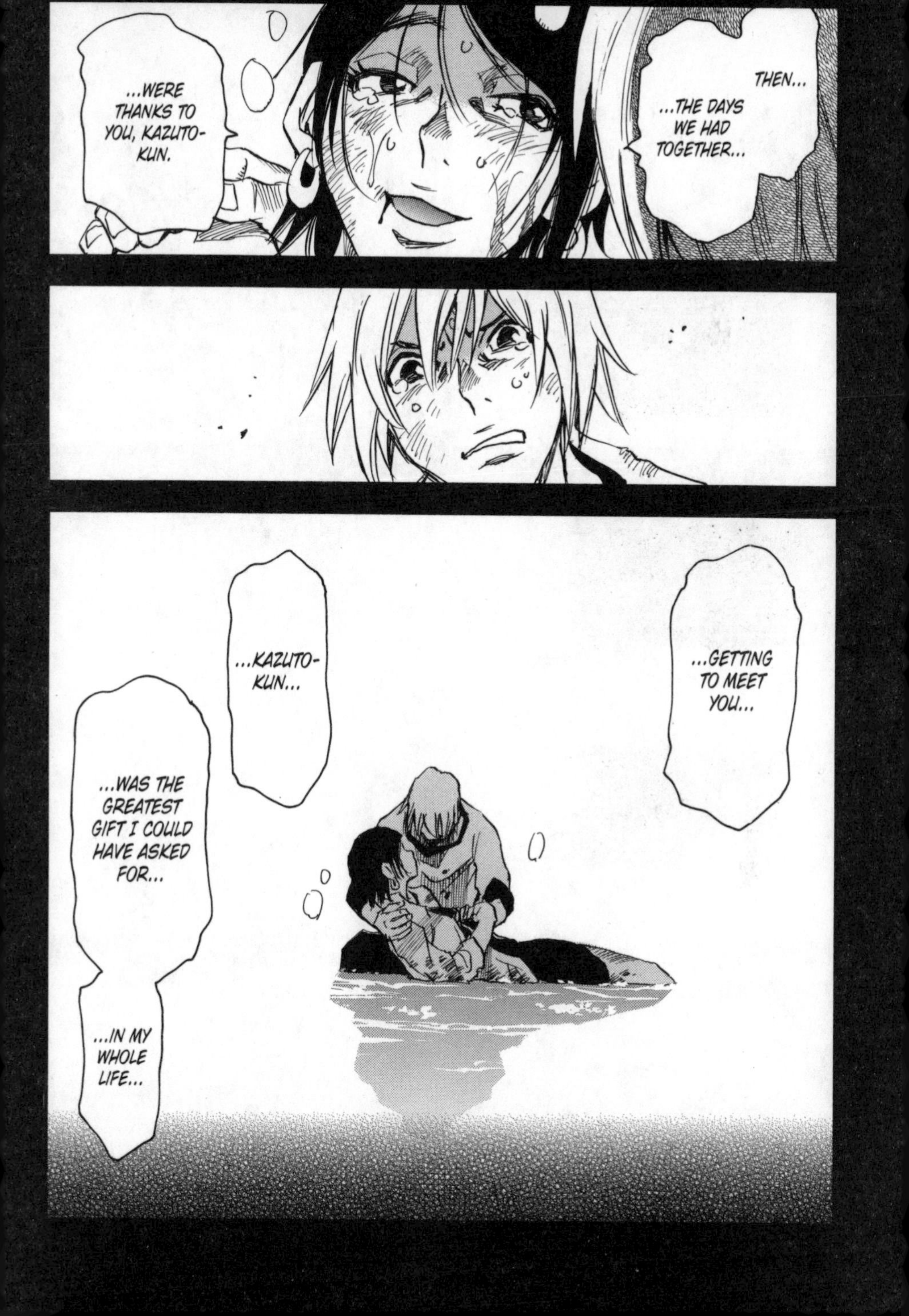
THEN... ...THE DAYS WE HAD TOGETHER...
...WERE THANKS TO YOU, KAZUTO-KUN.
...GETTING TO MEET YOU...
...KAZUTO-KUN...
...WAS THE GREATEST GIFT I COULD HAVE ASKED FOR...
...IN MY WHOLE LIFE...

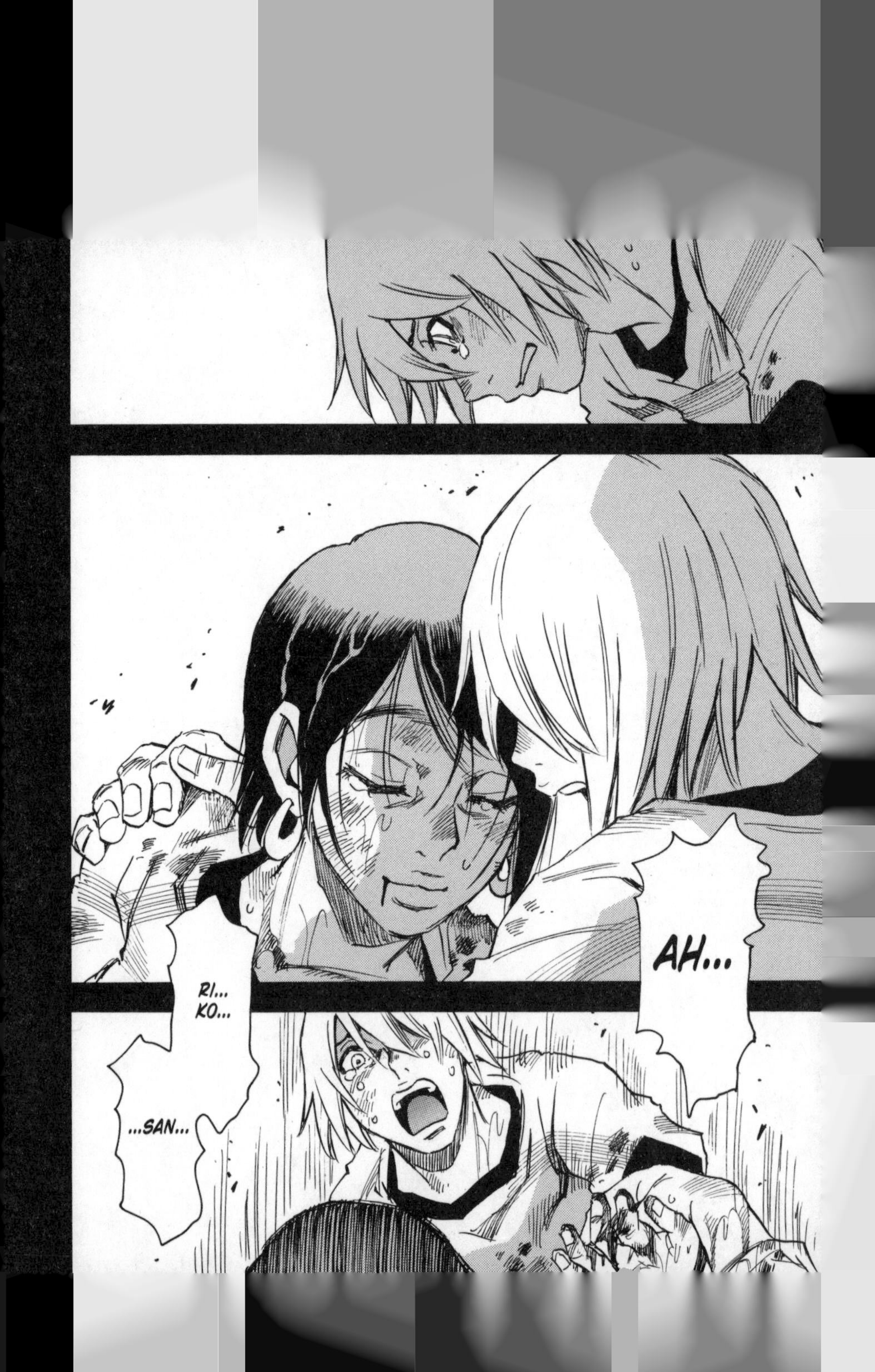
AH...
RI... KO...
...SAN...

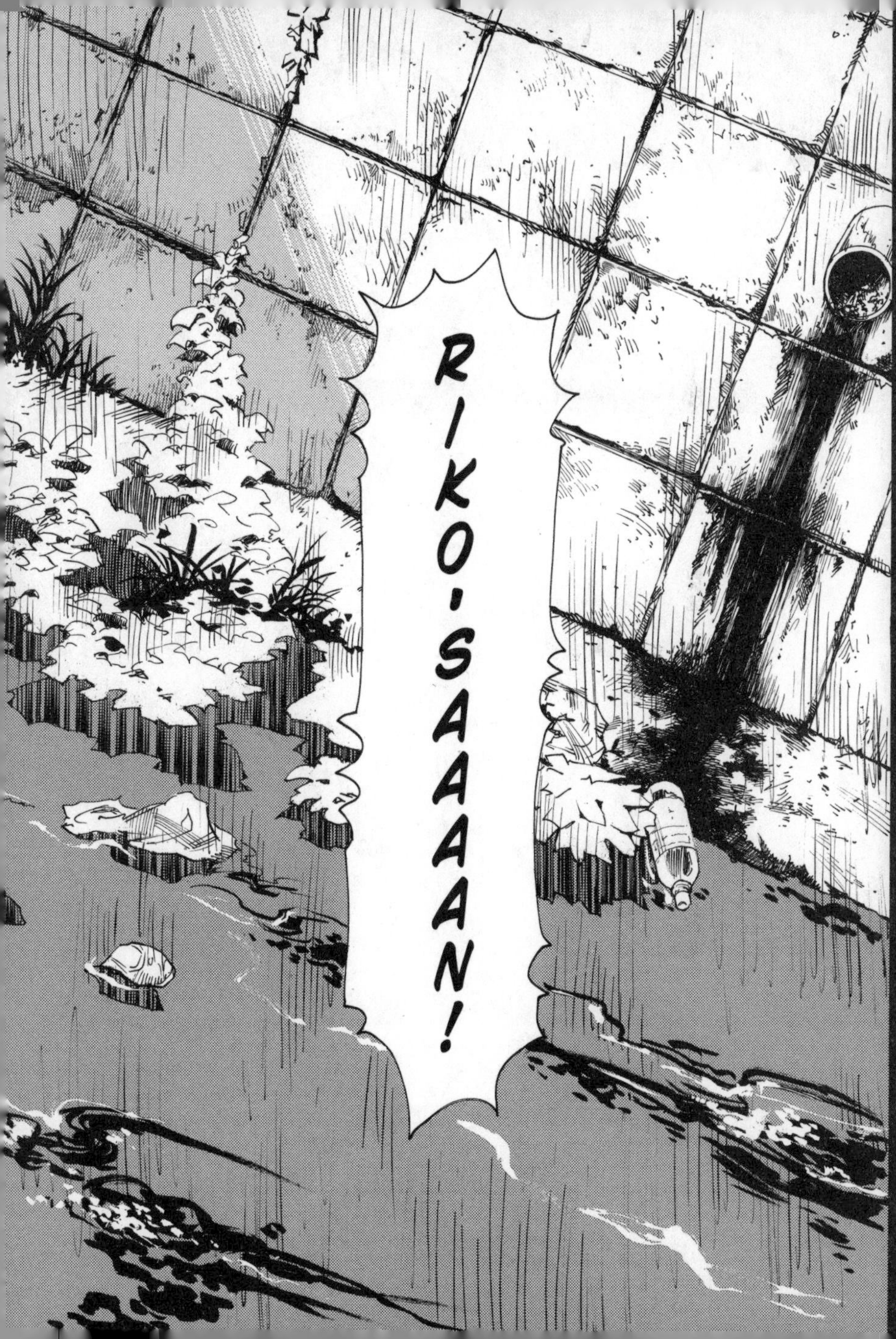
RIKO-SAAAAN!

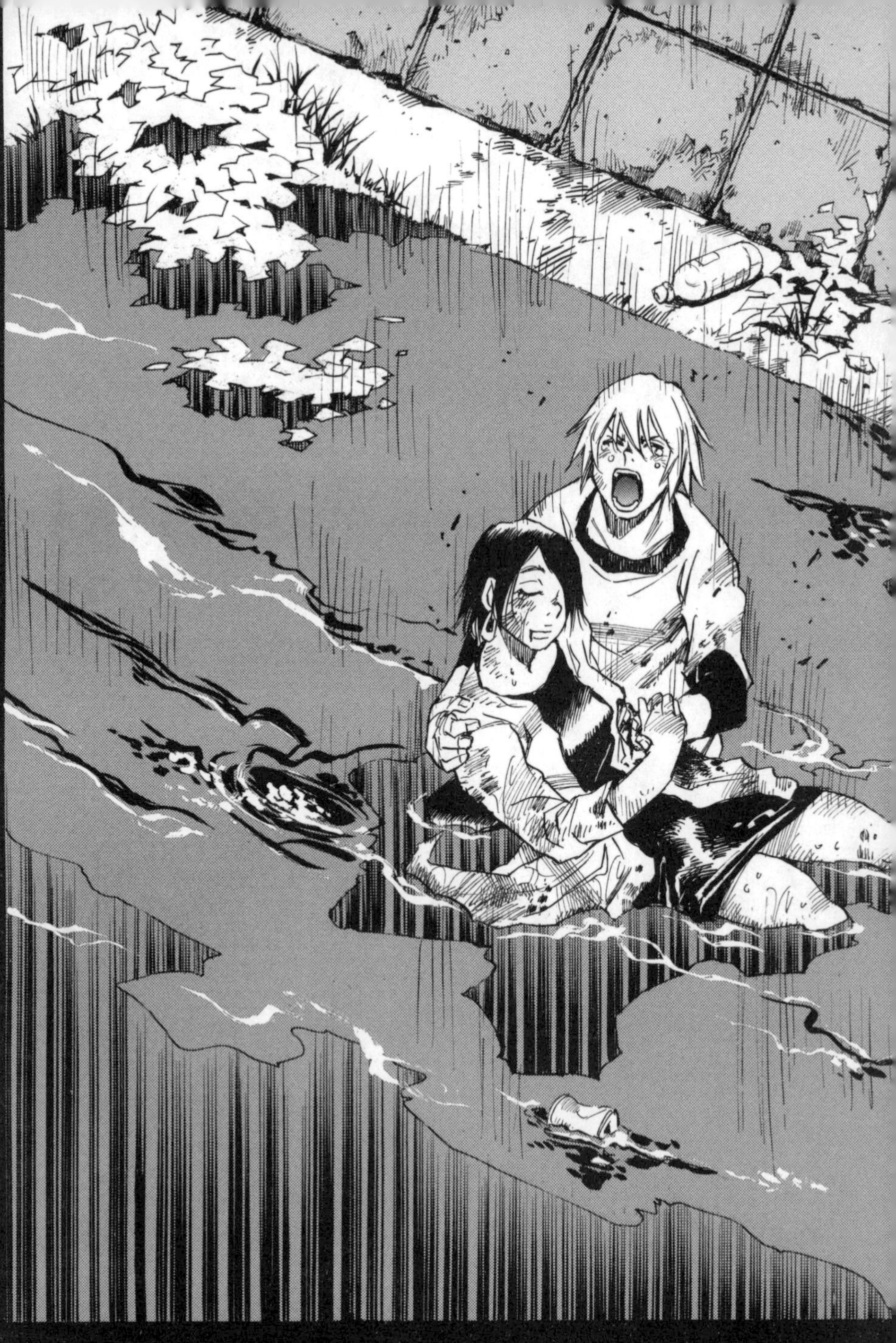

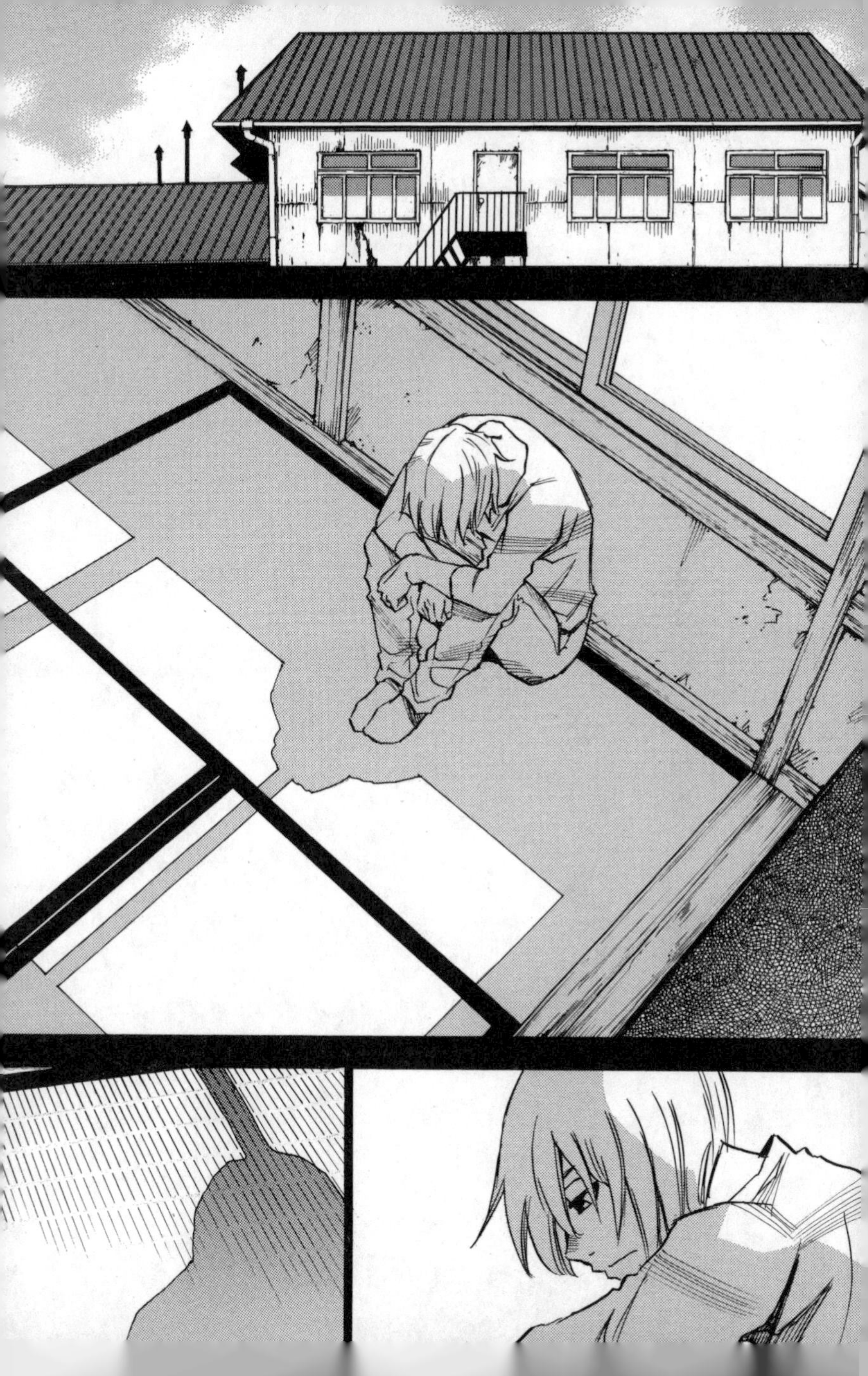

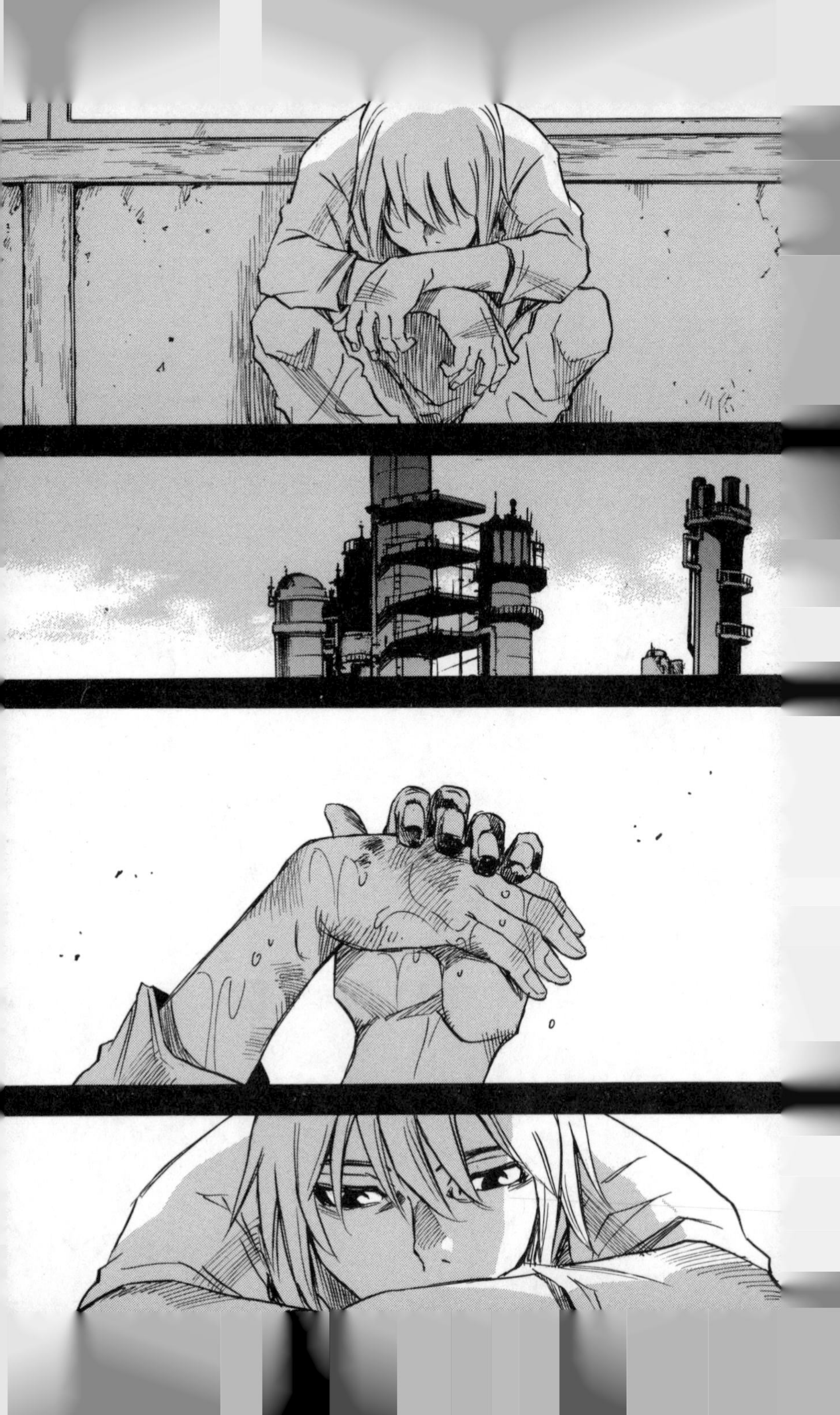

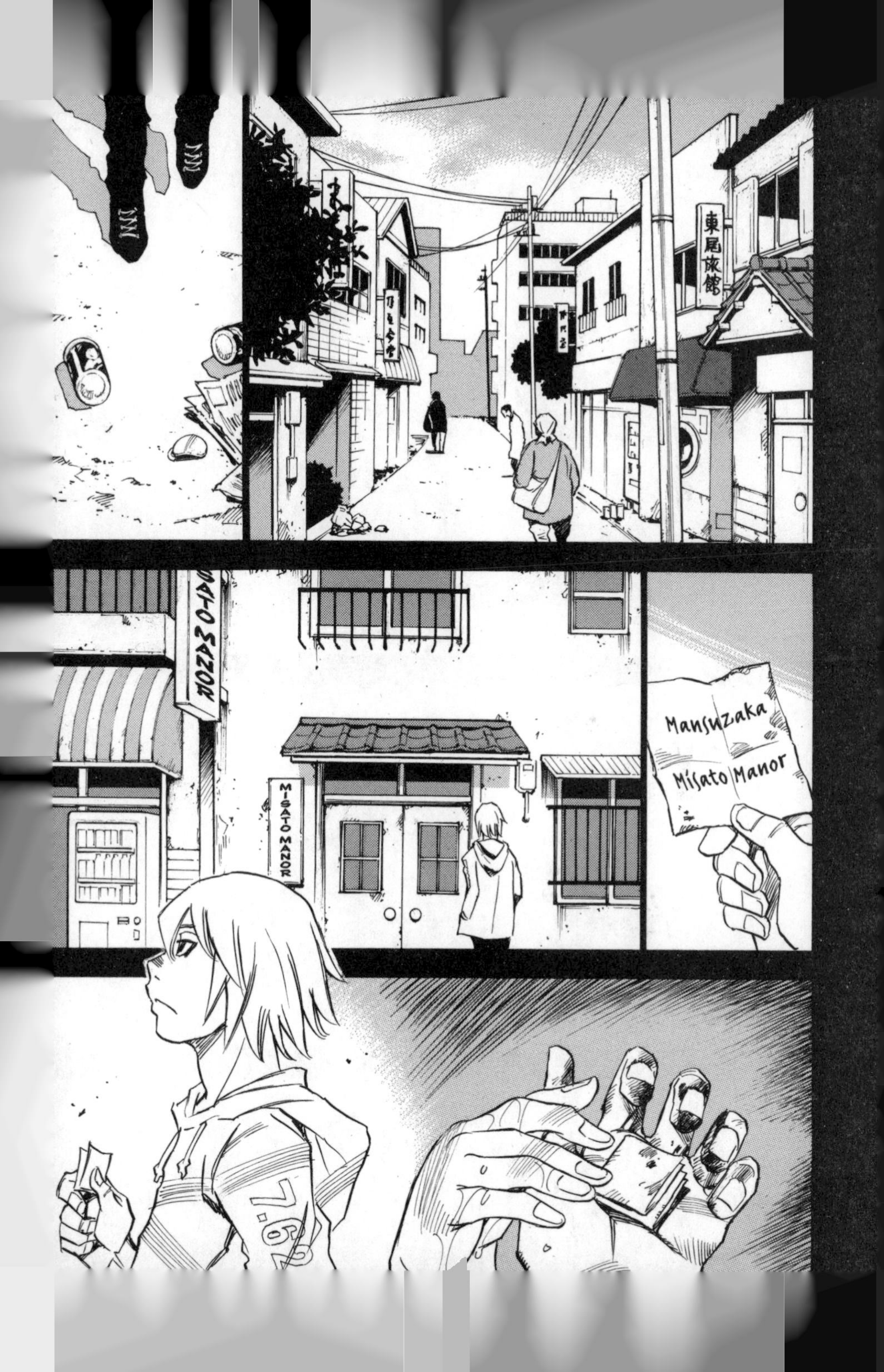
東尾旅館
Mansuzaka
Misato Manor
SATO MANOR
MISATO MANOR

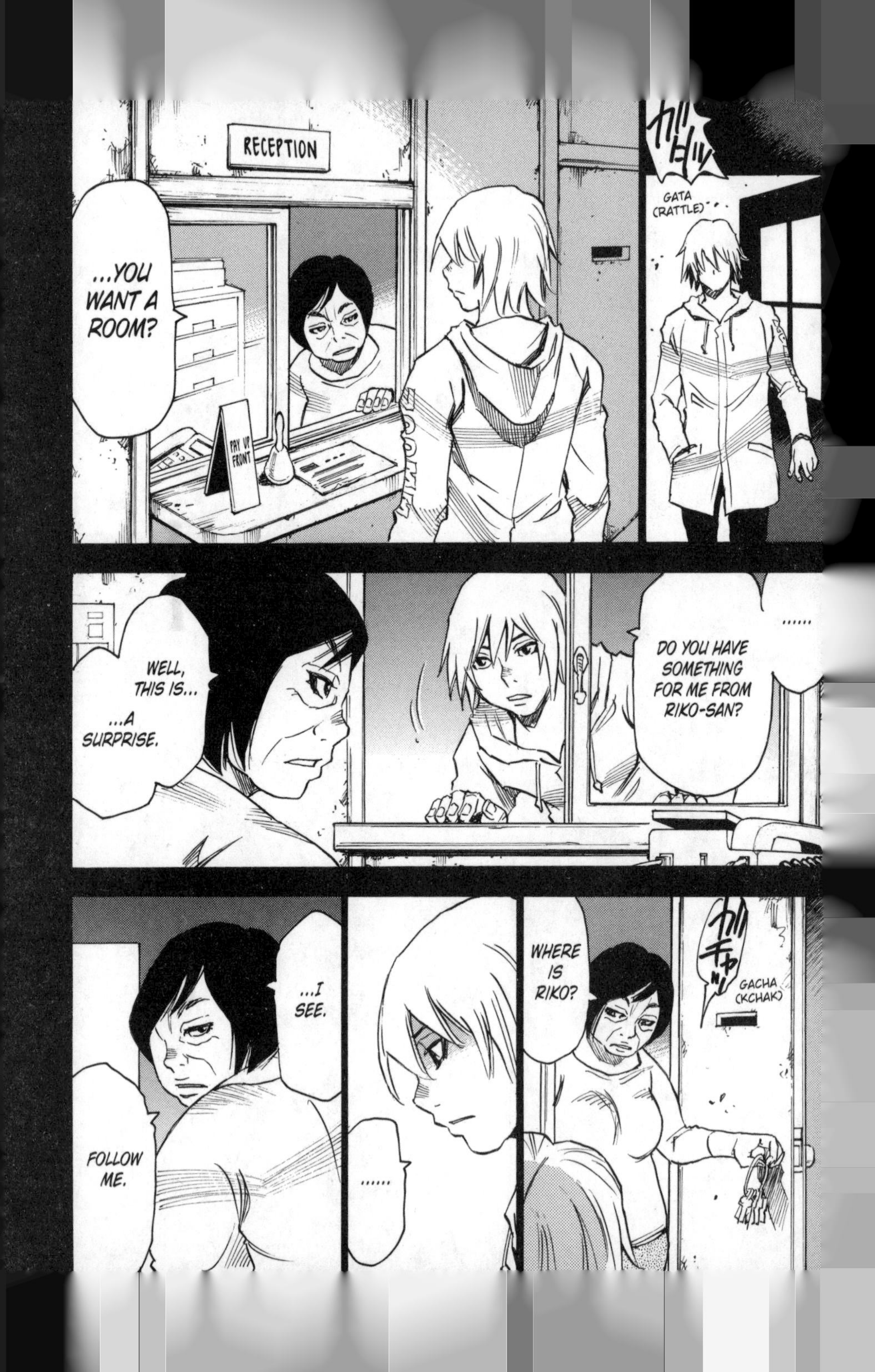
GATA (RATTLE)
RECEPTION
...YOU WANT A ROOM?
PAY UP FRONT
......
DO YOU HAVE SOMETHING FOR ME FROM RIKO-SAN?
WELL, THIS IS...
...A SURPRISE.
GACHA (KCHAK)
WHERE IS RIKO?
......
...I SEE.
FOLLOW ME.

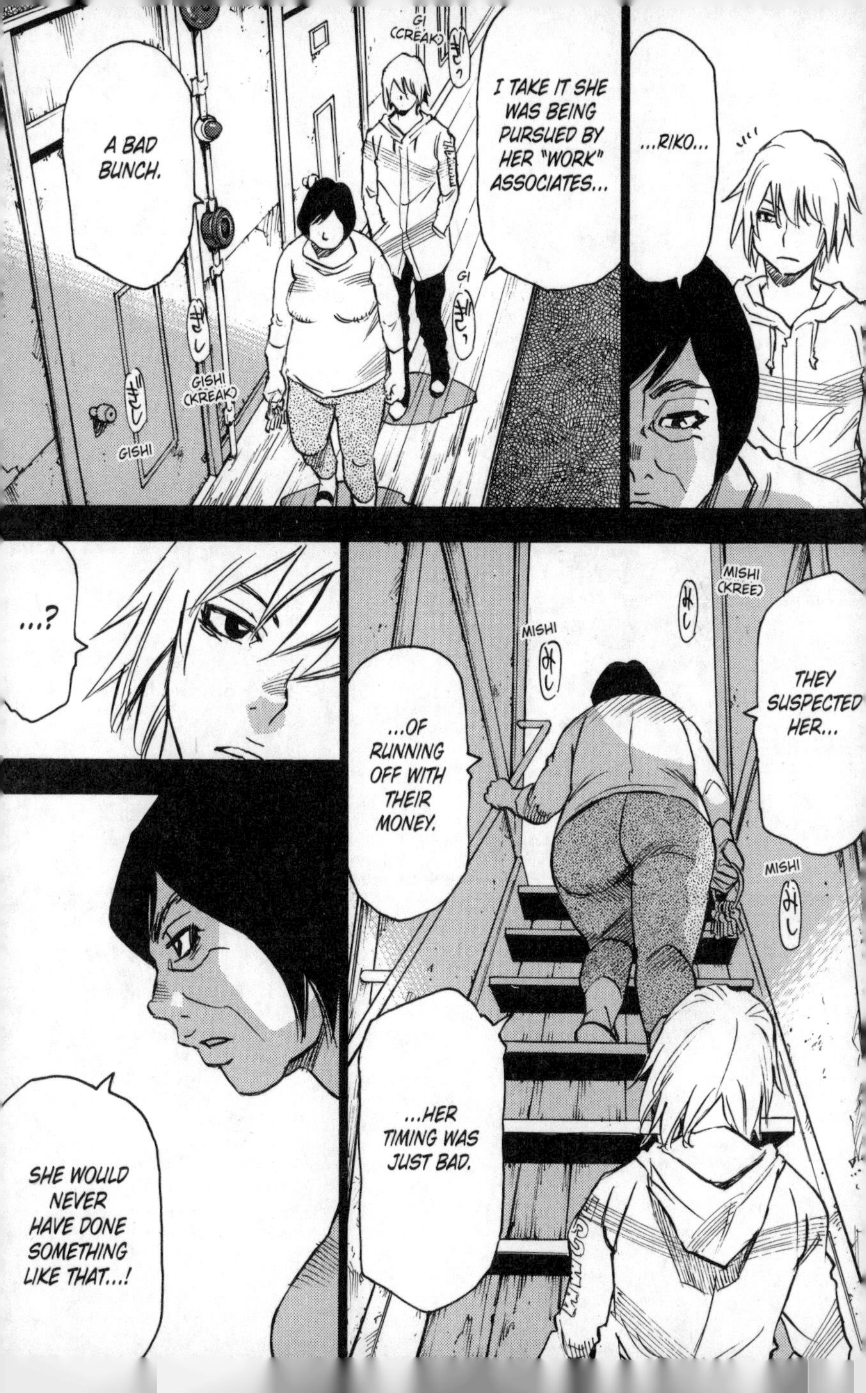
...RIKO...
GI (CREAK)
I TAKE IT SHE WAS BEING PURSUED BY HER "WORK" ASSOCIATES...
A BAD BUNCH.
GI
GISHI (KREAK)
GISHI
MISHI (KREE)
MISHI
THEY SUSPECTED HER...
...OF RUNNING OFF WITH THEIR MONEY.
MISHI
...HER TIMING WAS JUST BAD.
...?
SHE WOULD NEVER HAVE DONE SOMETHING LIKE THAT...!

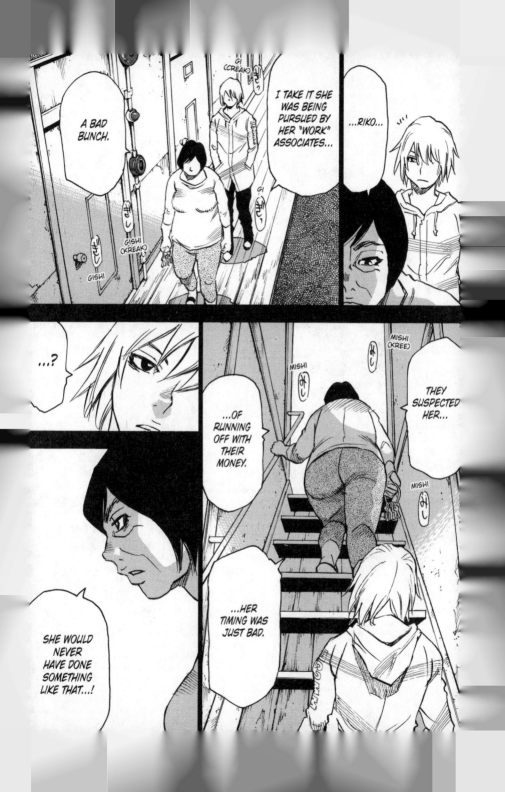

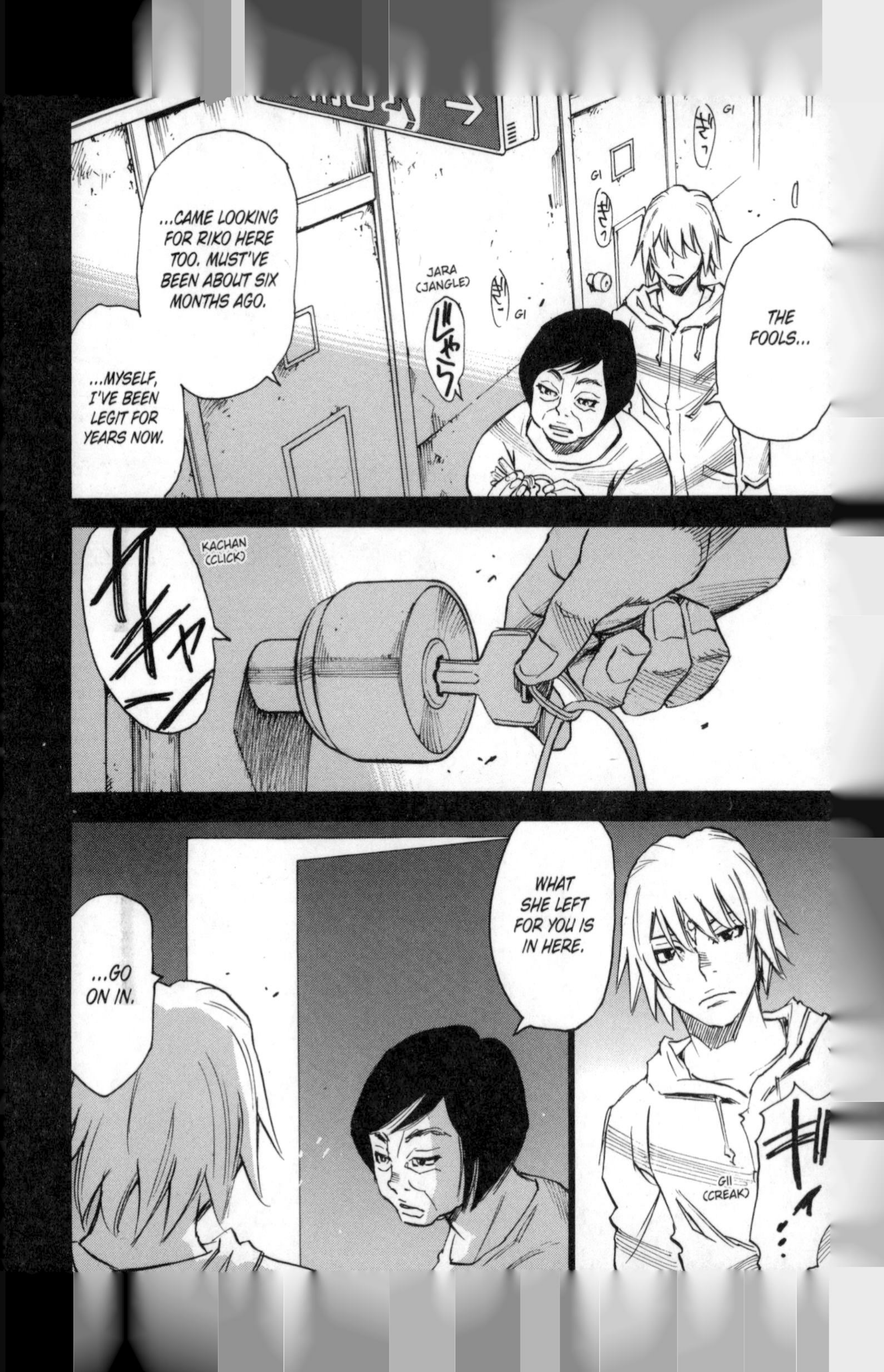

THE FOOLS...
GI
GI
GI
JARA (JANGLE)
じゃら
...CAME LOOKING FOR RIKO HERE TOO. MUST'VE BEEN ABOUT SIX MONTHS AGO.
...MYSELF, I'VE BEEN LEGIT FOR YEARS NOW.
KACHAN (CLICK)
WHAT SHE LEFT FOR YOU IS IN HERE.
GII (CREAK)
...GO ON IN.

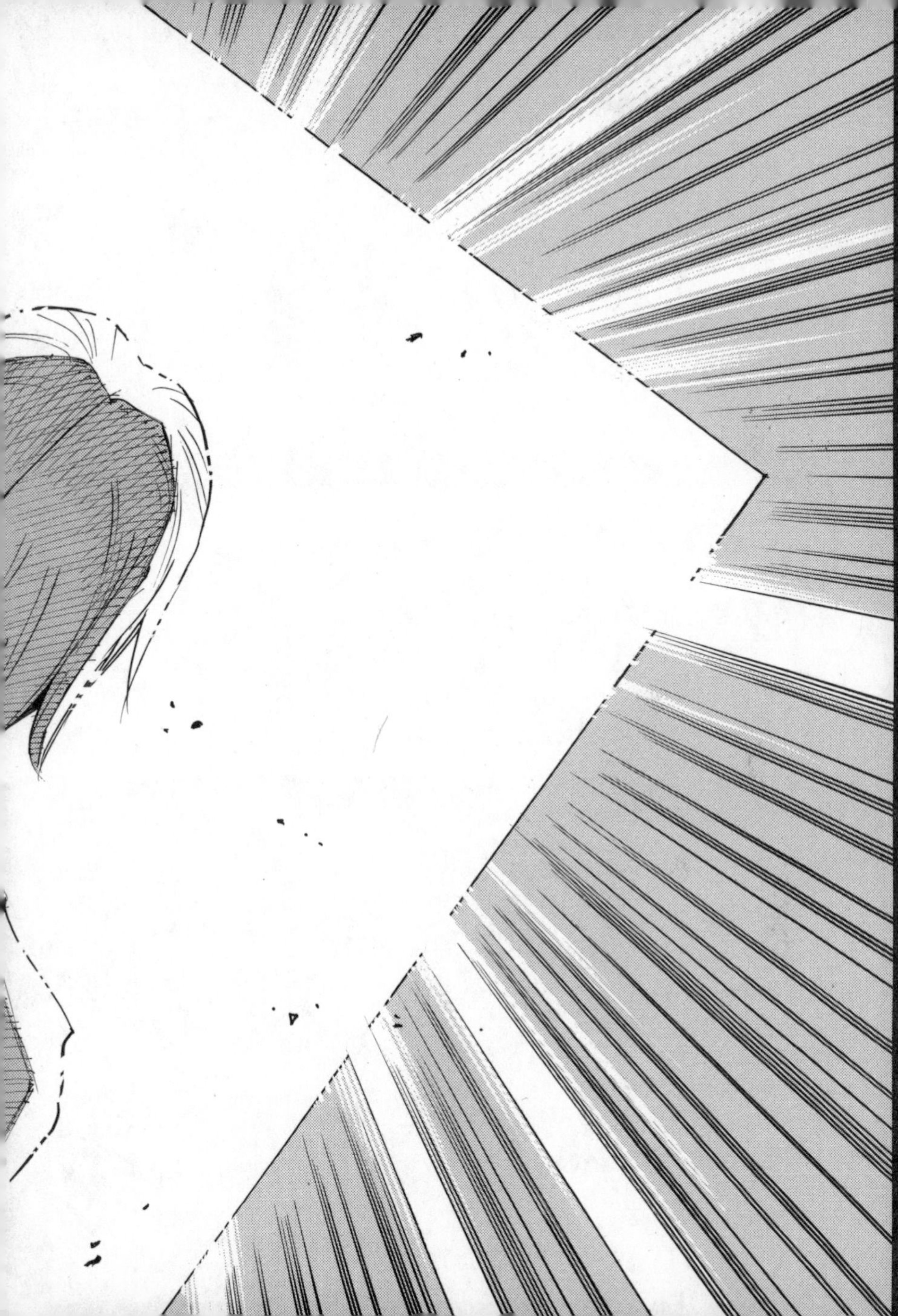

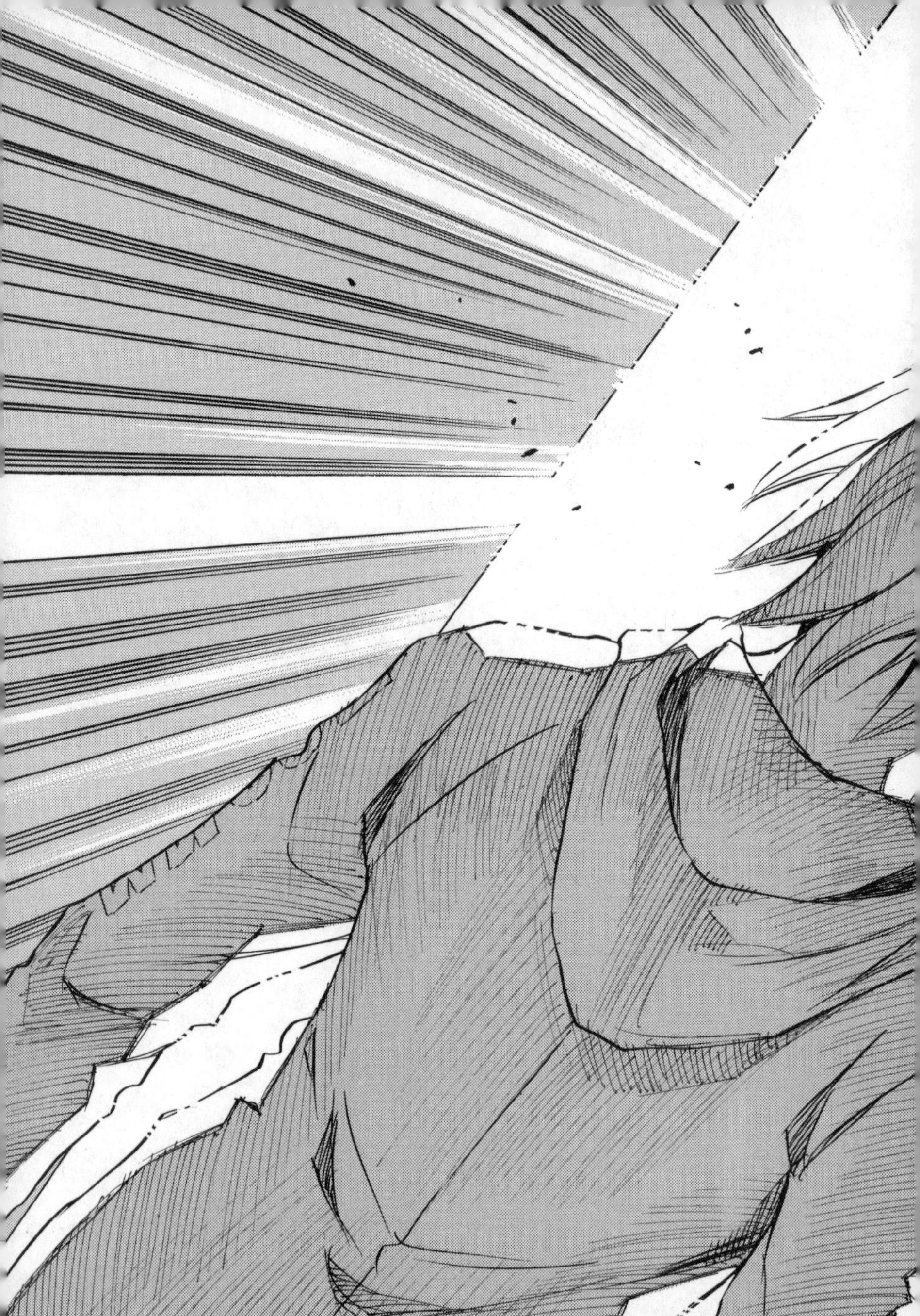

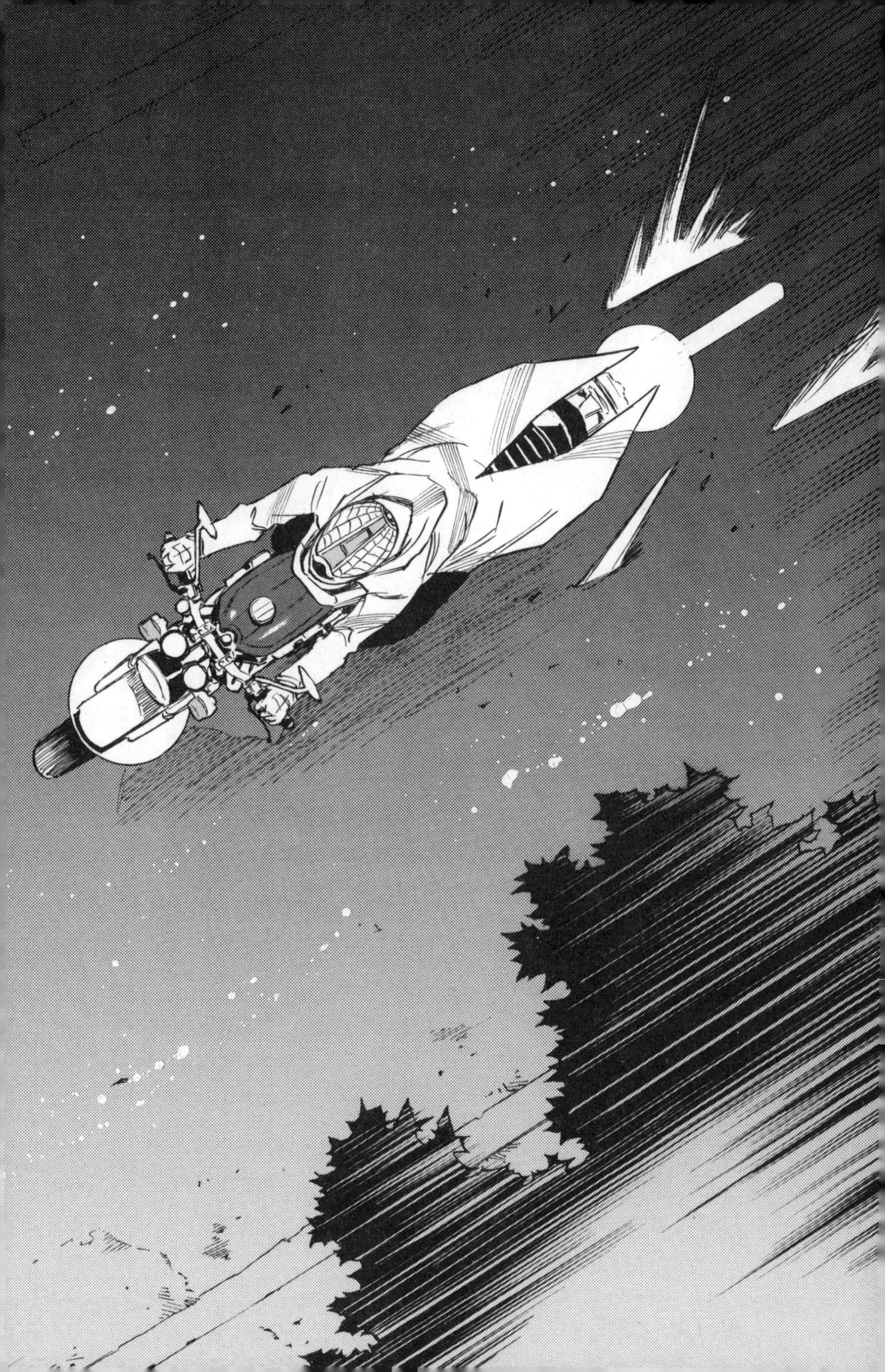

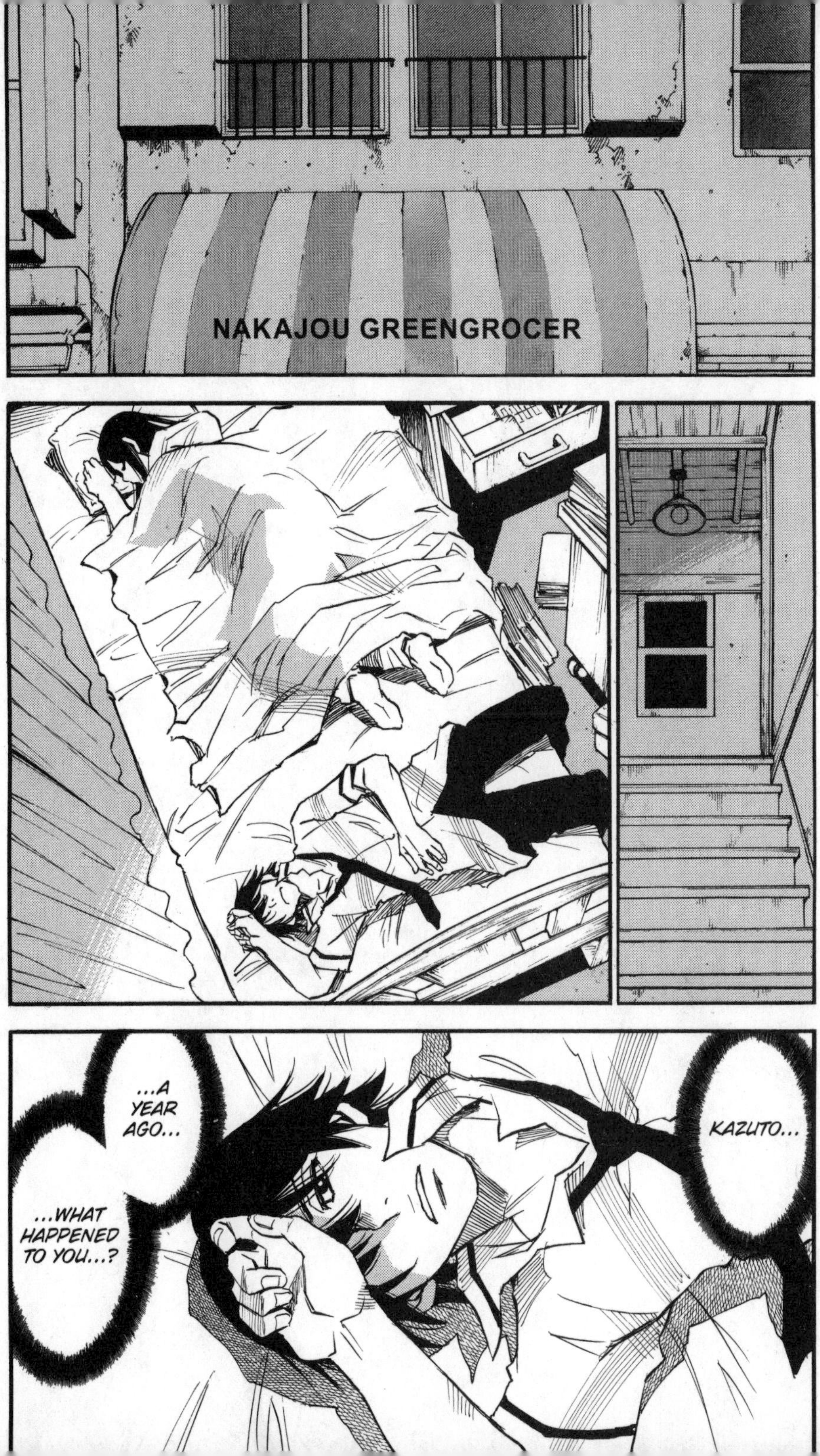
NAKAJOU GREENGROCER
KAZUTO...
...A YEAR AGO...
...WHAT HAPPENED TO YOU...?

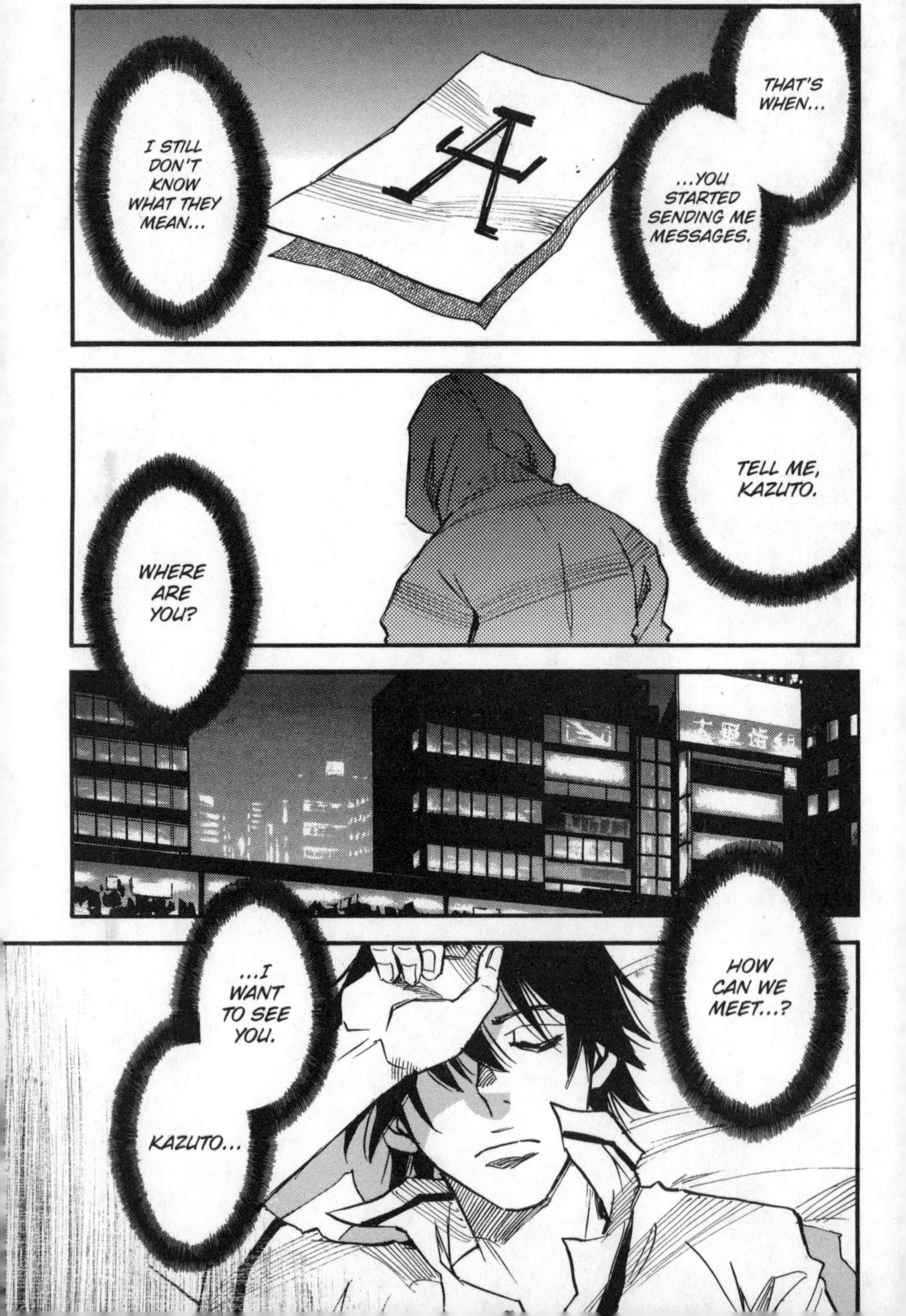
THAT'S WHEN...
...YOU STARTED SENDING ME MESSAGES.
I STILL DON'T KNOW WHAT THEY MEAN...
TELL ME, KAZUTO.
WHERE ARE YOU?
HOW CAN WE MEET...?
...I WANT TO SEE YOU.
KAZUTO...

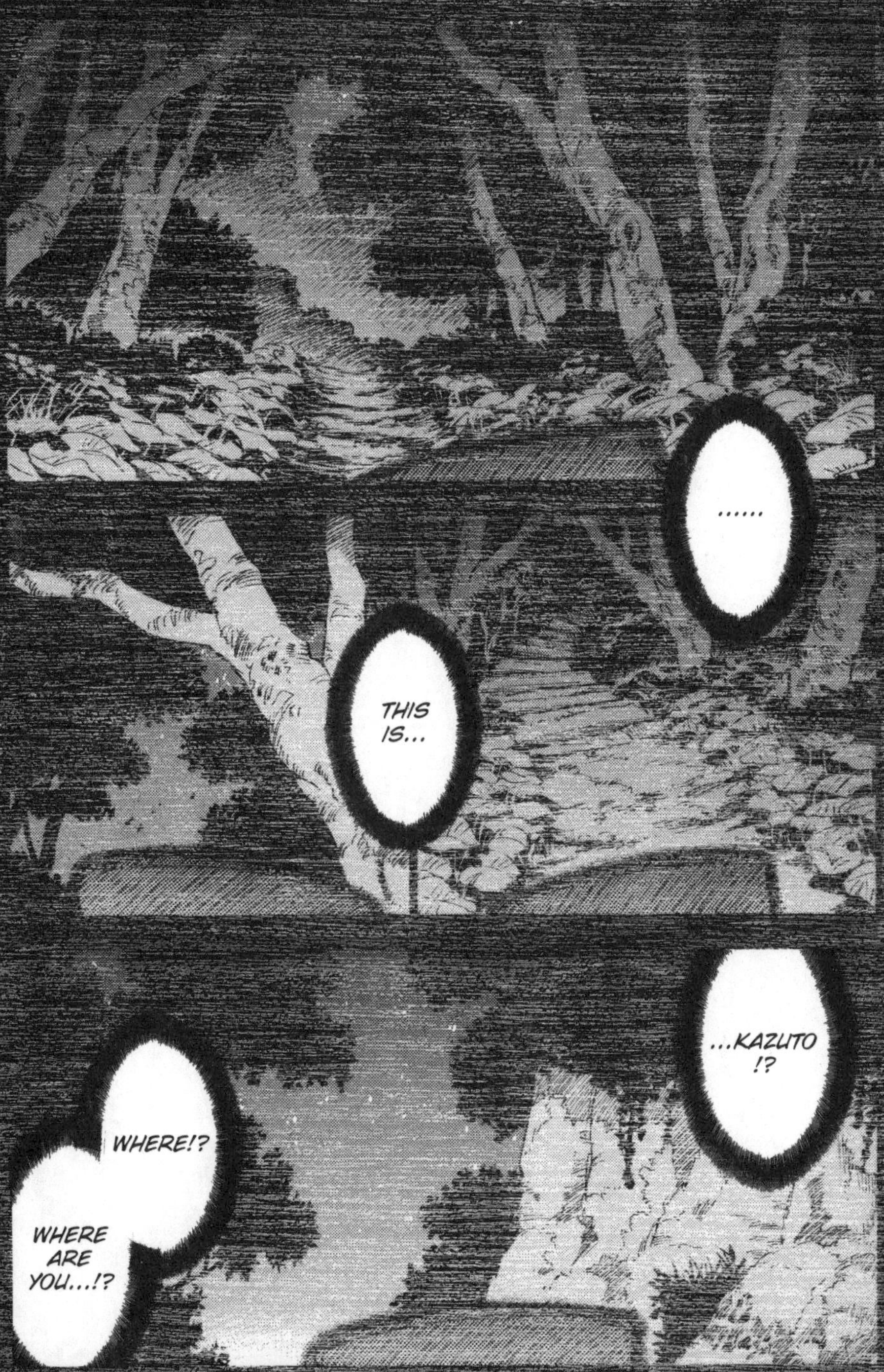
......
THIS IS...
...KAZUTO !?
WHERE!?
WHERE ARE YOU...!?

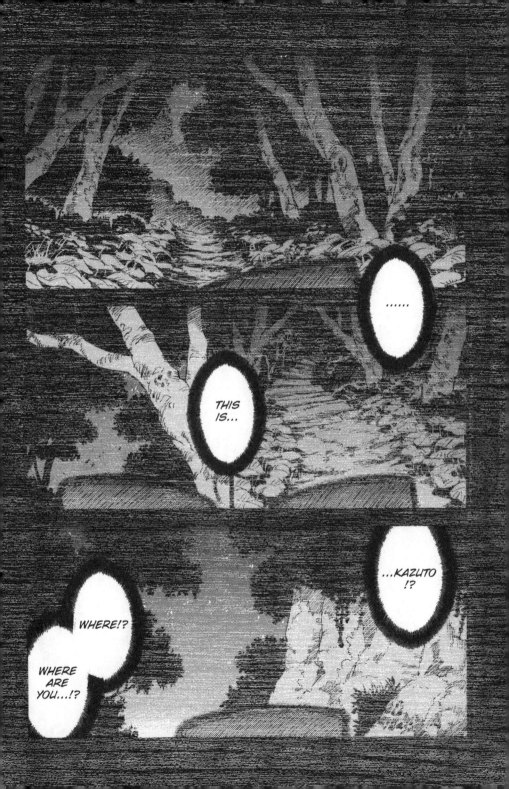

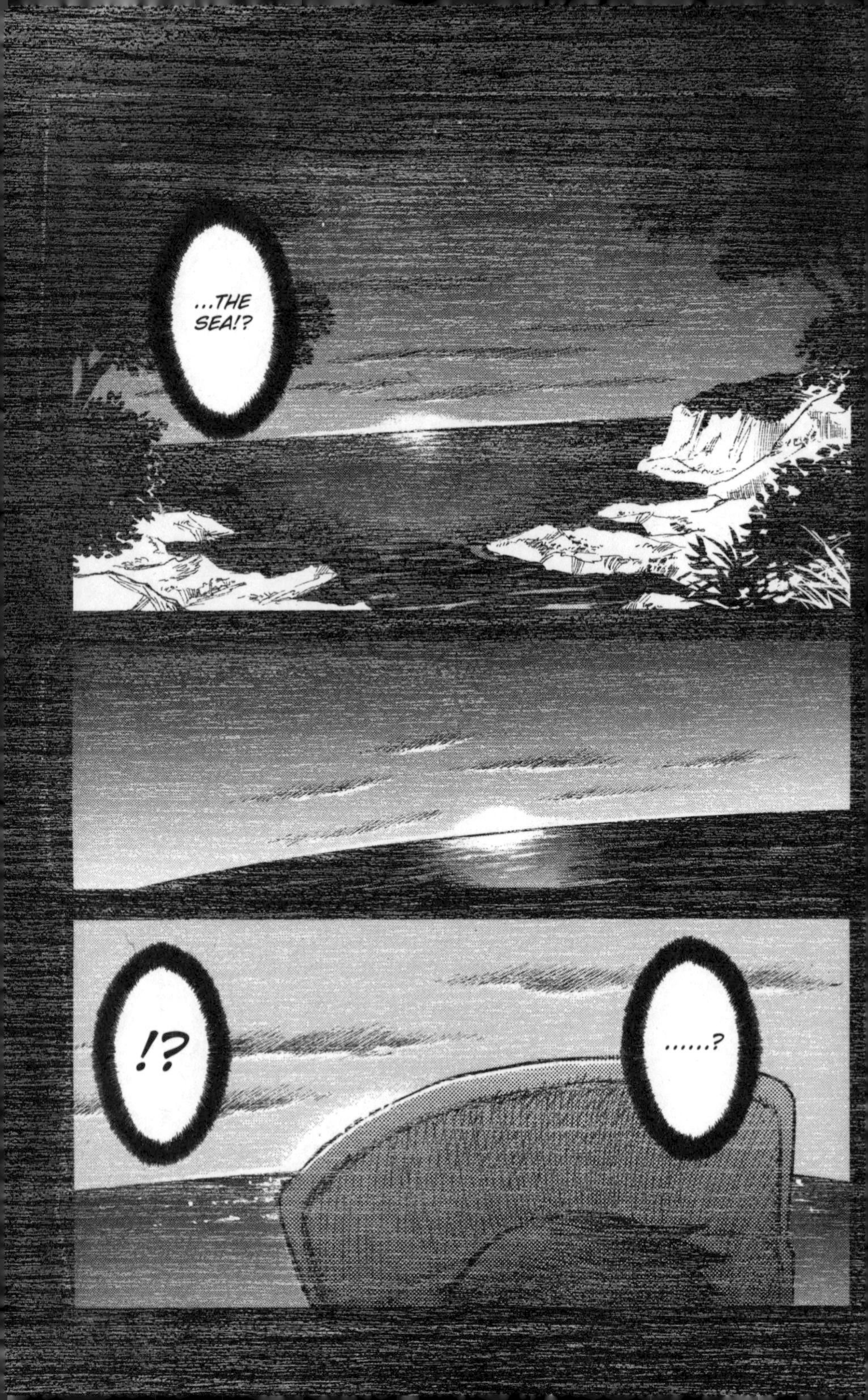
...THE SEA!?
......?
!?

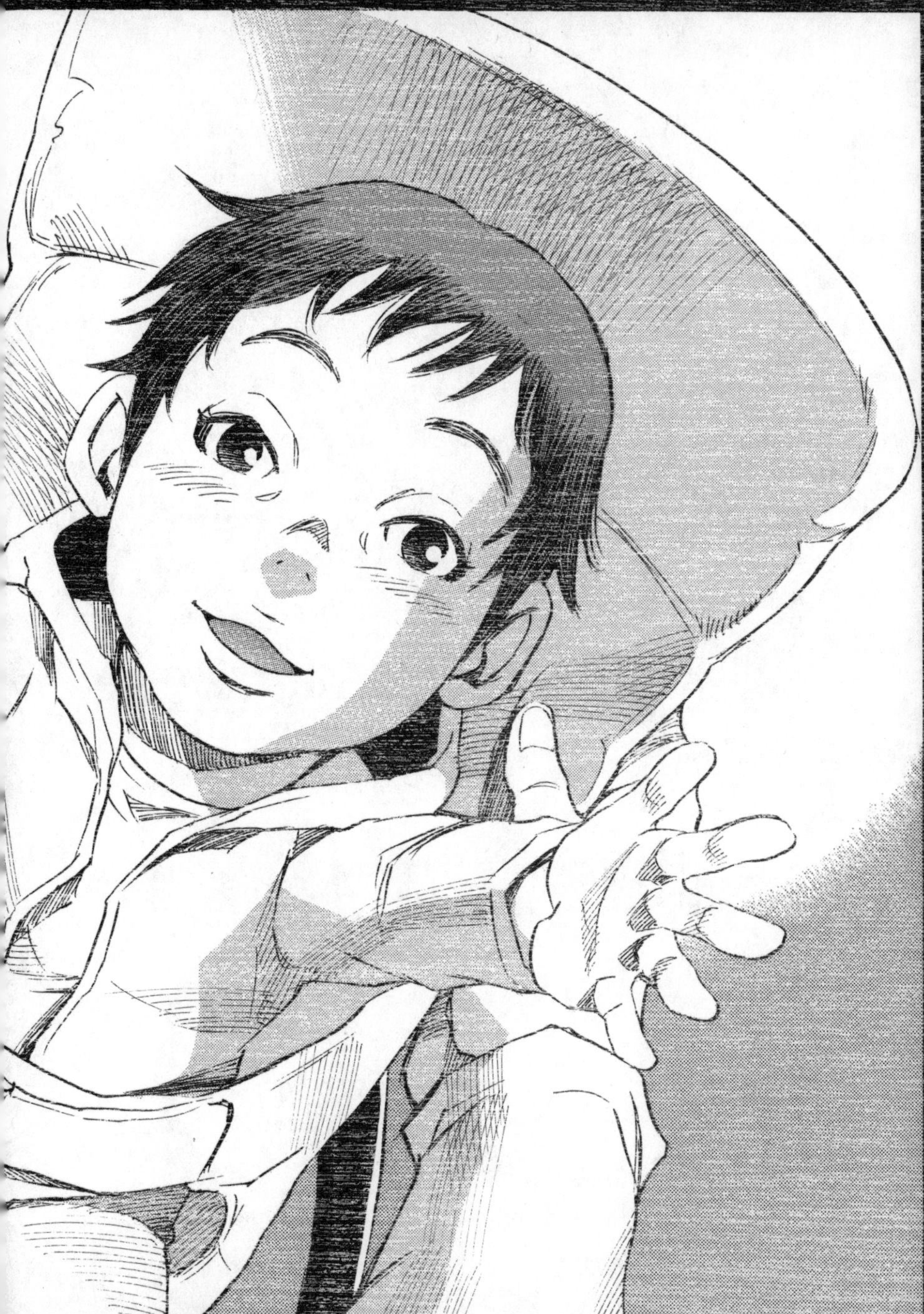

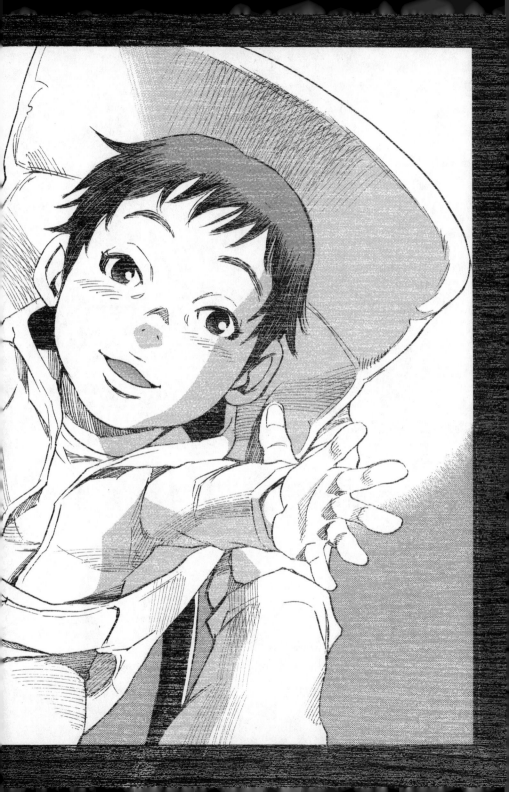

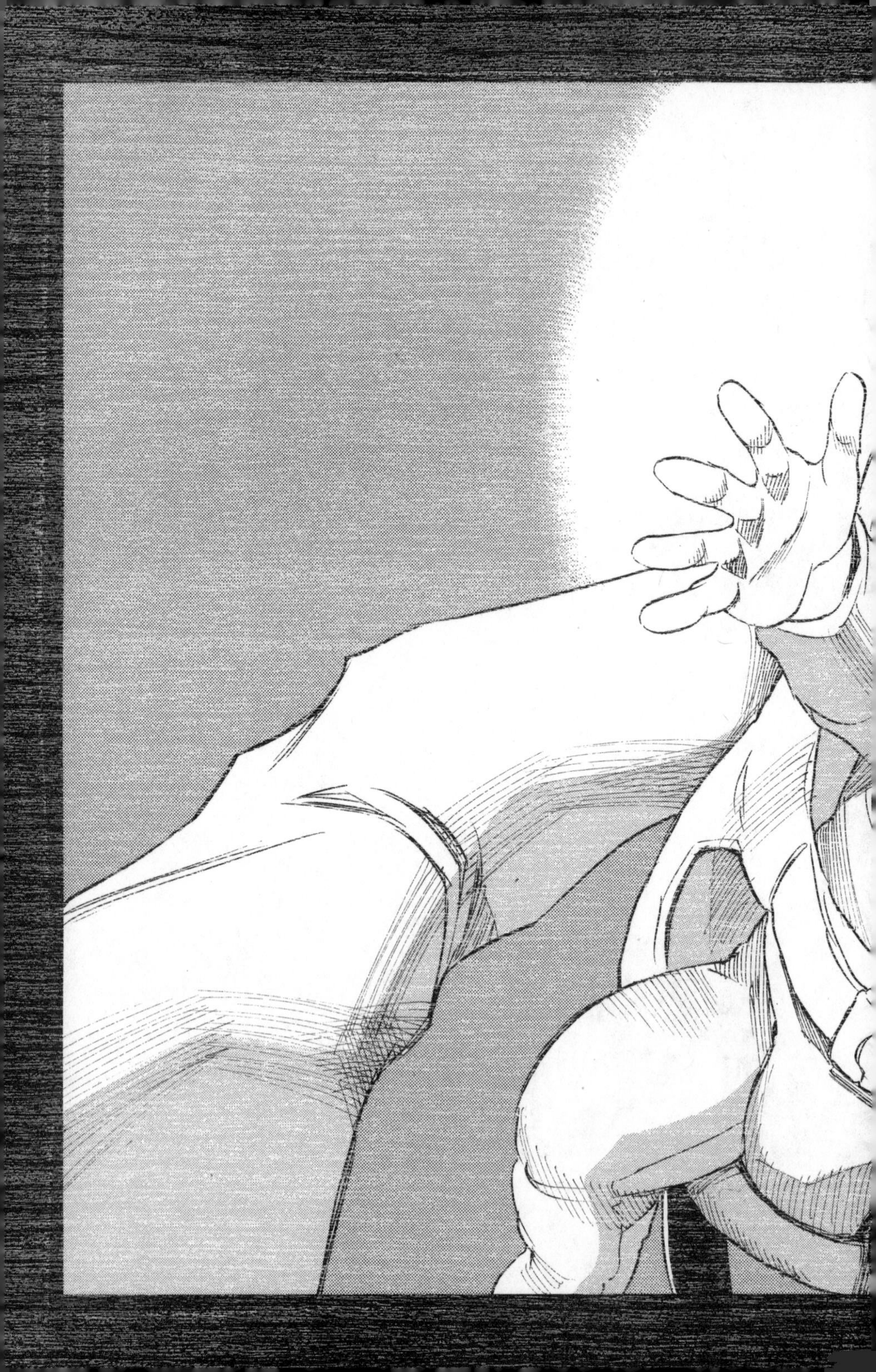

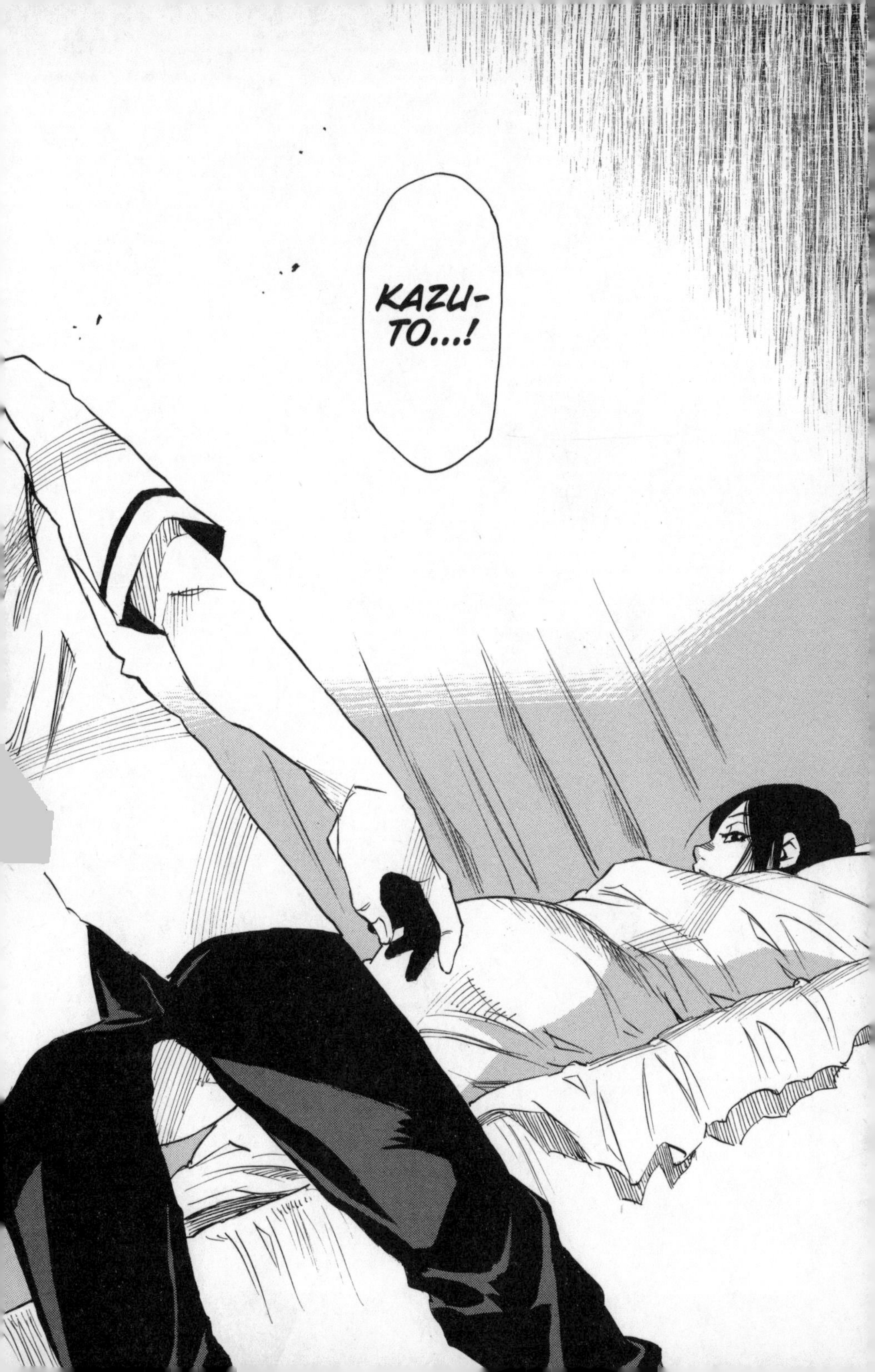
KAZU-TO...!

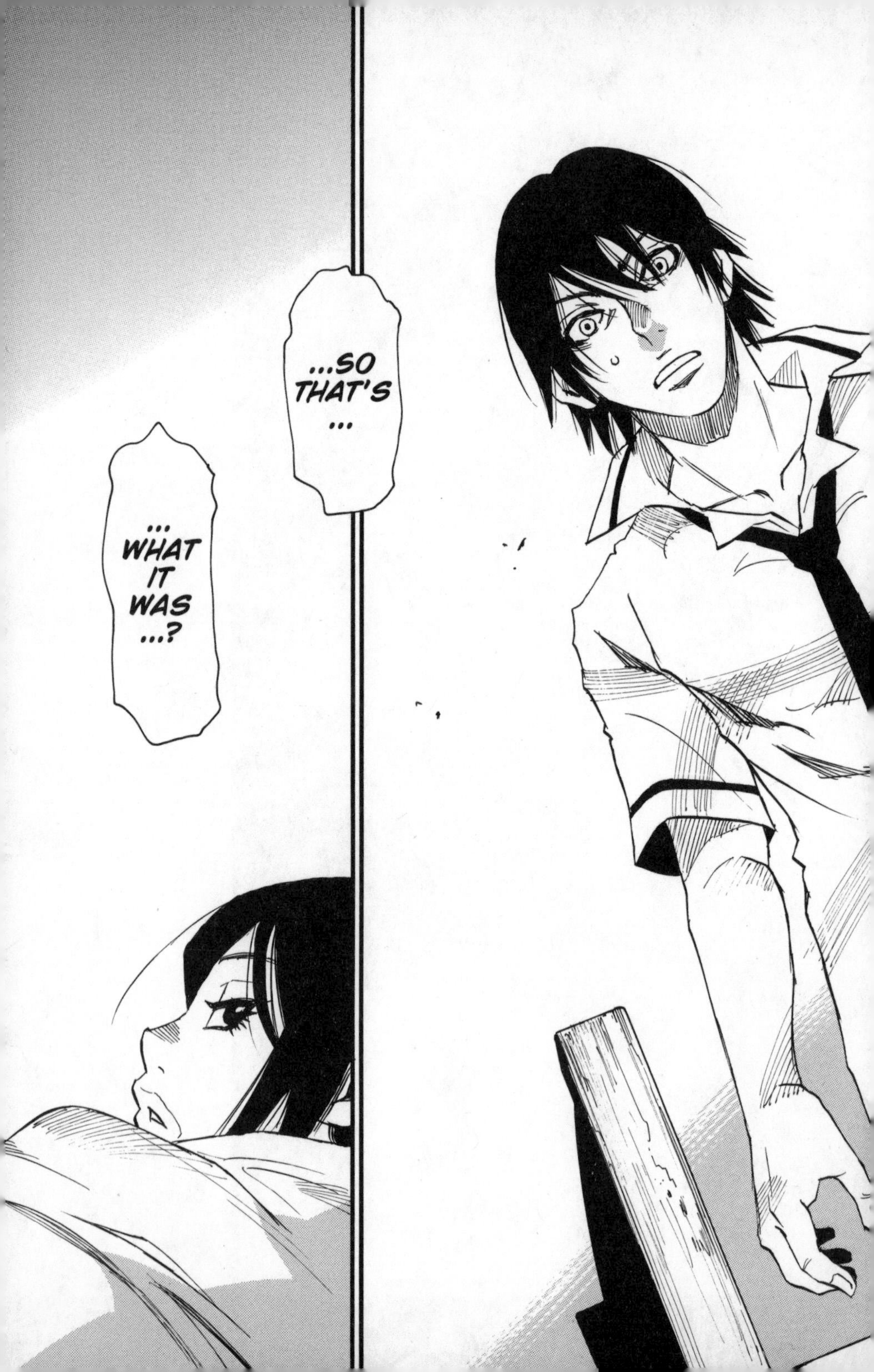
...SO THAT'S ...
... WHAT IT WAS ...?

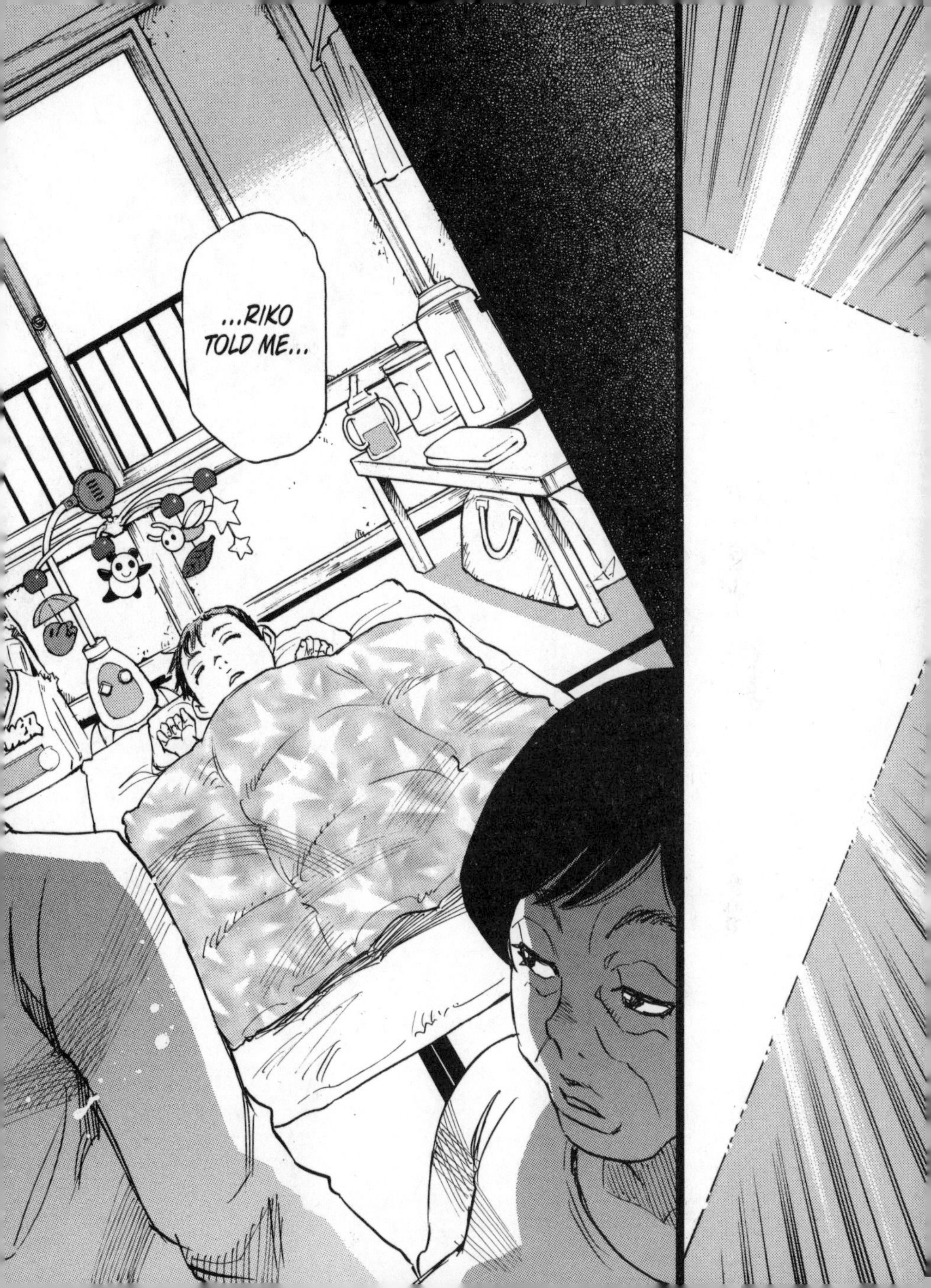
...RIKO TOLD ME...

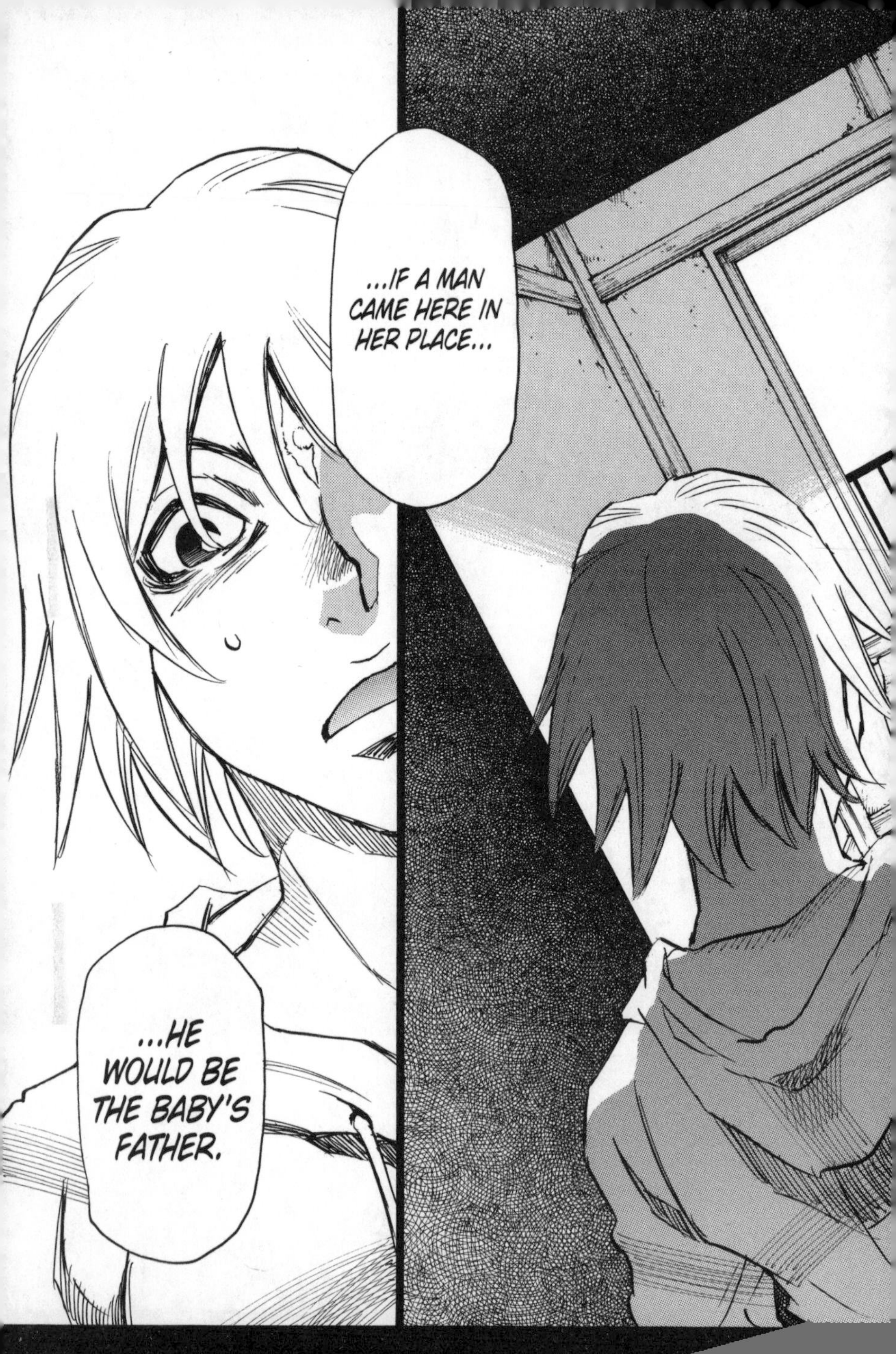
...IF A MAN CAME HERE IN HER PLACE...
...HE WOULD BE THE BABY'S FATHER.

I REALIZED WHAT RIKO-SAN'S LAST WORDS MEANT.

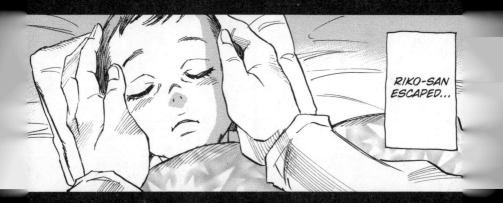

RIKO-SAN ESCAPED...

THE GREATEST GIFT OF HER LIFE.

...FOR THIS CHILD'S SAKE.

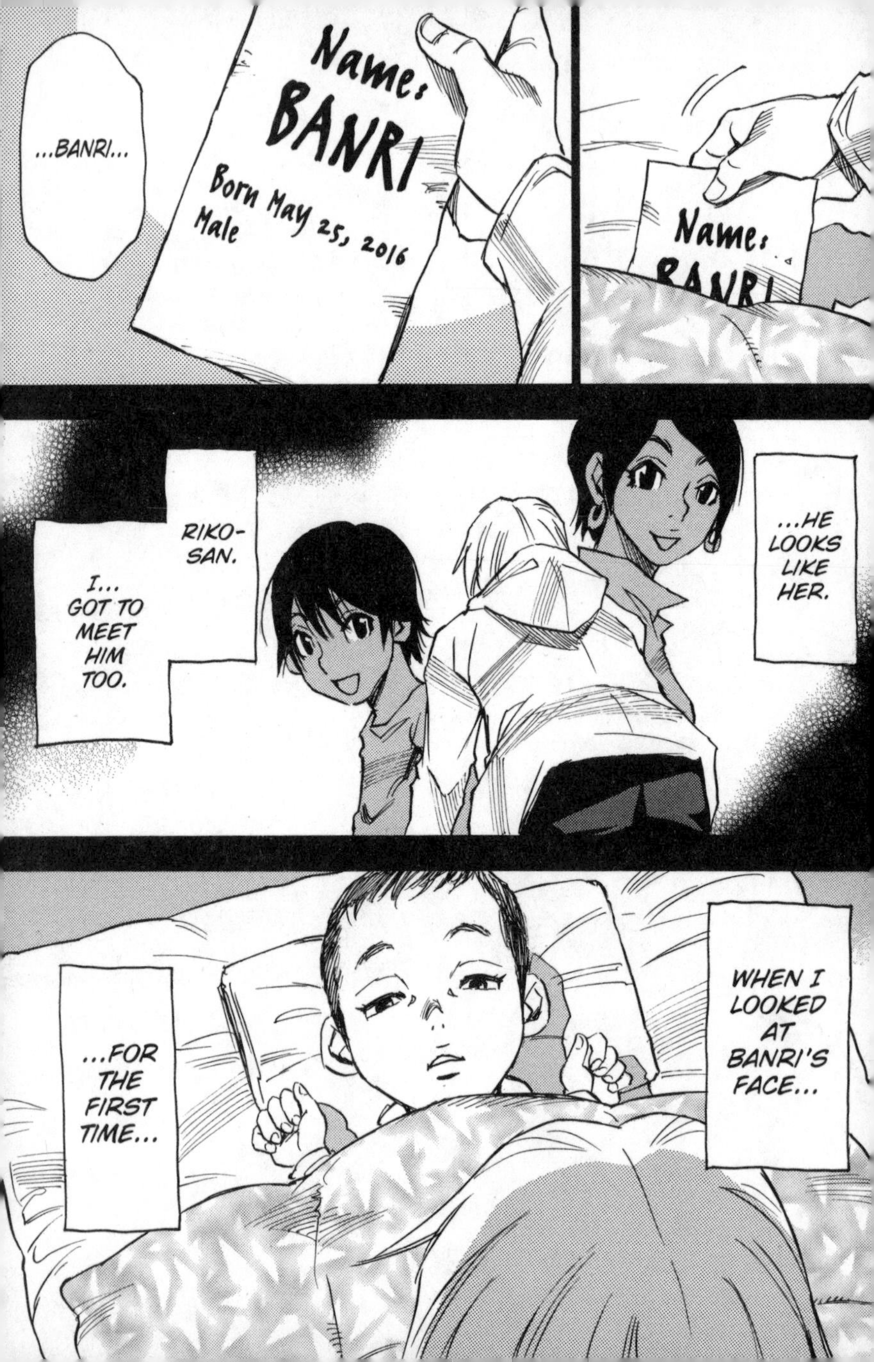
Name:
Name:
BANRI
Born May 25, 2016
Male
...BANRI...
...HE LOOKS LIKE HER.
RIKO-SAN.
I... GOT TO MEET HIM TOO.
WHEN I LOOKED AT BANRI'S FACE...
...FOR THE FIRST TIME...

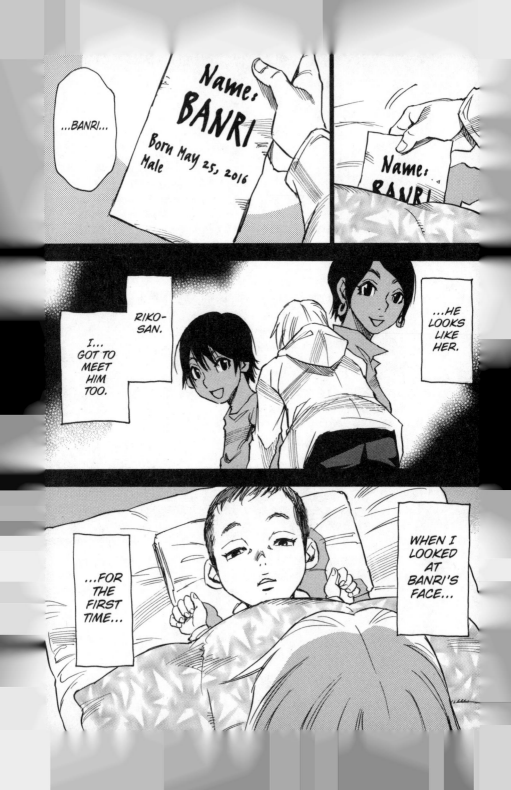

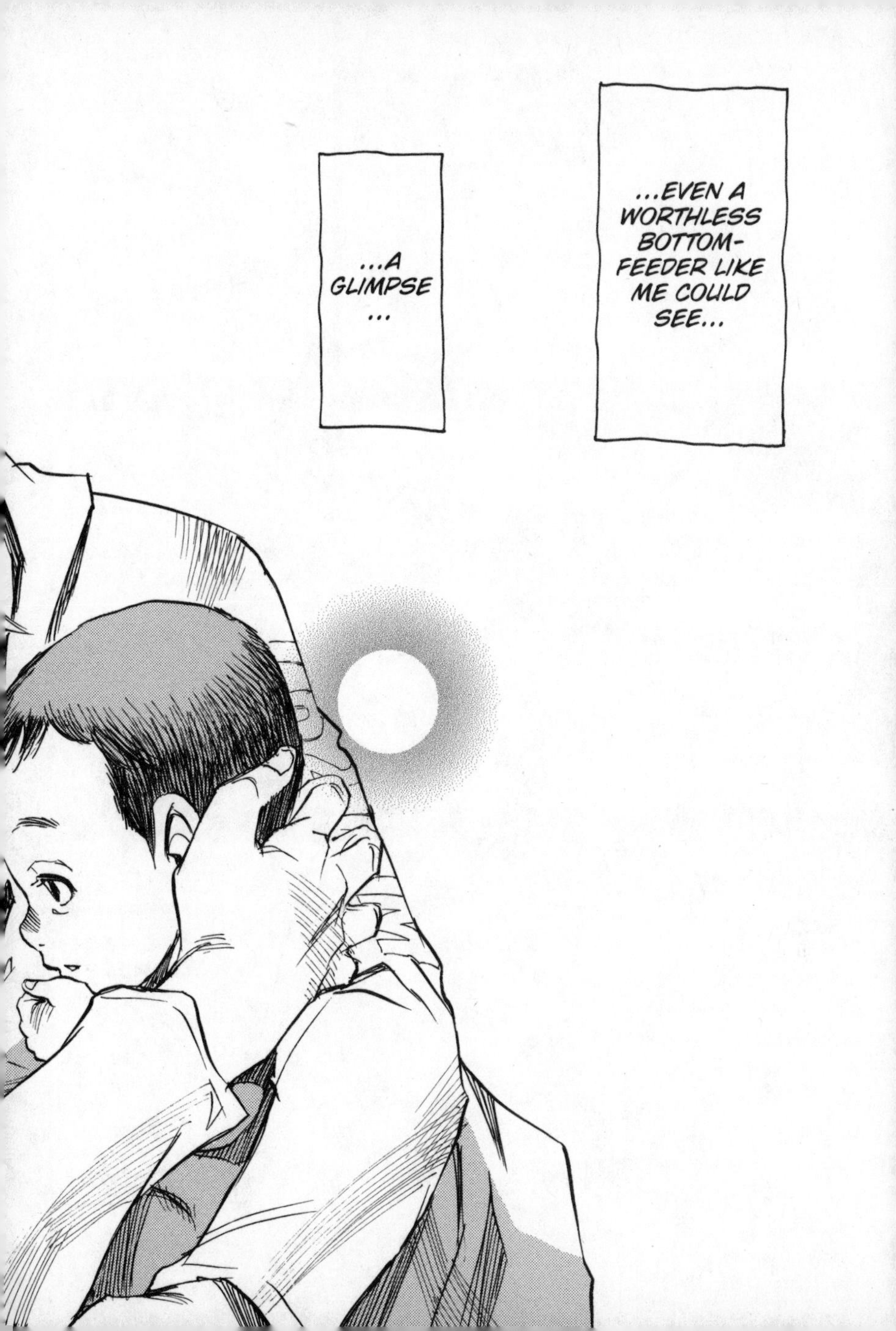
...EVEN A WORTHLESS BOTTOM-FEEDER LIKE ME COULD SEE...
...A GLIMPSE ...

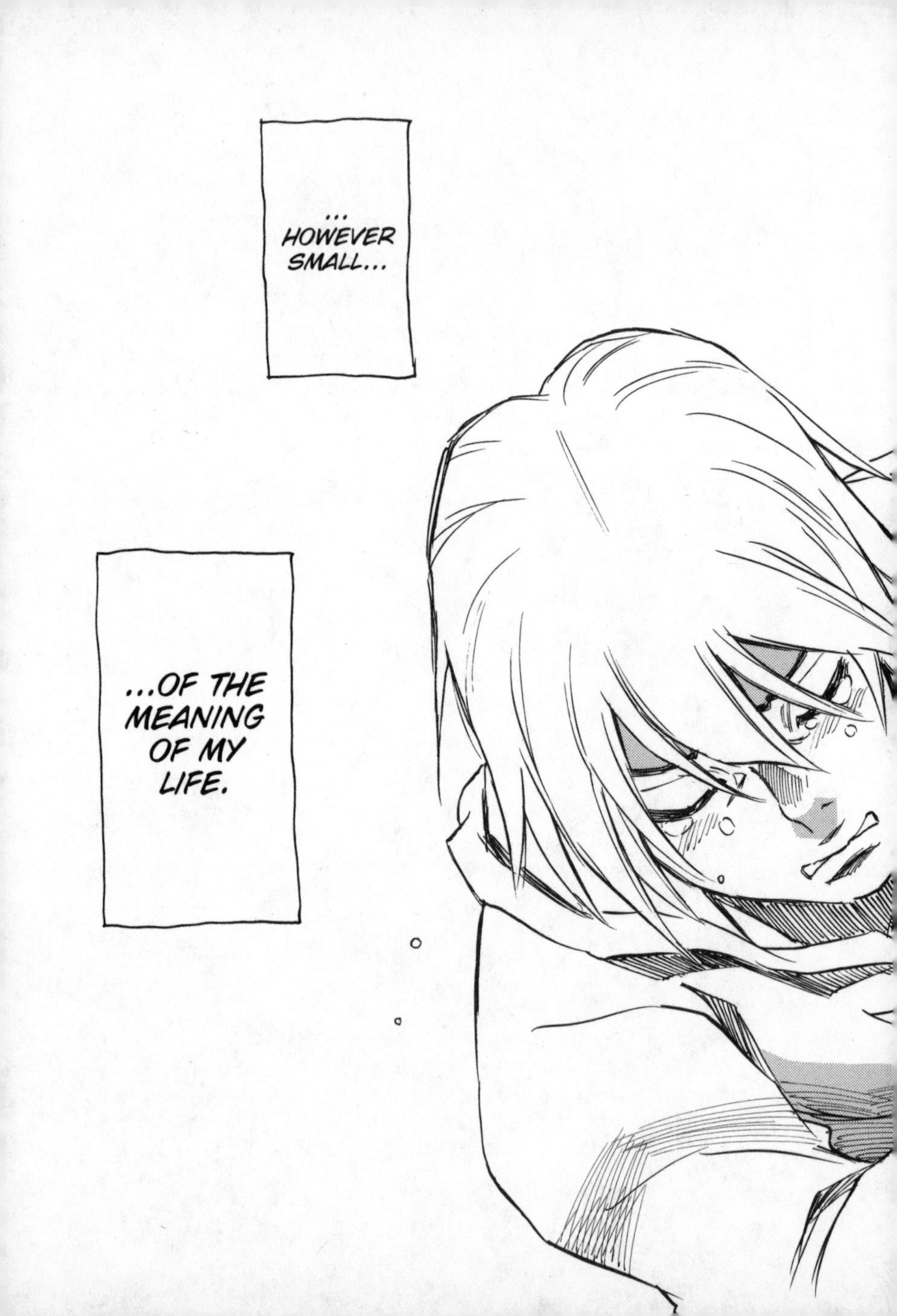

... HOWEVER SMALL...
...OF THE MEANING OF MY LIFE.

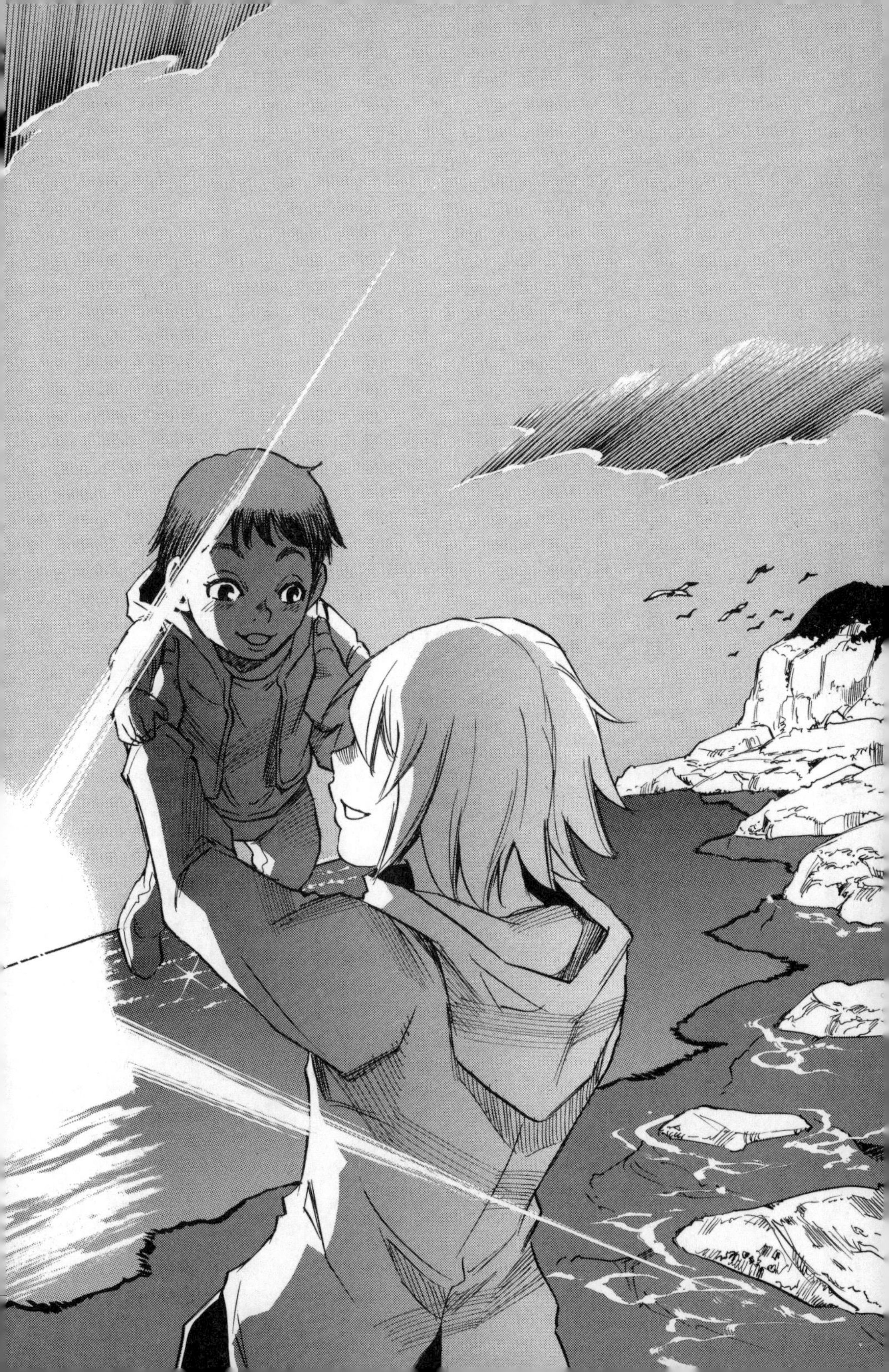

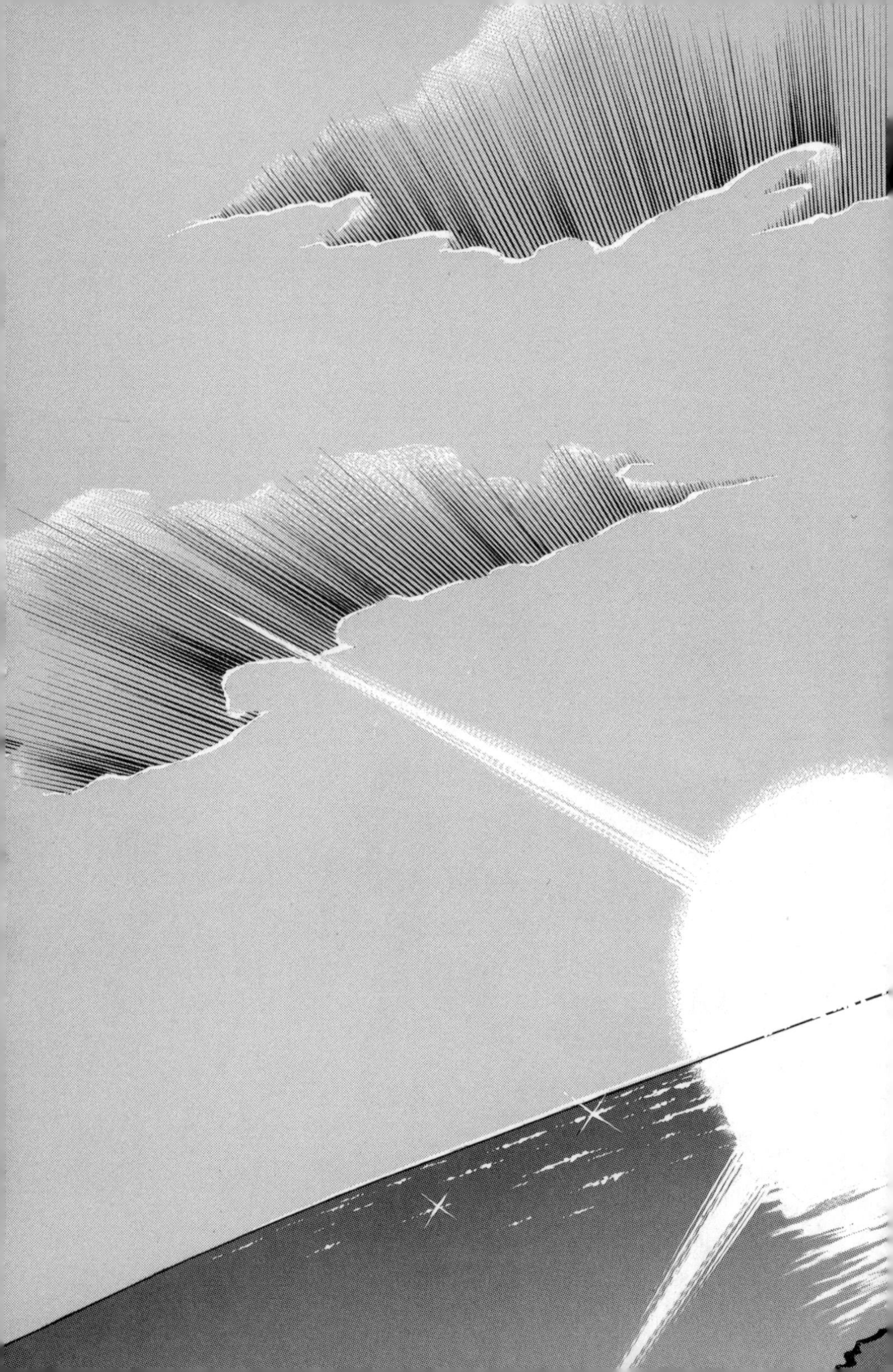

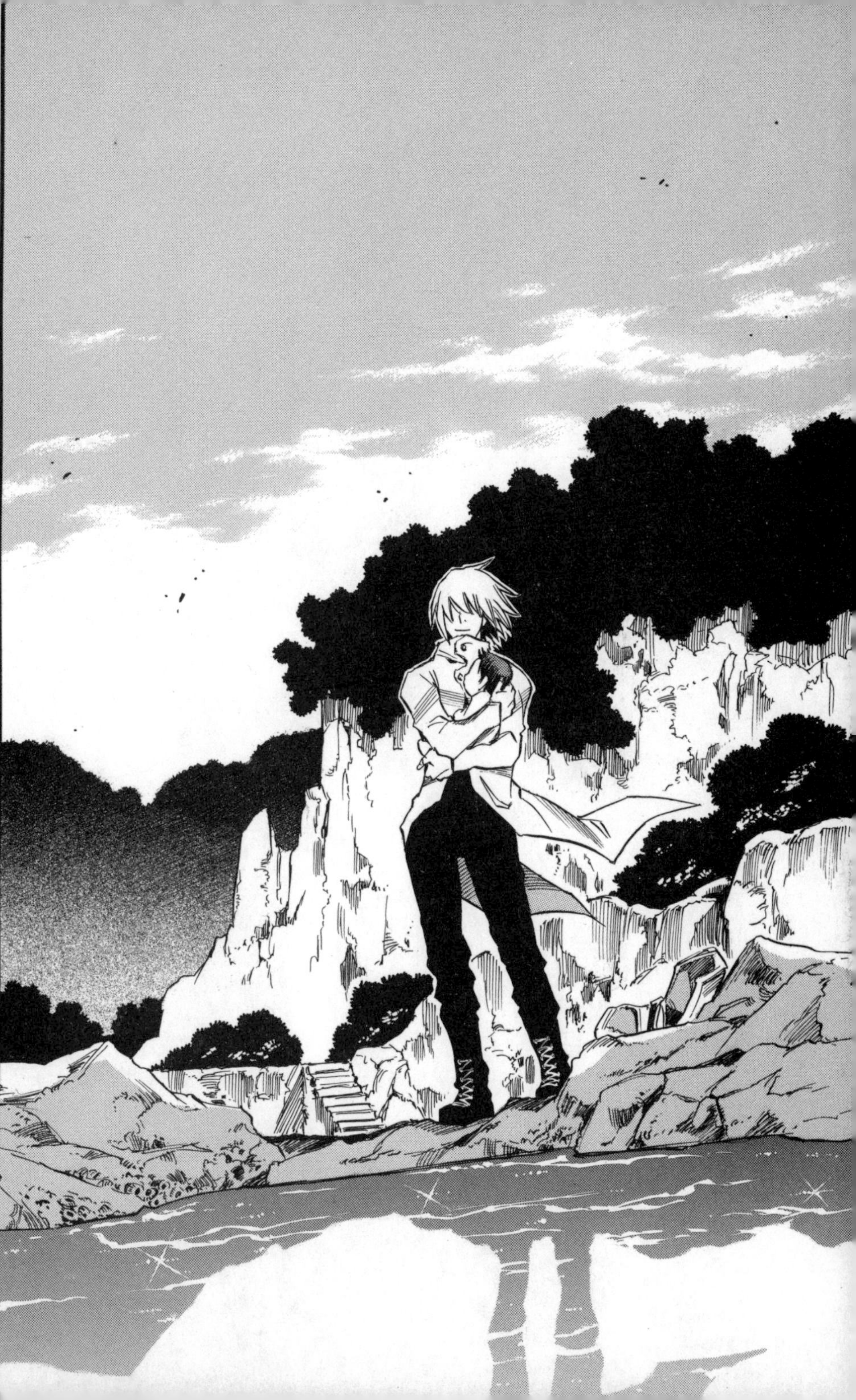

For the Kid I Saw in My Dreams ⑦ END

STAFF

Kei Sanbe

Yoichiro Tomita
Manami 18 Sai
Kouji Kikuta
Yasunobu

Keishi Kanesada

RESEARCH/PHOTOGRAPHY
ASSISTANCE
Houwa Toda

BOOK DESIGN
Yukio Hoshino
VOLARE inc.

EDITOR
Tsunenori Matsumiya

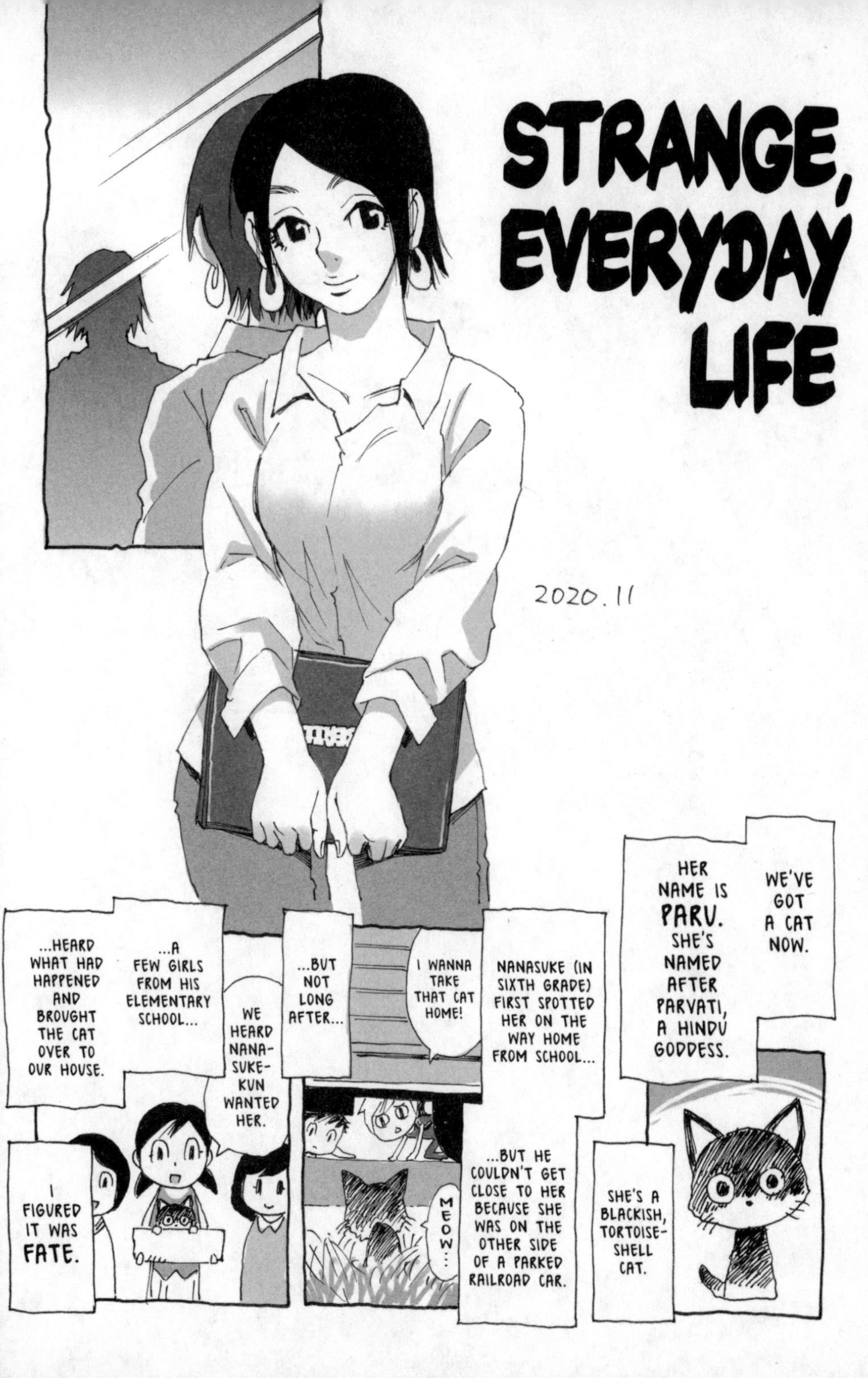
STRANGE, EVERYDAY LIFE
2020.11
WE'VE GOT A CAT NOW.
HER NAME IS PARU. SHE'S NAMED AFTER PARVATI, A HINDU GODDESS.
SHE'S A BLACKISH, TORTOISE-SHELL CAT.
NANASUKE (IN SIXTH GRADE) FIRST SPOTTED HER ON THE WAY HOME FROM SCHOOL...
I WANNA TAKE THAT CAT HOME!
...BUT HE COULDN'T GET CLOSE TO HER BECAUSE SHE WAS ON THE OTHER SIDE OF A PARKED RAILROAD CAR.
MEOW...
...BUT NOT LONG AFTER...
...A FEW GIRLS FROM HIS ELEMENTARY SCHOOL...
...HEARD WHAT HAD HAPPENED AND BROUGHT THE CAT OVER TO OUR HOUSE.
WE HEARD NANA-SUKE-KUN WANTED HER.
I FIGURED IT WAS FATE.

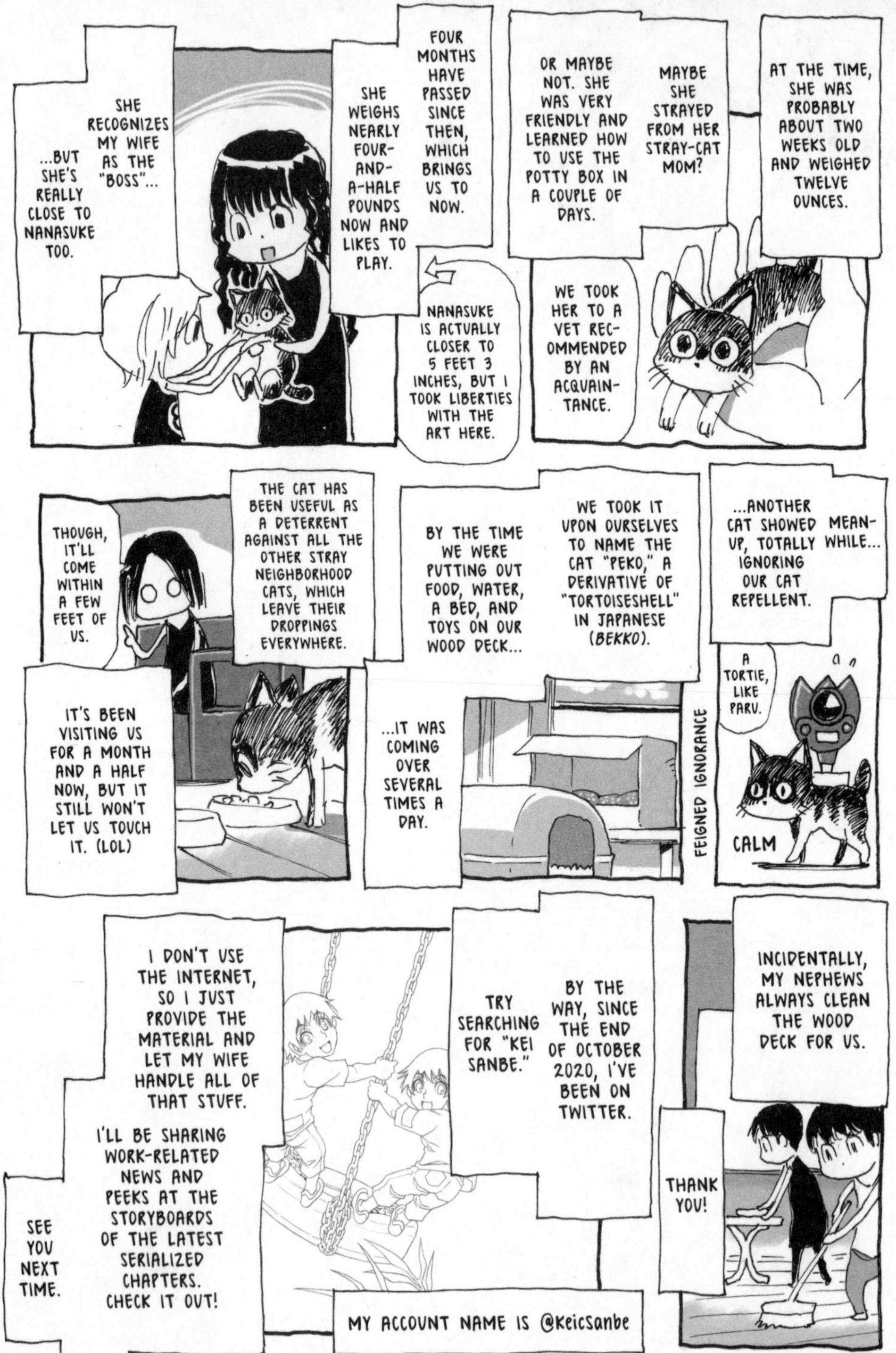

AT THE TIME, SHE WAS PROBABLY ABOUT TWO WEEKS OLD AND WEIGHED TWELVE OUNCES.
MAYBE SHE STRAYED FROM HER STRAY-CAT MOM?
OR MAYBE NOT. SHE WAS VERY FRIENDLY AND LEARNED HOW TO USE THE POTTY BOX IN A COUPLE OF DAYS.
WE TOOK HER TO A VET REC-OMMENDED BY AN ACQUAIN-TANCE.
FOUR MONTHS HAVE PASSED SINCE THEN, WHICH BRINGS US TO NOW.
SHE WEIGHS NEARLY FOUR-AND-A-HALF POUNDS NOW AND LIKES TO PLAY.
NANASUKE IS ACTUALLY CLOSER TO 5 FEET 3 INCHES, BUT I TOOK LIBERTIES WITH THE ART HERE.
SHE RECOGNIZES MY WIFE AS THE "BOSS"...
...BUT SHE'S REALLY CLOSE TO NANASUKE TOO.
MEAN-WHILE...
...ANOTHER CAT SHOWED UP, TOTALLY IGNORING OUR CAT REPELLENT.
A TORTIE, LIKE PARU.
FEIGNED IGNORANCE
CALM
WE TOOK IT UPON OURSELVES TO NAME THE CAT "PEKO," A DERIVATIVE OF "TORTOISESHELL" IN JAPANESE (BEKKO).
BY THE TIME WE WERE PUTTING OUT FOOD, WATER, A BED, AND TOYS ON OUR WOOD DECK...
...IT WAS COMING OVER SEVERAL TIMES A DAY.
THE CAT HAS BEEN USEFUL AS A DETERRENT AGAINST ALL THE OTHER STRAY NEIGHBORHOOD CATS, WHICH LEAVE THEIR DROPPINGS EVERYWHERE.
THOUGH, IT'LL COME WITHIN A FEW FEET OF US.
IT'S BEEN VISITING US FOR A MONTH AND A HALF NOW, BUT IT STILL WON'T LET US TOUCH IT. (LOL)
INCIDENTALLY, MY NEPHEWS ALWAYS CLEAN THE WOOD DECK FOR US.
THANK YOU!
BY THE WAY, SINCE THE END OF OCTOBER 2020, I'VE BEEN ON TWITTER.
TRY SEARCHING FOR "KEI SANBE."
MY ACCOUNT NAME IS @keicSanbe
I DON'T USE THE INTERNET, SO I JUST PROVIDE THE MATERIAL AND LET MY WIFE HANDLE ALL OF THAT STUFF.
I'LL BE SHARING WORK-RELATED NEWS AND PEEKS AT THE STORYBOARDS OF THE LATEST SERIALIZED CHAPTERS. CHECK IT OUT!
SEE YOU NEXT TIME.

TRANSLATION NOTES

Common Honorifics

no honorific: Indicates familiarity or closeness; if used without permission or reason, addressing someone in this manner would constitute an insult.

-san: The Japanese equivalent of Mr./Mrs./Miss. If a situation calls for politeness, this is the fail-safe honorific.

-sama: Conveys great respect; may also indicate the social status of the speaker is lower than that of the addressee.

-kun: Used most often when referring to boys, this indicates affection or familiarity. Occasionally used by older men among their peers, but it may also be used by anyone referring to a person of lower standing.

-chan: An affectionate honorific indicating familiarity used mostly in reference to girls; also used in reference to cute persons or animals of either gender.

(o)nii: A familiar way to refer to a older man close in age.

-sensei: A respectful term for teachers, artists, or high-level professionals.

Currency Conversion

While conversion rates fluctuate daily, an easy estimate for Japanese Yen conversion is 100 JPY to 1 USD.

Page 9

Nezumi Kozo: A Japanese thief and folk hero who stole from the rich and gave to the poor—or so the legend goes—much like a "Robin Hood" figure. In reality, Jirokichi Nakamura was a prolific thief with a fifteen-year career that ended with his execution in 1831. The fact that he died destitute helped give rise to the story that he must have given away all of his loot to the less fortunate. His nickname translates literally to "Rat Brat."

Edo Period: The era from 1603-1867 when Japan was under the rule of the Tokugawa *shogunate* instead of an emperor. The first *shogun*, Tokugawa Ieyasu, established his headquarters in the city of Edo, which grew to be the center of political power in Japan and was later renamed Tokyo in the subsequent Meiji period.

For the Kid I Saw in My Dreams

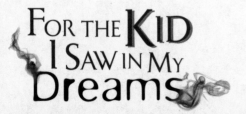